THE COMMUNITY DEVELOPMENT READER

History, themes and issues

Edited by Gary Craig, Marjorie Mayo, Keith Popple, Mae Shaw and Marilyn Taylor

First published in Great Britain in 2011 by

The Policy Press
University of Bristol
Fourth Floor
Beacon House
Queen's Road
Bristol BS8 1QU
UK

Tel +44 (0)117 331 4054
Fax +44 (0)117 331 4093
e-mail tpp-info@bristol.ac.uk
www.policypress.org.uk

North American office:
The Policy Press
c/o International Specialized Books Services (ISBS)
920 NE 58th Avenue, Suite 300
Portland, OR 97213-3786, USA
Tel +1 503 287 3093
Fax +1 503 280 8832
e-mail info@isbs.com

British Library Cataloguing in Publication Data
A catalogue record for this book is available from the British Library.

Library of Congress Cataloging-in-Publication Data
A catalog record for this book has been requested.

ISBN 978 1 84742 704 5 paperback
ISBN 978 1 84742 705 2 hardcover

Cover design by Qube Design Associates
Front cover: image kindly supplied by www.alamy.com/www.istock.com
Printed and bound in Great Britain by Hobbs, Southampton
The Policy Press uses environmentally responsible print partners

FSC
www.fsc.org
MIX
Paper from
responsible sources
FSC® C020438

Contents

Sources of extracts

Chapter 4.3   Community development at the crossroads: a way forward
From: Miller, C. and Ahmed, Y.(1997) 'Community development at the crossroads', *Policy & Politics*, vol 25, no 3, pp 269-84.

Chapter 4.4   When 'active citizenship' becomes mob rule
From: Thomson, J. (2000) 'When "active citizenship" becomes mob rule', *Adults Learning*, September, pp 23-4.

Chapter 4.5   Inequalities in health: contested explanations, shifting discourses and ambiguous policies
From: Carlisle, S. (2001) 'Inequalities in health: contested explanations, shifting discourses and ambiguous policies', *Critical Public Health*, vol 11, no 3, pp 267-79.

Chapter 4.6   The significance of global citizen action
From: Gaventa, J. (2001) 'Global citizen action: lessons and challenges' in M. Edwards and J. Gaventa (2001) *Global citizen action*, London: Earthscan, pp 275-89.

Chapter 4.7   Whose problem? Disability narratives and available identities
From: Cameron, C. (2007) 'Whose problem? Disability narratives and available identities', *Community Development Journal*, vol 42, no 4, pp 501-11.

Chapter 4.8   The changing terrain of multi-culture: from anti-oppressive practice to community cohesion
From: Shukra, K. (2007) 'The changing terrain of multi-culture: from anti-oppressive practice to community cohesion', *Concept,* vol 17, no 3, pp 3-7.

Chapter 4.9   Community capacity-building: something old, something new ...?
From: Craig, G. (2007) 'Community capacity-building: something old, something new ...?', *Critical Social Policy*, vol 27, August, pp 335-5.

Chapter 4.10   Reclaiming the radical agenda: a critical approach to community development
From: Ledwith, M. (2007) 'Reclaiming the radical agenda: a critical approach to community development', *Concept*, vol 17, no 2, pp 8-13.

Chapter 4.11   Community participation in the real world
From: Taylor, M.(2007) 'Community participation in the real world', *Urban Studies*, vol 44, no 2, pp 297-317.

Chapter 4.12   Community development and the politics of community
From: Shaw, M. (2008) 'Community development and the politics of community', Community Development Journal, vol 43, no 1, pp 24-36.

Acknowledgments

The editors would like to engage in a mutual admiration society, thanking each other for hanging together despite some twists and turns over the two years it took to put this book together. They are all still friends.

They thank the publishers who kindly gave permission to reproduce the extracts in the book. In addition they are grateful not only to the 'front of house' staff at The Policy Press, especially Emily Watt, for helping to support the emergence of the book with a light but clear touch, but also the unsung heroes and heroines of publishing in the backroom, particularly – as far as we can tell, and in no particular order – Dave Worth, Jo Morton, Charlotte Skelton, Laura Vickers, Leila Ebrahimi and Kathryn King. Marjorie Mayo also wishes to place on record her gratitude to Maria Dumas and Jonathon Fox at Goldsmiths College for turning unusable chapters into usable extracts; and Mae Shaw thanks Lesley Spencer at the University of Edinburgh for similar help. Gary thanks Gill for her forbearance and support as he worked through what seemed like a never-ending process of book production – and not just on this one!

Section I

Introduction: community development in the United Kingdom

Community development[1] began to emerge as a recognisable paid activity in the UK in the 1950s, legitimised by its recognition also by the United Nations, which produced its own definition in 1953 of 'a movement to promote better living for the whole community, with active participation and if possible on the initiative of the community' (UN, 1953: 33). Generally, the practice of community development was seen as taking place in the so-called 'developing' countries, many of which were then emerging from colonial rule. In the colonies, however, community development – often badged then as adult education or rural extension – was as much a means of controlling local populations as of liberating them.

> In short, any humanitarian act of any colonial power towards the 'ward' is merely to enhance its primary objective: economic exploitation – the attitude of Britain towards what they call 'participation' by colonial peoples in colonial governments are half-way measures to keep them complacent ... social projects merely serve as means to one end: the perpetuation of foreign rule. (Nkrumah, cited in Craig, 1989)

Although this book does not set out to be a comprehensive history of community development in the UK, it is perhaps useful to sketch out some important milestones in its historical development. The origins of community development in the UK from the 1950s onwards lay in three tendencies, each underpinned by a set of values, skills and a body of knowledge. These overlapped or, in some cases, were in conflict. The first lay in the continuing interests of 'community developers', returning from newly independent countries, particularly in Africa, Asia and the Caribbean, wanting to apply their practice to the rapidly changing social and economic fabric of post-war Britain. Secondly, there was the need, recognised by governments, for some form of social development in the new communities, housing estates and New Towns which were built to replace Britain's slums and war-damaged cities. Thirdly, there was the growing awareness of community development and community organising in the US, reflected in the influence of American literature (Ross, 1955; Biddle and Biddle, 1965; Marris and Rein, 1967; Arnstein, 1969; see also Craig, 1989).

Early literature available in the UK was dominated by writing from post-colonial returnees such as Batten and Batten (1967), and by the American literature, either from a more community work and rural extension tradition in poor agricultural communities in rural US states or a more radical –

albeit pluralist – community organising practice, developing within the US's (largely black) inner cities, exemplified by the writing of Alinsky (1971). Students taking early community development courses in the UK were offered a strange mix of these contributions, with virtually no indigenous literature at all, or, for those proposing to work overseas in what was becoming known as social development, a heavy dose of post-colonial practice. (This in part accounts for the presence of some early US literature in this volume.) This was to change in the 1960s, as observers of some of the early UK practice began to draw together reflections on the lessons learnt from this practice: for example, Goetschius 1969, writing on the work of the Association of London Housing Estates, and early texts such as those of Kuenstler (1961), Thomason (1969) and Leaper (1968) (see Section 2, Introduction). As this writing began to emerge, a struggle developed for the soul – or at least identity – of community development in the UK. This struggle took a number of forms: one was a debate, vigorous at times, which sought to distance community development – through the emergent Association of Community Workers (formed in the late 1960s) – from the practice of social work and its own professional body, the British Association of Social Workers. This struggle continued for some time as community development – along with casework and groupwork – was seen as part of a threefold approach to social work. Ironically, much early writing about neighbourhood community work and the training and skills required for it emerged from the National Institute for Social Work (for example Thomas and Henderson, 1976). For many community workers, a paradox was clear: if community development was about empowering local communities and thus effectively 'working the community developer out of a job', how could it lay claim to a continuing professional practice which, with its entry requirements, codes of ethics, training requirements and so on, sought at the same time to distance itself from the communities it was developing by the attributes and, more importantly, mystiques of profession. The Association of Community Workers continued almost to the present day as a useful focal point for debate and discussion, publishing a long-running series of short Talking Points together with occasional editions of its hefty *Skills Manual* (Harris, 2010), successfully avoiding becoming a professional organisation in the tradition of, say, law, social work and medicine.

In 1968, the government had established a national youth volunteer organisation, then known as the Young Volunteer Force Foundation (YVFF), sending small teams to deprived communities throughout the UK to 'harness the energies of young people through voluntary service'. Many of these young workers rapidly came to the view that such social work-oriented voluntary service would not address the problems they were facing on a sustainable basis and turned to community development as a more appropriate form of practice. Local projects were transformed into community development projects, many of them creating a degree of irritation at both central and local government levels for raising questions about the nature and origins of deprivation. YVFF became the Community Projects Foundation, now the Community Development Foundation (CDF). Increasingly subject to strong control from central government in its funding stream and terms of reference, the organisation has become positioned over time as a delivery agent for government policy rather than as a sponsor of autonomous community development activity. Thus, although CDF was seen at one time as a mouthpiece of community development vis-à-vis government, by the late 1980s, this was far from the case. By that time, various pressures – including concern that CDF was becoming too close to government and a recognition that 'expertise' lay throughout the field of practice and should not be represented by one national body – had led to the creation of the then Standing Conference of Community Development (now Community Development Exchange – CDX; www.cdx.org.uk), an autonomous federal membership organisation representing thousands of community development workers nationwide.[2] One pressure leading to the creation of SCCD was a proposal to establish a National Institute of Community Development, paralleling the institute that already existed for social work. There is now within the UK a range of organisations each active in managing and supporting independent community development initiatives: apart from those mentioned above, the most significant include the British Association of Settlements and Social Action Centres (BASSAC; www.bassac.org.uk), the Urban Forum (www.urbanforum.org.uk), the Development Trusts Association (www.dta.org.uk) and Community Matters (www.communitymatters.org.uk), the latter focusing more on the interests of activists than paid workers.[3]

The second, less wide-ranging but highly symbolic, struggle took place on the Editorial Board of the *Community Development Journal* (CDJ), then as now, the major international journal reflecting the theory and practice of community development. The CDJ had emerged in 1965 from a newsletter which circulated largely among those returning from the colonies and which continued to be dominated by their perspectives and experience until the early 1970s when an increasing number of those with experience predominantly in UK urban settings joined the Board. By the late 1970s this latter grouping emerged as a dominant force on the Editorial Board and the then editor, Brian Taylor, and Board Chair (Reg Batten), sensing perhaps a literary version of Macmillan's winds of change, resigned in short order. From that point, the CDJ set out to operate as a truly international journal, reflecting practice across the world, both North and South, including a substantial volume of material which reflected ways in which community development was being used in a 'Southern' context, to provide a voice for the poor and dispossessed against new ruling elites. Popple (2006) has contributed a short history of the CDJ published in its own pages.

The third struggle followed the emergence of the very substantial and influential writing of the workers on the National Community Development Project. An influential caucus of CDP workers developed what came to be known as the 'structural analysis' of the decline of inner city areas (where most of the 12 projects were based), pointing to industrial disinvestment and the rundown of public services as the major reason for poverty and deprivation in these areas, rather than, as the governmental literature would have had people believe, the fecklessness of inner city residents (CDP, 1976; 1977). This analysis – and its implications for community development practice – was taken further by a number of later writings such as *In and Against the State* (LEWRG, 1980) and Cynthia Cockburn's *The Local State*. (Cockburn, 1977) For many community development workers and writers wedded to a neighbourhood approach (for example, those then most closely associated with the National Institute for Social Work), this structural analysis was seen either as a betrayal of what they were doing or, even worse, as completely negating their years of hard work on and off housing estates and in inner city areas.

This response was, however, a misreading of the CDP's writings and of CDP workers' own practice. Virtually every one of the total of 100-plus workers on the local CDP projects was engaged in some form of neighbourhood work: their point was that without an understanding of the structural causes of decline, neighbourhood work could be misdirected and ineffective. The analysis, taken forward by others later on, argued instead for the need for alliances, across neighbourhoods, between community activists and trades unions, between women's groups and what had historically been male-dominated organisations, and across ethnic divides, in order to use the analysis for effective political action at local level. This analysis of course was scarcely popular with government since it completely challenged its version of the reasons for urban (and rural) decline (Loney, 1983). Not surprisingly, government never again embarked on a national programme of well-funded community development which gave project workers such a degree of autonomy, without, as with the New Labour New Deal for Communities (NDC) programme, having available a substantial degree of control over local projects if and when 'the natives became restless' (Dinham, 2005).

This analysis has continued to be influential, indeed, we would argue, particularly so at a time when public expenditure cuts of an unprecedented nature are being proposed and when government now uses the term 'community development' to badge a range of activities which have little to do with the empowerment of local communities (Craig, 2007 – Ch 4.9, this volume). The CDP analysis was limited in some respects and was rightly criticised for having a very limited gender or 'race' dimension, for example

(Green and Chapman, 1992). Nevertheless, it made a huge impact and helped in particular in clarifying the place of community development within a wider range of social and economic policies which, in a class-based analysis, it argued, were put in place to protect the interests of capital. It also made an important contribution to thinking about the role of action-research in community development work (Lees and Smith, 1975).

Community development, in reality, as we argue below, has always had an ambiguous nature. We believe this book will make a vital contribution to resourcing and informing an ongoing argument about purposes and values, which keeps the practice of community development sharp and relevant to changing policy contexts. It is also important to acknowledge the broad church nature of community development – from state-sponsored, well-resourced programmes to small-scale, poorly resourced, but independent community action – and the themes outlined later are ones which have recurred frequently within a variety of organisational settings. The downside of its ambiguity of course is, as many writers acknowledge and we emphasise later, that it can be colonised by those working with different values and objectives, often leading to confusion about what community development really is. One example of this is in the emphasis on consumerism – in reality an individualistic rather than a collective enterprise – which was associated with government initiatives in the late 1980s onwards and, for some, appeared to occupy community development territory (Berry, 1988). Another is the recurring interest in voluntarism (now sheltering under the ideological umbrella of the Big Society), which again has little to do with community development but is often misleadingly badged as such.

Community development now is not only a practice, involving skills, a knowledge base and a strong value base. It is also a goal, self-evidently the development of communities, in the context of social justice agendas, notwithstanding the different interests at work in defining what this is all about and why it matters. There has never been a 'golden age' of community development although there have been times when practice has been less under pressure from political and ideological confusion to clarify its boundaries. It is perhaps better to see community development as an 'embodied argument', a continuing search for new forms of social and political expression, particularly 'at the grassroots level' (within a participatory paradigm), in the light of new forms of political and social control. This acts as a strong reminder that community development fundamentally is not a neutral intervention but is ideologically contested. With a strong historical bias, this reflects the present editors' assumption that you cannot understand present debates about community development without reference to the past.

One critical problem for the practice of community development has been that those writing about – and practising – community development have struggled over the past 50 years even to define what 'community' means in practice (Shaw, 2008 – Ch 4.12, this volume). Paradoxically, while these debates continue, the context of community development practice has also changed in part to reflect these differing understandings. In the current global discourse about community development, 'community' has three basic meanings: first, it refers to a *geographical community*, a collection of people living within a fairly well-defined physical space. This has historically been the most common usage of the term and one which has shaped – and continues to shape – the job descriptions of many community development workers.

Community development workers from both North and South, however, came to recognise from the 1960s that seeing 'community' simply as a geographical entity did not adequately deal with the realities of conflict or tensions between different interests within spatially-defined communities (Baldock, 1977; Craig, 1989). These tensions might take the form of religious or ethnic conflict (as in Northern Ireland or Bosnia, for example), disagreements based on class or age, or the desire of some groups to assert specific needs, based perhaps on sexuality, gender, ethnicity or disability. Community thus properly incorporates axes of diversity which may generate conflicts. The second cross-cutting type of community thus is that of *community of identity*. Through the 1980s, community development was strongly criticised for still failing to incorporate a strong dimension of race, gender or disability in its work, thus contributing in part to the development of autonomous social movements focusing on these social divisions (although the municipal left was then also active in funding such work). Within and between geographical communities there might be a wide range of communities of identity that may have these differing needs and interests. Seeing community as a site of conflict between competing interests later presented a challenge in particular to the political approach of communitarianism, a political philosophy strongly promoted by New Labour in the early part of the 21st century and which strongly informed its own approach to community development (Dwyer, 2000).

However, while 'community' is of central importance to communitarians, New Labour's communitarian-inspired view of community was one which, as Driver and Martell (1998) argue, is characterised by conformity, conditionality and moral prescription driven by top-down policy solutions rather than those developed through democratic dialogue from within communities themselves. Government – perhaps learning in its own terms from the experience of CDP – does not therefore respond to agendas set from below, or allow the political space for alternative explanations of inner city decline and poverty but shapes policy programmes from above, *for* (rather than *with*) communities. This has enormous implications for the practice of community development since it effectively places government-sponsored community development in collision with the value base of community development as historically understood by many of those practising it.

Thirdly, community workers have often found themselves engaged in relatively short-term work, focused on particular issues such as improving housing conditions, improving road safety at school crossings, or protecting aspects of the environment through campaigns around river or industrial pollution. These groups constitute *issue-based communities*.

The concept of community development has itself therefore also been used to cover a range of differing understandings of practice and outcome. In the late 1980s/early 1990s, many governments and international organisations 'rediscovered' community development, although not labelling it consistently as such. Thus the World Bank viewed community participation as a means for ensuring that Third World Development projects 'reached the poorest in the most efficient and cost-effective way, sharing costs as well as benefits, through the promotion of self-help' (Craig and Mayo, 1995: 2). Their programmes, better known for fiscal conservatism than for political and social risk-taking, frequently led, however, to the undermining of local community social and economic structures while appearing to advocate the importance of 'community', a further example of the confusion which surrounds this and related terms such as 'community empowerment' or 'community capacity-building' (Craig, 2007 – Ch 4.9, this volume; Cornwall, 2008). The United Nations Development Programme (UNDP, 1993) commented that it had 'people's participation as its special focus. ... [It] ... is becoming the central issue of our time' (Craig and Mayo, 1995: 2). In reality, however, these international agencies and national governments driving the process of structural adjustment (Edwards and Gaventa, 2001) have too often failed to give effective attention to issues of social justice. For example, they demonstrate little concern with the dignity and humanity of the poorest, with their right to participate in decisions that affect them or with mutuality and equality: all principles which underpin the philosophy and practice of community development as it is understood by practice-based organisations (see, for example, definitions advanced by CDX in a national context: and by the International Association for Community Development, www.iacdglobal.org, in an international one).

These tensions and contradictory understandings represent one of the dominant and continuing themes in the history of community development within the UK. Nevertheless, attempts continue to be made to defend the practice of community development from the consequent linguistic and ideological confusion surrounding it. For example, a wide-ranging definition of community development was agreed at a conference convened in 2004 by a group of community development organisations. This Budapest Declaration is significant because it was drawn together by participants from more than 30 countries, mostly from across Europe but also from Asia, Africa and North America. This definition suggests that:

> Community development is a way of strengthening civil society by prioritising the actions of communities, and their perspectives in the development of social, economic and environmental policy. It seeks the empowerment of local communities, taken to mean ... geographical communities, communities of interest or identity and communities organising around specific themes or policy initiatives. It strengthens the capacity of people as active citizens through their community groups, organisations and networks; and the capacity of institutions and agencies ... to work in dialogue with citizens to shape and determine change in their communities. It plays a crucial role in supporting active democratic life by promoting the autonomous voice of disadvantaged and vulnerable communities. (IACD, 2004)

Thus, in order to serve the interests of local communities, community development should promote local 'voice', encouraging the ability to be critical of established policy and political contexts, driven by the twin underpinning values of social justice and a desire to change power structures in favour of the 'excluded'.

As noted, both national and international 'community development programmes' have too often failed to allow this political space to develop, as programmes from the ill-starred UK Home Office CDP onwards have learnt to their cost, and have imposed their own understandings of what community development is. Such programmes are not really, in the sense outlined by the Budapest Declaration, *community* development programmes because they allow little control by the community itself, with 'top-down' policy prescriptions taking precedence over 'bottom-up' community analyses. They also fail to understand potential divisions within communities, differences which may be increasingly overlaid with issues of 'race', gender and class (Meekosha, 1993 – Ch 3.7, this volume).

These contradictory messages from government continue to be reflected in present debates. The official document, part-sponsored by New Labour's Department for Communities and Local Government, *The Community Development Challenge* (CDF, 2007) argued as follows:

> Community development is a set of values and practices which plays a special role in overcoming poverty and disadvantage, knitting together society at the grassroots and deepening democracy. There is a community development profession, defined by national occupational standards, and a body of theory and experience going

back the best part of a century. There are active citizens who use community development techniques on a voluntary basis and there are also other professions and agencies which use a community development approach or some aspects of it.

… this is underpinned by a set of values, principles and roles. Community development also works with public authorities, services and agencies, to enable them better to understand, engage with and respond to communities … so a fuller definition would add that community development also works with public agencies to increase their ability to strengthen, engage with, respond to and work jointly with communities.

This document, interestingly, was strongly shaped by representatives of some of the key organisations active in the field including CDX, FCDL and CDF. The Community Development Foundation – accurately reflecting one of the core tensions in community development – has, as noted earlier, steadily moved over the past 20 years from being a voice for the community development profession to an agent for the delivery of government's understanding of community development.

It is important to emphasise that the warm consensus implied by the provenance of this document is, in any case, contradicted by the past record of UK governments, as demonstrated throughout this Reader. On the few occasions that government has in the past directly funded major community development programmes, it rapidly moved to close them down, as soon as the challenges posed by community empowerment became apparent. Government support for community development then was exposed as rhetorical. The same situation, we have observed, has obtained in relation to the New Deal for Communities, one of New Labour's flagship social policy programmes, where communities were allegedly to be empowered to take more control of the processes and policies that affected them. The literature beginning to emerge from this well-funded national programme also suggests that, despite a stated objective of 'putting the community "at the heart" of the initiative' (DCLG, 2010b: 5), in those cases where communities have organised to demand greater control of policy and strategies affecting them, frequently pressure has been brought to bear for them to stay 'on message'; at the same time, a 'bottom–up' approach was undermined by monitoring and measuring requirements which crowded out the 'community' contribution (Taylor, 2003). Such programmes have increasingly been managed from the 'top down', with financial management in particular as a mode of control to ensure that local community voices are marginalised (Diamond, 2004; Wallace, 2010). Typically, these projects have, in any case, defined the range of issues and policy options that are up for discussion, ensuring that more fundamental policy challenges are firmly ruled off-limits (as in the case of social housing, for example, where the role of local authorities in construction and maintenance has been clearly restricted, whatever the preferences of the local communities in question).

This evidence also highlights the contradictions inherent in the role of the community worker who is expected to support communities to have an autonomous voice even where that voice may articulate messages unwelcome to those with formal authority, or may have to act surreptitiously in doing so (Jones, 1991). Contradicting the rosy picture portrayed in official government publications such as *The Community Development Challenge* (CDF, 2007), then, the picture on the ground is thus rather less supportive, again reflecting the gap between community development rhetoric from government and the reality of community experience over many years.

During the early 1980s, largely as a result of the policies of the Thatcher governments, community work as an occupational form was put under severe pressure and the number of professional community development workers appears to have reduced substantially. The picture was, however, increasingly confused as many posts – including within local authorities – were created which had the term 'community' in their title, a substantial number of them being short-term, poorly paid jobs within the growing 'makework' sector funded by organisations such as the government employment quango, the Manpower Services Commission. One response from within the occupation of community development, reflected in the writing of the time, was for community workers to pursue the values and, as far as possible, the practice of community development from within other organisational and occupational settings and this undoubtedly contributed within these other settings to a growing awareness of ways in which the community development approach might inform better practice, particularly where there was a genuine desire to involve local communities in shaping policy formation and service delivery (Waddington, 1983).

Faced with the reluctance of central government directly to fund community development activity after the 1970s, local government took an increasing role in supporting community development activity at a local level. This did not, in the event, release community development workers from the pressures of working 'in and against the state', although it did at least keep community development, as a distinct 'professional' activity, in the public gaze. However, much of the work supported by local government operated as a slightly exotic version of social work within the new social services departments and there is no doubt that the pressures of working within local government reduced the tendency towards radical action (Barr, 1991). Community development posts were also funded through other parts of the state apparatus, such as the community health workers funded through the Health Action Zones programme of the 1990s or, even more recently, the mental health community development workers funded also from 2007 by the Department of Health under its Delivering Race Equality (DRE) programme (Walker and Craig, 2009). Local government, although again unevenly, also continued to fund a greater number of community development posts in the more recent past, some linked to the growing interest in community care (Barr et al, 2001). From the mid-1990s onwards, local government asserted the importance of community development through a series of publications sponsored by the various local government associations (AMA 1989; 1993). In Scotland, community development – badged in some contexts as a component part of a wider community education service – was mainstreamed on a statutory basis into the work of local authorities but still offered, in the view of some, opportunities for the empowerment of local communities (McConnell, 1996). (In England, some innovative community development work was also badged as adult education in further and higher education colleges such as Northern College in Yorkshire and Ruskin College at Oxford.) In Northern Ireland, community development practice continued to be a special case, linked to the difficulties of bridge building between hostile and sectarian communities (Lovett, 1993). Community development in Wales continued to develop, particularly around regeneration and anti-poverty work, but in a way which was less distinctive from that in England than practice and structures in the other devolved administrations (see, for example, Adamson, 2003).

In general, however, locally funded community development has been equally a site of contestation over values, methods and goals. This has caused continuing confusion about the goals of community development, as the term 'community' was attached to a huge variety of jobs, many of which – in contexts as diverse as the NHS, local government and education – turned out to have had little to do with the values of community development (Taylor, 2003).

In recent years, community work has grown again as a profession, however, at least as measured by the number of workers with this kind of designation for their role (Glen et al, 2004). This has been the consequence in part of apparently increased governmental commitment – albeit, as we argue, restricted in the pursuit of top–down agendas and at most times in any case rather shallow – to the values of participation and empowerment. These values have apparently also been more strongly asserted in recent years by mainstream government departments and programmes associated with them. However, commitments to community development and the empowerment of children and young people, for example, reflected in the Children's Fund, to communities in the New Deal for Communities and the Community Empowerment Funds, promoted by the former Office of the Deputy Prime Minister, and the emphasis on community involvement in the Health Action Zones programme, funded by the Department of Health, to take some random examples, have all turned out, in practice, to be rather more insubstantial than community development workers would have wanted. 'Community' is everywhere used as a badge to give legitimacy to programmes but as one commentator warned many years ago, it is usually no more than a 'spray-on additive' with little political or financial substance underpinning it (Bryson and Mowbray, 1981).

As Mayo has noted (2005), although spaces have been opened up for community activists to become more engaged as a result of investment in these various 'community development' programmes, there remain, at best, ambiguities and contradictions about the values and motives actually underpinning the community programmes which are targeted on them, particularly those programmes sponsored by the state (see also Cairns, 2003). An emphasis within regeneration on localism, for example, might simply mean imbuing community activists with responsibility but neither power nor resources. What government might describe as encouraging greater involvement of local residents might to local residents be seen as requiring them to take greater responsibility for service delivery (which they might not want) or to limit their capacity to become involved in the strategic direction of programmes (which they might want) (Cowden and Singh, 2007). The consensus within government is, some argue, not in reality so much about neighbourhood democracy as about neighbourhood management. For example, New Labour's ideological territory was defined by the consensual writings of those – such as Etzioni (1993) – who have propped up the Third Way, rather than by those who have provided a more radical and conflictual analysis, such as Bourdieu (Benington and Donnison, 1999). This is perhaps most obvious in the New Labour emphasis on community cohesion – seemingly continued by the 2010 coalition government – which seeks to manage those communities which have created the greatest difficulties for government in the recent past (Cooper, 2008). This emphasis has arguably been used again to obscure the structural causes of poverty and deprivation, especially among minority ethnic communities (Flint and Robinson, 2008). Here, the term 'community', while suggestive of bridge-building between minority populations and the majority UK population, obscures the rather less pleasant objective of mounting a 'war on terror', regarded by many inside and outside the Muslim community as a war on Islam (El Salahi, 2010).

Glen et al's (2004) survey collected data from 3,000 (self-defined) community workers. Interestingly, the *Community Development Challenge* (CDF, 2007), referred to above, suggested that there might be as many as 20,000 community workers in the UK, including many who use community development approaches as part of another job. This figure raises other troubling questions about the present practice of community development, questions which seem unlikely to be resolved by the coalition government's call for a new cadre of community organisers to be created. We return to this issue in the Afterword, albeit in a speculative manner.

The CDX survey itself also highlighted a number of important but disturbing issues, including the short-term nature of many posts (many of them generated by the various special government time-limited programmes, typically lasting only 2–3 years), the low salaries (and thus presumably status) attached to the posts, the lack of training of many community workers, and the fact that almost one-third of workers were supervised by someone with no experience in community work. This finding was reflected in the book edited by Banks et al (2003), *Managing Community Practice*, which found that the sustainability of community development at project level and as a profession remained then and now a major concern. So too does the extent to which community development values are not incorporated into the mainstream thinking of a range of employing organisations. In short, community development can be picked up and dropped as political mood takes governments and, when used by government, is structured in such a way that it supports the wider political, social and economic goals of government rather than allowing the voice of local deprived communities to influence policy development. Thus a 'community' approach in adult education might be used by government merely to enhance employability in the context of a low-wage 'flexible' labour market, rather than education being seen as a liberational tool in the tradition of Freire (1972). The changing picture was captured by Pitchford in his interviews with community workers, comparing practice in the 1970s with that of the 2000s, where 'community development [was felt to have] moved away from, what were felt by many to be idealistic goals in the 1970s of reducing poverty and inequalities ... [and] ... replaced by a more "realistic" focus on involvement within participation structures to influence the quality and delivery of public services' (Pitchford, 2008: 95).

Analysis of the CDX survey data also suggested a considerable anxiety within the profession that a quarter of all community workers were appointed to posts where neither experience, qualifications nor training were requirements for the job. This is also reflected in the employment conditions of the more than 600 community development workers now employed within the NHS in its DRE programme, to deliver mental health services to black and minority ethnic organisations (Walker and Craig, 2009). It is clear here that many such workers – whatever their other attributes – also came from backgrounds with little if any community development training or skills and worked within organisational settings where managers had no experience of community development. In addition, there was often no tradition of such work within the organisation. This suggests, at best, considerable and probably increasing confusion about the tasks facing community development. Such confusion is also reflected within contemporary discussion, creating a potential dilution in the professional/occupational focus of community work. The ageing of the community development profession was another area of concern emerging from the survey. Those with training and qualifications appeared to be those at the older end of the age spectrum and this suggests that many of those coming into new and short-term posts have no particular occupational or training commitment to professional community work. These are significant points to be made, while recognising, as has already been suggested earlier in this Introduction, that 'professionalism' has been contested, too, within wider debates about the nature of community development itself. Compared with the 1970s, there is now little formal training for community development, a disturbing situation at a time when there may be a new 'wave' of people described as community workers let loose in 'the community'.[4] On the other hand, a variety of innovative schemes have been developed for training and learning for both activists and paid workers, such as the Empowering Communities Programme linked to the notion of active citizenship developed in the North East of England (Banks and Vickers, 2006; see also www.fcdl.org.uk), which may provide models for those concerned about appropriate training opportunities.

Banks et al (2003) picked up some of these issues, reflecting on what is needed to support practice development – an approach which is based on an understanding of what works in community development. They suggest that it is a long-term and cumulative process but critically, this assumes that community development has a distinct identity. This latter is an important point because, again, as many commentators have observed, the 'spray-on' use of the term 'community' has often given a shallow veneer of participation and empowerment to programmes which have other, more state-directed, political and policy or service agendas, a process which has contributed to the undermining of the values of community development (Ledwith, 2005). The growing linguistic confusion about the goals and methods of community development was substantially added to during the New Labour period, with considerable government rhetoric about empowerment which actually translated into top-down initiatives (DCLG, 2006).

The issue of the effectiveness of community development is also one which is increasingly reflected in recent literature. This places the emphasis on process and outcome, in strong distinction to the government's Treasury-inspired focus on numerical inputs and outputs; the latter remained prominent in the New Deal for Communities programme where the final evaluation noted that 'it has sometimes been difficult for NDC partnerships to balance the desire to involve local residents with the need to meet milestones and delivery targets' (DCLG, 2010c:7). There is in fact a growing literature in community development which seeks to show how its effectiveness can be measured but this literature all points to the need for community participation in the determination of measures of success (Armstrong and Key, 1979; Barr et al, 1996; Craig, 2002; Skinner and Wilson, 2002). Most government programmes – as even the national evaluation of the

10-year long New Deal for Communities (NDC) acknowledged (DCLG, 2010a) – leave little time and space for such careful participative work to be undertaken over time, and remain dominated by a concern with inputs, outputs and targets.

Where national programmes did attempt to involve local residents, such as in the Sure Start programme for under-4s, government was critical of the fact that they fell behind schedule and were underspent (Glass, 2005). Perhaps, with local NDC projects managed quite strongly by professional interests – and a view that, in some cases, community views should be overridden by those of professionals – it is not surprising to find that there was 'little change with regard to some social capital indicators such as people thinking they can influence local decisions' (DCLG, 2010b: 28), even in relation to other deprived areas, and that radical forms of local involvement tended not to be encouraged (Dinham, 2007). Many of the lessons for policy-makers derived from this intensive and expensive programme – such as 'needing community engagement to occur from the bottom-up', and 'not making community engagement a numbers game' (DCLG, 2010a: 88), are those which community development practitioners could have identified many years earlier. The NDC evaluation also observed that communities tended to be the site of contestation as much as consensus, again an insight derived from many earlier years of community development theory and practice (Hoggett, 1997).

A strong theoretical base is important for preserving the distinctive identity of community development; yet, with some honourable exceptions, there remains a relative paucity of theoretical material about UK community development and this has also weakened its ability to develop a strong 'race' or gender analysis, for example. Although we have included extracts which focus on the dimensions of 'race', gender and disability, these are still not yet representative of rich seams of material in these territories. The editors believe this book may also prove to be useful in the context of a growing divergence of policy context in the devolved administrations. In addition, increasing attention needs to be focused on work with specific population groups such as black and minority ethnic communities as the population of the UK has become increasingly diverse and, in some cities, 'super-diverse'. This is a need highlighted by the growth of social movements from the 1990s which have been based far more on autonomous collective action than on the interventions of paid workers (Bunyan, 2009).

The goal of this book is therefore to reassert the identity of the occupation of community development in a UK context by drawing together key readings from the past 50 years from a range of sources (books, journal articles, monographs, policy papers) which have helped to shape this identity. While the majority of extracts are more analytical or theoretically oriented, we have also drawn on well-structured case studies of practice or policy that illuminate questions of value and general orientation. The need for this book is considerable at a time when the theory, values and practice of community development are in danger of becoming ever more compromised. In the context again of significant public expenditure cuts, community development risks becoming enmeshed in strategies to manage the growing shortfall in public service provision – inviting communities to participate in 'pulling themselves up by their own bootstraps'. Most importantly, therefore, this book explores the familiar gap between rhetoric and reality – between theory and practice.

At the same time, the aim of the book is not, as noted earlier, to provide a definitive 'official' history of community development in the UK. As also noted above, the context for this book is one where community development has moved in and out of fashion, has been promoted or undermined by the actions of successive governments, and, seemingly found in a wide variety of organisational contexts, is the subject of increasingly confused debates about its 'true' meaning, and yet apparently recently been enjoying something of a revival. We hope therefore that the book will provide a strong focus for these debates, providing a collection of key readings from the UK community development literature which will help to resolve many of the ambiguities about what community development actually entails in the UK, and provide guidance for new recruits to the profession in what is an increasingly bewildering time.

Even in a book as long as this, it is not possible to include every strong candidate from the literature. The extracts that are included, on average eight in each section, were chosen from long lists of about 40 pieces. The aim was to choose a selection which most accurately reflected the main currents of discussion in the literature for the periods in question. This is why, for example, several texts which are American in origin, are included in the first period when there was a paucity of home-grown urban literature in particular. The following sections reflect the three key periods, or milestones, in the life of community development in the UK, broadly, the period up to the 1970s, the late 1970s to the early 1990s, and the past 15 to 20 years. There is no sense therefore in which this collection could be regarded as either the 'best' of community development writing, or as a comprehensive account. What we think it does do as a whole is to reflect the continuities in debate – most of all about the ambivalent and frequently hostile relationship between community development and the state, and the latter's attempt to use community development as a tool to 'manage' urban deprivation and dissent; about the parameters of practice and the boundaries between that practice and related activities such as self-help; about the need carefully to interrogate the language of community initiatives to ensure that the values of community development are adhered to (see, for example, Craig, 2007 (Ch 4.9, this volume) in relation to the tendency to badge work as 'community capacity-building'; also Skinner, 1997; Henderson and Vercseg, 2010); and key changes – in status, in policy context, in the availability of literature, in the changing 'ownership' of community development, public understanding of its role, and in the freedom to act – which characterise the evolution of community development practice over the past 60 or so years. These intrinsic features – of continuity and change – are addressed in more detail within their specific policy contexts, in the introductory essays for each of Sections 2, 3 and 4.

The extracts here are organised in strictly chronological order, that is, in terms of the date of first publication. There are, as we have recognised, significant omissions in the collection here. This is partly because these can be found more appropriately elsewhere. We have attempted, however, to pick up some of the more significant gaps and milestone documents – such as the two Gulbenkian Reports of the late 1960s and early 1970s (Calouste Gulbenkian Foundation, 1968; 1973) and the corresponding Scottish report (SED, 1975), which helped put community development on a more professional footing – in the sectional introductions. There is little, however, that points to the influence of literature from other cultures after the 1960s. This is partly addressed in the international reader which some of us were involved in producing earlier (Craig et al, 2008), in the continuing output of the *Community Development Journal* and in the steadily increasing number of publications from the International Association for Community Development (IACD). We have not found room for material reflecting the growing interest in the evaluation of community development and, in particular, the important and innovative work of Alan Barr and his colleagues at the Scottish Community Development Centre (Barr and Hashagen, 2000) and of organisations such as COGs (Wilson and Wilde, 2003). In the late 1990s and 2000s, the Joseph Rowntree Foundation (www.jrf.org.uk) was also a significant contributor to the literature on community involvement in regeneration and housing programmes.

Some important issues and strands of interest are not sufficiently represented, such as the environment (for example, Warburton, 1998; Cannan, 2000), the field of arts and culture (for example, Meade and Shaw, 2006), or rural communities (for example, Francis and Henderson, 1992; Henderson and Kaur, 1999). Neither is the increasing role of the Church which, in *Faith in the City* (CoE, 1985) made a highly symbolic intervention into urban debates to challenge the hegemony of Thatcherite analysis and policy. Faith-based organisations in general have made an increasingly important contribution to community development work in the past years, a trend highlighted in the recent book on migrant workers in London (Wills et al, 2010), which shows how newly arriving migrants tend to gravitate more to church-based or faith-based groups rather than to political parties, trades unions and community groups, as their immediate post-war ancestors would also have done. We have also not been able to include literature reflecting an increasing theme of recent years, that of ethical questions (Banks and Gallagher, 2008) or a recent interesting trend in the literature and practice which focuses on assets rather than on needs, as a way of engaging with communities (O'Leary, 2008). Doubtless, other writers and practitioners could point to further serious omissions. In the next years, we will doubtless also identify literature which will turn out to be the precursor of significant new strands of the literature, for example reflecting different understandings of community in a globalised world, new sites of struggle, new issues to be addressed. Perhaps if we are lucky enough to be asked to undertake a second edition of this volume in a few years' time, these lacunae can be addressed!

Historically, as we have noted, there have also been a number of individual contributors to the UK literature who have had a significant impact in different ways and to which we have been able to pay limited attention: the early outputs of, for example, Robert Leaper (1968), George Thomason (1969) and Peter Baldock (1977), which helped develop a theoretical literature, the substantial volume of writing from David Thomas (for instance 1978; 1983) and, for many years, his collaborators, David Jones, and, most particularly, Paul Henderson, who developed a knowledge base around the kinds of skills and training needed for working in communities. The scope of Henderson's writing has been very considerable indeed (for example Henderson et al, 1976; Henderson et al, 1982; Henderson and Kaur, 1999; Henderson and Vercseg, 2010). The continuing work of Alan Twelvetrees, notably successive editions of his book on community work (Twelvetrees, 2009), Gilchrist's work on networking (1995) and Chanan et al's (1999) work on community development's contribution to regeneration have also been important. The need to balance perspectives with the space allotted to us has simply left us with some difficult choices which, doubtless, will not satisfy every reader. We hope, at least, to have signposted most of those who have made important contributions to the debates about community development in the UK.

At an historic moment in the political life of the UK, and one which might represent another key milestone in the history of British community development, with a radical coalition government embarking on a series of policies which may change the face of the country if carried through, it is difficult – not to say foolish – to predict where community development may be going. However, if we learn anything from its history, it is of a practice which reflects a commitment to the need for ordinary people to have more control over the policies and services which affect their lives, in ways which are more rooted in their own experience and expertise than simply through the mediation of an increasingly distant and unresponsive parliamentary system – and which will continue to adapt to the changing political climate in which it operates – while retaining and reviewing those values that support a process of real empowerment in the pursuit of social justice.

Notes

[1] Within this book we have chosen consistently to use the term 'community development' for simplicity: the terms 'community work', 'community action' and 'community organising' are related terms but often with nuanced differences. Some of the literature included in this book addresses these distinctions and there is substantial other literature on which the avid reader can draw, listed in our consolidated references section. We would encourage readers to draw on this exhaustive literature given that we could only include a small proportion of it here.

[2] Similar structures emerged in the devolved administrations later on such as the Community Development Alliance Scotland and CDCymru, together with a parallel structure to promote community development training, particularly for activists – initially the Federation of Community Development Training Groups, now Federation of Community Development Learning: www.fcdl.org.uk.

[3] Early in 2011, as a result of government funding cuts, BASSAC and DTA announced their intention to merge.

[4] This is even more the case for rural community development practitioners and activists than it is for urban practice: see, for instance, Craig, G. et al (2005).

Note on the editorial process

The book as a whole has been overseen by the entire editorial team but different members took responsibility for drafting introductions to the different sections and making a first choice of the extracts to be included. These initial choices were made, as noted, from long lists of possible extracts, and a consensus reached among the team as to which should be chosen as the selection most representative of the period concerned, and given the need for overall balance. No one author appears more than once, itself a hard rule to operationalise. Gary Craig drafted the main Introduction, Marilyn Taylor and Keith Popple that for Section 2, Mae Shaw and Marjorie Mayo that for Section 3, and Mae Shaw and Gary Craig that for Section 4. The Afterword was initially drafted by Marjorie Mayo. Given that these are extracts, we have edited them in a way that maintains the flow of key arguments as far as possible.

Section 2
In and against the state:
1950s to the late 1970s

Introduction

The period covered by this first section of extracts was a period of considerable change in international, social, cultural, economic and political affairs. It began towards the end of a period of readjustment throughout the world, dealing with the impact of the Second World War. The welfare state was at its height in many countries, establishing new perceptions of the rights of citizenship. The economic growth of the 1950s and 1960s fuelled both its expansion and expectations of what it could and should provide. The slogan of the Conservative Party at the end of the 1950s was: 'We've never had it so good'. But by the end of the 1960s, it was becoming increasingly clear that the problems of poverty and inequality had not been solved. This led, on the one hand, to increasing government intervention in the public sphere in Britain and elsewhere, including government initiatives targeted at local communities themselves; on the other hand, popular discontent grew with a wave of new social movements challenging the status quo. By the end of the 1970s, the picture was changing again, with significant cuts in public spending and the advance of a neo-liberal agenda, strongly committed to the market.

During the 1950s, the UK – along with other colonial powers – was beginning to emerge from a long history of empire. India, with the newly created Pakistan, had declared independence in 1947 and now in the words of the UK Prime Minister, Harold Macmillan, the 'winds of change' were sweeping across Africa, with the growth of nationalism on that continent. The community development tradition at that time was deeply embedded in colonial and post-colonial developments, the former seeking to perpetuate colonial domination and staving off growing unrest, the latter bowing to the inevitable and preparing its subjects for independence (Batten, 1957; Mayo, 1975 – Ch 2.5, this volume). On their return to the UK, however, Batten and his colleagues began constructing a distinct body of literature to promote community development in this country through what became known as the 'non-directive approach' (Batten, 1957; 1962; 1967), which was to influence the early volumes of the *Community Development Journal* launched in 1966 to replace an earlier newsletter.

In the 1950s, much of community development practice in the UK was concerned with youth, leisure and education. However, a large-scale programme of slum clearance and redevelopment, much of which was to deal with the remnants of war-time bombing and poor-quality rented residential property, was displacing longstanding communities, leading to concerns about fragmentation and isolation – a process documented by the newly founded Institute for Community Studies (Young and Wilmott, 1957, 1962). The need to 'restore community' on newly built but inadequately resourced post-war housing estates led to the growth of interventions to encourage community self-help and local support networks (Goetschius, 1969) and to the growth of tenants' associations, formed to tackle social and housing management issues.

Thomas (1983) documents a struggle for ownership of community development during these early years between the educational roots of colonial community development and an increasingly dominant social work profession. Although the colonial community education tradition was to remain influential in Scotland (HMSO, 1975), in England, it was social work that was gaining the upper hand. A strong influence was Dame Eileen Younghusband's 1959 report on training for social work, which identified community work as a third method of social work intervention, alongside case work and group work. This influence was to be reinforced in the late 1960s by the recommendations of the Seebohm Report (HMSO, 1968), whose proposals for a major restructuring of social services into large unified local authority social service departments included a recommendation that community work should become a key element in the delivery of social work services.

However, as the 1960s progressed, there were other influences at play. The election of John F. Kennedy as US President in 1960 was seen by many to herald the beginning of a new age of social change. The early 1960s also saw the growth of the black civil rights movement, with Martin Luther King's seminal 'I have a dream' speech on his vision of an equal and united America. Both the black civil rights movement and the growth of feminism in the US were challenging the white male domination of politics and power. At the same time, US foreign policy came under increasing public scrutiny and opposition, especially to its activity in Vietnam and Cambodia. Later in the decade, the certainties of the post-war period were to be further challenged by unrest and struggle in many major cities throughout the world, with student riots in Paris and the rise of the new left in Europe challenging capitalism, and the brief but iconic 'Prague Spring' in Czechoslovakia challenging the Soviet regime.

The UK too witnessed the growth of a new wave of dissent, from the foundation of the Campaign for Nuclear Disarmament and Amnesty International in the late 1950s to the formation of a range of campaign groups in the 1960s, including the Child Poverty Action Group, Friends of the Earth, Women's Aid and Shelter, the latter bringing the growing plight of homelessness to public attention. It was no surprise therefore when the long period of Conservative government since the beginning of the 1950s was brought to an end by the election of a Labour government in 1964 on a manifesto entitled *The New Britain*.

The 1950s also saw the eruption of 'race riots' in London and Nottingham and these racial tensions were to intensify over the 1960s, until they were brought to a head in a speech in 1968 by a leading UK Conservative politician, Enoch Powell, who predicted 'rivers of blood' on the streets of the UK.[1] The need for a government response was underlined by Africanisation policies in two former colonies, Kenya and later Uganda, which fuelled major new waves of immigration of Asian-origin refugees to the UK in 1968 and 1972.

Increasingly government became aware that it needed to respond to social change. During the 1960s, it commissioned a number of reports that exposed failures in the welfare state to eradicate the problems of poverty. These included, for example, the Ingleby Report (Home Office, 1960) on children and young people, the Plowden Report (DES, 1967b) on education, the Seebohm Report (HMSO, 1968) on social work, the Skeffington Report (HMSO, 1969) on planning and the Fairbairn-Milson Report (DES, 1969) on youth work and education. They were reinforced by independent academic accounts arguing not only that poverty had not retreated but that in some cases the plight of the poorest in society had worsened (Abel-Smith and Townsend, 1965; Coates and Silburn, 1970).

In 1964, the US had responded to growing urban unrest and racial tension by declaring a comprehensive War on Poverty, which included a range of measures, including a Community Action Programme providing for the 'maximum feasible participation' of the residents of these areas. Although by 1968, the flaws in this model were already emerging (Moynihan, 1969), this was to be a model for the UK response, which included a range of measures intended to ensure the maintenance of well-integrated communities and a well-managed workforce, as well as to improve the functioning of the expanding welfare state. In particular, the need to be seen to be responding to public panic in response to immigration and race relations, led the government to launch in May 1968, the Urban Programme (Foot, 1969: 112; Edwards and Batley, 1978). That year also saw the launch of the linked National Community Development Project (NCDP), located in 12 'deprived areas' of Britain. This was conceived as an action-research initiative, whose central purpose was to collect information on the impact of social policies in the selected neighbourhoods, to assist people to use local services more constructively and to encourage and support community innovation and initiatives (Mayo, 1975b).

Overall, this investment was to provide a significant boost to community development and community organisations more generally. The Urban Programme, for example, was to provide significant funding to community groups and organisations for years to come, although it failed to reach minority ethnic groups (Demuth, 1977). Indeed, as these initiatives were launched, community development was moving into the mainstream, with the terms 'community development' and 'community work' appearing more frequently in policy documents. This was highlighted by the findings of an influential study group, supported by a major foundation, which brought together some key players of the era. The first of two influential Gulbenkian Reports, published in 1968 and 1973, defined community work as encompassing both direct neighbourhood work and interagency coordination and put it on the map as a 'necessary full-time professional task' that 'should be recognised as part of the professional practice of teachers, social workers, the clergy, health workers, architects, planners administrators and others' (Gulbenkian, 1968:149). Thomas (1983) identifies this as the point at which community development finally broke away from its educational moorings although it had not totally lost its education roots. That year (1968) also saw the launch by the Labour government, under the auspices of the Department of Education and Science, of what is now the Community Development Foundation (then called the Young Volunteer Force Foundation), although it was to move in the 1970s to the Voluntary Service Unit at the Home Office.

Mainstream approaches to community development were, however, about to be challenged. In its original design, the NCDP assumed that a minority of people were caught in a 'cycle of poverty' and needed support to compete more effectively in the market-place and that it was communities and possibly failures of service coordination that lay at the heart of the problems of disadvantaged neighbourhoods. However, the CDP workers rejected these explanations. Instead they highlighted the wider inequalities consequent on gathering de-industrialisation and the contradictions of capitalism. Perhaps unsurprisingly, the articulation of these radical views led central government to withdraw its support for the projects (Loney, 1983). In this the NCDP experiment echoed the experience of the US War on Poverty, which foundered on the resistance of local mayors and the contradictions between a reformist agenda, on the one hand, and the aspirations of the people in disadvantaged communities whose participation the programme had sought, on the other (Marris and Rein, 1967; Moynihan, 1969; Miller and Rein, 1974 – Ch 2.6, this volume).

This more radical CDP analysis had a strong resonance for many community development workers on the ground. For many people, particularly young people, the 1960s had been a decade of growing idealism that the world could be changed for the better. During the 1970s, however, the clamour for large-scale and progressive change was followed by a sense of disillusionment as it was recognised that the struggles for real improvements had much to contend with.

The first challenge was the worsening global economic situation. The Arab–Israeli war of October 1973 led Arab oil producers to reduce their supplies and substantially increase the price of oil, which had a major impact on industrial production and consumption throughout the world. During the 1960s, world trade in manufactured products had grown tenfold; there was a significant increase in energy consumption; and a massive rise in the world's money supplies. However, these were all to be affected as economies throughout the world went into crisis with inflation and unemployment at their highest since the 1930s (Hobsbawm, 1994).

In the UK, a noticeable slump in economic activity at the beginning of the decade led to stagflation (high unemployment and high inflation), and wages struggled to keep up with inflation. The resulting industrial unrest – with a miners' work-to-rule – led to the introduction of a compulsory three-day week by the Conservative government of 1970–74 to conserve energy. Later in the decade, the dramatic slide in the pound sterling led the Labour government to seek a loan from the International Monetary Fund. The conditions that accompanied this loan demanded substantial cuts in the government's expenditure plans as well as increases in taxation.

Against this background, the 1970s witnessed the growth of a strong anti-statist element in community development, with the state as the fulcrum of discontent and target of many campaigns: strikes against proposed rent rises, campaigns to address poor housing conditions, demands for improved welfare provision, campaigns against redevelopment and so on. The march on the town hall was a common phenomenon. The social work tradition remained strong – community development established itself firmly at the National Institute for Social Work during the 1970s. But within the community development field, there was a renewed struggle for the soul of community development as community workers challenged the dominant community social work paradigm. This debate was carried out within the pages of a number of seminal publications. These included the output of the NCDP, but also notably the 'Talking Points' of the Association of Community Workers, founded in 1970, *Community Action*, a radical magazine launched by activist planners, and the Community Work book series published by Routledge and Kegan Paul. The Federation of Community Work Training Groups (now the Federation of Community Development Learning) was established with a grant from the Gulbenkian Foundation to provide community work training for both paid and volunteer community workers. The Federation's publications were to add to the growing body of knowledge in the field.

Inspiration for a more radical approach did not only come from the NCDP. In 1968, writing in the US, Jack Rothman identified three models of community work practice: locality development, social planning and social action. The first reflected the self-help tradition described above but also built on the work of Ross (1955), who sought to build the community's resilience in the wake of the dehumanising processes of urbanisation. The second was a more planning-oriented approach, reflecting perhaps how the NCDP was envisaged by the state, while the third sought to shift power relationships more fundamentally.

One important early influence on the growth of the social action approach was the US community organiser and writer Saul Alinsky (1909–72), who worked in some of the poorest communities of Chicago, California, Michigan and New York. His two seminal books (Alinsky, 1969; 1971) and his Industrial Areas Foundation were to inform community development writing and action in the US at the time, and much later, the ideas of the young Barack Obama. The late 1960s also saw the founding of ACORN and the Center for Community Change in that country, two more influential community-building organisations working with poor, which usually meant minority ethnic, communities for social justice.

Inspiration also came from the global South, where struggles against repressive governments were putting pressure on the North to recognise their demands and their place in the changing world order. One significant example was the struggle against apartheid, which became an international movement and eventually contributed to its overthrow. Also influential was the struggle in Latin America against US imperialism, especially after the overthrow of Allende in Chile. Liberation theology – and the work of Paolo Freire and Ivan Illich in particular – challenged traditional approaches to education and medicine but was to provoke considerable interest among community development workers and offer new approaches for community development practice (see, for example, Freire, 1972). Closer to home, however, the escalating conflict in Northern Ireland, where polarised and segregated Catholic and Protestant communities were engaged in bitter and often violent opposition to one another, was posing new challenges to community development. This conflict, euphemistically known as 'the Troubles', was to rage from around 1969 to the late 1990s.

Issues of race and gender were also beginning to surface in UK community development. Even the NCDP analysis, for example, whose focus was on alleviating poverty, was to be criticised for failing to highlight sufficiently the particular concerns of women in poverty or their role in community organising (Dominelli, 2006). Women were at the forefront (Rowbotham, 1990) of many community struggles, and were making a significant contribution to the community development literature. More generally, women on the political left in Britain were challenging the domination there of a traditional white male view of the world. This challenge was to grow over the coming years.

Much community action during the 1970s had seen the local and national state as its target. As the period came to an end, public services were under attack and the decade ended as it began, with increasing industrial unrest – the 1978–79 winter of discontent – which in turn was to open the door to a neo-liberal Conservative government under the leadership of Margaret Thatcher. In these circumstances, the anti-statism that some felt had characterised much of community development was to prove inadequate

(Lees and Mayo, 1984). Community development workers now found themselves campaigning in alliance with the public sector unions to preserve public sector services and jobs. Many found themselves in an ambiguous position, employed by the state and seeking to defend state services while feeling it was not 'their' state (LEWRG, 1980 – Ch 2.8, this volume).

Note
[1] Enoch Powell's apocalyptic speech suggested that racial tensions would increase to the point where there would be race warfare on the streets of urban Britain: for the text of the speech see www.martinfrost.ws/htmlfiles/rivers_blood2.html. See also Powell (1968).

The non-directive approach in group and community work

Reg Batten with Madge Batten

Although our definition of community work includes a very wide variety of purposes and programmes, they are all implemented through only two basic approaches: the one, which is directive in character; and the other which, for want of a better name, is usually called non-directive. Of these two approaches the directive approach is by far the more common. The non-directive approach is relatively new. It is still not very well understood and applied by most community workers, many of whom doubt its value.

The directive approach: planning and providing FOR people

The directive approach, as its name implies, means that the agency which adopts it itself decides, more or less specifically, whatever it thinks people need or ought to value or ought to do for their own good, and sometimes even how they ought to behave. These decisions become the agency's betterment goals *for* people. The agency will then provide whatever staff, equipment, premises, and programme it thinks are needed to meet the needs or interests of the people it wishes to help, in the hope that they will avail themselves of the services or activities it provides. This will bring them into contact with the agency's workers, who will then try to influence people in relation to the agency's ideas of betterment for them. It is the essence of this approach that the agency and its workers think, decide, plan, organize, administer, and provide *for* people. Always the main initiative, and the final say, remains with them.

While the directive approach is ... relatively ineffective as a means of influencing all the very many people who for one reason or another dislike it and resist it, it does at any rate bring the worker into personal contact with all those who are attracted to his programme. Many of these may not only not resent, but even welcome, direct advice and guidance from someone

From: Batten, T.R., with Batten, M. (1967) *The non-directive approach to group and community work*, London: Oxford University Press, pp 1-23.

they have learned to like, respect, and accept as their 'leader'. It is with this kind of person that the worker can do his most effective work.

But effective for what? Most effective, one might think, in meeting people's short-term needs, and least effective for the long-term goal of helping them to realize their full potentialities as persons. This is because the more effectively the worker succeeds in leading, guiding, and persuading them to accept the *results of his thinking* for them, and the more he provides for them, the less they need to think, decide, and provide for themselves. Thus he deprives them of many potentially valuable learning experiences and tends to make them more dependent on himself. This is a major weakness of the directive approach for agencies that aim to increase people's capacity for responsible and effective self-directed action.

Community work in its modern sense in Britain was begun in the nineteenth century by upper- and middle-class idealists and reformers who sought to ameliorate the often appalling conditions under which working-class people lived in the new industrial towns. Such people's material needs at that time were obvious and specific, and many of them were too poor, too ignorant, and too disorganized to do very much to help themselves. In this context the newly-formed social agencies necessarily took the initiative in planning and providing *for* people, and this directive approach was undoubtedly the most effective way of providing help.

Conditions today, however, are very different. Fewer people are really poor, and the main emphasis in community work has shifted from providing for people's material needs to helping them in relation to what, broadly speaking, one might call their psychological needs. Such needs may be stated in a variety of different ways: to find a real purpose in life; to control their emotional impulses; to think more objectively; to establish more rewarding relationships with others and thus acquire status with others; to make some more satisfying use of their increasing hours of leisure; or to learn how to choose from an ever-widening and often worrying range of choices those most likely to produce the greatest satisfaction to themselves. Experience has shown that the traditional directive type of approach has limitations as a means of helping people in relation to such needs, for reasons that have already been explained: and this is why many agencies are now experimenting with the non-directive approach. This is the subject of the next chapter.

The non-directive approach

The worker who uses the non-directive approach does not attempt to decide for people, or to lead, guide, or persuade them to accept any of his own specific conclusions about what is good for them. He tries to get them to decide for themselves what their needs are: what, if anything, they are willing to do to meet them; and how they can best organize, plan, and act to carry their project through. Thus he aims at stimulating a process of self-determination and self-help, and he values it for all the potential learning experiences which participation in this process provides. He aims to encourage people to develop themselves, and it is by thinking and acting for themselves, he believes, that they are most likely to do so. Moreover, the outcome will usually be a project designed to produce some change for the better in the people's lives. Thus two kinds of betterment result, and change in people and change in their environment go hand in hand.

At least, that is the theory, but stated thus briefly it leaves a mass of relevant questions unanswered. For instance, even if the worker succeeds in getting people to consider meeting some of their needs themselves, how can he be sure that they will agree on what these are? Or if they do agree, that they will decide on what is really best for them? Or even on what is practicable for them? And if, for whatever reason, their project fails, as it well may do since the worker is in no sense in control, how then does betterment of any kind result?

Conditions necessary for self-directed action

To answer these questions we need to look much more closely at the worker's role. First, let us note that people do quite often agree on a need, decide on a project to meet it, and carry it through successfully without any outsider's help. They may establish their own recreational or cultural or interest group, and decide on a programme quite independently for themselves; they may form a protest group to demand a playground or a safe road crossing for their children; or they may form a service group to help other people in need.

While this is true it is also true that many such groups have failed to meet the needs of their members. In fact, autonomous action by small groups of people will not occur, or if it does occur will not succeed, unless certain conditions are present. These are:

1. that a number of people are dissatisfied with things as they are, and are agreed on something which they all feel as a specific want;
2. that they realize that this want is likely to remain unmet unless they do something about it themselves;
3. that they have, or have access to, sufficient resources to be able to achieve what they want to achieve. This implies that they have (or can get):
   (a) enough knowledge to enable them to make a wise decision about what to do and how best to do it;
   (b) enough resources of knowledge, skill, and equipment actually to do it; and

35

(c) a sufficiently strong incentive to keep them together while they carry the project through.

If the want is strong enough, and the other conditions are all present, then people will act without outside help. Unfortunately, more often than not they are not all present. This is why many potentially valuable need-meeting autonomous groups either do not form, or if they do form, quickly die: and this is why community workers, if they wish, can find ample scope for using the non-directive approach.

The worker's role in groups

This kind of work is now being called *community development*, and workers who undertake it are often called *community development workers*. Such workers specialize in using the non-directive approach in the work they do with autonomous groups. The essence of their work is to create sufficiently favourable conditions for successful group action without in any way infringing group autonomy either by making decisions for the group or by doing for its members anything that they could reasonably be expected to do, or learn to do, for themselves. This means in practice that the worker will:

1. try to strengthen incentives for people to act – when these are weak – by stimulating them to discuss their needs in the hope that they will come to see them more specifically as wants
2. help by providing information – if people need it – about how similar groups have organized for action
3. help people systematically to think through and analyse the nature and causes of any problem they may encounter in the course of their project, and to explore the pros and cons of each and every suggestion for solving it; and
4. help by suggesting sources from which the group may be able to obtain any material help or technical advice in addition to what they can provide for themselves.

The worker has one other important role in groups. This is to help resolve any inter-personal difficulties that may arise between the members. However strong the incentive that has brought them together may be, and even perhaps just because it is so strong, every member will be personally affected by the outcome – good or bad – of any decisions the group may take. Yet some of them may hold very different views about what these decisions should be. Such disagreements may easily lead to friction between the members, and unless they are resolved may even break up the group. Should such a disagreement happen, the worker is often in a much better position than anyone else to help resolve it. He is present in the group but he alone is not a member of it, and he does not commit himself to support anyone's viewpoint. On the contrary, by asking questions, he tries to encourage the members of the group objectively to consider the pros and cons of *every* viewpoint in order that they should decide what best to do in the interest of them all.

The worker's role with individuals

What has been written above applies to non-directive work with a group, or with a committee representative of several groups. But a worker may also work with individuals in much the same way, for the underlying principle of enabling people to assume responsibility for implementing their own decisions for themselves is the same.

The potential advantages of the non-directive approach

Workers who use the non-directive approach do so because they believe that they can achieve their purposes better in this way. Its advantages, as they see them, are as follows:

1. It enables them to accomplish more with their limited resources
By encouraging people to organize to meet more of their own needs for themselves, the non-directive approach enables an agency to spread its own limited resources more widely, since the agency provides less and the people more. There is also the additional advantage that people will generally look after what they provide for themselves more carefully than what an agency provides for them.

2. It helps to 'develop' people
Many agencies have as their primary aim the development of people in the sense that they want to help them, both individually and in groups, to develop the will and the competence to manage their own affairs. They value this, not only because it enables people to meet more of their own needs for themselves, but also because in the process of doing so they can increase their status and feeling of self-respect.

3. It helps the emergence of 'we-feeling'
People who work together in a group on a project they have all chosen in order to meet some need they all share tend to get to know and like and respect one another, and to think and talk of themselves more and more as 'we' rather than as 'I' and 'they'; and thus, if it was previously lacking, the germ of a feeling of caring for the welfare of other members is born, which

may later extend to people outside the group. It is this change of attitude towards others, which *may* result from a project, which constitutes the core of all true community development.

4. It provides many opportunities of educating and influencing people
Although a worker using a non-directive approach does not try to lead or guide people to accept any preformed conclusion of his own, he does hope to educate them, and also to influence their attitudes and behaviour. He aims to educate them partly by asking questions intended to help them to think more systematically and relevantly than they otherwise would, and partly by providing any relevant information they need and would otherwise lack. He can also hope to influence their attitudes and behaviour indirectly, as we have seen above through what he contributes to the emergence of 'we-feeling'.

Its limitations

Whether the worker actually reaps these potential advantages of the non-directive approach or not will depend on the degree of skill with which he uses it: but however great his skill may be, he must always be ready to recognize that this approach has limitations.

Thus it is implicit in the use of this approach that the worker is never in control, and he has no guarantee whatsoever that, as the result of the thinking he has helped people to do, they will arrive at the conclusion he would prefer. All he can do is to trust to his skill in the hope that with his (non-directive) help, they will arrive at decisions which really are good for them. If they fail in this, e.g. if they choose goals they lack the skill or resources to achieve, they will lose confidence both in the worker and themselves, and the worker's efforts will have resulted in harm rather than good. A very great deal, therefore, depends upon his skill in helping them to think objectively and systematically about where their own true interest lies.

Another limitation is that people may sometimes dislike and reject the worker's non-directive approach because they do not want the trouble and responsibility of thinking and deciding for themselves. This may frequently happen when an agency changes from the directive to the non-directive approach, for one effect of the directive approach, as we have seen, is to make people dependent, irresponsible, and unpractised in thinking for themselves. Yet if the worker then tries to *impose* responsibility on them, however unwilling they may be, what then becomes of his 'non-directive' approach?

Factors affecting choice

As we saw earlier, a worker may either work *directively* by trying to get people to act on his conclusions about what is good for them, or *non-directively* by encouraging them to think out their own conclusions for themselves. The two approaches are therefore very different, but both are useful and neither is invariably 'better' than the other.

If both are useful, why then do so many workers use only one, and that in most cases, though not in all, the directive approach? There are many reasons for this which are quite unrelated to any normal criteria of efficiency. One is that the directive approach is the traditional approach to community work, and that like all established traditions it tends to perpetuate itself. Another is that the directive approach helps the worker to feel that he really is in control – however illusory in practice this feeling may sometimes turn out to be – and this is far more tolerable, even for people who are not authoritarian in outlook, than the feeling of strain and uncertainty that the worker so often has to endure when he is working non-directively. When working non-directively the worker can never feel entirely in control.

There are other reasons too. Even if a worker wants to adopt a non-directive approach he may not be free to do so. This is because many workers are not free agents. Their status in the community, or even with the agency which employs them, may depend on their ability to produce some quick and visible results which they cannot ensure, or ensure quickly enough, by working non-directively. Thus a youth leader, for instance, may feel that he has to work directively in order to satisfy his Management Committee or the parents of the young people that he is running 'a really worthwhile club'. Again, he is not really free to choose a non-directive approach unless he has acquired the skill he needs to use it. And he may have few opportunities of acquiring it for training of this kind is still, for most workers, hard to come by even if they want it.

But if a worker has skill in using both, how then does he decide which to use and when to use it? A great deal will depend on what he sees as the people's major needs and on what he thinks of the people who have these needs. If he thinks that they are either so ignorant or so young and inexperienced that they are unfit to decide for themselves where their own true interest lies; or so apathetic or irresponsible or lazy or dependent in attitude that they will not attempt to do anything to try to help themselves; or so hostile towards one another that they will refuse to work together; or so disorganized that they are incapable of working together: then he may well decide that the only way he can achieve anything is to decide, plan, and provide for them himself.

He will also be influenced by how he sees himself. Thus the more expert in diagnosing and meeting people's needs he feels himself to be, and the less he trusts the people he is working with to do this well enough for themselves, the more likely he is to choose the directive approach … this is true of many youth leaders who see their job mainly as one of leading and guiding young people who, because they are young and therefore immature, seem so much less well fitted to reach 'un-guided' good decisions for themselves.

It is more than doubtful, however, whether even a skilled and experienced worker is always safe in deciding for people just how their needs can best be met, or even just what these needs may be. As a worker his standpoint and his purposes are necessarily somewhat different from theirs, and therefore just because he is a worker he can never hope to become completely 'one of them'. Thus when he makes a decision for them he can only do so in the light of *his* purposes and of the relevant factors which *he* sees. Since he is not and cannot be one of them, however, he may quite easily overlook some factors which are relevant for them: and in that case his decision will not be truly right for them. And the greater the difference between him and the people with whom he works – whether in age, education, training, or experience of living as they do – the harder it will be for him to see their needs as they see them, or to judge how acceptable to them his ways of meeting these needs will be. Many agency-sponsored and worker-sponsored projects in communities have failed for no other reason than this. A worker using the directive approach needs to be able to identify himself with his clients very fully if he is to avoid making decisions which may involve him in difficulties of this kind.

To the extent that a worker realizes that such difficulties are likely to occur and wants to avoid them, to that extent he may be inclined to favour the non-directive approach. This has the advantage that it does not involve him in making any specific decisions for people, for it is then his job to encourage them to make these decisions for themselves. If he does this, however, he incurs the disadvantage, inherent in the use of the non-directive approach, of never being sure that the people will choose what he would like them to choose or act in the way that he thinks best. Thus to avoid the one disadvantage he will have to accept another: and only he is really in a position to decide in the light of the circumstances facing him at the time which advantage, together with its accompanying disadvantage, he will choose.

If this were all he had to worry about it would be bad enough, but in fact he is likely to have to face yet another dilemma. On the one hand the surer he is that he knows what is right, and the surer he is in his own mind that the people are not to be trusted to decide, plan, organize, and act quickly and efficiently for themselves, the more inclined he will be to choose the directive approach. On the other hand, if he then decides, plans, and provides for people, how does this help to meet their basic underlying need of learning how to think, plan, and act responsibly and efficiently for themselves? In fact, it is likely to have just the opposite effect, for the more the worker decides, plans, and provides for people, the more dependent and irresponsible they are likely to become. Thus once again the worker has a difficult choice to make.

It would be presumptuous for anyone to say what a worker should do when he faces a problem of this kind. All that can certainly be said is that he should desirably recognize that the dilemma exists and needs to be resolved. This means that he must carefully assess his purposes for people in the light of both their present and their long-term needs. In crisis situations, e.g. when people are homeless or hungry or diseased, their material needs are dominant and they may be in no position to help themselves. In such situations, the case for the directive approach becomes overwhelmingly strong. When, however, the people's needs are chronic rather than acute, and their attitude so irresponsible that they show no real willingness to try to help themselves, then the directive approach seems far less applicable: and the case for stimulating people to think and act for themselves, and thereby develop themselves, i.e. the case for the non-directive approach, becomes correspondingly strong.

There is one final complication. Whichever approach a worker may decide on, he cannot use it to really good effect unless it proves acceptable to the people he is working with. Thus if people would rather decide things for themselves, they may resent a worker's attempt to decide for them and withhold the co-operation he needs for success. Similarly, if a would-be non-directive worker seeks to impose on people the responsibility of deciding for themselves things they would rather have decided for them, then they too may feel resentful and refuse to co-operate. Somehow, whichever approach he chooses, the worker must make it acceptable to the people, and effective for his purposes with the people. For the worker the only sound criterion for assessing the value of either approach will be its effectiveness in helping him to achieve his purposes with people.

Hence although we believe very strongly in the value of the non-directive approach as a means of promoting development and growth in people, we also believe that workers should be careful to avoid imposing on dependent groups of young, or immature, or inexperienced people responsibilities for autonomous decision-making in excess of what they really are willing and able to bear. What the worker has to do with such people is to delineate initially only those areas of freedom and responsibility which he believes they will value and can learn to exercise with benefit and satisfaction to themselves. Then, as their confidence grows and as their competence increases, he will enlarge their area of freedom and responsibility accordingly.

Thus in some situations the worker may at one and the same time function directively in so far as he retains the power or intention to direct, lead, guide, persuade, or in any other way get people to conform to what he thinks they ought to do; and non-directively in so far as he defines and communicates to the people certain areas of freedom and responsibility within which he will leave them entirely free to act for themselves. Within these areas he will not express his own opinions and will not impose, or try to impose, any kind of veto, but concentrate solely on the non-directive functions of helping people to think, discuss, decide, plan, organize, and act responsibly and autonomously for themselves. And the more clearly he sees the development of people as his purpose, and the non-directive approach as the means of achieving it, the more he will want to use it with as many people and in as many situations as possible in relation to whatever wants and purposes they have or may develop.

There can be no question, therefore, of condemning one approach and supporting only the other. Neither can be judged good or bad except in terms of the worker's purpose, the relevance of this purpose to the needs and circumstances of the people, and the appropriateness of his choice of approach to the achievement of that purpose. However, when this has been said it may also be said that very many workers do habitually use the directive approach without ever seriously considering whether the non-directive approach might not sometimes, or often, help them to achieve their purposes better. Why this is so has been briefly explained earlier in this chapter, but the fact that it is so is unfortunate. One reason for writing this book is to explain both the uses and the disadvantages and limitations of the non-directive approach and thus provide some help to workers as to when to choose it; another, to explore what it implies in terms of role and function for workers who may then want to use it.

2.2

Working with community groups: using community development as a method of social work

George Goetschius

Forms of leadership

Experienced indigenous leaders

Leaders of this kind have usually been 'trained' by their previous experience. They may have been members of a trade union, a political party, a residential settlement, church or other body, and have been in a position of some responsibility, perhaps as a group or committee officer within a larger organisation. This kind of leader can often bring knowledge of how things are done, of committee procedure and an understanding of organisational matters, as well as an extremely valuable intuitive ability to get people to do things together.

Inexperienced indigenous leaders

Most of the local leaders encountered during the field work were inexperienced when they began to take part in the work of a group, and this affected their leadership in one of two ways. First, such a leader might feel hesitant and inadequate, fearful of making a wrong decision, slow to see what was needed, unable or unwilling to take sufficient responsibility for making things happen, in order to match the expectations of the membership with the activities of the committee. This kind of inexperienced leader either gradually developed the necessary skills and confidence, or grew anxious about his inadequacy and withdrew.

The second effect of inexperience was to lead to an over-estimate of the need for positive, visible leadership and for the 'boss' to make all the

From: Goetschius, G. (1969) *Working with community groups: Using community development as a method of social work*, London: Routledge & Kegan Paul, pp 48-52, 129-50.

decisions, and to be in on everything. This conception of leadership was sometimes due to insecurity in the new role, fear of failure or a genuine misunderstanding of the work of a leader in a self-programming group. This kind of leader can stunt the growth of a group and deter other potential leaders by his own fear of displacement or of losing control.

This fear can also hamper the group's relationship with the worker, who is seen as a threat by the insecure leader, and this may prevent the worker from offering effective help. There is less danger of an established group being, or feeling, threatened or overwhelmed by this type of leader, whose skills and energy can then be used to advantage.

The sociopathic leader

All leaders bring their own personalities into the work of the group and sometimes the personality is more valuable than any knowledge or expertise. Even a richly gifted personality, a charismatic leader, needs to bring something other than his personality to the group–some knowledge, skills, insights into human behaviour; also a recognition of the existence of a group as a group, and of the individuals within it and its responsibility to the membership, the residents and the community.

By contrast, the sociopathic leader usually comes to the group determined to remake it in his own image. He uses his endowments – sometimes neurotic, occasionally psychotic – as the sole instrument of leadership. This can involve an almost total disregard of the personalities of other members, of the validity of existing aims, objectives and procedures, and of the already existing pattern of social action. The sociopathic leader is not necessarily psychologically disturbed, but may be imprisoned within a particular situation, whether at home, at work, or in the social environment, that offers no scope for his potential abilities. He may suffer from inadequate educational opportunity and resent having to live below his potential. On the other hand, he may hold an exaggerated idea of his social role, far in advance of his ability to perform. He may try to act out a phantasy of leadership, without the necessary personal resources and with inadequate understanding and appreciation of the situation in which he is actually set.

A newly-formed community group often suffers seriously from the presence of such a leader. At first it feels the need of his determination and drive, only to discover later that his energy is disruptive of co-operative effort and that the group cannot extricate itself from his attachment. There were examples during the field work where the leadership behaviour of sociopathic leaders who had attached themselves to community groups led, or almost led, to the destruction of the group. The sociopathic leader often feels the need to deprive the group of the worker's services, as the worker is seen as a rival. The sociopathic leader can define leadership only in the singular. No other leader at any level must provide any service to the group but himself. All other leadership is unacceptable and, if it appears, is seen as competition or rebellion.

The indirect leader

The indirect leader is important to the work of the community group and is frequently present in the membership or in the wider community. He does not seek office as a committee member or as an activity leader but works quietly behind the scenes. He is often someone with previous experience of leadership in organisations unconnected with the estate. He encourages association among members and residents or, if he is from the adjacent community, he may help in the formulation of opinions about what is needed and what should be done. He may even be asked to speak at membership meetings and may often be useful as a mediator, helping informally to interpret the conflicting views. An indirect leader may sometimes be a disrupting influence on the work of the group if, for some reason, he has been wrongly excluded from the affairs of the group, is by nature a lone wolf, or is even an incipient sociopathic leader. It is important for the worker to find ways of helping the group to use the indirect leader to the best advantage in order to extend the opportunities for leadership as widely as possible.

Stages of group development

(1) The starting point

In fact, there is often no visible starting point. Spontaneous social interaction, the raw material from which groups develop, happens from the moment the new residents move on to an estate, and the worker's role is simply that of an observer.

(2) Exploration

At this stage, individuals meet informally, at first without definite purpose, in the ordinary occasions of social life. This loose network of personal relationships, from which the community group gradually emerges, is characterised by:

- Several small, nebulous, informal friendship groups, each with some idea about what should be done.
- No firm agreement within or among the groups on anyone proposal or on any set scheme for co-operation to achieve any of their aims.

- The presence of indigenous leaders-individuals with a definite idea, often without a formal following, or with a very small, loosely knit one.

Role of the Worker. At this stage the worker is occupied in making personal contacts, taking and creating opportunities for establishing his own role and probably only offering specific information. The worker must be able to draw on his experience of what other groups in similar circumstances were able to do, and to offer the necessary information should the group decide to take on a new task. Even before the group has reached any depth of cohesion and is still more or less a collection of individuals, the worker must make it clear that his service is offered to the group. Often a strong indigenous leader will attempt to 'use' the worker in the exercise of his leadership, especially if his authority is not already established.

The worker must make it clear that he is advising the *residents* and that the group, or groups, he is working with are to him representative of the entire resident population.

(3) Formation

By now the loosely-knit informal group has become more organised and is concerned to do something for the estate. They may even have regular meetings with a temporary chairman and have a fairly well-worked out proposal for some kind of activity. The gradual emergence of group feeling enables a definite programme to take shape. Some characteristics of this stage are:

- The group has begun to attract new members and it is possible for sub-groups to form, usually on the basis of common interests. age or place of residence on the estate. The group may choose a name for itself and may elect a chairman.
- Difficulties in getting co-operation. Occasionally after the initial enthusiasm has waned the sub-groups may compete with the larger group for status and power. Sometimes this takes the form of a conflict about what is to be done, or the nature of the authority vested in the officers.
- Deciding on aims and objectives. Many difficulties are partly resolved when the organisational forms are agreed upon and a general committee elected. Some difficulties may then be centred upon the roles of the various officers and the relations between the committee and the membership.

Role of the Worker. The worker should be able to show why formalisation is helpful, and to suggest forms of organisation which have been tried and found useful. The worker should recognise that, at this stage, some conflict is possible. The worker can point out that conflict experienced by the group is part of its development and not a sign that it will never work or that it is becoming less neighbourly. He should also be able to suggest how the conflict can be used, when it is recognised and accepted, to clarify the aims of the group and its preliminary tasks.

The worker should explain to the group the time and care necessary to establish the organisation. Often elements within the group want to begin work before the resources, manpower, money and organisation are available. The worker can suggest that the best thing is to concentrate on building an organisation capable of offering services. The social interaction arising from the attempt to build an organisation is just as valuable as that which occurs later when the service is offered.

(4) Development of programme

With some kind of organisation agreed upon, and something of its structure achieved, the attention of the group usually turns to the provision of service to its members. This period is characterised by increased cohesion and a sense of purpose. Early in this phase there is often pressure to make a vigorous start and to begin all the activities at once before the necessary money or manpower is available.

When the membership is fully informed and all the volunteers are available, then the committee is faced with the need to prove its usefulness. Excessive demands for service come in from the membership; the residents have exaggerated expectations, and dissenting groups within the membership add to the committee's problems. In such a situation the committee often overstretches its resources in order to offer bigger and better service, to exercise its authority and to prove itself. The committee, the membership and the association are attempting to establish an identity in their own eyes and in those of the statutory and voluntary bodies. It can be that so much is being done, so much attempted, that there is a general breakdown in communications.

Role of the Worker. The worker should suggest caution by pointing out the difficulties that may come from attempting to do too much. Anxiety can be allayed by assuring those directly concerned that the difficulties encountered are only to be expected; that going more slowly will increase the stability of the group and not endanger its 'identity'; that one activity well done can achieve more than several that 'don't quite come off'.

The worker can show the group methods of keeping the lines of communication open so that the various sections of the association and the community can be well informed and stress the importance of this. Help may be needed for the group to develop appropriate criteria for evaluating its work. Good evaluation is an aid to better service, a way of helping the group to see the value of the work and to achieve their own experience of 'success'. Often the criteria used are not relevant to the activity evaluated; for example, an outing does not depend for its success only on the numbers in the bus or the cost per person.

(5) The established association

This phase of the group's development produces strong group feeling stemming from established procedures. There are also relatively well-defined rules for individual and sub-group behaviour, and a sense of identity resulting from the successful attainment of some goals. Some characteristics of this stage are:

- Established Procedure. The group has settled down to a routine of group life; the role of the committee members, the work of each activity volunteer, and the channels of communication have been established. A tradition of how to do things in the association has grown up, a balance of responsibility and privilege has been achieved, and the provision of service to the membership and the estate has become almost a routine affair.
- Contact with Outsiders. The security of the established community group makes for easy contact and co-operation with the neighbouring statutory and voluntary bodies, with other housing estate community groups and with the Association of London Housing Estates.[1]
- Changes in Leadership. At this stage in the development of the group, it is possible that some of the early leaders have retired and have been succeeded by a new set of indigenous leaders. This may happen without undue difficulty, simply by the election of new officers. On the other hand, the group may experience a short period of adjustment while the new leaders are settling in, but usually leadership is replaced gradually.

Role of the Worker. In the early stages the worker had to help the group to come to terms with the intricacies of relationships between the elements that made up the association. Now he has to help the association to develop a pattern of response to the neighbouring community, and to help those in the established community and in the statutory and voluntary bodies to understand the nature and problems of the group.

---

[1] This book was written based on the experience of community groups in London. ALHE was a federal resource body supporting individual community groups.

In the early stages the worker helped the group to establish ways of dealing with recurring difficulties and to agree on principles of procedure. He may now have to encourage them not to become too set in their ways and so unable to respond to new circumstances or new needs. The worker should also encourage the group to offer service to less developed groups so that the association concerned has the opportunity to widen its sphere of activity by helping others.

(6) Integration with the wider community

In the final stage a community group can undertake wider responsibility on the estate in providing service to the members and residents and in its relationships with official bodies. It has a wide variety of activities with an equally wide variety of indigenous leaders and can often take comparatively heavy responsibility in the Association of London Housing Estates and in local affairs. The group is now one among many community groups and is, in fact, an established voluntary body which can associate and negotiate on an equal footing with other statutory and voluntary bodies in the community.

Role of the Worker. At this stage the role of the worker is to recognise and support the group as 'an established body' and to change the character of the service offered to the group from a *community development* service to that of *community organisation*.

The worker

Doing Too Much. The worker is continuously tempted to do too much for a group. Their many requests for help and advice may be phrased in such a way as to convince the worker that the situation is an emergency. The temptation to 'do it for them' is very strong. There is the odd occasion when only the worker can fill in and do something of importance in a group's life, but this is an exception ...

If the worker does too much himself, the group is deprived of opportunities of learning by doing. If he is too deeply involved with decisions made in the group and a project fails he will be blamed, and the group will miss the opportunity of assessing the failure in broader terms. When a project succeeds, the group may miss the full force of the experience of 'having done it ourselves'. This does not mean that the worker is not available to give information and advice, but that he has to develop a shrewd sense of how much or how little is actually needed compared with what the group actually requests ...

Acceptance. It may seem strange to suggest that a group's acceptance of a worker may be a problem for him. Experience in the field has shown this to be so, especially if the worker has been successful the first few times in helping the group to get something done, to work out a problem or to overcome a difficulty. The worker is invited and then expected to attend every meeting, take an interest in every affair, help in every situation and finally to take responsibility as a member of the committee and association. This is often a difficult situation because it may be the group's way of thanking the worker, and because it offers the worker an access he needs, a freedom and depth of contact that is beneficial to both parties. It may indicate that the group feels free to ask for, and take, advice and the worker can more effectively offer it. Yet it has its dangers on two counts, which the worker must learn to cope with. The first is that if he becomes too involved in the affairs of the committee of the association he may lose objectivity, and even if he does not, he may be thought to have done so. ... The second is that an unskilful rejection of the group's offer to join fully in the work of the association might be seen by the group as a rejection of themselves as persons and of their work. This can be especially disappointing for the group and the worker in cases where early acceptance of the group by the worker played so large a part in the group's development.

If the worker is aware that this stage is a passing phase, he may be able gradually to give less attention to the group without giving offence. This is the time for the worker to show the group a wider context of the work by discussing, confidentially and with care, his relations with other groups, his 'office work' commitments and other aspects of the work. This will also emphasise the necessity for strict allocation of time in his work schedule, and serve as an illustration of the worker's role as 'consultant' rather than full member of a group.

Rejection. Rejection is sometimes easier to handle than acceptance. Of course the inexperienced worker is often disappointed by rejection, but so often it is a sign that the group has worked out a satisfactory way of doing things and is ready to reject the worker in order to show that they have 'arrived'. (Rejection may be too strong a word to use.) It might be simply a temporary measure designed to get the worker out of the way while a 'private' affair was settled.

The agency

... Before any departure can be made from a traditional method of working, the agency must be willing and able to work in a different way. It must be willing to change, to alter patterns of service, to develop and adapt new ways of thinking and working. New criteria have to be worked out to define the areas in which the new service can be offered, and to assess the effectiveness and efficiency of the work. The agency may need to make only slight modifications to some of its established ways of working, but there may be real conflict with some of its traditional standards and procedures.

A willingness to alter and adapt must be present at every level of the agency operation. It must be shared by the management or executive committee, by the executive and administrative staff, and by those directly concerned with the day-to-day problems of the service and its operation in the field. But willingness alone is not enough. Willingness alone will not always provide the necessary support. The agency must also have the ability to offer the field workers adequate supporting services, supervision, in-service training, clerical help, and acceptance and support for the work in the field. The agency must also have the resources necessary to allow the worker to offer direct services in the field (duplicating, help with book-keeping, etc.) ...

[...]

Administration. Social work agencies never expect to operate within a strict 9 a.m. to 5 p.m. five-day week schedule, but the other extreme of 'constant availability' brings its own problems of staff and office routine. At the beginning of this service and especially in the early stages of field work, it was very important for staff to be available at all hours, evenings and week-ends, 'simply to be there so that we can talk to someone when we need to' as one committee member described it. To the onlooker, this seemed like spoon-feeding. 'Why can't it wait till Monday?' 'It's only a petty quarrel, it will sort itself out.' What seemed trivial to the onlooker might have been a momentous issue for the struggling group. Even the obviously trivial requests could not be dismissed, as they often represented a kind of testing out, 'Can we count on them if something were to go wrong?' 'Will they be there in an emergency?' To convince the groups that the offer of 'constant availability' was trustworthy was as important a part of the service as the more practical assistance with duplicating, publicity and accounting. The price of success was a certain amount of havoc in the office.

A typical day and evening in the central office of the London Council of Social Service may find field workers, office staff and consultant occupied in checking transport arrangements for an old people's outing, drafting letters of invitation to a residents' social, discussing with a delegation from an association the legal implications of a lottery they proposed to run. Treasurers from two different groups may be wanting to discuss the audit before the annual general meeting; someone may want advice on buying sports equipment, and someone else may want help in drafting a request to the local Council on behalf of the committee. One group may have taken a decision to circularise the whole estate about a special activity due to take place in four days time; as it is the first event for the whole estate to be attempted by the committee, it is important that it should be a success.

The necessity to take things as they came strained even the most flexible office routine. But even the overcrowding and confusion had some positive effects in introducing residents to a quite different set of problems from their own and also, incidentally, to residents from other estates ...

[...]

Interpretation. Every social work agency is in partnership with others engaged in social welfare work in the area and in the whole country. As a partner, an agency is responsible for explaining and interpreting its work to its colleagues and to the local and wider community, especially to those who provide the grant aid. In a Council of Social Service the necessity for interpreting the work is brought nearer home by the fact that many social welfare bodies are members of the Council.

Responsibility without Control. An agency inevitably attracts problems when it accepts public money for work with community groups when it cannot control the work of the groups. The agency has to justify its work to itself, to its donors and partners, and to onlookers; it has to carry out its work, offer the service, work with groups in the field, and evaluate its work, but with no formal control. The agency cannot 'command loyalty', 'exercise authority' or 'enforce discipline'. (The only possible control would be the withdrawal of the service, a very rare occurrence.) Its constitution might prevent it from raising money by any form of lottery, but this would not prevent the field workers from offering advice to an autonomous group on the legal requirements of running Bingo.

A sponsoring agency which is responsible but not in control must learn to live in an advisory capacity rather than as a superior authority.

Values and standards

The problems of the agency and the worker were aggravated by differences and conflicts in the values and standards of all those involved. These were the groups themselves, the neighbouring community, the voluntary and statutory bodies, the agency and the worker. The values and standards of the groups, especially in their early days of development, might differ considerably from those all around them (professional workers, officials and even the neighbouring community): the differences might cover a wide range, from attitudes about money, how to raise it and account for it; how to settle arguments; how to distinguish between a 'public' and a 'private' controversy, and between the use and abuse of power. There were differing interpretations of the meaning of 'independence', some meaning complete isolation, others very moderate co- operation. Group behaviour was conditioned by many other social attitudes which gave rise to differences in values and standards, which in turn affected the work in hand and the relation of the group to its co-workers.

Groups are also affected by the values and standards of the neighbouring community. If the longer-established community is hostile to the newcomers because they consider their standards to be lower, mutual suspicion arises. This is difficult to overcome. On the other hand, if the settled community feels rebuffed by the newcomers because of their need to establish their own identity and programme, suspicion may arise that will be equally difficult to overcome.

The values and standards of the statutory and voluntary bodies also differ from those of the groups and often give rise to unrealistic expectations about their behaviour and work. It is said, 'They keep changing their officers', 'They don't answer letters', 'They altered the day of the week on which they meet and forgot to let me know', 'Their meetings never start on time and never finish before 11 o'clock'.

The values and standards of the agency and its workers may also conflict with those of the group. For example, a group may decide to raise money by a method of gambling which is only just on the right side of the law; or it may decide to spend money lavishly on something which professional workers may think unnecessary. A more complex situation arises when the field worker supports a group in a course of action from which his agency must dissociate itself.

When a worker is involved in a conflict because of differences in values and standards, he is first of all non-judgmental. He does not reject the values and standards of the group, even when they are obviously 'wrong' either in themselves or in the way that the group applies them. He is non-judgmental, not because he has no values and standards of his own, but because he believes that his acceptance of the group 'as it is', is the only basis on which he can work with it. He is non-judgmental because he is aware that often the values and standards of neighbours, officials and even on occasions of the sponsoring agency, are inappropriate and inapplicable to the group at that particular stage of its development. This may result in a paradoxical situation where the worker is non-judgmental about the values and standards of the group, but considers those of the outside bodies as inappropriate and inapplicable. In fact the field worker must regard this as not so much a question of 'rights and wrongs' as of different pre-suppositions and ways of thinking. (This of course only applies to situations which do not infringe the law.) To say that a worker accepts the values and standards of a community group does not imply acceptance in any absolute sense of their standards and values. Only from an attitude of acceptance can the worker begin to help each side interpret its views to the other. To ascribe non-judgmental behaviour is not to suggest that no judgments at all are made. The worker is constantly trying to assess the adequacy of group behaviour and to be specific in his judgments of the committee's methods and relationships. It is the non-judgmental attitude which makes the judgments acceptable and useful in the group's development.

2.3

Rules for radicals: a pragmatic primer for realistic radicals

Saul Alinsky

Prologue

... young protagonists ... have no illusions about the system, but plenty of illusions about the way to change our world. It is to this point that I have written this book. These words are written in desperation, partly because it is what they do and will do that will give meaning to what I and the radicals of my generation have done with our lives. ... today's generation is desperately trying to make some sense out of their lives and out of the world. Most of them are products of the middle class. They have rejected their materialistic backgrounds, the goal of a well-paid job, suburban home, automobile, country club membership, first-class travel, status, security, and everything that meant success to their parents. They have had it. They watched it lead their parents to tranquilizers, alcohol, long-term-endurance marriages, or divorces, high blood pressure, ulcers, frustration, and the disillusionment of 'the good life.' They have seen the almost unbelievable idiocy of our political leadership – in the past political leaders, ranging from the mayors to governors to the White House, were regarded with respect and almost reverence; today they are viewed with contempt. This negativism now extends to all institutions, from the police and the courts to 'the system' itself. We are living in a world of mass media which daily exposes society's innate hypocrisy, its contradictions and the apparent failure of almost every facet of our social and political life. The young have seen their 'activist' participatory democracy turn into its antithesis – nihilistic bombing and murder. ... the young are inundated with a barrage of information and facts so overwhelming that the world has come to seem an utter bedlam, which has them spinning in a frenzy, looking for what man has always looked for from the beginning of time, a way of life that has some meaning or sense. A way of life means a certain degree of order where things have some

From: Alinsky, S. (1971) *Rules for radicals*, Random House (New York), pp xviii-vi, 113-30.

relationship and can be pieced together into a system that at least provides some clues to what life is about. Men have always yearned for and sought direction by setting up religions, inventing political philosophies, creating scientific systems like Newton's, or formulating ideologies of various kinds. This is what is behind the common cliché, 'getting it all together' despite the realization that all values and factors are relative, fluid, and changing, and that it will be possible to 'get it all together' only relatively. The elements will shift and move together just like the changing pattern in a turning kaleidoscope.

In the past the 'world', whether in its physical or intellectual terms, was much smaller, simpler, and more orderly. It inspired credibility. Today everything is so complex as to be incomprehensible. What sense does it make for men to walk on the moon while other men are waiting on welfare lines, or in Vietnam killing and dying for a corrupt dictatorship in the name of freedom? These are the days when man has his hands on the sublime while he is up to his hips in the muck of madness. The Establishment in many ways is as suicidal as some of the far left, except that they are infinitely more destructive than the far left can ever be. The outcome of the hopelessness and despair is morbidity. There is a feeling of death hanging over the nation.

Today's generation faces all this and says, 'I don't want to spend my life the way my family and their friends have. I want to do something, to create, to be me, to "do my own thing", to live. The older generation doesn't understand and, worse, doesn't want to. I don't want to be just a piece of data to be fed into a computer or a statistic in a public opinion poll, just a voter carrying a credit card.' To the young the world seems insane and falling apart.

On the other side is the older generation, whose members are no less confused. If they are not as vocal or conscious, it may be because they can escape to a past when the world was simpler. They can still cling to the old values in the simple hope that everything will work out somehow, some way. That the younger generation will 'straighten out' with the passing of time. Unable to come to grips with the world as it is, they retreat in any confrontation with the younger generation with that infuriating cliché, 'when you get older you'll understand.' One wonders at their reaction if some youngster were to reply, 'When you get younger (which will never be) then you'll understand (so of course you'll never understand).'

... What the present generation wants is what all generations have always wanted – a meaning, a sense of what the world and life are – a chance to strive for some sort of order. ... When [young people] talk of values they're asking for a reason. They are searching for an answer, at least for a time, to man's greatest question, 'Why am I here?'

... What I have to say in this book is not the arrogance of unsolicited advice. It is the experience and counsel that so many young people have questioned me about through all-night sessions on hundreds of campuses in America. It is for those young radicals who are committed to the fight, committed to life. Remember we are talking about revolution, not revelation; you can miss the target by shooting too high as well as too low. First, there are no rules for revolution any more than there are rules for love or rules for happiness, *but* there are rules for radicals who want to change their world; there are certain central concepts of action in human politics that operate regardless of the scene or the time. To know these is basic to a pragmatic attack on the system. These rules make the difference between being a realistic radical and being a rhetorical one who uses the tired old words and slogans, calls the police 'pig' or 'white fascist racist' or 'motherfucker' and has so stereotyped himself that others react by saying, 'Oh, he's one of those', and then promptly turn off ...

As an organizer I start from where the world is, as it is, not as I would like it to be. That we accept the world as it is does not in any sense weaken our desire to change it into what we believe it should be – it is necessary to begin where the world is if we are going to change it to what we think it should be. That means working in the system. There's another reason for working inside the system. Dostoeyevski said that taking a new step is what people fear most. Any revolutionary change must be preceded by a passive, affirmative, non-challenging attitude toward change among the mass of our people. They must feel so frustrated, so defeated, so lost, so futureless in the prevailing system that they are willing to let go of the past and chance the future. This acceptance is the reformation essential to any revolution ...

Our youth are impatient with the preliminaries that are essential to purposeful action. Effective organization is thwarted by the desire for instant and dramatic change, or as I have phrased it elsewhere, the demand for revelation rather than revolution. It's the kind of thing we see in play writing; the first act introduces the characters and the plot, in the second act the plot and characters are developed as the play strives to hold the audience's attention. In the final act, good and evil have their dramatic confrontation and resolution. The present generation wants to go right into the third act, skipping the first two, in which case there is no play, nothing but confrontation for confrontation's sake – a flare-up and back to darkness. To build a powerful organization takes time. It is tedious, but that's the way the game is played – if you want to play and not just yell, 'Kill the umpire.'

What is the alternative to working 'inside' the system? A mess of rhetorical garbage about 'Burn the system down!' Yippie yells of 'Do it!' or 'Do your thing.' What else? Bombs? Sniping? Silence when police are killed and screams of 'murdering fascist pigs' when others are killed? Attacking and baiting the police? Public suicide? 'Power comes out of the barrel of a gun!' is an absurd rallying cry when the other side has all the guns. Lenin was a pragmatist; when he returned to what was then Petrograd from exile, he said that the Bolsheviks stood for getting power through the ballot but would reconsider after they got the guns! Militant mouthings? Spouting quotes from Mao, Castro, and Che Guevara, which are as germane to our highly technological, computerized, cybernetic, nuclear-powered, mass media society as a stagecoach on a jet runway at Kennedy airport?

Let us in the name of radical pragmatism not forget that in our system with all its repressions we can still speak out and denounce the administration, attack its policies, work to build an opposition political base. True, there is government harassment, but there still is that relative freedom to fight. I can attack my government, try to organize to change it. That's more than I can do in Moscow, Peking, or Havana. Remember the reaction of the Red Guard to the 'cultural revolution' and the fate of the Chinese college students. Just a few of the violent episodes of bombings or a courtroom shootout that we have experienced here would have resulted in a sweeping purge and mass executions in Russia, China, or Cuba. Let's keep some perspective.

We will start with the system because there is no other place to start from except political lunacy. It is most important for those of us who want revolutionary change to understand that revolution must be preceded by reformation. To assume that a political revolution can survive without the supporting base of a popular reformation is to ask for the impossible in politics.

Men don't like to step abruptly out of the security of familiar experience; they need a bridge to cross from their own experience to a new way. A revolutionary organizer must shake up the prevailing pattern of their lives – agitate, create disenchantment and discontent with the current values, to produce, if not a passion for change, at least a passive, affirmative, non-challenging climate.

...A revolution without a prior reformation would collapse or become totalitarian tyranny. A reformation means that masses of our people have reached the point of disillusionment with past ways and values. They don't know what will work but they do know that the prevailing system is self-defeating, frustrating, and hopeless. They won't act for change but won't strongly oppose those who do. The time is then ripe for revolution.

Those who, for whatever combination of reasons, encourage the opposite of reformation, become the unwitting allies of the far political right. Parts of the far left have gone so far in the political circle that they are now all but indistinguishable from the extreme right ... It hurt me to see the American army with drawn bayonets advancing on American boys and girls [at the 1968 Democratic Convention]. But the answer I gave the young radicals seemed to me the only realistic one: 'Do one of three things. One, go find a wailing wall and feel sorry for yourselves. Two, go psycho and start bombing – but this will only swing people to the right. Three, learn a lesson. Go home, organize, build power and at the next convention, *you be the delegates.*'

Remember: once you organize people around something as commonly agreed upon as pollution, then an organized people is on the move. From there it's a short and natural step to political pollution, to Pentagon pollution. It is not enough just to elect your candidates. You must keep the pressure on. Radicals should keep in mind Franklin D. Roosevelt's response to reform delegation, 'Okay, you've convinced me. Now go on out and bring pressure on me!' Action comes from keeping the heat on. No politician can sit on a hot issue if you make it hot enough.

... A final word on our system. The democratic ideal springs from the ideas of liberty, equality, majority rule through free elections, protection of the rights of minorities, and freedom to subscribe to multiple loyalties in matters of religion, economics, and politics rather than to a total loyalty to the state. The spirit of democracy is the idea of importance and worth in the individual, and faith in the kind of world where the individual can achieve as much of his potential as possible.

Great dangers always accompany great opportunities. The possibility of destruction is always implicit in the act of creation. Thus the greatest enemy of individual freedom is the individual himself. From the beginning the weakness as well as the strength of the democratic ideal has been the people. People cannot be free unless they are willing to sacrifice some of their interests to guarantee the freedom of others. The price of democracy is the ongoing pursuit of the common good by *all* of the people. One hundred and thirty-five years ago Tocqueville gravely warned that unless individual citizens were regularly involved in the action of governing themselves, self-government would pass from the scene. Citizen participation is the animating spirit and force in a society predicated on voluntarism.

... Here we are desperately concerned with the vast mass of our people who, thwarted through lack of interest or opportunity, or both, do not participate in the endless responsibilities of citizenship and are resigned to lives determined by others. To lose your 'identity' as a citizen of democracy is but a step from losing your identity as a person. People react to this frustration by not acting at all. The separation of the people from the routine daily functions of citizenship is heartbreak in a democracy.

It is a grave situation when a people resign their citizenship or when a resident of a great city, though he may desire to take a hand, lacks the means to participate. That citizen sinks further into apathy, anonymity, and depersonalization. The result is that he comes to depend on public authority and a state of civic-sclerosis sets in.

From time to time there have been external enemies at our gates; there has always been the enemy within, the hidden and malignant inertia that foreshadows more certain destruction to our life and future than any nuclear

59

warhead. There can be no darker or more devastating tragedy than the death of man's faith in himself and in his power to direct his future.

I salute the present generation. Hang on to one of your most precious parts of youth, laughter – don't lose it as many of you seem to have done, you need it. Together we may find some of what we're looking for – laughter, beauty, love, and the chance to create.

The process of power

... Power is the reason for being of organizations. When people agree on certain religious ideas and want the power to propagate their faith, they organize and call it a church. When people agree on certain political ideas and want the power to put them into practice, they organize and call it a political party. The same reason holds across the board. Power and organization are one and the same.

The organizer knows, for example, that his biggest job is to give the people the feeling that they can do something, that while they may accept the idea that organization means power, they have to experience this idea in action. The organizer's job is to begin to build confidence and hope in the idea of organization and thus in the people themselves: to win limited victories, each of which will build confidence and the feeling that 'if we can do so much with what we have now just think what we will be able to do when we get big and strong.' It is almost like taking a prize-fighter up the road to the championship – you have to very carefully and selectively pick his opponents, knowing full well that certain defeats would be demoralizing and end his career. Sometimes the organizer may find such despair among the people that he has to put on a cinch fight.

An example occurred in the early days of Back of the Yards, the first community that I attempted to organize. This neighborhood was utterly demoralized. The people had no confidence in themselves or in their neighbors or in their cause. So we staged a cinch fight. One of the major problems in Back of the Yards in those days was an extraordinarily high rate of infant mortality. Some years earlier, the neighborhood had had the services of the Infant Welfare Society medical clinics. But about ten or fifteen years before I came to the neighborhood the Infant Welfare Society had been expelled because tales were spread that its personnel was disseminating birth-control information. The churches therefore drove out these 'agents of sin.' But soon the people were desperately in need of infant medical services. They had forgotten that they themselves had expelled the Infant Welfare Society from the Back of the Yards community.

After checking it out, I found out that all we had to do to get Infant Welfare Society medical services back into the neighborhood was ask for it. However, I kept this information to myself. We called an emergency meeting, recommended we go in committee to the society's offices and demand medical services. Our strategy was to prevent the officials from saying anything; to start banging on the desk and demanding that we get the services, *never* permitting them to interrupt us or make any statement. The only time we would let them talk was after we got through. With this careful indoctrination we stormed into the Infant Welfare Society downtown, identified ourselves, and began a tirade consisting of militant demands, refusing to permit them to say anything. All the time the poor woman was desperately trying to say, 'Why of course you can have it. We'll start immediately.' But she never had a chance to say anything and finally we ended up in a storm of 'And we will not take "No" for an answer!' At which point she said, 'Well, I've been trying to tell you ... ' and I cut in, demanding, 'Is it yes or is it no?' She said, 'Well of course it's yes.' I said, 'That's all we wanted to know.' And we stormed out of the place. All the way back to Back of the Yards you could hear the members of the committee saying, 'Well, that's the way to get things done: you just tell them off and don't give them a chance to say anything. If we could get this with just the few people that we have in the organization now, just imagine what we can get when we have a big organization.' (I suggest that before critics look upon this as 'trickery' they reflect on the later discussion of means and ends.)

[The community organiser – especially the paid organiser – has to] ... first rub raw the resentments of the people of the community; fan the latent hostilities of many of the people to the point of overt expression. He must search out controversy and issues, rather than avoid them, for unless there is controversy people are not concerned enough to act. The use of the adjective 'controversial' to qualify the word 'issue' is a meaningless redundancy. There can be no such thing as a 'non-controversial' issue. When there is agreement there is no issue; issues only arise when there is disagreement or controversy. An organizer must stir up dissatisfaction and discontent; provide a channel into which the people can angrily pour their frustrations. He must create a mechanism that can drain off the underlying guilt for having accepted the previous situation for so long a time. Out of this mechanism, a new community organization arises.

... a competent union organizer approaches his objective, let's say the organization of a particular industrial plant where the workers are underpaid, suffering from discriminatory practices, and without job security. The workers accept these conditions as inevitable, and they express their demoralization by saying, 'what's the use?' In private they resent these circumstances, complain, talk about the futility of 'bucking the big shots' and generally succumb to frustration – *all because of the lack of opportunity for effective action.* Enter the labor organizer or the agitator. He begins his 'trouble making' by stirring up these angers, frustrations, and resentments, and highlighting specific issues or grievances that heighten controversy.

He dramatizes the injustices by describing conditions at other industrial plants engaged in the same kind of work where the workers are far better off economically and have better working conditions, job security, health benefits, and pensions as well as other advantages that had not even been thought of by the workers he is trying to organize. Just as important, he points out that the workers in the other places had also been exploited in the past and had existed under similar circumstances until they used their intelligence and energies to organize into a power instrument known as a trade union, with the result that they achieved all of these other benefits. Generally this approach results in the formation of a new trade union.

Let us examine what this labor organizer has done. He has taken a group of apathetic workers; he has fanned their resentments and hostilities by a number of means, including challenging contrasts of better conditions of other workers in similar industries. Most important, he has demonstrated that something can be done, and that there is a concrete way of doing it that has already proven its effectiveness and success: that by organizing together as a trade union they will have the power and the instrument with which to make these changes. He now has the workers participating in a trade union and supporting its program. We must never forget that so long as there is no opportunity or method to make changes, it is senseless to get people agitated or angry, leaving them no course of action except to blow their tops.

And so the labor organizer simultaneously breeds conflict and builds a power structure. The war between the trade union and management is resolved either through a strike or a negotiation. Either method involves the use of power; the economic power of the strike or the threat of it, which results in successful negotiations. *No one can negotiate without the power to compel negotiation.*

This is the function of a community organizer. Anything otherwise is wishful non-thinking. To attempt to operate on a good-will rather than on a power basis would be to attempt something that the world has not yet experienced. ... The organization is born out of the issues and the issues are born out of the organization. They go together, they are concomitants essential to each other. Organizations are built on issues that are specific, immediate, and realizable.

Organizations must be based on many issues. Organizations need action as an individual needs oxygen. The cessation of action brings death to the organization through factionalism and inaction, through dialogues and conferences that are actually a form of rigor mortis rather than life. It is impossible to maintain constant action on a single issue. A single issue is a fatal strait jacket that will stifle the life of an organization. Furthermore, a single issue drastically limits your appeal, where multiple issues would draw in the many potential members essential to the building of a broad, mass-based organization. Each person has a hierarchy of desires or values; he may be sympathetic to your single issue but not concerned enough about that particular one to work and fight for it. Many issues mean many members. Communities are not economic organizations like labor unions, with specific economic issues; they are as complex as life itself.

To organize a community you must understand that in a highly mobile, urbanized society the word 'community' means community of interests, *not* physical community. The exceptions are ethnic ghettos where segregation has resulted in physical communities that coincide with their community of interests, or, during political campaigns, political districts that are based on geographical demarcations.

People hunger for drama and adventure, for a breath of life in a dreary, drab existence. One of a number of cartoons in my office shows two gum-chewing stenographers who have just left the movies. One is talking to the other, and says, 'You know, Sadie. You know what the trouble with life is? There just ain't any background music.'

... Let us look at what is called *process*. *Process* tells us *how*. *Purpose* tells us *why*. But in reality, it is academic to draw a line between them, they are part of a continuum. Process and purpose are so welded to each other that it is impossible to mark where one leaves off and the other begins, or which is which. The very process of democratic participation is for the purpose of organization rather than to rid the alleys of dirt. Process is really purpose. Through all this the constant guiding star of the organizer is in those words, 'The dignity of the individual.' Working with this compass, he soon discovers many axioms of effective organization.

If you respect the dignity of the individual you are working with, then his desires, not yours; his values, not yours; his ways of working and fighting, not yours; his choice of leadership, not yours; his programs, not yours, are important and must be followed; except if his programs violate the high values of a free and open society. For example, take the question, 'What if the program of the local people offends the rights of other groups, for reasons of color, religion, economic status, or politics? Should this program be accepted just because it is their program?' The answer is categorically no. Always remember that 'the guiding star is "the dignity of the individual."' 'This is the purpose of the program. Obviously any program that opposes people because of race, religion, creed, or economic status, is the antithesis of the fundamental dignity of the individual.

It is difficult for people to believe that you really respect their dignity. After all, they know very few people, including their own neighbors, who do. But it is equally difficult for you to surrender that little image of God created in our own likeness, which lurks in all of us and tells us that we secretly believe that we know what's best for the people. A successful organizer has learned emotionally as well as intellectually to respect the dignity of the people with whom he is working. Thus an effective organizational experience is as much an educational process for the organizer as it is for the people with whom he is working. They both must learn to respect the dignity of the individual, and they both must learn that in the last analysis this is the basic purpose of organization, for participation is the heartbeat of the democratic way of life.

We learn, when we respect the dignity of the people, that they cannot be denied the elementary right to participate fully in the solutions to their own problems. Self-respect arises only out of people who play an active role in solving their own crises and who are not helpless, passive, puppet-like recipients of private or public services. To give people help, while denying them a significant part in the action, contributes nothing to the development of the individual. In the deepest sense it is not giving but taking – taking their dignity. Denial of the opportunity for participation is the denial of human dignity and democracy. It will not work.

Community as fact and value

Raymond Plant

Most sociologists seem to have weighed in with their own idea of what a community consists of and in this lies much of the confusion. For sociologists, no more than other individuals, have not been immune to the emotive overtones that the word community constantly carries with it. Everyone – even sociologists – has wanted to live in a community; feelings have been more equivocal concerning life in collectivities, networks and societies. The subjective feelings that the term community conjures up thus leads to a confusion between what is (empirical description), and what the sociologists felt it should be (normative prescription).

This is not, as Bell and Newby (1972) seem to imply, something which may be avoided but rather something in the nature of the case with a contested notion like 'community' with its complex descriptive dimension. We should not be pre-occupied with looking at the language of community in a one-dimensional way, but be more alive to the 'open texture' of its use – its actual use in language and thought, in the description, interpretation, organisation and evaluation of behaviour. ... Community is so much part of the stock in trade of social and political argument that it is unlikely that some non-ambiguous and non-contested definition of the notion can be given.

To suggest that it is possible to formulate some scientific, non-contested descriptive meaning of community betrays a misunderstanding of the logic of the situation and an insensitivity to the extent to which the historical career of a concept structures our present understanding of it.

Community as a value in the sociological tradition

As Bell and Newby argue, the answer to the question of why community has the evaluative force that it has, is to be found by looking at the perspectives on community formulated by some of those thinkers who have been central in forming the sociological tradition. ... Fortunately a very great deal of the spadework has already been done in this field by Nisbet (1953,

From: Plant, R. (1974) 'Community as fact and value' in *Community and ideology: An essay in applied social philosophy*, London: Routledge & Kegan Paul, pp 8-36.

1966) Nisbet fixes the rise of the idea of community as an important ideal in social and political theory in the late eighteenth and early nineteenth centuries, particularly in the German thought of the period. The rise of the idea during this period has often been described as 'the rediscovery of community' and to put the point in this way invites the questions 'What went before?' 'What was it about what went before which led to the subsequent emphasis upon the notion of community?' 'What was it that was being rediscovered?' For many of the seminal social theorists of this period in Germany, particularly Herder, Schiller and Hegel, a sense of community had existed paradigmatically in the Greek polis, particularly in Periclean Athens. It was thought that in the polis was to be found a form of social organisation and interaction which went far beyond mere locality. The culture of the polis was regarded as homogeneous, participatory and open to all; religion, politics, art and family life were all intertwined in a close and tightly-knit fashion, and the Germans took this over-idealised image of the Greek city state as a paradigm in terms of which they could criticise the atrophied and enervated character of social life in western Europe. Indeed this image of community derived from the Greeks has been pervasive in Western social thought. ... As the Germans took their ideal of community from Greek culture it was felt that this reality of the homogeneous, participatory, rooted community had been lost sight of in the modern world.

Community and the whole man

It was widely felt by the Germans that the idea of community involved some notion of the whole man, in which men were to be met by other men in the totality of their social roles and not in a fragmented or segmental way. All interactions within a community take place within a web of inclusive ties – men are related to one another through more than one description. The modern world however, with its progressive division of labour and the development of mass urban society, had destroyed the idea of the whole man. In modern society man was now a narrow and enervated being and the nature of his social contacts had become more and more fragmented. ... This idea that community involves the notion of the whole man and not fragmented forms of human interaction, though connected with certain preconceptions of the German Romantic movement still plays a very major part in the idea of community. It is retained in the idea that community lifts man out of the particularity of his own personal and selfish interests so that in community he is given a less narrow and sectional sort of social experience and this gives force to those who see in community the concrete realisation of fraternity and co-operation. ... Wirth has argued this point particularly well. (1957: 54):

'Characteristically urbanites meet one another in highly segmented roles. They are to be sure dependent upon more people for the satisfaction of their needs than rural people and are thus associated with a greater number of organised groups, but they are less dependent upon particular persons and their dependence upon others is confined to a highly fractionalised aspect of the others' activity.'

This connexion between the loss of community and the loss of the reality of total personal contact in the social sphere, though closely related originally to central preoccupations of the German romantics has become part of the moral background within which and against which the notion of community makes sense. It is insisted upon again in one of the most recent studies of the notion of community, in Poplin (1972), in which he argues that members of communities regard each other as whole persons who are of intrinsic significance and worth whereas members of mass society regard each other as means to ends and assign no such intrinsic worth and significance to the individual. In its attempt at the rediscovery of the community the sociological tradition from the nineteenth century is therefore on this view to attempt to recapture some sense of the wholeness of human nature which has been lost sight of in modern mass society. It is this context among others to be discussed which has given the notion of community its singular evaluative dimension.

Community and social divisions

The division of labour did not lead just to the fragmentation of the human personality, the progressive differentiation of function also led to deep social divisions based upon identities of functional interest – the most ubiquitous of these being the development of social classes. Class relationships, so it was thought, divided the previously homogeneous community. If community presupposes shared values and interests, then the development of social classes and interest groups generally within society is inimical to the maintenance of the reality of community. Rousseau was one of the very first to see that the sectional interests developed as a result of the division of labour are inimical to the development of an homogeneous community and he put the point very succinctly in his *Premier Discours sur les sciences et les arts* (1964 edn: 26): 'We have among us physicians, geometers, chemists, astronomers, poets, musicians and painters but we have no citizens.' Marx took the same kind of argument much further, seeing the problem of the fragmentation of society and of the personality as part and parcel of industrial capitalism which replaced the communal virtues of co-operation and fraternity with those of conflict and competition.

Capitalism was seen as an isolating and separating process that stripped off the historically grown layers of custom and social membership and replaced these benign features of social life with competition and the cash nexus. … Thus the notion of community has been used by both conservative and radical critics of industrialism or industrial capitalism to formulate the predicament of man in modern society, and again this use has radically influenced the evaluative dimension of the word.

Community and the loss of political involvement

A further major feature in man's contemporary condition which preoccupied those who formed the sociological tradition of which our present understanding of community is a part, and which indeed has continued to influence contemporary thinking on community, has been the increasing organisation and bureaucratisation of life generally but in particular in the sphere of politics. In a community, so it might be said, a man is and feels an integral part of an overall way of life, he is not conscious of a division between his own attitudes to the community and the way in which that community organises and articulates its life. He is in a full sense a *member* of the community. However, the argument would continue, with the development of the industrial revolution, political, economic and social power has become increasingly centralised and in consequence men have come to feel less and less at home in the social world; they have become estranged from that social world in which they live, move and have their being.

Nisbet (1966) has stressed the political dimension to this problem. He argues that the state cannot provide the individual the sense of rootedness and security which he needs because 'by its very nature it is too large, too complex and altogether too aloof from the residual meanings which human beings live by.' Only some rediscovered reality of community in modern life will be able to provide the recognition, fellowship, security and membership which all men crave. This way of thinking about community, although it has deep historical roots, is still central. How much of the radical line in community work is inspired by a sense that social and political institutions in modern life are too distant, too remote and too bureaucratised to be responsive to the needs and wants of individuals?

Again the evaluative dimension of community becomes built in because the idea of community becomes the yardstick by which the atrophied nature of contemporary social reality is judged.

This general tradition of theorising about community, many of the forms of which have been only crudely noticed above, reached it greatest expression perhaps in Ferdinand Tonnies's book *Gemeinschaft und Gesellschaft*, published in 1887 (see Tonnies 1955 for the English edition), which was a paean to the lost community and an indictment of the baneful effects of many of the features of contemporary life noted earlier in this chapter. In this work Tonnies, against this evaluative background, preoccupied with the loss of community, tried to work out a typology for on the one hand real interacting reciprocating community, *Gemeinschaft,* and on the other hand the aggregation of individualistic atomistic society, *Gesellschaft.* This typology conceived in the thick of the ideological controversy and social criticism discussed above has dominated thinking about community ever since. In *Gemeinschaft*, human relationships are intimate, face to face and not discrete and segmented – they are with the whole man, not with a man under a particular description or acting from within a particular role. Each person knows the others in the round. Because a community shares its values there can be no fundamental moral conflicts, roles and relationships cohere and cannot conflict. The community is stable in that physical mobility between one place and another is not of any importance within this kind of society and there is very little or no mobility in terms of status. The ethic is very much of the 'my station and its duties' type.

On the other hand *Gesellschaft* relationships are characteristic of large-scale modern societies and institutions. The dominant image of relationship here is that of contract and not habit or customary observance. The authority of such a society is not traditional, indeed it is based upon the opposite – the legal, rational notions of consent, volition and contract, a view which implies a radically individualistic account of the genesis and authority of the legal order. …

Relations of the *Gemeinschaft* type are more inclusive; persons confront each other as ends, they cohere more durably …. In *Gesellschaft* their mutual regard is circumscribed by a sense of specific if not formal obligations. A transaction may occur without any other encounters leaving both parties virtually anonymous. (p. 184)

If Tonnies's distinctions are translated into current sociological jargon in terms of primary and secondary groups or in terms of organic and functional relationships we may see how far our contemporary sociological understanding of the community was laid down in the latter part of the nineteenth century in the thick of ideological controversies which still are part of our consciousness. At the same time, the above analysis may provide too homogeneous an impression. … Some of those who praised community, such as Tonnies, were basically conservatives who used the notion of community to diagnose the baneful effects of contemporary urban industrial society, seeing in the notion of community an encapsulation of the values of the rural community for which they had a considerable degree of nostalgia. Such conservatives took community to refer mainly to locality, to fixed modes and hierarchies of status and power with little physical or social mobility, embodying shared values based upon some shared, traditional way of looking at the world. Such a view of community embodied the static, orderly, rooted notions which were central to conservative thought. ... Others, less conservative, such as Hegel and Schiller, fully accepted the values which urban industrial society had realised, freedom to move, a growth in individuality and a wider capacity for consumption, but at the same time they wished to counterbalance these achievements with some reformulated notion of community experience which would negate the more baneful consequences of urban civilisation.

Their view of community was not so much nostalgic as progressive and liberal, attempting to assimilate the values of individuality within the notion of community. In doing so Hegel particularly put far less stress upon locality and the sense of belonging to a specific place than the conservatives, but saw the achievement of community in the modern world to depend upon functional groups, which he called Corporations, and upon greater political participation and awareness. Here again what is taken to be central to community is not, as it were, a set of brute facts discoverable outside of a particular framework of evaluation, rather the diminution of the stress upon locality and the increase of emphasis upon shared ends and the extent to which shared values are to be seen as a consequence of functional co-operation were necessitated by a basically progressive or liberal ideological framework. Others again, notably Marx and Rousseau, provided a very radical understanding of community demanding neither a return to a pre-industrial rural ethos nor an attempt to tinker with the social consequences of industrialism. On the contrary, only a fundamental change in social and economic conditions could regenerate those values which *they* took to be central to the idea of community, particularly those of fraternity and co-operation, but fraternity and co-operation based not upon some mutual recognition within a functional specialism but rather based upon some awareness of a common humanity, an awareness distorted by the hierarchical nature of rural community and by the competitiveness of community based upon specialisation of function.

Community: the British tradition

Whereas the German communitarians tended to look a long way back to the Greek polis for their image of community, British communitarians have more often than not looked back to the village community which was beginning to be destroyed in the second half of the eighteenth century, if they did not go further with William Morris and see in feudal society the appropriate image of community.

[There are] some within the British tradition who look to the notion of community for a radical answer to present social problems and discontents. Prominent here is Williams (1961, 1965) who has tried to defend a view of community in terms of co-operation, fraternity, participation, egalitarianism and a sense of membership. Williams' attempt to make coherent the idea of a common culture is egalitarian and much influenced by the views of Marx.

[In the British context,] the notion of community is being implicitly defined in a conservative way in terms of a way of life which has been *lost,* and which is further seen as being incompatible with the central ethos of modern society with its differentiation of function and anonymous form of social interaction. This point may perhaps be further reinforced by a *collage* quotation from easily the most influential book on community work and development published to date. In *Community Work and Social Change,* the authors define the context of community work thus (Calouste Gulbenkian Foundation 1968: 9-10):

'The intensified growth in economic, social and geographical mobility accentuated by the Second World War and its aftermath has created or made manifest new needs in the community field . ... These may be viewed from three angles: situations whose impact is clarifying the need for community work include the movement of large numbers of people to new towns and housing estates which creates a whole range of community needs and potential tensions which demand action ... ; the effects of these changes in terms of social change and its consequences for people: these changes mean that because of specialisation, diversity and mobility and because of the physical features of urban living, the kind of community life which traditionally was based upon the neighbourhood is rare . ... This frees people from what they do not like, but it leaves them on their own. Man wants the security which a large-scale organisation can afford, but at the same time he craves the ability to shape at least a part of his own destiny. These opposing tensions have not anywhere been reconciled and it is not only the hidden persuaders of the commercial world but also the scale of central and local government, of industry and the social services that limit opportunities for active participation and decision. ... There is also a need in community planning to think in terms of whole persons and of the satisfaction of the needs of persons in social interaction with others.'

In this quotation we are able to identify the features continually referred to in this chapter: the positive value of community life, thus endowing the notion of community with evaluative force and the realisation that this community life is in danger of being lost as a result of urbanisation and urban renewal, the specialisation of function, the growth of complex organisations and bureaucracies, the loss of the notion of the total person in the anonymity of urban life. In this sense there is no sharp break in the ideology of the contemporary community worker and those who formed the sociological tradition which has so structured our thinking about community life.

Freedom, individualisation and the loss of community

While it is true that the notion of community and its recovery has to a great extent dominated social thinking over the last 150 years and that community work may be seen as an extension of this theoretical concern to practical realities, it would be wrong to give the impression that the sense of loss of the community had only given rise to the kind of reaction discussed thus far in this chapter. Granted that there were, as we have seen, different sets of emphases among those imbued with the communitarian ideal, there were many thinkers and still are many who have taken the opposite view from the community theorists, namely that the loss of community is *no* loss at all, in fact it has been a liberating and emancipating development. Many thinkers, particularly in the seventeenth and eighteenth centuries, tried to come to terms with the new world – with incipient market society, industrialisation, specialisation and urbanisation, and attempted to provide an understanding of the nature of man and his place in the world which would justify the loss of the old communalities. This tradition of thought sought the basis of human association not in tradition, habit and custom but in the contract and consent of free persons.

As Nisbet has pointed out, not surprisingly, such thinkers were not at all sympathetic to the notion of community (1966: 48): 'Groups and associations which could not be vindicated in these terms were cast into the lumber room of history. Few traditional communities survived examination by natural law philosophers in the seventeenth and eighteenth centuries. The family was generally accepted of course, though we find Hobbes using a tacit contract type of argument to justify the parent child relationship ... Guild, corporation, monastery, commune, village community, all of these were regarded as being without foundation in natural law. Rational society like rational knowledge must be the very opposite of the traditional.'

The loss of community understood in this way was, therefore, a necessary condition of the emancipation of the self-conscious, self-directing individual and, as late as the end of the eighteenth century, by which time the reaction in favour of the reformulation of community had set in, Bentham, the great utilitarian philosopher, attempted to build up a whole social and moral philosophy out of a set of statements about the necessary trajectory of *individual* motivation.

This way of thinking certainly had very profound effects. Even among those imbued with the communitarian ideal there was a conscious attempt very often to reformulate an understanding of community in the modern world which would take account of the degree of individual freedom which the anti-communitarian thinkers saw as the chief benefit of the decline in the traditional community. The development of individualism has freed men from the constraints of the traditional primary community but there had been losses too. Parry implicitly points to the ambiguity in the value of the traditional community in a study of Locke's views (1964: 164): 'If this order gave the member little scope for independent action and offered little variety of life, it offered instead a degree of protection, established by law and group feeling, it offered the certainties of a fixed and predictable status and of well- established communally-shared beliefs and it offered a sense of solidarity with the fellow members of one's group.'

The constraints of community upon individuals have been removed but what has emerged in the view of the communitarian thinkers discussed in the last section is a *mass* society in which individuals are left alone without being able to draw on the support of primary community groups. The dilemma is, as Younghusband (1959) put it, that the decline of the traditional community 'frees people from what they do not like, but it leaves them on their own'. Is there some way of understanding community which will enable the freedom of the individual and the co-operation and fraternity of the community to be meaningfully held together? …is there an alternative? Is there a liberal theory of community, which will satisfy enough of the descriptive criteria of community to make it worthwhile to call it a 'community' and yet one which can take account of the liberal critique of the traditional *Gemeinschaft* type of community. This is quite a central problem in modern social and political theory and … is an issue which the community worker has to face.

2.5

Community development: a radical alternative?

Marjorie Mayo

Where has the notion of community development sprung from?

...The British concocted the term community development out of their attempts to develop 'basic education', later called 'mass education' and social welfare in the colonies. But why, after 30 or 40 years or so of colonial influence or rule in Africa (and very much longer in India), this dramatic increase in concern for the 'development', 'education' and 'welfare' of the subject colonial peoples? Colonial rule had, after all, been based on principles of metropolitan self-interest as well as benevolent paternalism – the dual mandate to 'civilize' while exploiting, which was recognized quite explicitly by that well-known colonial administrator and theorist, Lord Lugard (1922).

At the political level, there were clearly self-interested reasons for Great Britain's increasing concern for colonial social or community development. During the interwar period, the fear of the possible implications of self-government for the colonies began to be felt in earnest in the metropolis. In India this process had begun even in the 1930s; in Africa it began later although, before the end of the Second World War, there is evidence of the first recognition of the distant but eventual possibility of successful independence demands in that continent, too. The Colonial Office began to consider ways of coping with these demands by promoting the 'development of political institutions' or more generally of that most ambiguous term 'political development'. The British wanted 'to encourage democracy and local initiative', and 'to establish solid foundations for the approaching self-government' (see Brockensha and Hodge 1969: 164) which, as the United Nations (1958-9) explained, meant bringing the colonies in line with 'political, economic and social standards as established in the majority of democratic countries.' In other words, the colonies were to be protected

From: Mayo, M. (1975) 'Community development as a radical alternative?' in R. Bailey and M. Brake (eds) *Radical social work*, Edward Arnold, pp 129-43.

from communism or from other potentially unstable political regimes (which might eventually be too weak to contain the emergence of that same spectre of communism).

One of the best-known consequences of British policy was the Indian community development programme. This was developed by both British and United States protagonists before independence in 1947 and taken up (merged by then with the non-violent and anti-communist ideology of Ghandi) as a major plank of the Congress Party in 1952. The whole programme was quite explicitly an attempt to create plausibly democratic institutions without serious dislocation of the vested interests of the status quo.

During the Second World War, the British had become increasingly concerned about the political crisis with which they might have to deal at its end. What, the colonial administrator F. L. Brayne (1944) asked, would become of the returned soldier? – would he 'explode and become either a fervent reformer or red-hot enemy of all government or a violent and dangerous criminal?' The answer he thought, lay in a balanced community development and national reconstruction programme … An idealized and supposedly democratic version of village life, the 'Panchayat', was to be recreated, as part of this scheme to promote rural development, without offering any explicit challenge to existing property or power and caste relationships. (Brayne 1945; Mayer *et al.* 1958) Nehru himself (1957) made this quite clear in his own statements on the community development programme: 'We want an integrated India, not only politically but emotionally' (i.e. ideologically). Existing property (and particularly land-ownership patterns) were thus to be left undisturbed: Nehru would not give official support even to 'voluntary' programmes for land re-distribution. 'It is obvious,' he affirmed, 'that no government can go about asking people to give up their land.' Yet, as Barrington Moore (1966) has commented, to attempt in India 'to democratize the villages without altering property relationships is simply absurd.' As the United Nations evaluation team on their visit in the late 1950s were forced to recognize, despite all the efforts of the community development teams, the poorer peasants still lacked incentives, while the richer peasants and landlords were still able to appropriate their surplus, not to mention the additional material benefits that had been available from the community development programme. Thus social and economic divisions have actually widened and the underdevelopment of the poorer peasants' plots increased as a result of five years of community development. Nor was the Indian programme alone in having such political and social ideological intentions. Similar conclusions can be drawn, for instance, about British efforts in part of Africa and Malaya where, by 1953, there were 450 'new community development villages' as a result of the emergency resettlement of half a million people as part of the military operations against the communists.

The political implications of community development as an attempt to build up local bulwarks (and vested interests) opposed to communism, can be traced in the possibly even cruder policies of Britain's successor as an imperial power, the United States. As Brokensha and Hodge (1969) have explained, 'by far the greatest American expenditures on community development occur in those countries (Vietnam, Thailand, Laos) considered to be most threatened by communism.' Often community development was used to disguise counter-insurgency activities, including perhaps those projects as part of aid programmes to Latin America. 'The Alliance for Progress' and all the non-government sponsored United States projects are concentrated in politically tense, yet economically vital areas, for instance, in the Middle East, Jordan, Lebanon and Iran – and Greece, another critical sphere for political and military influence ... On the political level, then, as an American critic (Erasmus 1968) has commented, community development clearly has been used by both countries as a pacifier in the hopes of avoiding disagreeable agitation.

Underlying the political dimension and critically and causally linked to it, economic motivation has also been of key significance in the development of the colonial ideology of community development. The colonies had, after all, a crucial economic function for the metropolitan power. (see Lenin, 1966). Imperialism was economically vital for a variety of reasons, as a means of combating falling rates of profit at home by the more profitable export of capital abroad, but also, for instance, to provide and guarantee the supply of raw materials cheaply and to facilitate the export of metropolitan manufactured goods on favourable terms of trade. The British preferred to ensure that native labour was available to produce these raw materials and to facilitate this trade by economic pressure, for example, taxes to force peasants into wage labour and the use of ideological pressure rather than by the Portuguese method of naked brute force – forced labour. ...

Community development was a more subtle, potentially less troublesome way of achieving the same ends – the extraction of 'voluntary' and, of course, still unpaid native labour, to build up the infrastructure for further economic development exploitation... .

Community development was also significant, ideologically, in encouraging favourable institutions and attitudes, and in discouraging those unfavourable ones that might lead to the development of a radical challenge. To the economic and political establishment community development thus represented an attempt to create a capitalist 'free market', economic development on the cheap (development for the metropolitan interests anyway, even if that entailed underdevelopment for the colonized country), and colonized peoples sufficiently indoctrinated to participate voluntarily in accelerating this process ...

Community development as applied in contemporary United States and British urban situations

Could such a concept as community development have been applied for radically different goals in the very dissimilar situation of the cities of the West? In practice, the evidence from official programmes and the establishment community development literature in Great Britain and the United States demonstrates striking parallels with ... the colonial and neo-colonial experience.

These links can be traced particularly clearly in the programme to 'develop' the depressed black minority population in the United States. After the Civil War, in order to oust the southern Democrats, the Republican party was anxious to secure the newly available votes (at least until the blacks lost the vote again, in the subsequent period of reaction from the late 1870s onwards when the Jim Crow laws were passed and the Ku Klux Klan developed). So various Republicans were willing to support and encourage black self-help projects, as long as these were designed to develop agricultural productivity and a better skilled and disciplined black industrial labour force – not of course to generate black political or social demands. Some wealthy southern conservatives were also willing to support schemes of this nature. Probably the best-known black leader of this 'self-help only' genre was Booker T. Washington. (1967; Weisberger 1972). From 1881, he ran a black teacher training college in Alabama, Tuskegee, which became, from the point of view of the wealthy whites, the model for black self-advancement. As Washington explained, black education for agriculture and factory work could produce a more docile labour force 'without the strikes and labour wars' which were becoming endemic amongst the white proletariat in the north; and he was quite explicit in making no social or political demands. 'The wisest among my race understand,' he said, during the Alabama address which made his fame, 'that the agitation for social equality is the extremest folly.' ... As the militant black leader W. DuBois (1971) assessed him, 'Mr Washington represents in Negro thought, the old attitude of adjustment and submission. His doctrine has tended to make the whites, north and south, shift the burden of the negro problem to the negroes' shoulders and stand aside as critical and rather pessimistic spectators.'

Formally, the political situation was reversed in the 1960s when community action emerged as a major strand in the war on poverty. This time it was the Democratic Party which was interested in keeping the votes of the black migrants, who had shifted to the ghettoes of the northern and western cities. Alinsky (1969) has described this war on poverty as 'political pornography', a 'huge political pork barrel' patronage in the form of jobs and funds to be handed out to supporters – i.e. to liberal academics and social and community workers –whereas, in terms of the real issues of the redistribution of economic opportunities and of the redistribution of physical resources (such as adequate housing) and of political power, the programme represented, he considered, no more than mere tokenism. And, as tokenism, Alinsky thought it should be resisted to the death.

Even less vehement critics have had to admit that the war on poverty was an attempt to initiate reform in the inner cities without actually committing any major resources. (see Marris and Rein, 1967) Instead, self-help and resident participation were to stimulate cheaper solutions – a theme which, despite some of the negative conclusions of the American experience, has been taken up in contemporary British attempts at community development. ...

The movement for the development of community self-help can also be related to particular notions about the causation of poverty in the inner cities, and to theories of a poverty cycle or a cycle of transmitted deprivation or a culture of poverty. (see Moynihan, 1969) Essentially, for the proponents of these views, the absence of real opportunities is not so much the problem as the failure of certain types of individuals and families to take advantage of them. The remedy for families concentrated in inner city slums was community development to overcome their current alienation. Mike Miller and Martin Rein have criticized this interest in community development and citizen participation as 'community psycho-therapy', as opposed to an attack on the real structural problems underlying this alienation.

The notions behind community development are, however, still deeply embedded, having had a long history in western social thought. Some of their clearest manifestations can be found in a book which was until very recently considered a classic in the field: Biddle and Biddle (1965) define community development as 'a group method for expediting personality growth', i.e., another method of social work. Thus, on a project in a depressed area in the southern states they comment, 'Today there is little evidence that the problems of the area have been solved but, there is abundant evidence that the people have changed their attitudes ... [for the poor and] alienated must overcome their inner handicaps, partially through the cultivation of their own initiative.' Lest there be any remaining doubt about the political implications of such a conception, Biddle and Biddle (1965) are even more explicit ... 'The all-inclusive community calls for a multiple approach [i.e. consensus-cooperation]. The two-way division [i.e. conflict] is more reminiscent of the Marxian class struggle than of the reality of American pluralism ... Whereas the community development worker should NOT be or should never become a destroyer of the social order. By using or endorsing the idea of revolution, he can find himself disqualified to act as a mediator between factions in controversy.'

By this time the non-radical (i.e. the reactionary and repressive) aspects of community development should be sufficiently obvious. As a relatively cheap and typically ideological attempt to resolve various economic, social and political problems, it has clearly been attractive to governments and voluntary agencies both national and international for use not just in the Third World but also among racial minorities and indigenous poor at home. So why has community development appealed so much to apparently radical groups, particularly among students and young professionals? Part of the explanation seems to lie in the problems to which it is currently posed as a solution. Both the United States and the British official programmes recognize that all is not well with the present administrative and political structures of Western social democracies ... Part of this increasingly evident failure of the state mechanisms seems to be due to the increasing scale of state intervention.... In its attempts to regulate contemporary capitalism the state has ... been forced to intervene into more and more areas of the economy and also more deeply into an increasing number and range of social, political and ideological institutions. The more complex and technical its interventions and planning processes, the more difficult these become to oversee through the formal political processes which are increasingly seen as peripheral to the real sources of power and decision-making.

Meanwhile, in face of this evidently far from popular growth in official bureaucracy, western social democracies have been concerned to offer official antidotes in the form of citizen or public participation, community action and community development – to name only the most popular at present. These notions have enjoyed considerable popularity just because they do contain in part, if in idealized form, the outlines of potential counter-institutions. Their appeal, however, has probably been strongest among the growing numbers of young professionals and sub-professionals, themselves employed to operate the expanding central and local government services in question ... particularly at the lower end where the supposedly professional part of the job content is clearly becoming depreciated: the young professional is thus less clearly a professional and more obviously just another local (or central) government employee. (Mandel, 1972). These pressures are typically compounded with the frustrations caused by the gap between their actual job content and their professional aspirations. As a result, more and more young professionals are joining trade unions (for example, NALGO) and professional ginger groups (for example, Case Con). And these same pressures have also been pushing them to look for other ways of making their jobs more satisfying; which is why the notion of a return to the client population, implied in community development, has been so appealing.

But can community development be more radical than this: can it be more than a booster for the flagging egos of liberal students and young professionals who are unwilling to accept this devaluation of their professional status?

In practice, of course, any projects which dabble in social change can and frequently have backfired on the sponsoring agencies. The very ambiguity of the goals beneath the ideological rhetoric can be and has been exploited for other, more radical objectives. Even where in the short term official goals have apparently been attained, such changes can trigger off other, more far-reaching processes. So in the colonies, where community development led to successful promotion of popular education, this newly acquired literacy frequently became a source of strength to the emerging nationalist movements: in Ghana, for example, the mass literacy plank in the community development programme to improve cocoa growing in the 1950s was used to considerable advantage by Nkrumah's party in the struggle for independence. (Fitch and Oppenheimer, 1966).

Some of the most reactionary writers have also clearly been aware of the potential danger that their ideological weapons might be used for other ends. Biddle and Biddle, for instance, admitted that the community development 'process' could be hard to control, because once social change was on the agenda, Pandora's box would have been opened … . …it is clear from the experience of the war on poverty that some of the poverty warriors also saw this very early on, and planned to use the projects for more radical ends. Richard Cloward, in particular, related his own ideas to the considerably less radical, presidential interest in delinquency control, in the early period of the Kennedy administration; and he proceeded to use the ensuing experiments as a springboard for putting into practice his own, more radical ideas about changing not individuals so much as the opportunity structure.

Once citizen participation was let loose that too became part of a wider, more radical debate; and, despite official reaction in favour of putting control firmly back in the hands of city hall (as in the Model Cities programme), citizen participation could not altogether be conjured away. And of course all sorts of radical individuals and groups used Office of Economic Opportunity resources for other, more political ends. The Black Panther party grew around the North Oakland poverty programme office which hired Bobby Searle as foreman in the summer youth work programme in 1966!

Yet in spite of all manner of pockets of radicalism, the verdict on the achievement of community action in the United States so far seems to be that it did not offer any widespread or overall challenge to the established interests of power and influence. As a whole it has been incorporated by the status quo. 'So far from challenging established power,' Marris and Rein (1967) concluded, 'community action turned out to be merely another instrument of social services, essentially patronizing and conservative.'

2.6

Community participation: past and future

S.M. Miller and Martin Rein

Changing people

This point of view stresses that poverty is not so much a lack of material advantage, in the sense of insufficient economic resources, as it is a lack of power. It assumes that there was something wrong with the poor which left them unprepared to exploit the resources and opportunities available to them. Hence, what was needed was a program to prepare the poor so that they could more effectively use available community institutions and resources. Remediation, employability and citizen participation programs were needed to achieve this aim. All of these programs share a common rationale – the reduction of the dependence and the apathy of the poor in order to give the poor the opportunity to participate in the mainstream of American society. While participation played a prominent role in the early statements of the Office of Economic Opportunity (OEO), the federal anti-poverty agency, the dominating hallmark of its operating programs was training – training for work habits, training for skill development, training for citizenship and training for participation.

The poverty program, then, was essentially concerned with promoting compliance with American norms. The link between power and conformity was contained in the ideal of trying to promote a competent community. Residents of a community should be able to solve their own problems and control their own destinies by being able to influence the institutions which service them. When those who reside in an area lose the capacity to solve their own problems or the capacity to modify institutional performance in accordance with their needs, a breakdown in the institution of authority frequently results. This weakness in turn erodes mechanisms of social control. The grim product of the incompetent community is the collapse of its

From: Miller, S.M. and Rein, M. (1974) 'Community participation: past and future' in D. Jones and M. Mayo (eds) *Community work two*, London: Routledge and Kegan Paul, pp 3-24.

control system. Institutional incompetence leads to personal incompetence, with the consequences of the growth of crime, delinquency and social deviancy.

Apathy among the poor prevents them from effectively demanding that the institutions which service them accommodate to their needs. The result is that their plight worsens and their capacity for effective action is further weakened. A vicious cycle of poverty reinforces a vicious cycle of bureaucratic dysfunction. To break the cycle, the vigor of local democracy must be restored, and this can best be accomplished by expanding the freedom and the competence of local residents to respond to their local problems. Citizen involvement in local decision-making, through competent local leaders who understand how best to command the events and institutions which shape the lives of the poor, is a major ingredient of the strategy of building a competent community on the assumption that people change as they try to change their world.

Changing institutions

In almost every area of service, the level of performance in poor black areas was lower than in more affluent or in white areas. In education, less was spent per student and each dollar was utilized with less effectiveness than in the white sections of most cities. Sanitation pick-ups were usually less frequent, traffic controls less stringent.

Planning for the future of minority communities frequently tended to disregard the felt needs of the residents. Instead, city-wide rather than neighborhood interests determined their design and location. The most striking illustration is that of urban renewal, which decreased the number of low-rent dwelling units, replacing them with a smaller number of expensive units and office buildings. As a result, urban renewal was tarred as 'Negro removal'.

Black communities saw themselves as suffering from poor performance and poor planning. A third cause of attack on the planning and operating agencies was that they were largely manned by whites at both the decision-making and personnel levels.

What evolved in the sixties were ways of dealing with these issues of accountability, planning and employment. In employment, the non-professional emerged as a powerful social invention. This new occupational role not only provided employment opportunities for residents, a need inadequately met by most OEO programs, but also promised to improve the educational and social services by bridging the gap between the professional provider and skeptical neighborhood residents. And it provided one way for community residents to be involved in the service agency. But progress was uneven. ...

With the explosion of planning for change, two [further] difficulties became painfully clear: the technical base of planning was inadequate [technical support for planning was more often absent than present]; planning cannot supersede the question of values.

Political support for a general line of action is usually secured by ambiguity in statement of goals and the cloaking of the conflict among them. When more specific planning or action occurs, the underlying disagreements emerge. Any planning act helps some more than others; seldom do all benefit equally. Consequently, even highly competent professionals do not have scientific rules for decision-making which can substitute for the political will.

The limits of science reinforce the importance of community participation in the planning process. Participation affirms broad principles of intent and sets priorities, while science provides presumably the means for their implementation. … The move toward authentic involvement in planning and operations required that at least some disadvantaged citizens command positions of authority. Poor, black citizens began to sit on the central planning committees, on local advisory boards and on the staff of planning and service agencies. This theory of accountability repudiates the principle of professional objectivity and elite disinterest. Leading citizens sit on boards as presumably representing 'the public interest' in which they have no monetary or financial stake. It is based upon a vague notion of declared interest of the consumer.

Poor or black residents first sought accountability by publicly criticizing agencies for malperformance (as defined by the residents). Aggressive measures, such as demonstrations and sit-ins were used. With the growth of resources and political pressure, residents moved into positions on boards (a decentralized school board) and agencies (community action agency) where they had an institutionalized, legitimized base for questioning the performance of the agency. A fulcrum for changing institutions emerged or, as some critics maintain, a fulcrum for maintaining equilibrium by cooling off passions by promising pseudo-authority.

Both a pseudo-transfer of power and a transfer of pseudo-power frequently occurred. But participation did lead to some changes in the source of power as well as in service delivery and performance. Guttentag (1972) argues that community control, which has been widely and sometimes eagerly judged as a failure, was a success. The findings of later research are different from those of early studies. One of the aims (and many have argued, the prime aim) was to change the behavior, aspirations and attitudes of ghetto residents through a strategy of participation. People change as they try to change their world. While the Harlem experiment with community-controlled schools created deep conflict between professionals and consumers, it also changed the aspirations of adults and increased the educational achievement of the children who participated in it. …

Criticisms of participation

Participation and service delivery

It is important to recognize that improving public services is not easy. The long-term general situation of many low-income communities and neighborhoods is that they have long suffered from inadequate services. ... In any case, new organizations and leaders usually encounter difficulties in performing. Discussion may be delayed because of the excessive concern with having all issues, even very minor or detailed ones, debated and acted upon by the representatives of the residents. Conflicts may flourish, with the consequent making and unmaking of decisions. Inappropriate decisions may be made. Incompetent administrators may be chosen on political grounds. More important perhaps is that even highly committed personnel may be unable to overcome the basic lack of resources to meet local needs. ...

If inadequate resources cause fundamental and insurmountable problems, then service participation is not only distracting, but undermining as well. By directing energies to the use of present resources, participation may hinder the task of acquiring substantial new resources.

The choice seems to be between two different conceptions of participation. Political participation argues for the creation of effective political organization to make demands, while allocative operational participation is preoccupied with the distribution and use of resources already in hand. The history of participation in the poverty program shows that each without the other is insufficient ... yet they collide when pursued within the same organizational structure. The Welfare Rights Movement, committed to the creation of political organization among welfare recipients as a strategy of winning more resources and a more humane and adequate welfare system, confronted this dilemma. The national office accepted a quarter of a million dollars manpower grant in the Work Incentive Program, a job training program for women receiving welfare payments. The Pennsylvania chapter revolted, arguing that commitment to the running of a service program would undermine the organizing and confrontational tasks of the movement. Each organization committed to participation faces at some point in its history the need to make a choice between operating to deliver service or engaging in political combat to win resources and change. Public policy at the national level must decide whether it wishes to mix or keep separate these competing and complementary conceptions of participation.

Planning and accountability

In principle, the mayor appoints the board of a public agency and they are accountable to him; the staff of the agency in turn carry out the policy of the board and are responsible to them. Aggrieved clients or the disillusioned can appeal to the board and to the mayor. If they do not get satisfaction, they can elect a new mayor. The policy of the board and the mayor must take account of local needs and city-wide interests, but such an accounting in these theories does not require deep citizen involvement, only the chance of voters to present government and to review at some point the general performance of the elected officials who are held to be responsible.

But the theories have worked out poorly for the ghetto, and consequently new rationales have emerged with a new set of opportunities and difficulties concerning the role of the citizen, especially the resident of low-income areas. Do poorly-educated citizens have the competence to participate in planning? The experience of Community Action and Model Cities programs strongly points to the conclusion that they do. But that is not to say that technical competence is not needed or that residents are exclusive repositories of the wisdom of what needs to be done and how, in low-income communities. What has emerged is that ordinary citizens not only have usefully functioned to review plans developed by experts but have an important contribution to make at the level of the development of the plan. They are different kinds of 'experts' from the technically-trained, college-educated genre. In short, residents have an important but not exclusive role in planning. The model of advocate planners has developed a new relationship between residents and experts, in that experts now accept the leadership of low-income citizens, as earlier they accepted the obligation to operate within the mandates of their political, commercial or bureaucratic employers. The dominant role frequently no longer belongs to the professional or political head of an agency, but to that of the community's poorly-educated leaders. This model gives citizens a new role in planning in which they offer alternatives and competition to elite-derived plans.

One hoped-for result is that better plans will emerge from the competition of alternatives. Another contrasting result is inaction, as competing groups battle and the veto power of each group stops the activities of all.

A second type of criticism of participation in planning is that the neighborhood is not an appropriate unit for which to plan. How can a highway system or even a hospital system be planned only in relation to the needs and preferences of a neighborhood? In the former, the operation of the whole metropolitan area must be considered; in the latter, the distribution of labor in terms of specialties (does every hospital need a heart transplant facility?) is required for efficient deployment of scarce resources.

There is obvious merit in this contention, and it will be necessary to develop at least temporary alliances and coalitions among neighborhood units. Even metropolitan government is compatible with greater neighborhood participation; the neighborhood organizations and the formal governmental units of cities and towns can link up for some joint actions. But undoubtedly this development is difficult; metropolitan government has been achieved in very few places and inter-governmental compacts are scarce indeed. Hopefully, experience will drive even inwardly-oriented neighborhood units to respond to the need for joint action on a broader scale.

A third type of criticism is the undermining of the authority, and therefore the accountability, of the traditional city government. If mayors cannot make decisions, they cannot be held accountable: a common experience in many cities where power is already highly fragmented so that no one can be charged with the responsibility for failure. ...

In the community control version of participation, policy is set independently of city-wide concerns so that it can be most responsive to the demands of the ghetto. What is being called for is a separation between fiscal accountability (city, state, and federal) and administrative policy. Central bureaucracy tends stubbornly to resist the demands for autonomy. Local groups have secured resources with the support of federal agencies which offered them some basis of independence. The need for institutional change legitimates such steps. Three different approaches to neighborhood bureaucracies have been tried:

(a) Parallelism: a parallel activity program is developed which essentially carries out functions similar to those of the public bureaucracy, but under alternative auspices, e.g. Opportunities Industrialization Centers conducting vocational education programs run through the school system.
(b) Outpost of public bureaucracy: a local branch office is established with power to modify city-wide policy to the advantage of the local neighborhood (Model Cities).
(c) Community control: a mixture of (a) and (b). In the case of decentralized school districts in New York City, the financing has been at the city level with appropriations to the districts; the hiring of personnel is at the district level following city requirements and pay scales; the tenure of the teachers is city-wide; branch policy is a combination of city and state decisions with the growing importance of the districts.

Each approach poses special difficulties and opportunities; parallelism offers opportunity for experimentation but makes the system more complex and overlapping. Outposts can readily present an illusion of change with the reality of stability. Control reinforces racial, ethnic and class separatism, while it caters to local tastes.

Democracy

Participation on the basis of territoriality-residence in a geographic area leads today to racially and ethnically distinct units. The fear is that the drive for separatism will realize its objectives in the formation of new organizational units whose constituency is all black or all Puerto Rican or all Mexican-American.

The counter-argument is that the opponents of neighbourhood control of the new quasi-governmental units of community action are asking minorities to exchange any chance of greater immediate measures of power and autonomy for indefinite future hopes of integration and influence in the larger city units. It is nice to talk about an open and racially dispersed society, but as long as it is not achieved, minority groups should be able to exercise greater authority in their neighborhoods. This step runs the danger of permanent separatism. But it may be possible to offset this danger by keeping the boundaries of units fairly flexible.

Authenticity

The sixties can be seen as the time of political struggle to generate more public resources and to capture them for the black and the poor. Community participation in old or new established structures can be cooptative and may reduce the leverage which can be exercised to capture resources through dissensus or confrontational politics. Participation can become an end in its own terms, rather than participation in power. For the participants may become trapped in the details of scrimping with meager resources, rather than battling for larger and larger resources.

At some points, of course, coming into the seats of government is an important and positive step for the disadvantaged. Providing direction over existing resources is important, but the criticism is accurate in that the urgent aim is to expand resources.

Holding participation roles does not necessarily generate power. For strong roles, the representatives of the neighborhoods must be able to count either on the pressures of dissensus politics (which gets them into trouble as they will be operating against the power establishments at the same time that they are expected to be a part of them) or on conventional, electoral politics (where votes can be delivered). When both bases of power are weak, participation in the new structures is only limitedly effective. For example, Mayor Lindsay in May 1969 vetoed two of the three Model City programs because of excessive neighborhood participation roles; the belief is that he did this in a mayoralty campaign where white backlash was more important than black or Puerto Rican voting or confrontation. Authentic participation then requires a political base; to some extent this can be acquired through the quasi-patronage of the new institutions, but it probably requires wider political activity.

The future of participation

All over the world groups seek 'power' or 'participation' as an end in itself, concerned with controlling their destinies and protecting themselves against arbitrary or unresponsive rule. Student groups as well as poor groups express their concern for greater autonomy and self-determination.... We do not as yet have a sure formula for meeting effectively the participation drive, but it is clear that American society must accommodate to this concern more effectively than it has in the past. The forms of community participation that have evolved are, we think, important steps. But the particular structure is less important at this point than national and local commitment to invigorate governmental action with the involvement of citizens.

The issues of power are first raised in terms of the taming or curbing of arbitrary power. Next, they appear as a concern with the transfer of power to isolated and excluded groups. Finally, they are manifested in the effort to transform the relations between the power-wielders and the power-recipients. ... The concerns are strong, even if latent, and they will re-emerge as a political issue, for they are part of the effort to redirect and recontrol the great shift of governmental power that has taken place in the last few decades.

2.7

Gilding the ghetto: the state and the poverty experiments

Community Development Project Interproject editorial team

The 1960s saw the state turn to the thriving academic industry of the social sciences for a new framework to explain urban poverty. With education expanding and the social sciences going from strength to strength there was no shortage of respected academics who could run the commissions of enquiry and produce the reports that would set the tone for state policy. Nor was there any shortage of social science graduates to staff the new poverty programmes. But their task was not an easy one. In 1969 at the personal request of Harold Wilson, an Anglo–American conference was called at Ditchley Park (UK), to compare CDP and EPA with their enormous American counterpart the US Poverty Program. High on the agenda at the conference was the idea that social science had so far failed to deliver a reliable 'macro-theory' that could be used to provide the public with explanations about the urban problem and that this failure might be a basis for the public 'witholding consent'. The social scientists were unfavourably compared with the economists – this was 1969 remember –

> …the success of the economist in being absorbed into the political system lay not in his capacity to predict effects, but in his capacity to generate consensus about which results were worth achieving.
> *Minutes of the Ditchley Park Conference,* J. Rothenburgh

The economist had been able to build up a framework of theory that commanded widespread support and acceptance, irrespective of its accuracy. The restructuring of British capitalism to ensure profitability was meeting with little opposition, although it was quite clearly not in the interests of people in the older industrial areas who saw their jobs being lost and their neighbourhoods declining. Why shouldn't the social scientists do the same

From: Community Development Project (1977) *Gilding the ghetto: the state and the poverty experiments*, London: CDP Inter-project Editorial Team, pp 51-62.

and provide the state and particularly local government – which was having to pick up the pieces on the ground – with a rational objective and scientific research framework in which to develop solutions to the urban problem?

So the poverty initiatives emphasised survey techniques, statistical analysis and computer models. With touching faith the social scientist, with his finely calibrated measuring instruments, was expected to provide the precise answers to the problem.

The theories current at the time centred on the notion of the-'culture of poverty', the idea that people inherited poverty, not because they were victim of the process of industrial decline but because there was something about them, their lifestyle, their values, that made them unable to take advantage of the opportunities available to them. It was this idea that the social scientists were to pass on through the poverty programme ...The Charles Booths and other social reformers of the nineteenth century, through self-motivated rather than state-paid enquirers, had served exactly the same purpose for the state then in the furnishing explanations of what was happening to people in general and the working class in particular. What was different about this period was that because of the development of social science as a pseudo-scientific discipline in the post war period the sophistication and complexity of the explanation available had taken on a new lease of life.

Social scientists...had the 'objective' scientific language of multiple deprivation and stratification systems to draw on and had developed complicated methods of proving that the class division between labour and capital no longer exists.

It was this ideology or of ideas which the state mobilised in the form of the Poverty Programme to counter the day-to-day experience system of working class people in the inner cities. The initiation of the different poverty initiatives was itself part of the process. The existence of special projects, government departments etc. to deal with the 'cycle of deprivation', 'social pathology' and their like clearly proved that these things must exist. The institutions were the definition made concrete.

> CDP is based on the recognition that although the Social Services cater reasonably well for the majority, they are less effective for a minority who are caught up in a chain reaction of related social problems. *Home Office Press Release.* 16.7.69

Thus, the CDP brief carried home the idea that there's nothing wrong with the social services, but there is a minority who fall outside its efficiency. Built into the National Project's very existence, its twelve small area teams, was the proof that the unlucky minority live in isolated pockets dotted around the country in what are in effect very special circumstances. These were the 'areas of special social need' constantly referred to by the Home Office and the Department of the Environment. This idea of poverty affecting only small groups in marginal areas is a powerful one for it immediately reduces the scale of the problem. It also carries the implication that those who live outside these areas share no common interests or problems with the deprived within. The working class are effectively split into two and the scene is set for convincing those within that their problems have nothing to do with wider economic and political processes.

Drawing fixed boundaries around an area demonstrates the smallness of the problem. This is particularly misleading in inner city areas, but it is a good example of how the problem can be defined concretely for the local population. The boundary immediately sets them aside from the rest of the inner city, as small yet special. It turns them inwards and discourages them from seeking unity with neighbouring communities with identical problems.

Although the government has always stated that its projects were experiments, the small area focus has certainly diverted attention away from the scale of the issues. Liverpool Inner Area Study estimate that the inner cities of the large conurbations alone house 3,800,000 deprived people, or 7% of the entire population. Plowden wanted to see 10% of the country's children in EPAs by 1971 – an estimate that has been made redundant by Department of Education's insistence that it was for local education authorities to decide their own EPA boundaries. Yet when Birmingham, for example, wanted to designate 191 schools for 'educational priority' it was forced to cut this total drastically as' it represented almost half the total number *allowed* for the whole country!

Once poverty and exploitation have been defined as marginal it follows logically that only minor adjustments are needed to make it go away. The assumption that the policies of government and the exercise of economic power are determined by the interplay of separate interest groups in society is supported without question. If marginal groups are excluded through imbalances in, the democratic and bureaucratic system this just has to be remedied by the proper representation of all groups in the political process. So we get 'positive discrimination'.. .. But this idea was very quickly challenged. 'Positive discrimination' touched the state's Achilles heel in implying provision of greater resources, a concession it was unable to make in the late sixties because of the economic situation. So the later Poverty programme changed its tune and sang of the need to 'prioritise needs' instead.

But whatever the particular conception of the problem, the (state's) failure to deal with poverty is always presented as primarily a technical or administrative one). There is a continuing emphasis on management techniques – 'area management', 'community development', 'co-ordinated social plan' and most recently 'an urban deprivation plan'.

The implication is that the problems can be dealt with easily enough, once the right method or combination of methods have been found. Real solutions are seen to lie, not in the realm of politics, nor in the provision of extra'resources, but in improving administrative practice with modern techniques, like programme budgeting, corporate management, computers and cost benefit analysis. In this scenario there is no room for questions of conflicts, or debate about the fundamental issues involved. The ineffectual policies of the state are obscured by 'the apparent rationality of the way problems are to be dealt with'.

Although the major cause of poverty during the sixties was the decline of the industrial base of the older areas, few of the early poverty initiatives mention this fact. Instead poverty was called 'deprivation'. It was a problem of people, not of industrial change, and in case anyone was still in doubt, a typical example would be thrown in.

> ... ill-health – financial difficulties – children suffering from deprivation – consequent delinquency – inability of the children to adjust to adult life – unstable marriages – emotional problems – ill-health and the cycle begins again. *Home Office Press Release, 16:7.69*

In sociology literature this kind of description is known as a 'social pathology' model and at times the whole purpose of the poverty projects takes on a clinical connotation. The metaphor of the scientific experiment is implied in instructions about how to set up action projects:

> There are extremely intricate problems of measuring cause and effect in social action programmes, and the planning of project activities in each area will, therefore, need to be under-pinned by a research design which makes the social action amenable to evaluation by research methods and eventually it surfaces in the Neighbourhood Schemes where one of the aims is to 'act as a laboratory for CDP ideas as they develop'. *CDP Objectives and Strategy* September 1970

In the laboratory scientific rules must be obeyed. Dependence on the social services, for example, is viewed as some independent variable quite separate from any other factors affecting the people. The welfare state could solve people's individual problems, but when a significant number of those same people were concentrated in geographical areas – the old, the unskilled, the disabled, the unemployed left behind by the tide of industrial change – they become 'multiply deprived'. Whole families became caught in a 'cycle of deprivation' that was not only 'transmitted from generation to generation' like some hereditary disease but was also immune to the widely canvassed cure of 'equal opportunity'. Whole areas became affected, suffering from the 'social malaise' of 'urban deprivation'. The Lambeth Inner Area Study for instance talks of 'the environmental problems that arise in areas of poor and deprived people' and, like Booth,[1] suggests that the problems can only be ultimately solved by 'dispersing the concentrations'.

That such areas can be identified by physical overcrowding, high unemployment rates, dereliction and decay is not disputed, the distortion comes as the focus is turned on the people not the environment or the wider structural causes. The implicit metaphor of illness is ever-present: people are 'suffering' from 'chronic' deprivation.

[Success is to be assessed by] ... indicators of improved family functioning, community functioning, personal care, childrearing practices, education and support for young children and physical conditions. Nowhere is there any mention of increased incomes or resources. The kind of change envisaged is mainly in anti-social *attitudes:* for example, reduced damage to houses, increased marriage and cohabitation stability, reduced delinquency and crime rates, reductions in dissatisfaction with employment and reduction in abuse of social services through fraud and voluntary unemployment.

While it is true to say that over the last two or three years, academics and others have mounted some challenge to these explanations of poverty and pointed to the wider social processes which determine low wages, bad housing and unemployment, the pathological metaphors have become increasingly popular in local government circles.

... attempts to draw run-down working-class communities into a debate with local councillors and officials about their needs illustrates one of the starkest contradictions of the state's position. Here are areas where there has been a steady rundown of the traditional manufacturing industries – a process that has been deliberately encouraged by state policies. Although some new capital investment has been attracted for activities like warehousing and distribution, the general economic base and the supporting social infrastructure of the areas remains depleted. Yet, if left to rot even further, they begin to pose a direct political threat – both by their very existence and by their potential for social ferment.

So area management on the one hand and devices like information centres and community councils on the other, have been wheeled in to provide the illusion of political response. To quote Miss Cooper of the Home Office they were 'gilding the ghetto or buying time'.

... The emphasis on 'tackling social needs' in isolation inevitably distracts attention from the root causes of the problem, by focusing attention upon personal deficiencies. The people themselves are to blame for the problems caused by capital. It was doubtless disagreement around this point which caused the instant resignation of the first director of the Glyncorrwg CDP –

---

[1]   This is an allusion to Charles Booth's Victorian studies of poverty.

a child psychologist. Glwncorrwg is a small South Wales mining town with remarkable community spirit but unemployment of about 30% caused by the closure of all the pits in the valley. The Town Clerk and the psychologist had clearly different opinions about the nature of the problems in the area. After a stormy discussion, the psychologist caught the first train home and was never seen in the area again!

... Providing the definition of the problem alone was not enough [for the state]. If people were to believe in these explanations there had also to be a solution. Here the answer was ready to hand: social democracy could be made to work. In fact it was of vital importance to the state that social democracy should be seen as able to provide a solution because in these areas of urban and industrial decline people already appeared to have lost faith in it. The turnout of electors at the local Council elections, low in the best of areas, was typically very low indeed in these areas. Yet as the Redcliffe-Maud Report warned 'If local self-government withers, the roots of democracy grow dry. If it is genuinely alive, it nourishes the reality of democratic freedom.'

Participation and making local councillors more efficient were the ways in which belief in the political system – and thus the economic structure underlying it – could be restored. The need for *responsive* local government and for people to *participate* more was a constant theme of many of the official reports of the sixties, picking up and turning to their advantage the contemporary demand coming from students and the trade union movement for more participation in education and in industry, in the sense of more control.

... the state has a continuing need to keep its fingers on the working-class pulse to know what is going on particularly in those difficult unorganised sections of the working class where there are no established channels, unions, or leadership to deal through. It needed to know what to expect from the ghettoes and to have accurate information with which to update the diagnosis of the problems and so produce the next set of policies.

Despite the similarity of the different [state] initiatives, the feedback process can be seen at work even within the space of the poverty programme of the last decade: the 'action research' emphasis gives way to area management, 'positive discrimination' and to 'prioritising needs'. Even more clearly, the critical findings of CDP and some of the Inner Area Study reports with their insistence on the economic system as the root-cause of continuing poverty, can be seen today being fed back in mutilated form to the media via the 'structural' rhetoric of [the Labour MP] Peter Shore for example:

> The causes [of inner area decline] lie primarily in their relative economic decline, in a major migration of people, often the most skilled, and in a massive reduction in the number of jobs which

are left … Many facilities in our inner urban areas need qualitative improvement, and some need total and often expensive replacement.
Peter Shore, 17.9.76

while the old, now unpopular 'personal pathology' approach is faded into the background.

Keeping the initiative is essential to the state's success. It has to update its ideas and change definitions to keep abreast with critical comment, working-class pressure and the inevitable failure of its piecemeal measures, if it is to maintain its own credibility and public consent. The wide range of opinions and ideas represented by the professionals working for the state (never wider perhaps than at the height of the poverty programme) all go to help this process of ideological renewal on its way. While they seek new state 'solutions' to the 'problems' in good faith and genuine concern, the state has within itself a valuable reserve of alternatives to turn to. To the outside world they create the illusion that government is really trying to do something to alleviate the problems and that given the *right* ideas social democracy does work. As the needs of the poorer sections of the working class are defined as 'realistic aspirations' and the blame is diverted away from the real source and onto those who suffer the consequences of decline, the institutions' of the state reorganise and revitalise themselves.

… Nowadays we hear a great deal about the need to save money and cut back public expenditure on the 'unproductive services'. In many ways this seems a far cry from the atmosphere of the sixties when the growth of public spending was at its peak. Yet by the time CDP and the Urban Programme were being set up there was already a growing concern in some parts of government that public spending was getting out of hand. How to cope with the 'bottomless pit' was already a central theme of the early poverty initiatives. And it has become the keynote of the recent schemes, with their concentration on saving money co-ordination of services, cost-effectiveness and prioritising needs.

Today with the economic crisis considerably worsened the approach is out in the open. 'Explanations' of the economy are served up in the newspapers, on radio and television almost every day now. We know there is a 'crisis', we must all 'tighten our belts', we know about 'lack of investment', 'low productivity', unemployment. We are convinced that the 'national interest' is indeed our interest, even if it means unemployment and declining living standards for us and increased profits for the national and international corporations.

In the sixties, though, the basic concern about finding ways of saving money was being introduced into a very different ideological climate. The state's main concern was the enormous increase in local authority spending. Central government, hard-pressed by huge borrowing to maintain public spending, became concerned about the increase and took steps to integrate and control it within the total pattern of state spending, recommending a vast range of new management and technical devices to improve the local authorities' budgeting. But at the same time public expectations were high and had been encouraged to rise by the optimistic rhetoric of the fifties and sixties. People were expecting more from the Welfare State, especially in high-cost services like housing and education. White collar workers were becoming tougher about pay increases; militancy worked, as traditionally respectable groups like the hospital workers found. More women going out to work meant increased demands for nursery care; the unpaid work they had done before – looking after the elderly and their sick relatives, as well as their children – put additional demands on local government services.

The government's own advisors, often echoing the wisdom of liberal academics, were also recommending increased spending. The official reports described earlier were designed to update the services organised by the state to maintain a healthy labour force, which also had the necessary manual and intellectual skills. They called, in effect, for extra spending. Milner Holland wanted more local authority housing in London; Plowden, more and better primary schools; Robbins, big increases in higher education; Seebohm, extra resources for the personal social services. The list was endless.

... the poverty initiatives were primarily experiments with and on the residents of the older industrial areas. But they were also experiments with and on the local authorities themselves. Above all they were experiments *on behalf of* the central and local state. In this respect they were most important in providing a laboratory for both civil servants and local government officials to test out current and developing ideas not only about how to cut up the cake and distribute it, but how to get the best value for money. As ever the issue was presented as a problem of administration. The government however was quite clear about the political nature of resource allocation issues.

> It would also be an essential part of the experiment to assess how far, and on what criteria of need, policies involving positive discrimination in the use of resources could be pursued without loss of financial control, and without provoking 'backlash' effects from other communities or areas of need. The latter consideration would be particularly important where the CDA [later CDP] contained a high proportion of immigrants: we should wish to include two or three such areas within the experiment. *Report of an Inter-Departmental Working Party,* chaired by Derek Morrell, 21.5.68

Taken at face value it might seem that the state ignored the findings of its programmes, but with economic context and the real concerns of the state understood, it becomes clear that they were far from ignored. In fact the state has taken up the poverty programme suggestions in a systematic and highly selective way that reveals precisely its own interests. Recommendations to do with increased resource provision have been carefully ignored – the priority was not to improve the material conditions of the working class in the 'affected areas' in this way. But suggestions which have helped in the better management of urban problems without involving extra resources have been taken on board – the management of the poor is to be streamlined.

[Co-ordination] ... at all levels – between local authorities and voluntary agencies and groups, between local and central government' and even between central government departments. Within the context of local government as a whole this idea was enshrined in 'corporate management'. The poverty initiatives focussed principally on the co-ordination of service delivery aspects of the local authority. A 'total approach' was needed – an idea later redefined as area management – 'extending corporate management down to an area level'.

... But good co-ordination, at best, only provides an efficient baseline; and in most situations, as many local authorities have discovered, good co-ordination actually costs more. Much bigger savings can be effected by increasing productivity. In local government language this is called 'cost effectiveness'. The focus of the poverty initiatives however was not on work study for social workers, teachers or planners, but on getting more out of the *community itself* and out of short, one-off, professionally-run schemes which would initiate voluntary work on a longer-term basis. This 'multiplier effect' was the main principle behind Urban Aid and the EPA projects. The theory is that an adventure playground, for example, employing one or two play leaders, will organise activities for the children which are useful because they keep the kids off the street. Meanwhile the parents of the children will get together initially as a playground committee but later to use it as a focus for other neighbourhood activities – Christmas parties, summer coach trips, visiting old people, fundraising for a community centre and so on.

EPA, especially in Liverpool, was very involved in pre-school playgroups (which are usually run by local parents) and with the concept of the community school. This embraces Plowden's idea of teacher aides (teachers on the cheap) but also seeks to link up the community and the school curriculum. The spin-off for the state would be improved education standards.

> CDP again echoes Seebohm with its aim of creating community spirit in order to ... 'take some of the load off the statutory services by generating a fund of voluntary social welfare activity and mutual help amongst the individuals, families and social groups in the neighbourhood, supported by the voluntary agencies.' CDP: Objectives and Strategy 1970

Urban Aid was to have a similar role.

> ... the co-operation of parents in the running of the project can be of considerable importance in helping to foster the community spirit. The potential here is as yet largely untapped, and its value should not be underestimated. *Urban Programme Circular No. 6* December 1971

Though none of the projects are explicit, it is clear that parents usually means mothers, and voluntary social welfare workers are always women. Although there were growing numbers of women going out to work there were still plenty at home who could be roped in as an alternative to employing full-time, paid nursery teachers or social workers.

The ideas of self-help and participation, too, had a potential pay-off for local government. Re-creation of community identity and feeling could perhaps lead to informal pressures on tenants to maintain their houses in better condition. Community activity around children would perhaps encourage adults to keep a tighter rein on the young people and discourage them from vandalising public property.

In and against the state

London Edinburgh Weekend Return Group

We are a small group of people who work for the state or for organisations which receive money from the state. We are socialists. We believe that the struggle for socialism includes a struggle against the state – one in which we, as state workers, hold a key, and at the same time contradictory, position. If we are to work in and *against* the state, we must find ways of bringing the struggle for socialism into our daily work.

The class position of some state workers is clear. Many public sector manual and clerical workers are the lowest paid of all employed people. For others it is equally obvious: they are highly paid management staff, top civil servants, directors of nationalised industries. But what about nurses, teachers, social workers? Their position seems ambiguous.

Those of us writing this book fall into the middle group of workers, who are often termed 'professional'. We are social community/advice/research workers. Often these types of job might seem as though they were above class. But our jobs have become increasingly disciplined, especially since the cuts in public expenditure which are pushing us all into positions and attitudes that are similar to those of workers for private capital.

We do not want to make some easy assertion that we are working class. That overlooks the real differences between people's oppression, for class derives from all sorts of hidden advantages and disadvantages as well as our jobs. But, the changes in the jobs that we do over the last 15 or 20 years have brought us like thousands of others in similar jobs to see ourselves as part of the working-class movement. Like many others we have made a choice. If we don't choose to be part of it, we inevitably choose to work against it. The point of this book is that we choose to be part of the struggle for socialism *within our own jobs* by the way we do them. We write from within our own struggle, the struggle against the state.

Some of us are women and feminists. For us the struggle to change relations within society is not just against capitalism but against sexism as well. The subordination of women by men existed long before capitalism, but is reinforced by the capitalist system and the state. The fight for a change

From: London Edinburgh Weekend Return Group (1980) *In and against the state*, London: Pluto Press, pp 3-6 and 140-7.

in the relations between man and women must go hand in hand with that for socialism. It cannot be assumed that sexism will automatically disappear in a socialist society.

In our group some of us are tenants, some are parents, all, at one time or another, have been patients. We know we have no choice but to enter into routine relationships with the state to obtain money, resources and services. We depend on and are controlled by state provision, rules, demands. As 'clients', too, we feel the need to organise to fight against the state.

The state is not neutral. It does provide services and resources which most of us need – education, health care, social security. But it does not do so primarily for the good of the working class. It does it to maintain the capitalist system. Although the state may appear to exist to protect us from the worst excesses of capitalism, it is in fact protecting capital from our strength by ensuring that we relate to capital and to each other in ways which divide us from ourselves, and leave the basic inequalities unquestioned.

We believe that it is essential that capitalism be seen not just as, an economic system, but as a set of social relations. It determines the way we see ourselves and others, the way we treat each other, the way some people have control over others' lives.

The state, too, is more than a structure which administers numerous services and programmes. It is a complex set of social relations which must be maintained if capitalism is to 'continue'. It is characteristic of the state that it treats us as individual citizens, families, communities, consumer groups – all categories which obscure class. By this process, the state seems to define us and our problems in ways which confuse us. It helps hide the fact that it is the *capital relation* which is the root of our problem and shapes our lives. The state also establishes a hierarchy of power and decision-making. This hierarchy is one of class, but it included the subordination of women and people of certain races and religions. These groups have a special experience of state oppression and must sometimes organise autonomously as well as together with other parts of the working class.

Those of us who work for the state are inevitably part of the state. We must find ways to oppose it from within our daily activity, which means breaking out of the social relations in which the state involves us and creating alternative forms of organisation as we struggle for socialism. If we do not, whether we recognise it or not, we are perpetuating a capitalist society – one which is exploitative, sexist and racist.

Struggle against the state – against the social relations it perpetuates – goes on all the time. The state is an often frustrating and threatening part of our daily lives, and struggle against it is instinctive. But it is often individual, risky and ineffective. Struggle must be collective. It is important that we understand what forms of collective action will most effectively challenge the state form of relations and provide a basis for building socialism, and then organise ourselves around them.

Because parties and trade unions on the whole have devoted little attention to the problem of how a state worker's hours of employment can be directed against capitalism and towards a transition to socialism, we have found that when we join them we are limited to 'after-hours' socialism. We spend our evenings and weekends struggling against capitalism, and our days working diligently as agents of the capitalist state to reproduce the capitalist system. Like Penelope, in the Greek myth, we stitch the tapestry of bourgeois society every day and attempt each night to unravel it before dawn.

Is there any way out of this hopeless dilemma? Can we shape our daily activity in such a way as to avoid stitching capital's tapestry, can we hinder rather than promote the reproduction of capitalist social relations? Does the fact that our work is situated in the state give us special opportunities in this respect, or is that merely a reformist illusion? These are the issues that we want to discuss. The aim of this book is to provide a framework for that discussion.

… The Conservative Government elected in summer, 1979, is apparently attacking many aspects of the state, cutting state expenditure yet further, causing the loss of state jobs. This confuses many people who feel the need to defend the state, yet do not feel that it is 'their' state and know that the state itself oppresses them. It is all the more urgent, therefore, that as socialists we look for ways of fighting back oppositionally, rather than simply defending a state we know to be indefensible.

Anger, resistance and the making of socialism

Search for new forms

The failure in socialist organisations and strategic thinking … has its good side as well as bad. There is a new openness around. Nowadays you have to delude yourself very badly if you think you have all the answers. For example, a book written by three socialist feminists, *Beyond the Fragments,* has, by its questioning of standard left assumptions, created more of a stir than any similar work for many years. It has had its impact, not because it provides answers that will solve all our problems, but because it raises questions that people were asking silently. … What can we do about the fact that many of us, as committed socialists, find existing socialist organisations inadequate?

The call for a renewed reliance on traditional trade union and labour party politics is partly based on the misconception that what we are experiencing is a return to the thirties. We have already pointed our some of the ways the emerging situation differs from the pre-war decades. Now there is an entirely new technology of control, from nuclear power to psychotropic drugs, a new mode of domination, different groups of people bearing the brunt of capital's offensive – in particular black people (scarcely present in the UK before the war), women, school leavers, pensioners. There are new issues and new groups at the focal points of class struggle.

The old forms of organisation have simply not adapted to the new circumstances – not that they ever did give adequate expression to the anger of many groups. New forms of struggle are needed which answer to the needs of *everyone* involved, both in terms of appropriate forms of organisation and of defining what it is we are fighting for. Take women as an instance – since half of us writing this are women. We are the ones who will be expected to cope as living standards fall and nurseries, hospitals and old people's homes close down. It is also women who are losing their jobs fastest and who may well turn out to be at the core of the struggle over the new technology. What autonomy and control over their own fertility women have succeeded in establishing over the last few years is also being undermined. For these reasons it is now quite impossible to conceive of a movement of mass resistance to capital's offensive which does not have women at the centre, especially when it comes to struggles in and against the state.

All of this is nominally recognised by socialists. Yet too often, men, and sometimes women too, see the problem as one of 'how to draw women in'. ...Those whose history has been in the labour movement are steeped in a form of organising that has been developed primarily by men, with committees, delegate structures, representatives, negotiators and so on, procedures and roles in which women often feel at a loss. Women, however, are not without characteristic ways of organising: many have brought much courage and inventiveness to direct action, in Ireland, in urban communities. Women also have more experience than men of working co-operatively, especially in small, mutually supportive groups.

Nor are women as passive as is often assumed. Women are struggling all the time. Making ends meet, pressing for a nursery place, securing an exceptional needs payment, getting the electricity reconnected, trying to stop the children being taken away, securing an adequate share of the wage for housekeeping. The problem is that women's many bitter struggles are often very isolated and individual ones. ... The problem is to find ways of de-individualising these struggles and strengthening collective organisation where it does exist.

Beyond questions of organisation, however, we should recognise that almost all these issues that concern women involve deep-rooted and complicated feelings; the cuts, for example, often affect nurseries, homes and hospitals which look after people who would otherwise be looked after by their families. Socialists oppose the closure of these institutions: caring for dependent relatives at home can impose intolerable burdens and there is no reason why this should be women's unpaid work. At the same time we must recognise that having our relatives cared for by the state often involves deeply ambiguous feelings, including guilt about admitting there are limits to our loving and caring and anxiety about poor standards of care. ... In this kind of situation we need to find ways of organising that don't trample on our feelings, which face up to and work through the contradictions.

Holding to what we have learned

As the crisis deepens and many socialists call for a return to the traditional politics of the labour movement ... we must hold onto what we have learned – in the squatting movement, the women's movement, in actions as diverse as Rock Against Racism and community publishing. In particular there are four crucial points.

1. Socialist practice must be rooted in people's own experience.
What we have learned, particularly from the women's movement, is that our struggle is strongest when it is based on a shared understanding of what brings people to the struggle in the first place, when our forms of action correspond to the personal needs of those involved. We have learned, too, that paying attention to the complexities and contradictions in people's lives will in the long run be a source of strength. People's views and feelings cannot simply be dismissed as 'false consciousness'. There are often coherent and plausible reasons why people turn to private medicine or want to buy their council house. Unless we listen to these and take account of them in formulating a socialist approach to health care, or housing, as the case may be, it is quite unlikely that we will ever be able to build a mass movement.

We have been saying that the capitalist state individualises people, that it denies the fact that we have a common problem and in doing so undermines our potential collective strength. We have to accept, then, that people *are* divided. People are racist and sexist, we often blame and fight each other rather than capitalism and those who control it. We cannot write people off for turning against each other, pensioners for hating punks, or punks for hating pensioners. We have to find a way of bringing them into a shared struggle.

2. Socialism cannot be built without a vision of what is possible.
In the past we have sometimes thought that if only we explain to people that their problems arise from living in a capitalist society, this alone will be enough to bring them to a commitment to socialism. It is increasingly clear, however, that people's commitment to fight back is in part related to the extent to which they can see a way out. ... The unpalatable fact is that for most people socialism means nothing better than the monolith of Soviet

Russia, or the drabness of the welfare state writ large. At the moment it is the radical right who are making all the running when it comes to 'new values'. ... It doesn't have to be like this ... We need to talk about what we are working for – about a life where we can be free of the fear of war, where we have time for ourselves and the people we care for, where we can live in unpolluted places and uncrowded houses, eat good food and enjoy good health. We know what we want to have – a society where each person can be equally valued, equally in control – and it is necessary to spell it out, to imagine it, to make it real ...

A hospital campaign, say, need not be a merely rhetorical defence of an institution which people never really felt was theirs anyway. Hospital occupations have been made into opportunities to try out new ways in which hospital workers of different kinds, workers and patients, workers and community, can relate to each other, giving a glimpse of how it could be. Besides, many more people will be willing to throw their strength behind a struggle of this kind. ... Resistance is more than the refusal to be dominated. It is also about positively asserting how things could be. For too long socialists have been silent about what our struggles are *for*. We should break the silence.

3. Our whole lives are subject to capitalism.
In the last decade we have learned that the personal is political. We have found that capitalist domination penetrates every aspect of our lives: schools, hospitals, the law, technology, what we eat, even the air we breathe. Through the interlocking systems of male supremacy, of racial domination and religious authority with the oppressive structures of capitalism, our most personal domestic relationships are deformed. There is no politics-free zone.

This insight is fundamental for our politics. ... We do not need to seek out extreme cases of police brutality or starving children to demonstrate the evils of capitalism. We can simply recount to ourselves our everyday experience of oppression. Our struggle is about everyday opposition to the *normal condition of things*.

4. Socialism is about transforming power relations, not about capturing power.
One sure thing we have found out from all the 'participation' exercises of the Keynesian years, whether it was a matter of tenants co-opted to the housing committee, the TUC sitting at the table with the government, or left Labour MPS voted into Parliament, getting 'our' people into 'their' structures rarely brings the gains we hoped for. Worse, in complicated and subtle ways, it somehow actually reinforces our powerlessness and confuses our struggle. However excellent the socialist credentials of the people who have taken their place in these structures, they have only been able to make an impact when they have challenged their terms of reference or forms of

organisation … The question of who dominates cannot be separated from the form of domination.

Power is maintained in our society not because there are unpleasant individuals in control whose interests are not our interests, but because the *relations of control* have been shaped by capital in its own image. Our struggle is therefore in part the assertion of our own ways of doing things, ways which are rooted in people's lived experience rather than betraying it, ways that strengthen rather than whittle away people's confidence, and foster collectivity rather than individualism.

The hopeful thing about the passage of the last ten or fifteen years is that we have had some very positive as well as negative experiences on this question of power. For instance, squatters dramatise homelessness not by getting their elected representative onto the council's housing committee, but by practical action which challenged the relations of property itself, contested the fact that the value of houses arises from their standing empty, claimed instead that it rests in their potential for use. …

The process in the health movement has been similar; we have gained strength to confront the experts by sharing our personal experience, learning about our own bodies and discovering common patterns in our illness and our interactions with the health service.

In each of these situations we have made positive gains not by 'winning' power' in any formal sense but by taking a degree of control, counterposing our forms of organisation to theirs … because a struggle waged in our own way is the only possible point of departure for a world we can live in on our own terms.

Section 3

In and against the market: mid- to late 1970s to early 1990s

Introduction

Throughout the 1970s, the political and theoretical arguments around social policy in general, and community work in particular, were conducted within a frame of reference in which the central role of the state was assumed. In contrast, throughout the 1980s and 1990s, the British welfare state was subjected to a systematic process of institutional and ideological restructuring which reconfigured the terrain of community work in unique and unprecedented ways. In order to locate community work in this period, therefore, the starting points selected for this section are twofold. The first is the publication of *In and Against the State* – in 1979 and again in 1980 (LEWRG, 1980 – see Ch 2.8, this volume). The subsequent edition was an expanded version of the first, to include a prescient Postscript which sought to 'analyse what is happening to us' in light of what the authors foresaw as a 'new mode of domination' which was changing the relations of the state and the possibilities for progressive action in the new context. The second arises from a conference held in 1979 'Looking ahead: Community work into the 1980s' which concerned itself with the same terrain, but which focused explicitly on the prospects for community work in the coming decade. These publications need to be set in the context of the election in 1979 of a 'radical rightwing' Conservative government led by Margaret Thatcher which was to reshape not only the state but also, and critically, the parameters of debate and discourse surrounding it. In this sense, the context of mid- to late 1970s can be seen as the canvas upon which the new vision was being sketched out, and which provided the context in which the contradictions of state-sponsored 'empowerment' began to be seen as particularly sharp.

Waddington, in his contribution to the 1979 conference, highlighted what he regarded as the major shifts produced by the 'developing crisis of western economies' which had been under way since the 1960s (Waddington, 1979). In particular he referred to 'the end of the post-war era with its confident expectation of steady growth and full employment and its consensual faith that social democracy and liberal reformism offered an adequate framework for the solution of all important social problems'. Cynthia Cockburn (1977), in her seminal work on corporate management and community development, *The Local State*, had already identified the deeply ambivalent nature of community work in the emerging context, but particularly the way in which the local state was becoming less local in its political loyalties while, simultaneously, 'the community approach' was becoming a central policy strategy in 'reproducing the relations of authority' through cheaper and more ideologically effective means (p 131). For Henderson et al (1980) (Ch 3.2, this volume), the boundaries of change presented an opportunity to reassert the distinctive role for community work in the 'interjacence' between different demands and interests, although the dangers of incorporation this posed were acknowledged. Debates such as these about the relationship between community work and the state would become increasingly important as democratic political processes were gradually and systematically being reframed as managerial procedures in the restructuring of welfare which characterised the early 1980s.

Although the rhetoric, and some would say the appeal, of Thatcherism was premised on a promise to 'roll back' the frontiers of the state, the reality was rather different. The Thatcher government was, as Craig pointed out 'one of the most centralizing and interventionist of governments for a very long time' (cited in Miller and Bryant, 1990: 318). Embarking with stern conviction on a programme of privatisation, deregulation and trade union 'reform', the Conservative government sought to redefine the terms of democratic citizenship itself. In this process the 'state bad/private good' formulation was aggressively advanced in all aspects of social welfare and supported by significant sections of the media. The passively dependent state client would be transformed into the enterprising, property-owning, shareholding customer. This shift would be achieved politically through a realignment of the rights and responsibilities of citizenship, with the emphasis on individual 'self-help' as the first line of accountability. Thus, as Clarke (1996) noted, 'what from one angle can be viewed as the diminution of the state's role can be seen from another as the extension of state power, but through new and unfamiliar means'. As the infrastructure of services was being systematically dismantled, an ideological apparatus was put in place so that more people were encouraged, or driven, to look for individualised and private solutions to social problems. The famous announcement by Margaret Thatcher that there was in her view 'no such thing as society' marked the beginning of what came to be known as the cult of the private.

Ironically, in this new context community workers found their faded professional legitimacy revived – as strategic carriers of the new social order, delivering the community responses which would effectively act as a substitute (or alibi) for a rapidly declining public welfare sector. In this context, debates about the deficiencies of the social democratic state, which had been a constant theme in theory and practice, suddenly seemed almost traitorous as it was being dismantled and re-formed. Those who had previously attacked the state for its paternalism now found themselves in the unaccustomed position of defending it (Jacobs, 1994).

It has been argued that there were two distinct eras over this time which produced quite different responses to these changes (Miller and Bryant, 1990). In the early 1980s, for example, there were attempts to mobilise against the growing marketisation and its consequences. Action against cuts in services continued well into the middle of the decade – around jobs, housing, health and education (for example, Colenutt, 1979 – Ch 3.1, this volume), although these attempts were in some cases subject to criticism for their failure to adequately represent black people or to acknowledge racism (for example, Manning and Ohri, 1982 – Ch 3.4, this volume). There were also experiments in local municipal socialism, the most celebrated example being that of the Greater London Council (GLC) under its colourful leader, Ken Livingstone. Similarly, many Labour local authorities across the UK used their relative autonomy to support community groups in their resistance to national government policies.

Perhaps the most significant example of solidarity work between political institution, workplace and community in the UK was to be found in the epic struggle between the National Union of Mineworkers (NUM) and the Thatcher government over the pit-closure programme of 1984/85, the last major industrial struggle to command large-scale public support (Beynon, 1985). Communities up and down the country organised themselves in support of what they saw as a just cause, with many such groups drawing specifically upon women's action in defiance of their traditional domestic role (for example, Holden, 2005). Where the strike coincided with experiments in municipal socialism, local councillors in certain areas joined forces with mining communities and, in some cases, put public resources at their disposal (Blunkett and Jackson, 1987).

It could be argued that the defeat of the NUM and its allies marked the end of the first phase of restructuring and, as the decade proceeded, the possibilities for independent local government action and trade union activity were gradually closed down through a series of legal and financial instruments which made resistance more difficult and less attractive. The GLC – along with other metropolitan county councils – was simply abolished. Although other social and political struggles emerged – including the successful campaign against the Poll Tax (an extremely unpopular local tax) in Scotland in the late 1980s – the legacy of a string of defeats for oppositional politics was the creation of an hegemony of resignation among the public at large: the perception that nothing could stand in the way of what was coming (Miliband, 1994). This was, of course, precisely the argument put forward by the Thatcher government itself: 'there is no alternative' ('TINA', as this view came to be described) to a neo-liberal approach if the UK was to compete within the now globalised 'free-market' economy. This had a dramatic effect on community work, like everything else.

Several commentators have argued that community work theory and practice left practitioners unprepared for the dramatic consequences of these restructuring processes. Bryant and Bryant (1982), for example, argued that a simplistic view of the 'repressive state' inhibited strategic analysis when it was most necessary. Nick Derricourt too was concerned about what he described as 'arrested development' in the sense that the 'painfully learnt lessons' of the 1970s had been set aside (cited in Miller and Bryant, 1990: 320). Waddington (1979) lamented the 'increasing impatience with theory' in a context in which theoretical analysis seemed to be more critical than ever. At the same time, however, alternative approaches elsewhere were providing influential challenges, particularly the developing literature on the relationship between education and political mobilisation (for example, Horton and Freire, 1990 – Ch 3.5, this volume). Freirean ideas in particular seemed to resonate for many in the new context. For example, the necessity for social and cultural action – to break the culture of silence or resignation – was seen to be in dialectical relationship to macro-analysis. The widespread institutionalisation of participatory development approaches worldwide during this period was also influential on community development. On the one hand, they provided support for rolling back the state by putting greater emphasis on non-governmental organisations as providers of services previously supplied by the state, but in some cases they also provided the context for the development of alternative approaches to neo-liberalism, both in the UK and internationally (Cooke and Kothari, 2001).

There was also a growing recognition that, if the state was no longer in a position to offer comprehensive or effective solutions to intractable social problems, then community development should be supported in encouraging local solutions. The Association of Metropolitan Authorities in England produced a report *Community Development: The Local Authority Role* (1989) addressing this very subject. The report, which emerged through consultation with a wide range of voluntary sector and national agencies in England, advocated that community development 'be taken seriously and resourced properly', and that it should be seen 'as a key element in any democracy since it stimulates and supports participation and involvement and thereby encourages effective and responsible citizenship' (p 7). The idea that such inclusive participatory processes should inform the work of a range of local authority departments had previously been advocated in the Worthington Report in Scotland in 1978, leading to the embedding of community development as council policy in what was then Strathclyde Regional Council. These developments and the decade or so in between reflect what has always been an ambivalent attitude towards community development by local government – advocating, supporting and, inevitably, regulating its activities.

In another development, in 1985 *Faith in the City: A Call to Action by Church and Nation*, was published by the Archbishop of Canterbury's Commission on Urban Priority Areas. The report came in the wake of much concern about what was happening in the UK's inner city and outer council housing estate communities. *Faith in the City* was crucial in sparking new awareness of the emerging gaps in society, gaps which had become painfully apparent in the 'riots' of the summers of 1981 and 1985. In line with faith-based work in the United States, the community organising approach of Saul Alinsky was rediscovered in some urban areas, particularly in England (Henderson and Salmon, 1995).

It is also notable that policy developments in this period stimulated new and oppositional forms of politics (Manning and Ohri, 1982 – Ch 3.4, this volume). Thus, as responsibility for welfare shifted from the public to the private sphere, new issues and sites of struggle were actively constructed by and through policy. For example, the new emphasis on 'consumer choice' and 'voice' in education, housing and health arguably provided the stimulus for mainstream service providers to re-examine their practices in progressive ways (Taylor, in Miller and Bryant, 1990), while the introduction of 'user-involvement' strategies created a potential space for those previously disenfranchised to influence policy (for example, Croft and Beresford, 1992 – Ch 3.6, this volume). In this respect, the gap between intentions and outcomes of policies such as Community Care could be said to have created new communities of interest whose identities were defined by their previous marginalisation or exclusion, such as disabled people and carers (Shaw, 1996).

A distinctive feature of many such groups, as they developed their political platform, was their primary focus on gaining cultural recognition – often posed against a limited and exclusive view of redistributive universalism. For some this represented a potentially diversionary focus on diversity at the expense of communality (Miller and Bryant, 1990). For others, it was a necessary corrective to an overly deterministic understanding of 'class' which had, in any event, dominated community work for too long (Dominelli, 1995). In response to the post-modern challenge to 'grand narratives' which were no longer regarded as coherent, there was an attempt to develop a basis for practice which would 'move beyond the simple respect for difference on the one hand or the uncritical acceptance of the push for equality on the other' (Meekosha, 1993 – Ch 3.7, this volume). In any case, and for entirely different reasons – the individualisation of social relations and competitiveness over reducing funds in particular – the emphasis in policy was increasingly on 'difference', which seemed to chime with the new political demands, producing new contradictions for community work.

As the decade progressed, those class-based organisations which had been accorded some corporate legitimacy in the social democratic welfare state found themselves largely excluded, presented increasingly as the enemy of the modernised state, to be replaced at the table in due course by an ad hoc conglomeration of community organisations in the move towards a new neo-corporatist form of governance. Community work, once a relatively marginal activity on the edges of the welfare state charged with 'picking up the pieces', was now poised to occupy a strategic role in the 'enabling state', ready-made to assist with the process of 'community empowerment'.

Community action over local planning issues

Bob Colenutt

Introduction

The ideas that the residents of working-class areas are engaged in struggles about the environment but not much in workplace and employment struggles; and that conversely, the local workforce is not much concerned with environmental issues may now be a myth. This is the conclusion that is emerging from community actions up and down the country where local residents and workers have participated together in local planning issues.

Plans for local areas, whether 'informal plans' or those required by law (District or Local Plans as they are often called) have provoked more interest and stimulated broader alliances than local authorities may have bargained for. In this article, we shall look at the growth of opposition to planning policies in Southwark; first, towards office development, and then policies towards public services, discussing the reasons for the alliances that have emerged and the scope for further collaboration between residents and the local workforce. We shall also refer to the role of community work in this process.

Conflict over office development policies

Back in 1971, when Southwark council prepared a plan for the Thames-side area in the north of the borough, there was little conception among the planners or politicians in the Town Hall that the plan was controversial or that it would create a movement of grass-roots opposition that would have wide political repercussions. The Strategy Plan for Thames-side affected an area of a square mile bounded on the north by three miles of wharves and warehouses and tapering south towards the Elephant and Castle. It was an where industry and housing were mixed, small shopping parades and

From: Colenutt, R. (1979) 'Community action over local planning issues' in G. Craig, M. Mayo and N. Sharman (eds) *Jobs and community action*, London: Routledge and Kegan Paul, pp 243-52.

corner shops were prolific, and open space was confined to patches of grass and courtyards in housing estates. The area also carried (and still carries) the main roads heading for the bridges across the Thames, in particular Blackfriars Bridge and London Bridge leading to the City of London, and Tower Bridge linking access to the East End. The thirty thousand people then living in this area did not constitute a single community but a number of smaller communities distinguished by the type of housing (council or trust property), location (old metropolitan boroughs of Southwark or Bermondsey), their length of residence in the area and their connections with the major local industries.

Local politics had been dying in Southwark and Bermondsey since the war. Membership of local ward parties was at a low ebb and the Labour group on Southwark Borough Council exercised control with little opposition either from within the Labour Party or from outside, in the community. Local councillors were likely to be nominated by a tiny handful of Labour Party members. Some tenants' associations did exist on the estates but they were almost exclusively concerned with rehousing from slum tenements. There was little awareness in Southwark or elsewhere of the meaning or possibilities of planning and participation in planning.

The Strategy Plan changed all that. The plan itself was an 'informal' plan which altered the land use zoning of the riverside and the adjacent area from industrial, commercial, shops and housing to 'City and West End Uses' – i.e. offices, hotels and other commercial developments. Its purpose was to give the council authority to grant planning permission for the increasing applications for offices. These applications were building up as the property boom triggered an overspill of office demand from the City of London across the river to North Southwark. The social and economic implications of this spreading office development were of importance to the local residents and workforce. Basically the area would cease to serve the needs of the old working-class communities, providing houses, jobs and shops, and would become part of the financial, commercial and tourist centre of the capital instead.

However, the council reckoned without the upsurge of community action that accompanied the property boom in London and other cities. Word was spreading about other protests against speculative development and community workers were beginning to encourage such movements in some areas. An action committee was formed in North Southwark in response to the Strategy Plan, consisting of tenants' associations, trades councils, and individual residents. The committee was assisted by community workers based at a project run by the National Institute for Social Work Training. Later this committee, called the North Southwark Community Development Group (NSCDG), was able to obtain a five year grant under the Urban Aid Programme to set up a Community Planning Centre staffed by two full-time workers. The presence of the Centre and its workers in the community played an important part in the protest movement because they were a resource of facilities, energy and skills for NSCDG.

But what tied the local groups together was the glaring conflict between local needs for reasonably-priced housing, shops, open space and industrial jobs on the one hand and the pressures for speculative development on the other. These pressures were (and still are) helping to drive out some of the industrial firms and local shops. By bidding up the price of land they were also inhibiting local authority intervention.

The battle between the local groups and the council was focused on the future of major development sites such as Hays Wharf and also over the effects of 'hope values'[1] created by the council's planning policies for North Southwark. Opposition to the council centred, initially, on the lack of public consultation over the Strategy Plan. The controversy about the inadequacy of consultation was an important factor in drawing local residents, the trades council and other local groups together. In fact, it was this aspect of the council's policies which, at the beginning, caused the most hostility towards the council – a distrust that only increased when planners and council members tried to justify themselves at public meetings.

Later on, the opposition concentrated on individual office developments and the policies of West End and City zoning. For example, the North Southwark Community Development Group attacked the council's own plans for a site called Bankside, where it was proposed that the council go into partnership with developers to build a large office block and a theatre. On this prime riverside site, the Group wanted to see council houses with gardens. The council's initiatives obliged them to submit their own planning application for housing. The purpose of this move was to force a public inquiry over the use of the site and to challenge the council's overall strategy at the same time.

The Community Planning Centre undertook surveys of industry, shops and housing in order to reveal what was happening to the area. Help was also given to tenants' associations undertaking their own household surveys to find out what people thought of the area and what they would like to see on particular sites. Planning applications were investigated and information passed around to the tenants' associations most affected. When there were public inquiries over development proposals, vigorous and well-researched contributions were made by local groups.

---

[1] The 'hope value' of a piece of land refers to the practice of speculators buying land at inflated prices in the expectation that values generally will rise rapidly in the near future. It can also be used to denote the 'hope' that a change of use, for more profitable purposes, will be allowed by a council's Planning Department. For a more detailed exposition see Ambrose and Colenutt (1975).

Without support inside the council, all of this activity and ammunition was to no avail in changing council decisions. Between 1970 and 1976 585 planning applications for offices were submitted for sites in North Southwark, of which 466, affecting 349 different sites, were allowed. Only on a few notable occasions were office applications turned down as a result of local protest. But each of these successes and each delay effected merely strengthened the determination of local groups. The very consistency of the council itself in supporting offices, hotels, tourism and prestige schemes sustained and stimulated the opposition forces.

This experience convinced local activists that a change of tactics might add a further dimension to the struggle. They felt that a voice in the council and better representation for local people was needed. So the membership of local ward Labour Parties was slowly built up until the community groups were in a position to replace five of the councillors representing the area. The biggest build-up of membership was in the wards closest to the riverside where most of the development pressures were evident. The differences between the new councillors and the old ones was principally that the new members had their base in the tenants' associations, trades councils, and the NSCDG while the old guard were suspicious and separate from this movement, having become part of the Town Hall establishment. It is important to add that trade union delegates to the Labour Party played an important part in this political change-over.

The closeness between trade union activists and tenant activists in the Labour Party was not always matched when pressure was being mounted by community groups against the Strategy Plan and individual development proposals. Even though this part of Southwark provided jobs for nearly seventy thousand people and was experiencing a rapid run-down of industry (a survey of fifty industrial firms in 1974 was repeated in 1978 and showed that thirty per cent of the jobs had disappeared in four years), many workers did not regard Southwark's office strategy as a threat. In well-organised workplaces, the trade unions were able to negotiate substantial redundancy payments for longer-serving workers. Alternatively they accepted the closure as long as some of the workforce were transferred to other plants or moved with the company. The real losers were the least organised members of the workforce – women generally, unskilled workers, short-term and part-time workers, especially if they were employed in non-union firms.

For these reasons only a few workplaces responded to overtures from community groups to take a stand on redevelopment issues. At Courage's bottling and brewery plants, for example, both simultaneously affected by plans for run-down and closure allied with office development plans, the union made no response to offers of help and co-operation from the NSCDG and the trades council. The main concern of the branch appeared to be obtaining promises from the management about the size of redundancy payments and transfer to other Courage plants. On the other hand, the postal workers at the large sorting office in North Southwark joined with community groups in opposing a large office block scheme in Borough High Street.

Much of the trade union response was located in the Bermondsey and Southwark Trades Councils. They affiliated to the NSCDG, made use of the facilities at the Community Planning Centre and joined fully in the protest about the Strategy Plan and various office developments. Not all members of the Trades Councils felt strongly about these issues; but dockers who had worked on Hays Wharf and the Surrey Docks were particularly incensed by Southwark's collaboration with companies who had seemingly 'sold their workers down the riverside'. On the other hand, representatives of some of the blue-collar unions hardly seemed to care. Local residents who were also active in their trade unions, however, took the issue to the Trades Councils, and those trade unionists living elsewhere in the borough who were concerned about the employment base of the borough became involved in the protest movement. In particular, members of the civil service and local government unions took an interest in council policies. Politically, then, the issue became a focus for a wide range of trade unionists active in Southwark politics.

The Trades Councils were able to complement the environmental arguments made by residents by concentrating on the employment implications of more and more office development. The Southwark Trades Council formed an Employment and Planning Committee to monitor and analyse employment changes in the borough. A major report, *Employment in Southwark*, was produced with the help of the Community Development Project. This document examined the reasons for the decline of industrial jobs in each sector and the growth of the office sector. It pointed to the wastage of skilled workers, the reduction in earnings for industrial workers who had moved to office occupations, and the decline in apprenticeships. Southwark Trades Council proposed an alternative employment strategy which combined a halt to further office development with a major effort by the Borough Council to protect remaining firms, where possible, and to construct and modernise factory buildings. These ideas were publicised as widely as possible and used when lobbying the council.

The impact of this on employment in the borough was limited, not just because the council was hell-bent on its own policies but because the forces responsible for the loss of industrial jobs and the invasion of offices were so powerful. The borough had by this time accepted the need to develop factories, albeit by going into partnership with private developers. The major remaining areas of disagreement were over the amount of offices and the extent of municipal intervention but the Trades Councils could do little more than try to create some sort of public debate about the issues.

Perhaps the most important outcome was the strengthening of the political network stretching from tenants' associations and trades councils into the Labour Party by the formation of a general set of common policies, or at least common attitudes, towards employment.

The trade unions have not yet called for industrial action. Only one resolution has threatened such action. This came from the Greater London Council (GLC) direct labour branch of UCATT (the construction workers' union), which resolved to 'black' a site in Lambeth near the river where the Tory GLC had decided to scrap the previous Labour plans for council housing and seek a massive office and hotel development. Whether this union branch or the Trades Council will be able to stop other building workers going onto the site of the office remains to be seen. But it is an important new step and gives encouragement to those in the community who have been battling against such schemes for several years without much political or industrial muscle behind them.

Yet there is scope for other kinds of industrial action from the public sector unions which are close to the Trades Councils. These unions recognise that planning policies which place office buildings before open space, council housing and community facilities have implications too for jobs in local government. Further steps towards active trade union criticism of council policies are taking place only slowly. Perhaps the explicit link-up between land use planning and public expenditure in Southwark's 'CommunityPlan' and the Local Plans for North and Mid/South Southwark will draw in these unions more completely.

Conclusion

The experience we have gained in Southwark over the past six years suggests that, at least in our area, the much-discussed dichotomy between local residents and the local workforce may no longer be such a great divide. Although there are circumstances, as we have noted, in which the workforce did not join in community actions, there are important links. Plans such as the Thames-side Strategy, which have serious employment implications, and Local Plans, which raise a very wide range of issues, have brought community and trade union activists together. The demand for more adequate consultation over plans has been another meeting point for different groups. The co-operation has not so far led to industrial action over planning issues but it led to the development of close links, with the sharing of information and mutual support.

Joint action over planning issues whether employment, jobs, public expenditure, or housing has taken place in the arena of local politics. With a strong representation of local tenant activists in Labour Party and trade union delegates attending the General Management Committees of the constituency Party, political alliances between trade union delegates and ward delegates have developed. Similarly, the Trades Councils are forums where trade unionists and community activists are working together over employment and other planning issues. The Trades Councils have not been able to involve many of the branches affiliated to them, but the network is there for future developments.

The debate about public expenditure has also created new alliances between tenants' groups and trade unionists. When the effect of cuts or controls over spending is evident in both the community and in the local authority workforce, the two groups have something in common. Moreover, in inner city areas like Southwark, where the key to regeneration lies with the public sector, public spending is the critical factor both for residents and workforce. Local authorities may well be forced to develop their own local economies by building factories, setting up industries, and expanding public sector employment. Equally, the shops, community services and environmental maintenance that residents need must be provided by the public sector. As local councils take more control over the management of their own areas, the alliances between trade unionists and residents are likely to be strengthened.

3.2

The boundaries of change in community work

Paul Henderson, David Jones and David Thomas

Alone

If
You are mortar
It is
Hard
To feel well-disposed
Towards
The
Two bricks
You are squashed
Between
Or
Have
A sense of
Community.

Ivor Cutler

The words and imagery of the poem by Ivor Cutler stimulate sociological interpretations. The bricks seem to represent the different components of which our society is composed – its people, groups, classes and institutions. The stability of the bricks, and the forms they have been used to create, are related to the nature and composition of the foundations. In our society, views of its components, their relations and the ways in which they hold together to create political and sociological forms are rightly influenced by the basic assumptions – one of the foundations – of that society.

From: Henderson, P., Jones, D. and Thomas, D. (1980) 'Introduction', in P. Henderson, D. Jones and D. Thomas (eds) *The boundaries of change in community work*, London: George Allen and Unwin, pp 1-10.

There are a number of ways of understanding what mortar represents in this poem. It may be seen as the individuals, groups and interests that are squeezed by the big bricks of society. On the other hand, we could view the mortar as the bonding, integrative elements of society, one of which may be taken to be community work. The integrative nature of community work will be applauded or deplored depending on one's political views and one's appraisal of the basic assumptions upon which one sees society constructed. On the one hand, some might call for more bonding material – even buttresses – to make society more secure, whilst others may choose to press for a falling wall.

Many of the case studies in this book suggest situations in which community workers are caught between various community interests and organisations and yet strive to bond them together (not necessarily without disagreement and conflict) to work on a community issue that transcends particular concerns and boundaries. The bringing and holding together of people in a neighbourhood action group or interdepartmental planning group is, like the mortar in a wall, an essential though sometimes unrecognised job. When we appreciate some fine building, it is not the mortar that our eye naturally lights upon; we ignore its presence, and take for granted the skills and care with which it was prepared and laid. So, too, with community work; it is the organisational forms facilitated by community workers to which we rightly give most of our attention. The most fundamental task for community workers is to bring people together and to help them create and maintain an organisation that will achieve their goals. All other tasks are, in our view, secondary to those of organizing people – whether residents or agency staff – into some form of stable and achieving collective.

The task of organising people into a collective has to be achieved by the community worker whilst he or she stands between people and organisations, rather than being of them. Like mortar, their structural position is almost always one of interjacence, carrying out their work on the boundaries of groups and organisations in the community. Community workers have to be with the people, whilst not being of them, and have to develop the additional skill of being able to equilibrate (Halmos 1970) between the various individuals, groups and organisations that make demands upon them. We wish to develop the notion of community work as an interjacent activity, lying between other components of society, and in relation to which it has some function. We suggest that ideas and insights about interjacence may be useful for a better understanding of the function and practice of community work, both at a societal and local level.

There is considerable emphasis in the theory and practice of community work on resources, and, in particular, on redistributing them. The resources in question are, on the whole, public resources administered by local and central government departments, other public bodies and voluntary organisations and it is between these bureaucracies and people that community work stands. Community work is, on the one hand, interjacent between organisational interests and, on the other, between individual and collective interests 'out there' in local communities. These individuals and collectivities need not necessarily be of the poor; social action, sometimes involving community workers, has become as much an instrument of the relatively advantaged, as exemplified in campaigns about schooling, motorways, airports, and transport. It is, in effect, an instrument of the powerless, whatever their income and relationship to the means of production; and precisely because of its interjacent nature it is also an instrument that can, and is, employed by the powerful – in this case, local and central government departments.

This perception of community work as lying between people ('clients', 'consumers', 'victims', 'residents') and bureaucracies is not original. It is a perception that occurs in accounts, for example, that point to the isolation and detached position of community workers, and their dual and sometimes multiple lines of accountability to local groups and the agency that employs them. The notion of interjacence is implicit, too, in analyses of community work that suggest its function as a feedback mechanism to corporate and agency management in local authorities. One of the most useful sociological analyses of interjacence is provided by Litwak and Meyer (1966); they write of the antithesis between bureaucracies and community primary groups, and suggest a balance theory of co-ordination between them, one of the links in which may be a detached expert such as a community worker.

We have, then, a picture of community work (at a societal level) and community workers (at a local level) inhabiting the space between local groups and individuals and local and central organisations. In this space, community work and community workers are not static; they move around as they are pushed and pulled by various forces that emanate either from community groups or from bureaucracies. They are impelled, too, by their own internal energy; important policy debates inside community work, or within a group of local workers, will produce a new position in the interjacent space, moving, for example, a group of community workers closer to a chief executive's department or a local trades council. The different members of the bureaucratic environment will differentially push and pull community work and workers; this is a source of anxiety that is revealed in discussions about professionalisation, the 'takeover' of community work by social work and youth work and in fears of co-option and absorption into particular departments. There will always be a concern in community work, if it is to be effective, with 'keeping one's distance' and a fear of being contaminated or sucked in by established professions and agencies. We are not suggesting that the location of interjacence necessarily leads, or should lead, community workers into playing the part of go-between or mediator between community interests. Rather, it is a continually testing drama for community workers both to be in an interjacent location and to resist the temptations of playing the role of link-person where it undermines the authority and competence of community groups. The antipathy in community work to the role of go-between is, perhaps, a justified over-reaction to many of the ambiguities inherent in interjacence.

The effects of the push and pull forces on community work and its practitioners will vary with factors such as the cohesiveness and sense of security that is present at any given moment within community work, and with the levels of disorganisation affecting the bureaucracies: The period that followed the establishment of Seebohm departments of social services, for example, may be seen as one in which these departments were able to exert very little cohesive influence on community work. It would be wrong to suppose that the forces or influences that are exerted by bureaucracies or community groups have a uniform effect on community work and community workers. It is our view that the different elements of community work are differentially affected by the push and pull forces in its bureaucratic and community environment; that is, the effect of these forces is to move the 'parts' of community work in different directions from each other. We put parts in quotation marks because we do not want to suggest something that is necessarily tangible.

We want now to consider community work in terms of the tensions that exist between its culture, process of practice, and method of change. We shall take these three for the purposes of introducing the themes and content of this book. The culture of community work is predominantly other-centred; not only is it in business to serve others, but considerable value is given to the autonomy, power and responsibility of those others, particularly when they are members of community groups. Community work is defined in terms of the struggles of others, and the help and resources that community workers can bring to these struggles; it is difficult to define community work in terms of a corporate professional identity as we can do with social work, teaching and medicine which, unlike community work, expend many resources on their own system's maintenance and development. Its other-centredness is not, on the whole, mitigated by a concern with professional structures and issues, or with identification and affiliation with departments or agencies. The development and expression of itself is not a central feature of community work at the present, though such a concern is becoming apparent in the recent developments connected with training in community work, and referred to in several chapters in this book. Its other centredness is essentially self-effacing and even subservient, and it is this commitment to others that helps workers to tolerate the isolation, stress, suspicion and lack of support that is often a feature of their work.

The process of the doing of community work, however, is worker-centred; the effectiveness of a worker's transactions with local people depends so much on his or her personality, energy, stamina and skills in the way the worker uses his or her self and resources in a purposeful and disciplined way. The worker has no statutory authority or inducements that facilitate entry and contributions to community groups. If local people or agency staff are turned off him (or her) then there is very little the worker can do, no matter how relevant his or her skills or knowledge, to help a group. The central importance of the worker as an instrument of personal and group change is implicit in the concern in community work with role; in particular, the debate about directiveness and non-directiveness reveals the potency of the benign and adverse effects workers themselves may have on a group.

We do not wish to be misunderstood on this point: we are not suggesting that the worker is or ought to be more important than the group; or that his or her contribution is or ought to be the most central one in achieving the goals that a group has set itself; or that the development of a personal relationship with group members is a more important goal than helping them to organise for effective action. We are rather suggesting that in transactions with a group, or interagency committee, the worker's capacity to be of help to them is primarily a function of the power of person, and through which other bases of influence, such as expertise, are mediated.

The methodological approach to change through community action is we-centred; that is, the values and the instruments of change are essentially those that involve the egalitarianism, fraternity and potency of the collective. The primacy of the collective in community work has three aspects. First, community work is largely concerned with issues and problems in their public or social aspects and is less interested in working with individuals' experience of these problems. It is concerned more with policy than with case, more with collective situations and benefits than with services to particular individuals or families who are in need or disadvantaged. This is not to say, of course, that individuals do not benefit as a result of collective action; in the last resort it is often the individual's estimation of the costs and benefits of community action that may crucially affect the success or failure of collective efforts; secondly, if the beneficiaries of community action are a larger collective (a street, an estate, a neighbourhood) then, on the whole, benefits are not achieved through individual negotiations, petitioning or protest. The emphasis in community work is on groups of people, whether residents and/or agency staff, taking action in order to secure benefits for a wider population. These first two points suggest that there is in community work a concern with both moral and methodological collectivism.

Thirdly, community work is concerned with participation and with a spirit and methods of working that include people. It thus stresses a collective approach to problem-solving and decision-making about needs, goals, priorities and programmes. In particular, it seeks to enable marginal groups to migrate into 'the acting community' of decisions and decision-makers. This inclusive approach is as much apparent in the case studies that describe work with agencies as in those dealing with neighbourhood groups.

The commitment of service to community and other groups, the worker-centred nature of practice and the collective mode of action in community work combine as the thesis in a dialectic whose antithesis is a fundamental paradox at the heart of the activities of most, but not all, community workers. This antithesis-paradox is that community workers are aligned with the people by identification and principles but they are employed on the whole by local and central state agencies. Community workers stand between the world of welfare professions in which they gain the means to live and the movement for change to which they belong. They are in the welfare state but not of it (Baldock 1977), but they are also in community groups but seldom, if ever, of them.

One of the syntheses that this dialectic produces is a ragged and changing ideology that acts in its own right as a force that pushes and pulls community work and community workers in the space between local groups and state bureaucracies. The influence of this populist ideology in community work is pervasive and, amongst other things, it serves the purposes of helping workers to believe they are really of and with the people, and of facilitating the division of the world into those who are of and with the people, and those who are with and of the establishment. This division is often present in the debate about whether community work is a social movement or a profession.

Other effects of this ideology include, for example, the elevation of neighbourhood work and a distaste for social planning and organisational reform and development; a certain romanticisation of the power and abilities of the people; and, as Tasker and Wunnam (1977) have suggested, a radical ethos that produces a sense of moral superiority and self-righteousness in some sections of community work. This constellation of attitudes characterises players in a destructive Bernean game described by Claude Steiner in *The Radical Therapist* (1974) as 'Lefter Than Thou'. We do not want here to elaborate further on the effects of this populist ideology but rather to suggest that it serves the purpose of helping workers better to bear the paradox we have indicated above, and to disguise the truth about the shifting positions that community work and community workers actually occupy in the space between the people and organisations. The positions shift as community work and community workers are pushed and pulled between their groups arid their employers and agency colleagues.

Within each worker there is a constant tension: between his or her affiliations and accountability to local groups and those owed, and perhaps felt, towards the agency. Within community work, twists and turns in values, goals and ideas alternatively push and pull community work towards and away from the people; the interest in links with trade unions, for example, may be seen as a force that will emphasise the relationship of workers with local groups rather than with service organisations; the concern about the family as a place of reproduction, and the role of women within it, may also emphasise this relationship. On the other hand, the analysis from the women's movement about the impact of welfare bureaucracies on the family and on women may result in a greater awareness amongst community workers of their organisational affiliations and the opportunities they provide for agency reform and improvement.

Our primary hypothesis is that whilst community work and its practitioners will always be moving around within the space we describe, it will seldom be able or afford to become incorporated either by the people or by the organisations that employ workers. At best, community work and community workers will be anchored to the boundaries of community groups, organisations and professions, and the degrees of externality that are associated with this boundary role may be seen as necessary for the survival and effectiveness of community work. We want now to elaborate on these ideas of interjacence, boundary and externality.

Community work in the interjacence

Within society, community work occupies a marginal position in relation to major political, economic and social welfare institutions and forces. Community workers tend, on the whole, to work with marginal groups, particularly those left with little in the way of resources, status, power and ambition. Community work stands on the outside of so many important decision-making processes (including those of local groups), yet its function is to help others to move inside decision-making arenas. Community workers may be seen as people who help others to cross boundaries that they themselves invariably remain outside of. This interjacent location of community work is implicitly conveyed in some of the more common role descriptions such as mediator, broker, advocate, facilitator and interpreter. What are the implications for community workers in their practice of being 'outsiders'? We shall briefly examine the relationship of community workers to the local groups with whom they work.

The community group

The recognition of the boundary nature of community work can be traced time and again in a number of descriptions of community work; these emphasise that it is a process that nearly always involves the application of the skills and knowledge of an external 'expert' or change-agent to indigenous resources in order to undertake action that meets the felt and expressed needs of the local people. Such a conception of community work appears, for example, in Thomason's work, where he writes:

> the basic theorems which underlie the whole process of community work are those which relate to three elements of an influence process; the agent of influence, the influence process; and the recipient or respondent to influence. In the nature of community work, the community itself functions as an agent in its own (self-) influence, and shares with the external agent in the influence attempt. (1969: 24)

The boundary role of the community worker is also implicit in the notion of autonomous community groups that informed the work of the community workers of the London Council of Social Service in the 1960s. Goetschius describes how work with groups was influenced by the four following points of policy:

- advice should only be given on the invitation of the tenants' committee
- a worker could only act for the group at its request
- a worker would offer service to a 'protest' group only if it was willing to discuss its problems
- workers could not join groups as regular members or serve as elected officers. (1971: 15)

This policy is, in effect, a series of prescriptions to ensure both the autonomy of the group and the necessarily related externality of the community worker. There is a clear message in many community work texts (e.g. Jacobs 1976) that it would be 'out of role' to do anything or to assume a position of membership or leadership that infringed 'group autonomy either by making decisions for the group or by choosing for its members anything that they could reasonably be expected to do, or learn to do, for themselves'. (Batten 1967: 13). To be in role in community work is precisely to be external to the group.

The externality of the worker to the community group is viewed in community work theory and practice as both desirable and inevitable. It is desirable because it safeguards the members of a group from the undue influence of the views, values and knowledge of the professional worker; it is in accord with salient values in community work to do with participation and self-determination; and externality is the only status, with its associated roles, that ensures that people learn for themselves how to do things in groups. In addition, the status of externality is essential to foster the long-term independence of the group of the worker, who has to be committed but detached and able objectively to view the activities of the group and its relationships with other systems such as its constituency and the local authority.

Community workers are also outsiders because they are frequently so different from those with whom they work in local groups. With rare exceptions, community workers are outsiders to the groups and their constituencies because of class, education, income, life-style and opportunities. They are professionals come to help others, usually living outside their area, and committed to them for a relatively short period of time. At the outset, community workers are also likely to be more politically aware than the bulk of constituents, or at the very least, more optimistic about the possibilities of collective action and change.

As outsiders, their personal experience of the problems facing local residents is likely to be non-existent or limited, and their analysis of these problems will often be related to events and situations outside of the local community. The experience of these neighbourhood issues of a professional middle-class community worker who has chosen to live in the community is not the same experience of them that is had by working-class residents, who may not be resident in the area through choice but rather through economic circumstance.

The labels that are used to describe various roles in community work – enabler, catalyst, encourager, educator, and so forth – tend to suggest the contingent nature of the community work intervention, and the status of the worker as someone who is less than a full member of the community and of the groups with whom he or she works. The externality of the community worker will vary with several factors. For example, it will be affected by whether or not he or she is an indigenous worker, and by the nature of the services or product offered by the worker (and how far these are seen as usable or desirable by many local people). Many of the ambiguities and tensions of interjacence are present even when the community worker is employed by community residents.

It is, of course, unsatisfactory to draw attention only to the 'outsideness' of the community work role. The situation for the worker, and for community work within society at large, is more complex. Community workers have also to build up working relationships with community group members; in order to be effective they have to become accepted, trusted and valued as contributing something to the work of the group. They have to get close to people and issues, being seen as committed to the goals and interests of the group. Being accepted as an 'insider', albeit a temporary one, is undoubtedly a condition for effectiveness in community work. This suggests that one of the skill areas in community work is that of maintaining a creative tension between the 'in' and 'out' aspects of one's role, and being able to manage the ambivalence both of the role and of the feelings that it creates in oneself and group members.

Much the same may be said of workers' relationships to their employing agency. Being effective in achieving change within the agency may equally depend on workers being accepted and valued as members of the group, even though this perception of the workers by others (and by themselves) will necessarily co-exist with their reality as marginal or boundary persons in the agency. The externality of the community worker may also be an important requirement for effective work in the field of inter-organisational relationships. The success of workers in facilitating joint planning and co-ordination between agencies may depend on their being seen as the 'disinterested middle-man', not associated with the particular interests of any one of the agencies involved in the co-ordinating process. There is a strong sense that the worker's abilities successfully to bring people together and to provide essential back-up tasks is a function not only of the worker's 'time, effort, energy, thought and imagination' but also of his or her interjacence and externality of role.

The boundary nature of the community work role may be seen as a purely developmental phenomenon, associated with the relative newness of community work in this country. Our view, however, is that the role of community work in acting upon, and moving between, the boundaries of organisations, may also be understood as a structural factor that is a function of the very nature of community work itself. It may be more appropriate to realise that the kind of contribution that community workers are able to make to community groups and their service agencies is in important ways dependent on the preservation of their 'outsideness'. Incorporation into any of the systems that are worked with may endanger the integrity and the vitality of the community work role by diluting the critical and supportive faculties that community workers bring to bear on the situations of community groups and community organisations. Co-option is justifiably a suspect word amongst community workers; the emotions it arouses epitomise a fear of all states of incorporation. The community work task has to remain external to community groups and service organisations because it is an operating condition that supports the survival and distinctive contribution of community work. The community worker is a marginal person and an intermediary precisely because that is what he or she is and what he or she has to be in order to be an effective change-agent within a pluralist community environment of competing interests.

We hope that some of the ideas that we have tentatively raised here – of interjacence, boundary and externality, for example – are of sufficient interest not only to encourage the reader to explore them further in relation to community work, but also to provide a broad theme for the book that will hold together and provide continuities between the different chapters. Such continuities will sometimes be explicit where an author uses, for instance, the notion of boundary-ness to highlight a particular point of interest in his or her work. More often, perhaps, these continuities in the book will be there waiting to be discovered by the reader who is willing to think about some of the key concepts discussed here and bring them to bear on what he or she finds in the chapters in the book. We suggest that the notions of interjacence, boundary and externality provide a potentially productive set of analytic tools for thinking about community work. We have only been able to signpost in this Introduction some of the possible areas of discussion and insight that they make possible; a map has been provided for an intellectual journey that others can undertake.

Change and conflict: a defence of local community action

Barbara Bryant and Richard Bryant

The salient characteristics of the Crossroads approach to community work almost fit the identi-kit profile of a variety of local community action which re-emerged in Britain during the late 1960s and early 1970s: the emphasis on grass-roots organizing and intensive neighbourhood based work; the uneasy ideological mixture of socialism and libertarianism; the commitment to learning through collective action and a scepticism about abstract theory; the focus on issue-centred groups and the mistrust of political parties and established organizations. This style of local community action has been a prominent strand in British community work over the last decade, and, after a lengthy period of action and experimentation, it is now being subjected to critical examination from many quarters. Local community action has failed to live up to some of its early, over-ambitious rhetoric – the poor have not 'transformed the world' and 'power' is still far removed from the 'people'. This has been one factor in the development of two ideologically divergent schools of thought, which we have termed the social planning approach and the radical left approach, both of which are critical of local community action and suggest revised or alternative models for community work practice.

The social planning approach to community work

Whereas local community action focuses, in its goals and strategies, on the development of the social and political potential of groups, the social planning approach is primarily concerned with changing the organization of welfare institutions and producing a more sensitive fit between social policies and the needs of clients. The community worker operates mainly at inter-organizational and intra-organizational levels, working to stimulate collaboration between established services and seeking to modify the internal structure and policies of formal institutions.

From: Bryant, B. and Bryant, R. (1982) 'A defence of local community action' in *Change and conflict: A study of community work in Glasgow*, Aberdeen: Aberdeen University Press, pp 211-22.

As social planners, we should be able to bring a new vision and breadth to agencies and help release agency workers, especially in the social services, from a narrowness of approach caused both by their own specialist training and the burdens of their daily routines and responsibilities. Besides new concepts and perspectives, the social planner may also introduce alternative technologies to agencies. (Thomas 1978)

There is nothing novel about the social planning approach to community work. It has, for many years, been a central strand in American community work, and, in Britain, a social planning dimension has always existed in the work of co-ordinating bodies within the voluntary sector, like Councils of Voluntary Service. What is relatively new about the approach is its emergence, over recent years, as a dominant feature in local authority-based community work, a trend which owes much to the re- organization of local government and the development of corporate management policies. This trend was apparent in Glasgow when, after the re-organization of local government, the Strathclyde Region began to develop an ambitious community work programme, closely linked with the Region's 'areas of need' policy. By the late 1970s the Region's social work department was employing over fifty community workers in the city, with funding mainly coming from the urban aid scheme. Although these staff operate at a variety of levels – citywide, district and local neighbourhoods – the guiding philosophy placed a central emphasis upon the social planning task of producing a more sensitive and responsive fit between the policies of local government and the needs of local groups.

> Community workers working with local communities on a broad range of issues appear to us to carry out an important pivotal role between Councils and people (similar in many ways to that of an elected member in his constituency), and they must be concerned to activate channels of communication with local authority members and officers in the same way as they do with community groups. (SRC 1978)

Consistent with this linking role was an emphasis upon working through institutional mechanisms and defining the processes for change within boundaries which are acceptable to power holders.

> We feel that community workers employed or supported by the Council must seek to interpret 'conflict' in terms of constructive challenge, and, through negotiation, to reach a consensus, wherever possible, between the community's aspirations and the financial,

political and other constraints which bind the authorities so that expectations are not unrealistically raised beyond the capacity of the authorities to fulfil them. (SRC 1978)

A defence of local community action

The social planning approach represents a significant move away from the traditional community work focus on local organizing, towards the full incorporation of community work within the managerial structure of statutory services. For some observers this move will represent a 'coming of age' for community workers – a winning of their professional spurs and a hallmark of official credibility. For others, like ourselves, the trend is viewed with some criticism and suspicion.

The social planning theorists are guilty, at times, of caricaturing the limitations of local community action. Specht's criticism of British community workers for allocating a low priority to working for social policy changes and their failure to develop skills in the 'structuring' of change is not, in our experience, an accurate one.

Much of locally-based community work is concerned with a dual process of organizing groups and attempting to change the policies and practices of state welfare institutions. The external work of many community groups is directly concerned with social policy issues and much time is devoted to plotting out strategies and developing 'action systems'. The crucial difference between the social planning approach and the community action approach is not over whether there is an involvement in working for change in social policy but, rather, over the way in which social policy change should be approached, and who should be involved in the process. The community action approach emphasizes change coming from the mobilization of working class groups which operate outside of formal power structure. The social planning approach, in contrast, tends to emphasize change coming from professionals and elected representatives in consultation with local groups. Both approaches are concerned with changing social policy, but they differ sharply in political analysis and the priority which is given to different groups in the action process.

Although we would question the criticism that local community action is not concerned with changing social policy, the theorists of the social planning approach are right to suggest that local community has only had a marginal impact on the formulation and administrative practice of major items of social policy, such as the supplementary benefits system or the financing of council housing. Linked with this justified criticism is the implication that the scope for the community worker to influence social policies is enhanced within the social planning approach. While we would not doubt that working at managerial levels does have considerable advantages in terms of access to information, making political contacts and command over technical resources, we would question whether the influence of the worker is as substantial as some of the literature tends to suggest.

Working within state institutions should not be confused with an effective ability to influence the major policy-making functions of these institutions. The scale and hierarchical structure of local authorities, allied to the impact of corporate management regimes, has resulted in a tendency to concentrate formal policy-making powers in the hands of relatively small elites of senior officials and politicians. While social workers and community workers can enjoy considerable autonomy in their day-to-day work, they can also be relatively detached from the major decision-making processes which are concerned· with budgeting and the definition of overall policy adjectives and priorities. Their professional influence on policy-making can be limited and, rather ironically, aggressive community groups can, on occasions, reach the senior administrators and politicians more easily than can employees or even backbench councillors.

A more serious question for the theory and practice of community work arises over whether community workers should directly seek to influence policy-making and occupy roles in the process of local government which, arguably, should be filled by the representatives of local groups. Implicit in much of the theory of social planning is the role of the community worker as an advocate for policy change – a professional broker who, through negotiation and bargaining with other officials and politicians, has an active involvement in the policy-making process. This role is sharply at variance with much of the traditional community work theory which eschews policy-making roles for the professional worker and emphasizes, instead, the worker's role in enabling or organizing direct representation from client and local groups. Working as the link person between state agencies and community groups, the social planner can easily become a surrogate spokesman for community opinion, acting as a mediator of local needs and a filter for the flow of ideas and information.

This role of 'speaking for' the community is made explicit in a Strathclyde Region policy paper:

> It is essential to have a team of officers at local level to monitor the needs of an area from the viewpoint of the community and to speak for that community. (SRC 1978)

We would suggest that the social planning approach can seriously limit and control the scope for direct representation by community groups. This containment of participation can be further reinforced by the social distance which can exist between the community worker and local areas. Community workers employed at managerial levels do not, in our experience, operate from locally accessible offices – and, more importantly, by the practice in local government of interpreting community consultation and participation mainly with reference to the more formal and constitutional types of community organizations.

As the above observations imply, the social planning approach tends to operate within a political framework which only permits disagreement within institutional boundaries. The obvious question which arises, for both the community worker and local groups, is what do you do when the normal channels of consultation, bargaining and negotiation are exhausted and fundamental disagreements still remain between the parties involved? These situations are not readily amenable to a bi-partisan approach and are likely to confront the community worker with an acid test of loyalty.

The social planning literature tends to hedge around this issue, or hints that more sophisticated knowledge, technical skills and professional competence can safeguard the worker from 'the enervating effects of the bureaucracy on their idealism' (Thomas, 1978). For the worker, who is caught in the crossfire of local group-power structure conflicts, a dexterity at juggling competing loyalties is certainly required but, in our experience, we would seriously question how long this form of gymnastics can be sustained without a serious loss of credibility in the eyes of community groups. Improved training and skills will not resolve the political contradictions which are inherent in professional community work roles. Such contradictions require a political response and, for the community worker, the most appropriate avenue for action is through trade union and other collective responses both inside and outside the workplace.

All approaches to community work have boundaries which define and limit the degree of challenge to the state with which it is considered legitimate for the workers, in their professional role, to be identified. In this respect the distinction between the local community action approach and the social planning approach is one of degrees and not absolutes. Both operate within an essentially reformist model of political change, but vary significantly with regard to the activities and strategies which are defined as legitimate for community workers and local groups. By ruling out conflict, in terms of confrontation and contest, the social planning approach provides a more restricted political basis for the practice of community work.

The radical left approach

Although the social planning approach is a reflection of a current trend in the state sponsorship it is still relatively weakly represented in the British community work literature. It is an approach which is more practiced than written about. The reverse could be said of the radical left approach, examples of which have formed a vigorous and dominant thread in the literature, but which rarely finds a clear-cut expression in the work or philosophy of agencies which employ community workers.

The 'radical left' is a convenient shorthand expression to denote a range of criticisms of community work, and it is not a description of a clearly defined and ideological cohesive school of thought – from Marxists of various types to libertarians of widely different political persuasions. Irrespective of the different ideologies which might inform them, however, there are commonplace and recurring criticisms.

According to such criticisms, the dominant role of state sponsorship in the promotion of community work predisposes it to exercise a social control function which belies the radical rhetoric of many projects. Community work is part of the software of capitalism – an expression of repressive tolerance which encourages citizen participation providing it acts as a safety valve for working-class discontent and not as an avenue for political activism.

The locality focus of community work produces material results which are of marginal value to working people, encourages the development of a parochial 'community consciousness' rather than a class consciousness, and fosters a divisive set of relationships between localities as they compete with each other over scarce public resources. The work of many community workers substitutes unreflective action and simplistic moral concerns for hard-headed political analysis. The class dimension of community work and political educational role of the worker is confused by the emphasis which the community worker places on 'non-directiveness' and their quixotic tilts at statutory windmills serve to obscure the real targets of working-class exploitation – big business.

A focus on those community and welfare issues which are more immediately accessible for action – such as housing, welfare rights and recreational provision – deploys attention away from broader economic and employment issues and contributes to a separation between community and industrial action. Community action, taken in isolation, can be a diversion from building a united working class movement.

Prescriptions for community work which derive from these criticisms are many and varied. Some critics advocate a concentration on work-place organization as the only viable avenue open for working-class political action. Others have argued for a forging of links with wider political movements, linking community groups to the trade unions, the women's movement, the revolutionary left or the Labour Party. Also implied in much of the criticism is a concern to rescue community work from the social welfare establishment. Whereas the social planners are anxious that the political movement ethos of local community action will dilute its professionalism, the radical left critics have the opposite concern.

The tendency on the left to minimize the political significance of local community action can both exaggerate these limitations and, at the same time, serve to overemphasize the positive features which are claimed for other forms of working class activism, especially workplace organizing. Some of the gains derived from community action are far more than of marginal significance for the people involved such as rehousing from a damp, insanitary, flat; and, while the more militant areas may well win concessions in advance of other areas, there is evidence to indicate that 'knock on' effects do occur and that a process of mutual learning can happen. The Gorbals Dampness Campaign not only won a 'special case' status on rehousing and compensation but also provided a political precedent and organizational example to other areas in the city which suffered from dampness.

One of the major strengths of local community action is its potential to bring into collective action people who are often excluded or alienated from any organized form of political activity. For some groups, like housewives, pensioners and the unemployed, local community action represents the most immediate and accessible arena for political involvement. How to retain this participatory value and, at the same time, broaden the organizational context and political content of community action presents a major dilemma for the left. Some of the prescriptions for change which have been advocated could well sacrifice the participatory value at the expense of developing an improved organizational and political sophistication.

All community work is selective in terms of issues, groups and strategies. We are not doubting here the legitimacy of selecting to work intensely with the more politically aware groups, but rather we are questioning the implications this concentration might have for contact and work with those people in working-class areas who are on the margins of politics and who comprise the vast majority of residents. Community workers can, in our view, be politically selective in another direction. They can make strenuous efforts to encourage involvement from those people who have been 'written off' by the formal political system, and who are also assigned a subordinate and passive role in vanguard theories of change.

Social control and the welfare establishment

The present structure of the British welfare state is the product of more than a century of class conflict, political compromise and administrative innovation. Embodied within its legislation and policies are elements of universal provision and elements which are being reinforced at the present time, of selective provision which negatively discriminate against the poorer sections of the working class. The welfare state is not, as some optimistic Fabians once claimed, a triumph for socialism but neither is it, as Marxist critics often imply, a triumph for the incorporating powers of the capitalist state. To identify and locate community work only within the social control dimension of the welfare state is to impose a uni-dimensional analysis upon a multi-dimensional reality. It fails to define community work within a political arena where a constant battle is being fought between forces for change and forces of reaction.

Community work can certainly have a social control function and the history of British community work is littered with examples, such as the conservative ideology of the Victorian settlement house movement, and the soup kitchen and 'no politics' approach of some Councils of Social Service during the depression years of the 1930s (Dennis 1958). But the hegemony of conservatism has not always been as all-pervasive as some critics have suggested. (Lees 1972; Leat 1975) Just as the 1942 Beveridge Report, the foundation of the modern welfare state, contained a mixture of progressive and conservative measures, so the personal social services have embraced a variety of approaches and political ideologies. The balance between these competing elements is never static and equal. It changes according to wider political trends, and gains which are won during one period can swiftly disappear during later periods of reaction.

In a sense, this has been the recent history of community work in Britain. A period of trial and error experimentation, informed by a mixture of political motives, was initiated during the late 1960s and this has been followed by a period of backlash and political re-assessment. While the limits of radical action have now become more sharply defined and the sponsorship trend is away from the more controversial styles of community work, it is too simple to argue that this was always what was intended to happen. If the sponsors of community work had only wanted to encourage a 'bread and circuses' variety of community work, it is puzzling why so many of the early projects were given, at least initially, so much autonomy in their day-to-day running and management. Community work in Britain has been of an essentially pluralistic nature and this has been reflected in its sponsorship, as well as in the activities of different projects. This pluralism can be advantageous in providing a legitimacy for the more radical varieties of community work and the freedom to manoeuvre which it granted is sorely missed, when, as at the present time, the trend in central government is towards a more clear-cut and ideologically pure form of welfare policy.

While we have raised critical questions about the political constraints which can operate in state agencies, it is too sweeping a judgement to suggest that community work loses all its radical potential by an association with state welfare and social work. This view assumes that the work of employees within the social services is uniformly conservative and that employment settings permit little freedom for developing counter-ideologies and approaches. Apart from those activists who operate purely on a voluntary basis, or who fund projects through private means, the alternative left projects are faced with having to bargain for state funds or with negotiating grants from charitable trusts. It is arguable, in any case, whether money which comes from charitable trusts is any less-constraining than are funds from the welfare establishment.

Conclusion

The social planning approach and the radical left approach provide the outline for a broader organizational and conceptual framework for community work, at the risk of limiting the scope and opportunities for participation, especially from those working people who are on the margins of collective action. This is not an argument for retaining an exclusively localized-base for community work. Rather, it is a warning that value conflicts and choices will arise when attempts are made to overcome the political and social policy limitations of local community action. If community work has a distinctive role to play, it is in terms of the commitment to participatory ideals in the struggle for social change. Community workers who abandon this commitment, for whatever reason, only serve to reproduce a form of paternalism which is all too familiar to working people.

Racism: the response of community work

Basil Manning and Ashok Ohri

It is essential that all in Britain, including community workers, accept the fact that racism is a dynamic force in this society, which unchecked, will continue to exploit and subordinate black people. Once these premises are accepted, they have serious implications for community work. If not accepted, they have dire results for the community workers' understanding of race issues which inevitably will lead to diversionary initiatives which do not address the fundamental need of the black community to be free of white racism.

Unfortunately major central government reports in the 1960s which addressed the issue of the objectives of community development work, made no direct reference to the issue of racism. These reports make reference to now generally-accepted objectives for community work, those of working with people to assist in the identification and articulation of needs to enable development of skills and the mobilisation of resources to contribute to community well-being.

Many innovations and experiments in social policy were based on the assumptions that poverty can be eliminated by (a) improving the co-ordination of existing social services, and (b) by individual social pathology, and by the involvement and participation of the poor in policy-formation. The Plowden Report (1967) on education, the Seebohm Report (HMSO 1968) on the reorganisation of social services, and in Scotland, the Social Work (Scotland) Act (1968), the Skeffington Report (HMSO 1969) on citizens' participation in planning, the Alexander Report (SED 1975) and the Russell Report on adult education (HMSO 1973), are all based on these assumptions, encouraging local government to greater involvement in community work.

Community workers focus on such fields as housing, education, social services, unemployment, play and recreation and welfare rights. Usually they work with small groups such as the tenants or the residents' associations

From: Manning, B. and Ohri, A. (1982) 'Racism – the response of community work' in A. Ohri, B. Manning and P. Curno (eds) *Community work and racism*, Community work 7, London: Routledge and Kegan Paul, pp 3-33.

which might have good aims and objectives, for example, the welfare of the community or with particular interest groups with very specific aims, for example housing action groups. The interest of these groups tends to be the improvement of their neighbourhood. Some community workers assume that the neighbourhood is homogenous, and that by working through issue-based groups they will attract a cross-section of the people who are concerned or affected by the identified problem. Of course, the experience in practice is different. Community groups tend to be small groups of self-selected, usually more articulate, members of the community. More often than not they do not represent or involve the black people and the poor section in their neighbourhood. White community workers take account of the fact that poverty is a consequence of fundamental inequalities in our present political and economic system, but do not recognise that racism is also rooted in the social structure.

Recently, prior to the formation of Community Work Training Groups in 1979, there appeared on the list of objectives for community work, as a last thought, a euphemism: 'Breaking down stigmatisation of minority groups.' That objective, in the absence of any other, demonstrates that in traditional community work circles the fundamental concern is still with racial prejudice rather than racism itself. This may explain why the predominant response of white community workers is to organise 'multi-racial festivals' in order to break down stigmatisation. Addressing the issue of racial prejudice is a necessary task in white community groups, but should not be confused with addressing the issue of racism itself. Notwithstanding that reservation, it is difficult to determine how white community workers are breaking down stigmatisation in practical terms. Nor can one recollect any guidance on possible methods emanating from academics or professional bodies on how a community worker could 'break down stigmatisation'. The issue of racial prejudice, let alone racism, is still treated as marginal by community workers. It is an activity which is not directly related to their work with white groups, but one which finds expression in the worker 'joining' other anti-racist organisations, at a campaigning level, and in few cases supporting black groups.

It is unlikely that a group of white people in a neighbourhood will choose the issue of racism and its effects on the black community to organise 'as one of the human resource contributions to the process of decision-making about material resources in and on behalf of their neighbourhood'. 'Their' neighbourhood is invariably one which excludes 'the blacks' who live next door or over the road. For this very reason most community work groups end up being white with a white worker. If the white community group will not immediately focus on racism, if community work training has developed little expertise on addressing this issue, if professional bodies seem to be afraid to articulate possible ways of addressing it, if the workers' consciousness is already affected by a socialisation process in a racist society, who then, in community work terms, will develop an initiative to challenge racism? The answer is clear: 'What we need here is a black project'; or is it?

If white community workers are to take a more directive approach, at present the only possible approach to racism if it is to be challenged, they need to understand the dynamics of racism. Part of the apathy and inaction on the part of community workers relates to their lack of understanding of how racism operates at an individual and institutional level. Whilst it is important to point to the effects of racism as evidenced by the extent of racial disadvantage, it is equally important to be able to identify how it is operating as an effective force in the life of a community. It would be useful to start with a look at some of the concepts.

Whenever the issue of race is talked about in a variety of contexts, a number of words are used interchangeably, as though they have the same meaning, but they are different:

Prejudice

The most accurate dictionary which goes to the root of the word is 'unfavourable opinion or feelings formed beforehand without knowledge or reason. Racial prejudice is where such unfavourable opinions or feelings relate to a particular group based on colour, race or ethnicity. So both black and white people can be 'prejudiced in Britain. Contrary to popular belief, prejudice is not 'natural' (you are not born with it) or 'inherited' or hereditary, but part of our environment formed by a socialisation process, caused by suspicion, fear and insecurity. It is both contagious and expensive; people pass it on and it wastes time, energy and money.

Racism

Is, in the view of the US Commission on Civil Rights of 1970, where *prejudice* combines with power to inform 'any attitude, action or institutional structure which subordinates, a person or group because of colour, race or ethnic differences'. Clearly, racism is not just a matter of attitudes; actions and institutional structures and practices can also be a form of racism. It involves having the power to carry out practices whether awarely, unawarely, overtly or covertly to subordinate a person or group. In Britain, therefore, black people can be prejudiced, but not racist. Once institutionalised, it has a dynamic or momentum of its own, which, unaddressed, will continue as a motive force.

Discrimination

Whereas racism implies a positive force to subordinate however un-consciously, discrimination is, again in the US Commission 's words, 'any action which deprives an individual or group of their rights because of race, colour, religion, national origin, sex or age[1]. It has the negative effect of withholding that which is theirs by right. Like racism, if not specifically reversed, in its institutional form discrimination will be a dynamic force of its own and will often occur through doing what is 'traditional' or 'what we've always done'. It also occurs through the taking of a narrow view of the make-up of our community and regarding those of a different ethnic background as 'outsiders' who have no rights and to whose needs we have no responsibility to respond.

In the minds of most white community workers 'racism' is predominantly that phenomenon which finds expression in the National Front. That overt form of racism is easily identifiable and therefore receives most attention both in terms of media time and organisational effort. However, for the average black person who experiences the sharp edge of racism daily, there is little difference between those policies espoused by the NF and the reality of institutional racism in Britain today. Stokely Carmichael, speaking of the situation in the USA, stated it in sharper terms: racism is both overt and covert. It takes two closely related forms: individual whites acting against individual blacks, and acts by the total white community against the black community. We call these individual racism and institutional racism. The first consists of overt acts by individuals, which cause death, injury or the violent destruction of property. This type can be recorded by television cameras; it can frequently be observed in the process of commission. The second type is less overt, far more subtle, less identifiable in terms of specific individuals committing the acts. But it is no less destructive of human life. The second type originates in the operation of established and respected forces in the society, and thus receives far less public condemnation than the first.

When white terrorists bomb a black church and kill black children, that is an act of individual racism, widely deplored by most segments of society. But when in that same city – Birmingham, Alabama – five hundred black babies die each year because of the lack of proper food, clothing, shelter and proper medical facilities, and thousands more are destroyed or maimed physically, emotionally, and intellectually because of conditions of poverty and discrimination in the black community, that is a function of institutional racism.

Most community workers would not wish to associate themselves with overt racist acts like the petrol-bombing of black shops and projects. However, there are a variety of ways in which they collude with covert forms of institutional racism through apathy, fear and non-action. Some equally racist positions taken by community workers are as follows:

(a) The unawarely racist or 'non-racist' position

This position has many forms. Fundamentally it is a position which fails to acknowledge the dynamics of racism as a pervading force within institutions and groups. Community workers who hold this position are fundamentally taking a neutral stance on racism and can more accurately be described as 'non-racist-racists', in that their neutrality does nothing to challenge the force of racism. Neutrality on this issue is in effect a vote for the status quo and is therefore collusion with racism. Among the forms that this position takes in community work is the 'this community group/centre/ resource, service is open to all sections of the community' approach. This position assumes non-discrimination and equal opportunities for all. It often expresses itself in the 'colour blind' approach – as community workers we do not discriminate, we see neither black nor white, only people. In neighbourhood settings the community worker might feel more comfortable either to encourage or to collude with a 'same for all approach' which might be espoused by the community group who falsely believe that there are no differences in need because there are no differences. This notion obviously stems from a confusion in most people's minds that to notice a difference is in itself discriminatory. Appreciating difference and taking fresh and rational initiatives to meet differing needs is not negative discrimination. The reduction of all needs to the 'same for all' approach will result in specific needs, which stem from the additional factor of racism, being marginalised.

The 'non-racist-racist' position also comfortably combines liberalism with reaction. On the one hand a community worker may help a group to recognise that racism does result in subordination and disadvantage, but will they go on to place the responsibility for challenging it in the institutional forms entirely on the black community. This inevitably leads to white community workers abdicating all responsibility for work on racism. It then becomes the prerogative of 'specialists', the local 'race-relations project' or 'the CRC' to be the only organisations to be concerned about racism.

(b) The anti-racist-racist position

By the very definition this position is difficult to comprehend. It takes the form of community workers being very active in campaigning organisations against the National Front, whilst being involved in little or no activity to challenge institutional racism. Obviously such workers need to be commended for recognising that racism is a cancer which should be reckoned with, but they fall into the trap of becoming Sunday-anti-racists.

Such workers either fail or refuse to recognise racism as a reality in situations where they hold either power or responsibility. It blocks the possibility of such a worker being able to evaluate how her/his current community work at a neighbourhood level either colludes with or challenges racism. The worker begins to assume that being anti-racist at a campaigning anti-NF level will automatically translate itself into anti-racist work at a neighbourhood level without monitoring her/his actions or the strategy of the group. It also becomes unsafe for anyone to raise the issue of racism in an honest, self-critical and constructive way, because of the defensive stance which such workers take, believing themselves to be committed anti-racists, but fearing to put that to the test.

A further anti-racist-racist position with which community workers collude is that of assisting community groups and tenants' associations to adopt constitutions which make declarations of intent not to discriminate on the grounds of race (sex, political opinion). Both the community worker and the group then delude themselves that they are not racist because the constitution says so. On the other hand, there is no effort to monitor what positive action is being taken to ensure equal access to all. It assumes that once that clause is included in the constitution, people start from a position of equality and have equal access. It also results in a community worker and group (e.g. a tenants' association) assuming that the levels of deprivation in an area are the same for all. In other words, they fail to take into account the additional factor of racism when organising around an issue. Add racism to classism to understand the double oppression of the black working class; add racism to adultism to understand the double oppression of young black people; add racism to sexism to understand the double oppression of black women. In reality it is necessary when considering any oppression or indicator of deprivation to add the factor of racism, if any initiative is to avoid marginalising the needs of the black community and in so-doing collude with racism itself.

Such collusion, however, is widespread. Often it results from fear and uncertainty on the part of a white community worker about what to do. Fear and uncertainty is partly engendered by the racist context in which the community worker finds him/herself. That context is influenced by a number of current trends which is affecting both the community and the worker. These trends include a lack of positive leadership on the issue of racism in Britain. It is a sad reflection on this society that it can produce so many passionate racists like Enoch Powell and John Tyndale, or a Prime Minister [Margaret Thatcher] who can whip up latent racism in the white community by claiming that 'white people in this country have legitimate fears of being swamped' by the black 3 per cent of the population. There is in this country no equivalent-white 'leader' who will stake career, electoral prospects, popularity, on passionately speaking out for racial justice. Political, ecclesiastical, trade union or community leaderships are 'astute' enough to sense the racist mood within the country to be sufficiently careful to pay only occasional lip-service to the need for racial justice. When it is done, it takes the form of vague references to 'equality for all' or the need to live in racial harmony, rather than an admission of how deeply racism is woven into the fabric of this society and what white people with responsibility and power, be it formal or informal, need to do to turn the country back from the racist path which it now follows.

Combine the lack of leadership with the immigration debates, the immigration laws and procedures, and the entrenchment of racism into the proposed Nationality Law, and the result will be a country in which licence, however subtle, is given to individuals and institutions to discriminate against those, the like of whom, after all, every effort is being made to keep out. Those racist measures affect the white communities' perceptions of the black community and open the door for all the irrational blame and scapegoating of the black community, for bad housing and high unemployment, poor schools and lack of amenities in inner-city areas. It is into such areas and armed with the racist ammunition freely given by government leaders and others that the fascists move to play out their war drama, with the knowledge that other racists will join in the fray.

Neither white community groups nor community workers are immune from these current influences which reinforce deeply held prejudices which stem from 'settler' consciousness which Sartre (1970) alludes to. Perceptive as most community workers are about the risks involved in confronting racism, they are inclined to take the easy option of colluding with racism and allowing it to be an unchallenged force in community groups and organisations.

From the above analysis, pertinent questions for white community workers may be 'what is my role in combating racism? I recognise that I have been affected by racism and this may express itself in paternalistic racism (i.e. setting white standards to which all people are expected to conform) or patronisation. Is it not best to leave it to the black community or black community workers?' Let us look at this first. Black self-help is traditionally interpreted as a 'development of self-reliance', the right of the black community to solve their own problems. A recent Home Office study (Home Office 1979) blames the demoralising, practical and psychological effect of 'discrimination and disappointment' among the ethnic minority groups as being the major factors contributing to the growth of the black self-help movement. Yet the report comes to the startling conclusion that black self-help is primarily about 'self-improvement', and divides the groups into five categories:

1. Government-sponsored organisations such as Community Relations Councils.
2. Ethnic (sic) Cultural Groups including dance, music and more recently, drama.
3. Ethnic (sic) religious activities groups.
4. Community care groups running hostels, education tuition, youth clubs etc.
5. Umbrella groups or political pressure groups.

However, it may be easy to fall into the trap of losing sight of what the primary goal for the black community is, i.e. a struggle against racism. Both white and black community workers who lose sight of that goal could easily busy themselves and the groups in activities which forever 'pick up the pieces' as a result of racism. The self-help initiatives in the black community, the organising of separate and alternative services should be recognised for what they are in the main: a commentary on the levels of racism in British society.

There is sufficient evidence in community work that groups committed to institutional changes need to organise as umbrella groups and have very specific political objectives. Groups with a service orientation normally do not have the resources to concentrate on other objectives. They are too busy working away at providing services. For example, many black projects are running temporary employment or training schemes, without analysing why youngsters are unemployed. Others, while working towards remedying the situation, are also mobilising people and building alliances to fight racism. Such groups have developed projects and activities which have a service orientation to collect evidence to use to keep up the momentum for the struggle.

Community workers working with the black groups need to assess their roles and objectives in the light of evidence available. The resources and energies of the black self-help movement must be directed towards tackling racism. The task is to identify issues that can demonstrate the hidden working of racism in the state services and other institutions, black community.

This requires a close collaboration within the black community. Not all groups work together and the division among the black community needs to be understood in the context of historical experience of colonialism and oppression. To undo the effects of this history is a long and painful process. Black people have to go through a painful reappraisal, to evaluate their worth and their positions in society. The values and attitudes of whites about themselves and about black people are upheld and reinforced by a complex structure of lies, misconceptions of imperial grandeur and invalid assumptions about their place in society. White people too need to go through a similar painful self-evaluation.

The community worker must realise the classist and racist nature of every aspect of the society that she, and the people she is working with, are living in and use every opportunity to make sense of the world in those terms. In the process of consciousness-raising there is a necessity to start as one means to continue. You certainly do not start with service-orientated groups and projects, but develop opportunities for analysis and education which should be grounded in the community's everyday experience. This process of political education, with the objective of development of political consciousness, could be the only way in which community work with the black community can develop at this stage.

Now turning to the role of white community workers in combating racism: This strategy, of course, depends upon the awareness of the community worker. Every community worker needs to go through racism awareness training. This kind of training should be available to all workers and not only those working within multi-racial areas. Having gone through such training themselves, the workers should learn how to set up training programmes so that they can provide similar opportunities for local groups.

Some guidelines for white community workers follow:

1. Start from the point of recognition that racism is a reality in British society. It is accurate to assume that no institution, group or organisation you work for/with is free of racism.
2. Be clear that racism is a white problem in Britain. It is a problem about white people, for which white people must take full responsibility.
3. Do not abdicate responsibility for racism in your work; it is not the task of the 'specialist' self-help black projects alone. Do not confuse the issues; appointment of black staff is essential to give effect to equal opportunities policies in employment, not to relieve white staff of the responsibility of anti-racist work or demonstrate racial harmony at work.
4. Recognise that the more you collude with racism (the overt expressions of it in your group, the all-white tenants' association on a multi-racial housing estate), the less likely you will be to intervene in future. Whilst you and other white people may want to resist the notion that Britain is a racist society, monitor the extent to which you intuitively act in the clear knowledge that it is, for fear of lack of support from other white people/colleagues, possible isolation and being accused of being 'over sensitive' or 'too passionate' about race.
5. Do not be misled by 'declarations' of commitment to 'equal oppor-tunity' in organisational statements and constitutions: more importantly, monitor the actions of the group: are its make-up, decision-making, and use of resources genuinely anti-racist, or subtly colluding with racism and largely marginalising, excluding, or abdicating responsibility for the needs of some residents.

6. Do not confuse 'picking up the pieces' with combating white racism itself. It may be necessary and easier to support a black self-help initiative, but your primary role as a white worker is to challenge white groups and institutions; to attack the racism which necessitates the growth of such self-help initiatives , with little or no resources. Resist the temptation to confuse relationships with black workers/people with anti-racism (male relationships with women are no proof of anti-sexism) and be clear that racial harmony is no useful indicator of racial justice.

7. Encourage other white community workers to focus on and to share anxieties, fears, confusion about white racism, and develop support for each other and strategies for combating it in the areas of work where each has responsibility, influence and power.

8. Community workers need to recognise the need to be familiar with the issues of concern to the black community. This knowledge and sensitivity, if sensibly used, could, in some instances and with hard work, provide a basis for collective action and solidarity among the white and black groups.

<h1 style="text-align:center">3.5</h1>

The difference between education and organizing

Myles Horton and Paulo Freire

Myles: One of the unsolved problems, even I think here at Highlander, is the difference between education and organizing, and that's an old question, it goes way back. Saul Alinsky and I went on a circuit. We had the 'Alinsky/Horton show' that went out on the circuit debating and discussing the difference between organizing and education. At that time Saul was a staunch supporter of Highlander, and I was a staunch supporter of him, but we differed and we recognized the difference. We had no problem about it, and we tried to explain to people that there was a difference. Saul says that organizing educates. I said that education makes possible organization, but there's a different interest, different emphasis. That's still unclarified. In my mind I kept them separate because I could function much better having a clear-cut idea about what I consider the difference in operating on that basis.

The reason it was such a debatable subject is because the overwhelming majority of the people who were organizing and who were officials of unions in the South had been at Highlander. So the public who only saw that, didn't know what went on at Highlander, and they assumed that we were an organizers' training school. But I kept saying no, no. We do education and they become organized. They become officials. They become whatever they are, educational directors. Basically it's technical training. We're not in the technical business. We emphasize ways you analyze and perform and relate to people, but that's what I call education, not organizing. When I wanted to organize – which I did at one period, something I'll go into later on – I resigned from the Highlander staff. I took a leave of absence from the Highlander staff because I didn't want organizing and education confused in the minds of the people. It was confusing enough as it was.

So Highlander's been in the situation where we were looked at from all kinds of different angles. We always had to watch not to accept the appraisal of other people, and try to make our own criticism relating to these critics. We just had to constantly keep clear about what we meant by education. One

From: Horton, M. and Freire, P. (1990) 'The difference between education and organizing' in P. Freire, M. Horton, B. Bell and J. Gaventa (eds) *We make the road by walking*, Philadelphia: Temple University Press, pp 115-29.

of the examples I used to use got me in trouble and still gets me in trouble when I use it. I'd say if you were working with an organization and there's a choice between the goal of that organization, or the particular program they're working on, and educating people, developing people, helping them grow, helping them become able to analyze – if there's a choice, we'd sacrifice the goal of the organization for helping the people grow, because we think in the long run it's a bigger contribution. That's still a hot issue. I used that illustration in a participatory research meeting when I was pushed on the difference. One woman there was organizing a hospital. She was just furious, because she thought it was inhumane to take that position, that my purpose was to develop people instead of particular issues. I would usually find there wouldn't be that contradiction, you see, but if it came down to it, then you have to make that distinction. That's how strongly I felt about separating the two ideas.

Paulo: Could I make a comment just about that? I think that mobilization of masses of people has or had, inside of itself, organization. That is, it's impossible to start mobilizing without organizing. The very process of mobilizing demands organization of those who are beginning to be mobilized. Secondly, I think that both mobilizing and organizing have in their nature education as something indispensable – that is, education as development of sensibility, of the notion of risk, of confronting some tensions that you have to have in the process of mobilizing or organizing. Knowing, for example, the dialectical relationship between tactics and strategy. You have to have some tactics that have to do with the strategy you have. You understand the strategy as the objective, as the goal, as the dream you have, and as the tactics you raise as you try to put into practice, to materialize the objective, the dream. In the process of mobilizing, of organizing, you need from time to time to stop a little bit with the leaders in the groups in order to think about the space you already walked. In reflecting on the action of mobilizing and organizing, you begin to teach something. You *have* to teach something. It's impossible for me not to learn. A good process of mobilizing and organizing results in learning from the very process and goes beyond.

Until some years ago, among the left groups and left parties, we had strong examples of how education was not taken seriously during the process of mobilization and organization, which were seen just as process. In fact they are educational processes at same time. Why this attitude? I think that the answer should be found in the analysis of or the understanding of education as something that really is superstructure and a productive reproducer of the dominant ideology. It's very clear, for example, in the seventies, the writings about education's power to reproduce the dominant ideology. It was, I think, because of this that left parties and the groups always thought, in America, for example, that education is something that comes *after* we get power. When we get power through the revolution, then we can begin to treat education. In this line of thought, this vision was not even to make a distinction between the schooling system as Myles has underlined and the activities *out* of the subsystem. In fact, nevertheless, even education inside of the subsystem of education is not exclusively reproducer of the dominant ideology. This is the task that the ruling class expects the teachers to accomplish. But it's possible also to have another task as an educator. Instead of reproducing the dominant ideology, an educator can denounce it, taking a risk of course. It's not easy to be done, but education cannot be exhausted exclusively as the reproducer of the subsystem of the dominant ideology. Theoretically it is not exclusively this.

Today I think that the tension is expressed in a different way. I know many people in the left parties in Latin America who discovered through practice what political education is. I think that the tension is being treated in a different way today. When we're in the process of mobilizing or organizing, it begins to be seen also as an educational problem of process and product, because undoubtedly there is a different kind of education in mobilization before getting power, and there is also the continuity of that. That's a mistake committed before, that education should come just exclusively after organizing. Education is before, is during, and is after. It's a process, a permanent process. It has to do with the human existence and curiosity.

Myles: If you're into having a successful organizing campaign and dealing with a specific project, and that's the goal, then whether you do it yourself or an expert does it or some bountiful person in the community does it, or the government does it without your involvement because that solves the problem – then you don't take the time to let people develop their own solutions. If the purpose is to solve the problem, there are a lot of ways to solve the problem that are so much simpler than going through all this educational process. Solving the problem can't be the goal of education. It can be the goal of organizations. That's why I don't think organizing and education are the same thing. Organizing implies that there's a specific, limited goal that needs to be achieved, and the purpose is to achieve that goal. Now if that's it, then the easiest way to get that done solves the problem. But if education is to be part of the process, then you may not actually get that problem solved, but you've educated a lot of people. You have to make that choice. That's why I say there's a difference. So when I went to organize for a union, I got a leave of absence from the Highlander staff. I wouldn't do that as a member of Highlander staff because I don't think organizing and education are the same thing. I do think participatory research and education are the same thing, but I think organizing and education are not the same. I think the goal is different.

Now a lot of people use organizing to educate people. That's what I was trying to do when I was organizing textile unions, but when it comes down to it, I wasn't free to make a decision not to get a contract, to sacrifice the contract and the organization for education because I was hired to organize the union. Organizers are committed to achieving a limited, specific goal whether or not it leads to structural change, or reinforces the system, or plays in the hands of capitalists. The problem is confused because a lot of people use organizing to do some education and they think it's empowerment because that's what they're supposed to be doing. But quite often they disempower people in the process by using experts to tell them what to do while having the semblance of empowering people. That confuses the issue considerably.

Third Party: Your description of organizing is a description of what most of education is. Most of education is specifying a specific objective and reaching that objective irregardless of how the process works.

Myles: That's right. Schooling.

Third Party: So most schooling is in fact analogous to what you call organizing?

Paulo: But, inside of the process of organizing, as Myles said, first we have education taking part of the nature of organizing. What I want to say is that it's impossible to organize without educating and being educated by the very process of organizing. Secondly, we can take advantage of the process of organizing in order to develop a very special process of education. Maybe I will try to be more clear. For example, when we are trying to organize, of course we have to try to mobilize, because mobilization and organization are together. But in the process of mobilizing and automatically organizing we discover as well, as in any kind of action or practice, that we must become more and more efficient. If you are not trying to be efficient in organizing workshops, the people will not answer you next year when you call.

That is, efficiency, without being an instrument of enslaving you, is something that is absolutely necessary. Inefficiency has to do with the distance between what you do and what you would like to get. Do you see that we manage with efficiency in this place? I have my dream. Then what did I do in order to materialize my dream? Then my evaluation has to do with this. Those who are engaged in mobilizing and organizing have to evaluate this process. In the process of evaluation, undoubtedly, there is an interpretive and necessary moment in which the leaders who are trying to mobilize and organize have to know better what they are doing. The organizers engage in critical reflection on what they did. In doing that, the leaders start participating in a process in the next stage of mobilization and organization, because they change. They tend to change in their language. Do you see? If they don't do that they are not capable. They will change their language, their speech, the contents of their speech to the extent that in mobilizing the people they are learning from the people. And then the more they learn the people the more they can mobilize. It's expected. They can mobilize the people. Then because of that I always see that it's absolutely necessary for mobilizers and organizers to be quite sure about the educational nature of this practice.

In a second aspect we can show, in an analysis process we call mobilizing and organizing – which implies organizers getting more and closer contacts with groups of people – that the organizers are engaged, if they are good, in a kind of participatory research.

The politics of participation

Suzy Croft and Peter Beresford

The marginalisation of participation

Participation would appear to be an important idea which demands our attention.

It is central to a number of key debates and developments. It is the primary objective of large-scale state-supported initiatives for public participation in planning, community development and user-involvement. Yet its achievements seem to be limited and it is surrounded by suspicion. Why is this? Why does participation seem to be marginalised? First, let's look at some of the expressions of this marginality.

However important we may think participation is, its development has been slow and uncertain. A bibliography of public participation in Britain published in 1979 included nearly 1,400 entries. The number has greatly increased since. Yet during this period only two books analysing and exploring the idea of participation have been published in Britain. Both the debate and developments around participation have been hesitant and unprogressive. There is now an enormous body of knowledge and experience, but often this is inaccessible or unavailable and this has made progress difficult. There have been practical problems in the way of recording participation's history. People involved in innovatory schemes often don't have the time or confidence to write about them. Those on the receiving end are even less likely to have the opportunity. Community and user groups have not often had the chance to develop and monitor their own initiatives.

There have been few systematic studies of participatory initiatives. There has been little cross-learning between different policy areas. For example, community social work initiatives which were intended to involve local people were slow to draw on the lessons learned by community work and community workers. Hoggett and Hambleton commented on the failure of decentralisation debates of the 1980s to draw on earlier practical and theoretical work on public involvement. If ever the cliche 'reinventing the wheel' epitomised an area of human activity, it is in the case of participation.

From: Croft, S. and Beresford, P. (1992) 'The politics of participation', *Critical Social Policy* no 25, Autumn, pp 20-44.

The predominant pattern of participation's history is one of cyclical development which rarely seems to build on, or go much further than what has gone before.

The debate about participation has rarely taken the lead in challenging the exclusions faced by women, black people and other groups. Unless specific initiatives are taken to ensure the involvement of such groups, they are likely to be left out, and frequently such steps have not been taken. Typically, participatory schemes have mirrored rather than challenged broader oppressions and discriminations. The average participant of traditional public participation in planning exercises has been typified as a middle class, middle-aged, able-bodied white man. Such participation is likely to have the damaging effect of reinforcing such biases. Pressure for change has come primarily from *outside* participatory debates and structures, from feminist and black organisations. Distinctions have not been properly drawn between the public and private spheres of participation and adequate consideration given to the ways in which women are restricted to the private sphere.

One of the student slogans in the 1960s headlined this: 'I participate. You participate. *They profit*'. Discussions of participation have frequently ignored or underplayed structural issues; the role of the state and market; and have been confined within services or 'communities'. When we look at the substantive purposes that participatory arrangements may actually serve, we discover that they are not always consistent with people's effective involvement and increased say. Instead a range of other functions are identified. These include:

Delay: Action is made to wait on people's involvement. The need to consult, to set 'self-advocacy' groups, is used as a reason for procrastination.

Incorporation/Co-option: People are drawn into participatory arrangements which limit and divert their effective action.

Legitimation: People's ineffectual involvement is used to give the appearance of their agreement and consent to pre-determined decisions and plans. Participation serves as a public relations and window-dressing exercise.

Tokenism: encouraging the minority involvement of members of oppressed groups, unrelated to the representative structures established by their organizations.

Arnstein included eight rungs in her influential ladder of citizen-participation. These were:

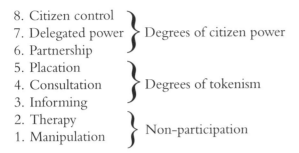

8. Citizen control
7. Delegated power } Degrees of citizen power
6. Partnership

5. Placation
4. Consultation } Degrees of tokenism
3. Informing

2. Therapy
1. Manipulation } Non-participation

Most of the current initiatives concerned with user-involvement fall into the last two categories.

But the demand for more say is widespread. Even people who can exert a negative influence over others less powerful than themselves may feel they have little control over the world in which they live. Indeed the two may be connected. One large-scale local study of public participation in planning, for example, found that the view that the council took little notice of local people extended to all social groups and was not confined to council tenants or the worst off. Another expression of such broader disempowerment and exclusion is the emergence of the new social movements of women, black people, gay men and lesbians.

The limited nature of most people's political and civic involvement is well-documented. The fact that citizenship seems to be an idea few people give much thought to, appears to reflect people's more general lack of involvement in the political process and public affairs. Official reports highlight this. One, for example, drew attention to the serious under-representation of women in Parliament, in public bodies, in recognition in the honours system, on Boards and Trade Unions Executives. Another government report showed that in 1985 less than 20 per cent of councillors were women. Home owners, professionals and managers are also greatly over-represented among councillors. Only 5 per cent of councillors worked or used to work in semiskilled or unskilled manual occupations, as compared with 25 per cent of the general population.

Participation, then is an idea whose development is restricted, whose role is ambiguous and whose focus has been limited. Are these arguments for ignoring or rejecting it? They may be, but a number of other arguments are also offered for paying it serious attention and trying to *increase* people's involvement and participation. They are both practical ·and philosophical: participation works and it is right. It:

• makes for more efficient and cost-effective services;
• ensures accountability;
• reflects the democratic ethos of our society; and

- encourages people's independence, and self-determination is consistent with people's human and civil rights.

Thus a set of strong economic, moral, political and psychological arguments are advanced for people's participation. Equally important, people want to be more involved. What research there is indicates that most people want more say and involvement. Three-quarters of a random sample of comprehensive school students said they wanted more say. Two-thirds of the people interviewed in the study of public participation in planning referred to above, expressed a desire to have more say in decisions affecting them. Two-thirds of a random sample of people interviewed in one neighbourhood as part of a study of local social services, felt that service users, workers and other local people should have more say in them. The desire of people for more involvement is also reflected in the large and growing numbers of community, disability, users, and rights organisations which are pressing for more say and involvement over issues and decisions affecting people's lives and neighbourhood and in the organisations and institutions which affect them.

How do we resolve the contradiction between the possibilities and the frequent reality of participation? The answer seems to be in untangling its ambiguities. At the heart of these lies the issue of power.

Participation and power

Generally people want to get involved to exert an influence and to be able to make change. Some of the features that are associated with people's desire for more involvement are:

- influencing decisions and outcomes
- changing the distribution of power
- ensuring equal access to marginalised and oppressed groups and constituencies
- providing for broad-based involvement, moving beyond the creation of new leaderships.

That is why terms like 'having a say' and 'empowerment' have become synonymous with involvement in people's minds. But as we have seen they are not necessarily synonymous with the practice of participation.

Let's look more closely at power. The model proposed by Lukes may be helpful here. For Lukes, power involves conflict of interest, though conflict may also be pursued by power and influence – falling short of the exercise of power. He assumes at least two parties in conflict and that power is exercised when one of them (call them A) gets the other (B) to act in a way which is against B's interests as perceived by B. The two parties need not be individuals.

Groups and institutions also exercise power between each other.

Lukes is also concerned with the hidden dimensions of power. Hidden power is exercised, he says, when a conflict of interest has been excluded from public debate and decision-making. As a result, though others appear to acquiesce in what happens, in reality their viewpoint has been prevented from being raised. The absence of overt conflict means only that they have been 'denied entry into the political process'. Lukes also proposed a third dimension of power, 'The complex and subtle ways in which the inactivity of leaders and the sheer weight of institutions – political, industrial and educational' – serves to keep people out of the process and from even trying to get into it.

Enabling people's participation represents a challenge to all this. It's an enormous challenge and one that is often very unpalatable to powerholders.

But involvement and empowerment don't only mean power being taken from one and going to another. They don't necessarily mean losing power. They are not a zero-sum; so that if I have more, then you must have less. Instead involvement can be concerned with changing the nature of the relationship between participants. Nonetheless, the idea of people's involvement is still frequently seen as threatening by organizations, institutions and their personnel. A way in which they can resolve this tension is by *manipulating* the *ambiguity* of participation. Participatory initiatives can be a route to redistributing power, changing relationships and creating opportunities for influence. Equally they can double as a means of keeping power from people and giving a false impression of its transfer. They can be put to two conflicting purposes, according to whether their initiators want to hold on to or share power.

Resolving the paradox of participation

Recognising the two faces of participation helps us to understand why it is so often treated as a rhetorical flourish rather than a serious policy and why it has become so devalued. But there may be a problem in then just dismissing the idea of participation out of hand. The answer may lie not in rejecting participation but first in being clear about its nature and objectives: where control lies and what opportunities it may offer. Then people can make rational decisions about whether to get involved. We also need to draw a clear distinction. Participation does not only mean participatory initiatives set up by state or service providers. It is also about people struggling to gain more say and involvement for themselves and working to enable the broader involvement of their peers in their own organizations. As people involved in community, rights, disability and user groups quickly learn from experience, power is generally not something that is handed over or can be given. It has to be taken.

As well as being clear about the nature and limits of participatory initiatives we also need to understand how to support people's involvement effectively. Two components seem to be essential here, if people are to have a realistic chance of exerting an influence and all groups are to have equal access to involvement. These are *access* and *support*. Both are necessary.

Access includes equal access to the political structure at both local and central government levels and to other organizations and institutions which affect people's lives. In the more specific context of services it includes physical accessibility; the provision of services which are appropriate for and match the particular needs of different groups; and access points providing continuing opportunities for participation within both administrative and political structures, including membership of sub-committees, planning groups, working parties and so on.

The need for support arises not because people lack the competence to participate in society, but because people's participation is undermined by or not part of the dominant culture or tradition. There are four essential elements to support. These are:

- *personal development*: to increase people's expectations, assertiveness, self-confidence and esteem;
- *skill development*: to build the skills they need to participate and to develop their own alternative approaches to involvement;
- *practical support*: to be able to take part, including information, child care, transport, meeting places, advocacy etc; and
- *support for people to get together and work in groups*: including administrative expenses, payment for workers, training and development costs.

A number of routes to achieving people's greater participation at both micro and macro level are already apparent. These include:

- People working for it in their organisations and social movements
- Gaining support for the enterprise from allies in public services and state institutions. For example, as Chamberlin has observed, the support of radical mental health workers has been one of the features which has characterised the growth of the mental health system survivors' movement in Britain.
- Clarifying the issue of participation in order to develop effective strategies to pursue it.
- Learning systematically from existing experience.

Conclusion

We do not underestimate the structural constraints restricting people's involvement or the obstacles that are likely to be in the way of increasing it. We, alongside many other people, have long experienced these in our own efforts to gain more say. Instead we are arguing the importance of *clarifying* and *highlighting* the issue of participation. Much work has already been done on supporting people's greater say and involvement in education, health care, social services and other social policies. But often this has not been pulled together as a basis for action or theory building. We are arguing for participation to be taken seriously in social policy. Then social policy may escape from its prescriptive past and come to have an empowering role in people's lives and in public politics.

3.7

Equality and difference – what's in a concept?

Helen Meekosha

Introduction to the debate

Over the last two decades two distinct trends have emerged within feminism. First we have seen the growing recognition of differences between women: black women, immigrant women, lesbians, women with disabilities, Aboriginal women, third world women, older women … at times the list seems endless. Some groups of women have reacted harshly to what they have perceived to be a privileged group of white middle-class women who have seemed to say they speak on behalf of all women. The theory and practice of feminism may not yet have come to terms with one of its unintended consequences - the power to exclude some women and include others.

Secondly, some women have moved to a position of celebrating their difference from men and have sought to re-establish a community of women where values of nurturing and caring are given prominence as women-only values. Yet such a position often denies or downplays differences between women on the basis of race, class and so on, with problematic consequences for women whose differences are not recognised. Furthermore the position says little about those sociopolitical and economic power relationships which sustain the unequal distribution of goods, services and wealth between men and women, and between women and women.

Along with the emergence of differences within feminism other social movements around identity have developed. From the early 1970s, Afro-Caribbean groups and Asian groups became significant political actors on the British scene and in Australia the ethnic rights and Aboriginal land rights movements gained momentum. The International Year of the Disabled Person (IYDP) (1981) marked the turning point for people with disabilities. Their struggle to organise around their shared sense of oppression took on a more structured and extensive framework, drawing on the campaign for

From: Meekosha, H. (1993) 'The bodies politic: equality, difference and community practice', in H. Butcher, A. Glen, P. Henderson and J. Smith (eds) *Community and public policy*, London: Pluto Press, pp 171-92.

civil rights articulated by other social movements. Similarly the mid- to late 1980s witnessed the rising political profile of older people, as well as a resurgence of the gay and lesbian movement around the politics of HIV and AIDS.

While the impact of post-structuralism may have decomposed the political thrust of a 'women's movement', it provided a crucial range of insights for theoretical understanding. Central issues of concern included the use of language, the rediscovery of 'the body' as a social construct – black, white, able or disabled – and the deconstruction of the universalising and homogenising consequence of the concepts of gender and race. This perspective raised a further question for community practitioners who are committed to 'responding to the needs of women'– which women in which context?

So public policy and community practice, traditionally based on a notion of equality and social justice, have had to be rethought in the light of these debates. While these ideas may be held at one step removed from community practice, they intrude through their influence on broader strategies of social change.

Conceptual and theoretical issues

There is a fundamental paradox to be addressed: any attempt to discuss commonalities undermines attempts to discuss difference and vice versa. (Spelman 1988: 3) Minority groups have experienced and attempted to work through these contradictions, often with considerable trauma, during the last two decades. Demands for equality with current power holders can often seem neither feasible nor desirable, indeed they seem a fantasy in a highly stratified society for those whose perspectives are strongly influenced by their differences from this hierarchy. Equal opportunity in its most liberal form has clearly not been about equality of outcome. The language of identity and discrimination avoids focusing attention on structural considerations, couched as it is in terms of individual and group rights. The valuing of and respect for difference has been developing as the humanitarian and political goal of the 1990s. Yet an emphasis on difference, in terms of developing theoretical analyses of the nature of social systems, could lead to the impossibility of making any generalised statements. One could ask whether this is a movement towards endless ethnographic reporting of difference, which is no replacement for the theory it seems to want to supersede. (Di Stefano 1991)

The concept of difference has become a substitute for more critical concepts such as privilege, conflict of interest, oppression and subordination. Difference can avoid discussions of power. For example, the experiences of Aboriginal women, immigrant women, 'black' women, women with disabilities, are not simply different; they are part of overall power relations and at the same time intersect with and influence each other'. (Gordon 1991:106) In some situations the same individuals or groups of women may have power and in some they may be powerless. Respect for difference also throws into relief issues of class, political and religious values and beliefs. Does respect for difference mean that we value all others' positions equally and uncritically - religious fundamentalism, nazism? Should we 'respect' differences that seek to become dominant and oppressive forces in themselves? (Connolly 1990a; Phelan 1991:136) The equality/difference debate is widespread; in community practice, public policy formulation and implementation, gender studies, sexuality studies, black studies and in the emerging area of disability studies. A variety of other conceptual tools has been brought into the arena, notably 'specificity', with its translation in public policy as 'special needs'. Yet in many ways the setting of equality as an alternative goal to difference and vice versa offers a false dichotomy, and advances neither theory nor practice.

The idea of specificity offers the potential to bring back together the currently diverse threads of feminism. Both equality and difference privilege the white male as generic and thus 'an emphasis on specificity aims at disrupting hegemonies, calling out differences for question and rendering everyone accountable for her positions and actions'. (Phelan 1991: 133) Yet such a view, while bringing forth ideas of the 'special group or individual', leaves dominant forces untouched, and can at the same time create for those who have been identified as 'special', a soothing and soporific sense of self. (Minh-Ha 1989: 87) In the context of policy-making, 'difference', 'specificity' or 'special needs programmes' can either legitimate inequality or hide inequality from view, as can be demonstrated in housing, health, education and welfare services that become even more selective and 'targeted' as time goes by.

The 'big picture' concepts – race, gender, class, community – become problematic under the influence of post-structuralist theory. If we cannot generalise about women in practice, can we theorise about 'women' at all? Theoretical debates focus on the shifting nature of socially constructed concepts. What constitutes the notion of 'Aboriginality' in Australia or 'black' in Britain or the USA, depends on the context in which the category is mobilised, either by the state or by claimants. (Pettman 1992; Lilley 1989) 'Gender' is often considered a central, fixed concept. Yet current campaigns in Australia to have the government recognise transexuality as a ground for complaints of gender discrimination demonstrate the malleability of the idea of gender and its highly contingent qualities. The possibility of a feminist practice as such can be destroyed if activists and practitioners avoid the use of the concept of gender.

'Community' has always been considered a problematic concept. (see Bryson and Mowbray 1981; Anthias and Yuval-Davis 1992; Butcher 1993)

It is a concept used by minorities to mobilise resistance, and for groups and community workers to claim legitimacy in the political processes. In the last decade more than ever before it has become integrated into policies of social intervention by governments at local and central levels. Yet that integration has had the curious effect of revealing a plurality of communities which share only their marginalisation from the assumed 'mainstream'. As the welfare state contracts under the influence of neo-Conservative ideologies of public policy, only those groups exposed as critically or multiply disadvantaged are sanctioned to seek specific community resources from the state. The 'community' can be said to be reduced to categories of equal opportunities, defined ultimately through their previous exclusion from the mainstream. (Cain and Yuval Davis 1990) 'Community' is now far more prevalent in discussion of public policy and practice than reference to class or poverty, or income and wealth differentials.

Current conceptual and theoretical frameworks are inadequate to deal with the context of contemporary politics and policy-making. For example, we have few ways of speaking about intragroup violence and conflict, such as in Aboriginal male violence against Aboriginal women in Australia, or black on black violence in South Africa. We need to refocus on theoretical developments which can contribute to a more aware practice. (Parmar 1990; Segal 1987) At the same time, we do need to substitute a feminist for a 'malestream' story, or an account of a colonised people for an imperialist world view; we should expect these accounts to be more valid. If we fail at this task, then we are set adrift in a sea of relativity. (Cockburn 1991: 212)

New theorising – implications for practice

Collective and organising implications loom large for practitioners and political activists concerned with social justice goals. Are individual experiences all that matter, and are inequalities and degrees of oppression simply questions of relativity? Everyone seems to be clamouring for 'difference', only too few seem to want any difference that is about changing policy or that supports active engagement and struggle. (another no-no word: hooks 1991: 54)

The language we are allowed to use, who is allowed to speak, organise, who is employed, all reflect these current dilemmas being debated within the walls of the academy. What is perceived as endless theorising by feminists at the level of the political correctness of concepts has contributed to political practice and policy-making, at times inhibiting action.

Criticisms of 'essentialism' in feminism and in particular feminist social policy, arise from a reaction to the assumption that all women have the same experience and needs, and that there is something innate and/or essential about the category 'woman' or 'black' or disabled. (Williams 1989;

Meekosha and Pettman 1991; Morris 1990, 1991) Other critiques reflect the perception that some women are not so much subsumed as excluded or shut out of the account. Essentialism serves to mask the privileging of women who were white and middle class in feminism, and the privileging of men in race arid ethnic politics. (Hence the title ofthe path-breaking book by Hull, Scott and Smith in 1982 *All the Women are White, All the Blacks Are Men, But Some Of Us Are Brave*). Meanwhile disability remains largely ungendered and lacking a race dimension. Might specific/category claims in social policy simply reinforce the essentialist nature of the category? Is childcare for women reinforcing a stereotyped role? Why is childcare not as important for men?

Demands for equality, and recognition of difference and specificity have together resulted in the emergence of 'additive strategy' (Meekosha and Pettman 1991), whereby different minority groups are added on to the 'mainstream'. Nowhere is this clearer than in some equal opportunities programmes, in particular where the category 'women' is privileged as in 'women and other minorities'. Such strategies leave the structures of inequality untouched; moreover it is not possible simply to add the experience of disability or Aboriginality to the experience of being a white or able-bodied woman.

Feminist theory has repercussions for practice, while practice continues to inform theory. Arguments for single-sex schools and arguments against women working in the dangerous workplace (such as the lead industry) are put forward by some feminists on the basis of 'difference'. Such arguments have also been put forward by conservative, anti-feminist forces. Feminist strategies in the workforce, such as the fight for 'comparable worth' (with men) in female-dominated industries as the basis for determining wage rates, and the entry of women into non-traditional jobs, reflect political choices along a 'difference-equality' continuum, with the emphasis shifting in accordance with the ideological positions of the women concerned.

The pursuit of 'difference' carries in its train the potential for separate women's development, in environments from which men are excluded. For some women, who have been forcibly segregated from both men and the outside world (as institutionalised women with disabilities) such a strategy is problematic. Current feminist discourses of difference rarely mention disability, as if celebration of difference was not able to encompass an experience perceived as only negative. The politics of race, class, gender and sexuality are often imbued with pride and self-affirmation. Disability politics are still seen by many activists and policy makers to lie solely within the province of welfare. The political debates about identity and difference have often led to a one-dimensional symbolisation of the complex needs of people – the multiplicity of categories brings in turn a reduction to crude equivalence between 'groups' and 'needs': women need childcare, disabled people need access, and so on.

The important contributions of the new theorising lie in the acceptability of analyses which illuminate the contradictions and conflicts within oppressed groups. Asian women who supported Salman Rushdie's position on *The Satanic Verses* in Britain (Connolly 1990b) demonstrate the existence of power struggles within oppressed groups, and the importance of their appearance in public debate. Issues of representation and accountability have materialised in the wake of feminist questioning of totalising concepts, raising again an exploration of the meaning of power on the margins and the implications when the powerless move into positions of power – as when Australian women bureaucrats ('femocrats') move into positions of control or influence in the institutions of the state. Is the empowerment of marginalised., groups sometimes only a way of changing the dominant 'bodies' at the top of the power hierarchy?

We have to reconceptualise ideas of power and authority; and move beyond the important arguments about whose voice is controlling and whose voice must be heard to political community and solidarity in difference. (Jones 1991) Two current understandings of authority – that it must be accessible to all women and men currently excluded so that we can each control our own lives, or that we should resist authority as a tainted practice antithetical to feminist principles – may contribute little to struggles for equality or recognition of difference. A redefinition of authority would move from a concept of 'border-patrolling and border-engendering [to] meaning-giving'. (Jones 1991: 123). Re-examining the concept of authority would open up a debate in community practice that is in danger of being closed – that of leadership and expertise. In this sense we can look at authority as having its basis in the possession of skills and knowledge which need to be passed on, rather than as an excluding power-ridden concept.

Community practice – difference and equality

A number of elements of analysis come together at this point. First, the emergence of arguments for equality in the earlier phase, and for recognition of difference later on, have been interpreted by the state and incorporated into public policies and programmes. Secondly, the influence of post-structuralist theory and developments in feminist thinking have interacted to produce layers of interpretation and interrogation of experience, with outcomes that are far from clear in, their implications for practice. In parallel to these discursive intersections, debates and struggles have been occurring within social movements, while for community practitioners the environment in which they operate has become highly coloured by the reflections of these debates.

There are wider issues raised by the diversity of women's voices, by anti-racist and multicultural analyses emerging from the black, Aboriginal and ethnic rights movements, and by explorations of the meanings and needs of people with disabilities and gay men and lesbians. While these may well be fairly widely discussed in the general literature in social and public policy, they have not been addressed in any sustained manner in relation to community work practice. Much professional practice material on community work tends to tell of how to undertake specific tasks. They are for the most part general skills guides rather than intellectually rigorous and theoretically-informed approaches to professional practice in a complex, multidimensional and culturally diverse social environment Indeed the poverty of articulation of identity issues with community work theory has obvious repercussions for practice, even though 'training' in community work often includes the compulsory sections on race, class, 'gender, and sometimes disability.

The 'community of bodies' is in many, ways the new heartland of struggle and gives rise both to the intellectual forment and to the increasingly complex responses within public policy. Declining and broken class-based movements have been overtaken by movements which are by and large concerned with identities – sexual, racial, ethnic, lifestyle, age, disability. Even within these movements there have been calls to difference, with even smaller and more fragmented identity groups emerging. (Meekosha and Pettman 1991) These differences have challenged the calls for equality, by eroding the clarity of goals espoused in earlier demands and supplanting them by modes of self-affirmation in separate identities: at times the desire to become 'equal' dissolved in the statements of individual uniqueness.

The very language and intent of community practice has changed considerably as a result of these developments. The language of difference has been embraced, although often in an 'add-on' way. Some definitions of community work call on workers to 'acknowledge the specific contribution of black people and women'. (Federation of Community Work Training Groups 1990) Others argue that they should confront 'practices or institutions which discriminate against black people, women, people with disabilities, religious groups, elderly people, lesbians and gay men and other groups who are disadvantaged by society'. (Standing Conference on Community Development 1991) Community workers have quite rightly addressed criticisms of the predominance of white, Anglo, male biases inherent in practice. They are working with a range of identity groups composed of women, blacks, immigrants and so on, in the community and inside local authorities and local councils in Britain and Australia, as well as continuing to argue for the legitimacy of these activities.

Within the arena of race and ethnic politics, a number of distinct trends have emerged in what has been termed the 'ethnic revival' (Smith 1981) and the rise of nationalism. The weakening of class-based political action in the face of the strengthening of, post-war capitalism in western democracies has highlighted the social awareness of inequalities which take 'ethnic' as tile line of social cleavage and oppression. One consequence has been for ethnic groups to form and mobilise around the push for the maintenance (in some cases re-creation) of ethnic heritage, and the search for an 'essential ethnicity' to which they can lay claim. Here we see the intertwining of the demands for equality and 'freedom', with ideas of ethnic separation, resulting in quite novel constellations of actions and ideologies – in some cases with horrendous consequences, as in the former Yugoslavia. The privileging of essentialist claims – as for instance in the acceptance of fundamentalist and ethnicity-linked religious groups – has brought with it very real dangers as these ideologies and beliefs are allowed to flourish unchallenged in a climate apparently more tolerant of difference.

The primary objective of attacking essentialist notions of community (which assume white privilege) by highlighting race issues has often resulted in treating race as a homogenous category, thereby creating a new essentialist category with its own problems. In Australia, community workers with ethnic groups have for the most part focused on the ideology of multiculturalism, raising awareness of cultural values, norms and heritage. They have often failed to examine internal power within ethnic communities on the one hand, and racism within the wider community on the other. In this context a simplistic, superficial and ahistorical practice based on respect for difference can reinforce inequalities.

If a woman is 'different' her feminist loyalty can be called into question by the most powerful segment – usually white middle-class women imposing their own definitions of legitimate feminist practice. One example can be found in those anti-rape organisations in Los Angeles established in the early 1970s which included very few black women; the situation led black women to establish rape crisis programmes specifically for the black community. These organisations became primarily community service-oriented, leading to accusations by white women in the anti-rape movement of black women's conservatism and having too close an association with the bureaucrats responsible for funding. (Matthews 1988) On the other hand, the assumption of the need to be different can elicit the opposite response. In Britain, an attempt to set up separate girls' nights in a youth project for black women was unsuccessful. Young Asian women did not go to separate groups as they believed it would reinforce an identity harmonious with their families' wishes and they wished to rebel against such ideas. (Connolly 1990b)

White, Anglo able-bodied community workers and community groups ask why 'they' (the 'others') do not join, come to meetings, organise? These workers and groups often assume apathy as the reason, without addressing issues of who is setting the agenda, does the group dispense power equitably and what is the relevance of the existing group to the 'others' being requested to join? For instance, few voluntary and community organisations have made much headway towards equal employment opportunity. (Meekosha *et al.* 1987; Cockburn 1991: 230) So while the paid workers may be either drawn from the dominant groups in society or 'community leaders', those who are clients or make up the constituency of the organisation may remain marginalised.

An awareness of these tensions has played a part in the development of a politics of identity. Identity politics has provided a decisive response to the assumptions and ethnocentricity of much mainstream theory and community practice. First, it has provided a critique of notions of community and shown that community is indeed permeable with ever-changing boundaries. Secondly, identity groups have become actors in community politics rather than disadvantaged objects of community work intervention. Thirdly, non-directive community work, with the role of the worker as facilitator rather than leader or spokesperson, has been shown to be an idealised and unhelpful notion in understanding the role of, for example, gay workers organising around AIDS or disabled workers around public transport.

We do not expect these workers to come value-free to their positions, carrying a bundle of neutral skills with which to aid the community. Workers who share the characteristics of their 'patch' or constituency group are usually more able to understand the issues and relate to the individuals affected than benevolent outsiders who have often put themselves in the position of mediating between the authorities and the oppressed group. While acknowledging these advantages, it is important to note that identity carries three possible dangers. First, it has at times become the qualification for the position. Bitter and conflicting scenarios have developed , regarding the role of those not part of the identity group. Employing a member of the category at all costs has led to-workers being set up to fail as a result of inappropriate appointments coupled with lack of support and training.

Secondly, there is a, danger that this interpretation of the 'respect' for difference will allow no role for those outside the category. It can become an excuse for white workers not dealing with racism, men not dealing with sexism, and so on. If the only legitimate speaking position on such issues is accorded to those individuals/agents directly experiencing the situation/ problems, then 'experts' are demobilised. As a consequence, the constitution of the criteria for legitimate speaking and/or acting positions has become a central tension both in community organising and action, and in social planning.

Thirdly, the recent shift towards the funding of community groups around identity has resulted in pressure exerted by the state for the groups to respond to bureaucratic demands, with clear outcomes which may erode the original political goals of the constituency. Groups become trapped by the need to continue to demonstrate oppression or disadvantage or victim status for funding purposes, rather than continue the project of social change. At the same time given the fiscal and legitimation crisis of the state, some types of community practice with discrete groups has met with little resistance. It is cheaper to develop services for specific groups than provide good, accessible universal services.

Crossing boundaries

Community development in Britain, the USA and Australia tended in the 1970s to concentrate on working-class neighbourhoods and the development of networks and the organisation of local action to achieve locally-articulated goals. As we have seen, this pattern of intervention has become transformed in recent years under the impact of social movements which, transcending locality, have now focused on a politics of difference and the specificity of smaller group experiences of discrimination and disadvantage.

As community work becomes increasingly moulded by the pressures of market models of welfare, the historic focus of community work as a profession of activism and commitment to the achievement of social justice becomes translated. It has now become a mode of work in which ever-more tightly delineated minorities and sectors of society experiencing discrimination are channelled into organising the provision of specific, usually volunteer-operated, services. Despite these pressures, innovative practice is occurring, with community workers and activists taking risks, crossing boundaries and re-examining practice in the light of both theoretical influences and direct experience.

Major questions confront community practitioners as we move through the 1990s. How do we transcend the political moralism of separatist tendencies of identity politics in community practice on the one band and the 'additive approach' on the other? How can we prevent the relentless task of maintaining good relations with government and external funding bodies on whose funding we rely, eroding the energy needed to develop and maintain the community empowerment process at the local and national levels? How do we establish priorities for community practice in the face of 'market-driven' community work and ever increasing demands on what the 'community' can achieve? How do we move beyond the doubt, uncertainty and sense of defeat characterising much of community work in the 1980s? The important task may. not be constructing unity, but achieving solidarity from the vantage point of our differences.

Dominant groups have a great deal invested in people staying in the correct categories for the purposes of policing, immigration, social security administration and justification of state surveillance/violence, to name but a few examples. It is therefore important that fixed and repressive aspects of categories are challenged as part of strategies of resistance. This flexibility should not cause a lack of commitment or direction vis-a-vis a transformed set of social relations. It should not be reactive for its own sake, but should be part of an alternative vision; new categories can be forged in the process of resistance as in the case of the Australian Aboriginal Gungarakyn people who re-evaluated power relations between men and women, allowing women 'to assert their importance as reproducers of people-land-society' for the purpose of land claims. (Lilley 1989: 90) Thus, challenging and crossing boundaries allows us to move beyond the paralysing effects of identity politics without moving back to a mainstream practice largely undifferentiated by race, gender, disability and so on.

Moving beyond 'additive' strategies requires reassessment of concepts of universalism, collective provision, multiculturalism and responsible citizenship. Demands on governments to respond to the specific needs of identity groups in terms of the provision of housing, social security, education, health and so on have been a double-edged sword. On the one hand, notable victories by groups making claims on the state have improved services. In some cases they have allowed segments of distinct communities such as Aboriginal people and immigrant groups in Australia and Asian and Afro-Caribbean groups in Britain to follow desires for self-determination and collective provision. On the other hand, ghettoised provision has protected the mainstream services, and in some areas new services are moving in the direction of specific provision only. Universal entitlement to quality, cheap, accessible housing, education and health is only debated in what remains of progressive left circles in industrialised countries.

The practice of the 'politics of location' (Mani 1990; Zavela 1991) has emerged as a strategy for working around simple categories which have become rigidly interpreted and imbued with political and community moralism. There are many sites of power, many sites of resistance, and struggles are temporary and changing. This has implications for community practice. It means that the social location of each group, project or activity is as important as the substantive issue. Following this argument, community practitioners need to articulate their location vis-à-vis the 'community' with whom they work. For example, where do workers themselves stand in terms of race, gender, class and education? Similarly gaps and commonalities between individuals within the group need to be articulated. The social locations of members of the group are taken as points for departure, for it is increasingly the case that the social response to an individual's identity leads to his or her involvement in community politics. Thus identity is an important but not the sole factor in community practice. While identity may be the point of departure – single mothers getting involved in a campaign for childcare – identity demands need reformulating in a way that does not reinforce their essentialist nature, in this case that childcare is an issue only for women.

Is there a danger that the emphasis on the politics of location is simply a return in disguise to the politics of localism, a method of working much criticised in earlier literature (Mowbray 1984; Dyen 1989) for failing to come to terms with systemic problems that go beyond the immediate situation? The politics of location and position also need long-term liberating goals and alternative visions of a more just society. There is a continuing problem that the emphasis on the politics of location could further highlight the current preoccupation with the individual at the expense of collective, national and international solutions, so that one is left with fragmented activity, typified by 'Generalization is out; particularity is in'. (Di Stefano 1991: 91)

Many community workers and feminist activists increasingly believe in the need to revive the idea of coalitions, alliances and networks between marginalised identity groups. In some ways the philosophy and practice of coalition work runs counter to the intent of identity politics, insofar as the interests of the minority may, be sacrificed in the interests of the majority; so new forms of networking, alliances and coalition structures need to be discussed. Some argue this is a crucial way to fight back following the demoralisation of feminist and popular community movements suffering the unprecedented effects of 'uncaring' governments.

Coalition building has been compared to leaving home; leaving the safety of your own barred room. 'You don't go into coalition because you like it. The only reason you consider trying to team up with somebody who could possibly kill you, is because that's the only way you can figure you can stay alive'. (Reagon 1983: 357) As we have seen, diversity has been used in recent years by governments to divide and rule, so there is clearly value in taking the alliance route. Alternatively some argue that their distinct needs are best met by organising autonomously (Radford-Hill 1986: 165); they fear the loss or marginalisation of their 'claims' by premature entering of coalitions and alliances. Universal 'sisterhood' as an unwelcome spectre can easily re-emerge when some groups are less powerful than others.

The effort, time and energy required for coalition work may also threaten the survival of your own group and compromise your goals. This is particularly true for some people with disabilities whose capacities are limited by shorter days and reduced physical endurance. It is notable that disability is the last 'cab off the rank' in identity politics. Sadly, too often the simple requirements for the involvement of people with disabilities, such as access, are still avoided when organising coalition work. Within the more institutionalised practices of feminism there is still much fear of women with disabilities. Some feminists, in the rush to move gender issues away from welfare, can refuse to be in alliances with women with disabilities. Alliances between identity groups are still the exception. Not all the new social alliances are progressive in nature; they can easily be co-opted by conservative and business groups on the new Right. There is similarly nothing inherently caring or progressive about being a disabled person, an immigrant and so on. For instance, a campaign in Haringey, London, occurred where the Black Pressure Group on Education and the Parents' Rights Group took a homophobic stance against policies directed towards educational equality. 'Was it a paradox of the postmodern condition or just everyday life in post-colonial Britain that what resulted was an 'unthinkable' alliance between Black People and the National Front? Welcome to the jungle, welcome to the politics of indeterminacy in the twilight of modernity.' (Mercer 1990: 48-49)

Conclusion

In the final analysis, post-structuralism has drawn us into many deep divides and has not indicated new forms of practice capable of dealing with the complexities of the post-modern world. It has, however, led to the experiences and knowledge of many of the marginalised, hitherto overlooked, being recognised for the first time.

It has ensured that community practitioners have begun to challenge the old ways and old texts. What remains is to devise new structures to bridge the divides and new forms of collective action to transform the many destructive, sources of power in society. Community practitioners should be able to move beyond the simple respect for difference on the one hand or the uncritical acceptance of the push for equality on the other. The invocation of the equality litany – race, class, gender, disability, age, sexuality – carries a great danger, that all these differences are understood to incur the same quality of disadvantage. The majority of the population encompassed by these categories in their totality suggests a very real potential power, even though in practice there may be hostility and tension between and within them. While the issues formulated by these groups have been very important in reframing the practices of the welfare state and the provision of communal services, it is important to be aware of what has been let slip and the effects of this dissolution of earlier views of social needs including universal provision. We have seen the individualisation of social relations, the competitiveness between categories introduced in order to reduce overall state expenditures in the name of respect for difference, and in particular in regards to community work practice, the loss of the capacity to mobilise communities for action through struggles for power rather than the cheaper management of targeted state services.

Women in the community: feminist principles and organising in community work

Lena Dominelli

Woman and community. Two words that make a powerful combination. Since time immemorial, women have worked in the community, stitching the threads of everyday life together. Most of the time, this work goes on unnoticed, except when it is not done or is the subject of complaint. Without women's work in the community, life as we know it could not exist. But what is the nature of this work? Why is it women who do it? And what has feminism got to do with community work? Wilson (1977) claims community is a 'portmanteau' word which conveys a wide range of activities without revealing their most fundamental features. So, Bell and Newby (1972) compiled 98 definitions of community without revealing that women had a crucial role to play in its formation, maintenance and reproduction.

Women have been responsible for undertaking the day-to-day work which keeps communities together and adds to the quality of daily life. Enhancing the substance of everyday life forms the crux of women's action in the community, replicating and drawing upon the labour women undertake in the privacy of their homes and in waged work. For women, the notion of community is not bound by territorial terrain. It encompasses those social relationships and networks constructed around the needs of those under our care and involves mediating and negotiating with private individuals, state agencies and commercial enterprises to fulfil the obligations that nurturing others imposes on us. For women, organising in the community often revolves around family life and entails: stretching scarce resources to their limit through self-help networks; providing day-care facilities; getting access to decent, affordable housing; preventing school closures; securing rights to minimum incomes; and a host of other issues linked to women's caring

From: Dominelli, L. (1995) 'Women in the community: feminist principles and organising in community work', *Community Development Journal*, vol 30, no 2, pp 133-43.

roles. Curno (1978) labelled such activities 'soft' issues which, as 'women's work', were accorded secondary status in the community work hierarchy. For him, 'hard' issues addressing the provision of jobs and the restructuring of the local economy were the prerogative of men and considered of primary importance. The indifferent assessment of women's work – in the community, like work at the domestic hearth – reflected their subordinate social status and preoccupation with private life. It contrasted sharply with the high status given to men's involvement in the public sphere.

Until feminists highlighted the gender-blind nature of community work (Mayo 1977; Wilson 1977; Dominelli 1990), its theory and practice took women's contribution for granted and scarcely mentioned women's actions, whether these were high profile campaigns seeking to prevent the closure of nursery places and secure low-cost housing for working class people, or more low key affairs such as setting up carers' groups for those looking after adults with physical disabilities. Feminists revealed not only the conceptual gaps in community work theory and practice, they identified the sexist nature of the working relations prevailing amongst community workers. Feminist analyses exposed the ways in which men community workers collared the most important decision-making posts whilst women were relegated to the servicing roles like making tea and writing minutes. (Curno *et al*. 1982) Feminists also castigated the language which made women's contribution invisible, for example, calling a group leader 'chairman' even if she were a woman. (Spender 1976) Feminists had the task of making women's community work visible by securing spaces in which women could speak, tell their own stories and develop forms of community action which were less hierarchical and alienating than those based on the organising strategies so favoured by male community workers.

In Britain, women's action in the community has spanned several centuries and included the activities of Octavia Hill seeking to improve life in the working class slums of Victorian London, Josephine Butler organising to repeal laws blaming prostitutes for the spread of venereal disease, Marie Stopes trying to establish easily available birth control measures for women and Eleanor Rathbone arguing for family allowances to be paid to women. Its most widely-publicised recent examples cover campaigns against men's violence against women; campaigns for women's reproductive rights; campaigns for the provision of shelters for women assaulted by men; the women's peace campaign; and women's campaigns against pit closures. Like earlier campaigns these have been woman-centred affairs. However, the latter initiatives have differed substantially from their predecessors in challenging women's role in society as the 'helpmeet' of men and engaging women in devising new visions of the world, one not bound by patriarchal social relations, but guided by non-hierarchical ways of women organising with each other as women, implementing the prefigurative forms of our alternative social order in the practice being elaborated here and now. In other words, 'second wave' feminists have sought to transform social relations in egalitarian directions rather than merely adapting women into the roles created by men for men. The argument is no longer abut women making it in men's world, but about women creating a new world for both men and women, regardless of age, 'race', sexual orientation or disability. (Segal 1987) The principle guiding this vision is one of egalitarian social relations replacing hierarchical patriarchal ones; a world which 'celebrates diversity and sees it as a source of enrichment rather than inferiority'. (Lorde 1984)

Feminist principles of organising

What principles inform feminist community action? And, what relevance do these have for people in general? Partly as a reaction to the invisibility of women's contributions, the neglect of women's specific needs as women under patriarchy and the unpicking of hierarchical gender relations which lies at the heart of feminism, feminists have placed 'women' at the centre of their agenda for social change. Identifying women's experiences of any particular situation to clarify women's needs and develop women–inspired solutions to them has been the main concern of feminist community action in recent decades. Women are the starting point of such activities. However, feminist analyses have unearthed the problematic nature of men's experience of patriarchy and set an agenda of change for them too. It is my firm belief that unless the social transformation envisaged by feminists encompasses both women and men, gender oppression, or the subordination of women by men, will not be eliminated. Men can draw on feminist principles of organising to help them in this task without either controlling women or usurping women's power and autonomy.

Feminism is well placed profoundly to alter our social order because it places the inegalitarian gender relations characterising patriarchy in the crucible of change. Feminism covers a variety of different schools of thought – probably as many as there are different groups of women. These tend to get variously categorised primarily as liberal feminism, bourgeois feminism, socialist feminism, Marxist feminism, black feminism and radical feminism. Each of these has a different philosophical standpoint and corresponding practice from others: radical feminists see 'men' as the enemy and concentrate their energies on developing women-only alternative forms of social organisation; socialist feminists feel capitalism distorts both men and women's lives and whilst insisting on women's right to autonomous spaces when they want them, are willing to work with men to change society; black feminists have incorporated classism, racism and sexism in their struggles. So, a key feminist principle of organising in the community is taking action to end inegalitarian social relations. Social change is the ultimate aim of feminist social action.

Starting from where women are at is another principle of feminist organising and is critical in living up to another feminist principle – making space for women to discover for themselves the nature of their reality through discussions with other women rather than having expert professionals or volunteers impose hierarchical relationships upon them. This approach to organising in the community is central to another feminist principle – that of promoting egalitarian relationships in their work with others. Feminists are reluctant to endorse placing one woman in a leadership position over others. Even if a particular woman has skills, resources or knowledge not available to the others she works with, her main concern is to share her source of power and expertise with them, so that the other women can acquire these for themselves. Such an attitude makes it easier for women to work cooperatively and collectively with each other. However it does not guarantee the absence of power differentials amongst them, only that their presence will be acknowledged and worked upon. Feminists as products of a society founded upon inegalitarian social relations and socialisation processes can also reproduce and reinforce inequality. Life is a constant struggle against the indignities and humiliations caused by the internalisation of hierarchy. Barker (1986) cites an example of how subtly and unconsciously the process of 'putting other down' can arise when she describes the 'false-equality' trap.

Another integral aspect of feminist organising is the principle of self-reflection and evaluation after listening to what women themselves have to say. Feminists accept that the unfinished and flawed nature of their work makes its critique by oneself and others a necessary and ongoing feature. A willingness to accept criticism and use constructively in further developing feminist social action has enabled feminists to improve their sensitivity to issues. For example, heterosexual women have responded, albeit slowly, to lesbians' analysis of the homophobic nature of their writings; white feminists have begun examining their racist reactions to the agenda placed before them by black women and taken steps to counter these. The dynamics contained within such an approach lend feminism its capacity to constantly regenerate itself and reinforce its commitment to more egaliatarian social relations. Additionally, such openness has enabled feminists to acknowledge *difference* and accept that women's experience of gender oppression varies considerably according to the social divisions which impact on their lives. Women's experience of sexism therefore, varies according to whether they are black or white, able-bodied or disabled, old or young, heterosexual or lesbian or any combination of these. Gender oppression is being conceptualised as an experience which affects women across the globe, but its manifestation differs according to the culture, country and social grouping applying to the women concerned. Sisterhood must be worked for rather than assumed.

Consequently, women are working to recognise and acknowledge their differences as well as establishing their commonalities. Celebrating this diversity gives feminism its non-dogmatic and flexible approach.

The relevance of feminist principles of traditional community work

Traditional community work can draw lessons from feminist community work and develop them in its own practice. Most people feel excluded from key decisions affecting their community and powerless in challenging them, whether these concern school closures, road widening schemes, factory sell-outs and mass redundancies, the destruction of the immediate environment or the lack of leisure facilities. The main difficulty they encounter is that of redefining the issues so that they transcend the individualised, fragmented responses to definitions of the problem promoted by the media, the state and powerful others. Definitions constructed by the powerful are usually dominated by economic considerations rather than social needs and are plucked out of their social context to provide a neutral technocratic problem that can be addressed primarily by experts, not ordinary people. The discussion which then occurs in any public forum is closely regulated by bureaucratic procedures which hinder free flowing creativity and control the nature of the discussion which ensues. People leave such meetings feeling frustrated, angry, humiliated and powerless. The roles which the powerful ascribe to the ordinary public are largely passive – receiving information and taking the situation as given.

Redefining the problem in ways which empower community residents requires that the problem be placed in its social context and links made between the structural determinants of their situation and their personal experience of it. Redefining problems in this way gives people a modicum of control in the matter and brings politics back into it, thereby highlighting a key feminist principle: that personal and public life is political and that political life is also personal. (Segal 1987) Reconceptualising the problem also empowers individuals in their questioning of the experts and opens the way for a real exchange of information between them. It also allows for the possibility that professionalism can be redefined as more of a servicing activity than a controlling one, enabling the balance of power between them to move in more equal directions. Such shifts in the relationship between community workers and residents are essential if real community empowerment is to enable the voice of the people to come to the fore. Working according to feminist principles, particularly those endorsing power-sharing, collective working and redefining professionalism, requires community workers to be more accountable to the groups they work with, work more effectively collectively, share skills and develop more participatory mechanisms. Such approaches encourage the continued involvement of participants, refuel their commitment to the task in hand and boost their morale. They also facilitate using their own skills and taking personal responsibility for the decisions each adopts as a member of the group. Community workers also need to promote consciousness-raising exercises enabling individuals to redefine their personal reality in social terms and acquire the freedom to express affective responses and emotions which connect external decision-making with their personal experiences.

Giving gender issues a central place in the community work agenda also allows community workers to confront the ideology of the heterosexual nuclear family which defines family norms and ties people to a sexist division of labour, and address the barriers to women's more equal involvement in mainstream community work. Were this to happen, women would not be placed in the position of seeking their male partner's approval to take direct action, or finding someone else to care for dependent children and elders. Neither would women be relegated to a subordinate status in the life of the group. Collective action would flow more freely, and non-oppressive gender relations rather than inegalitarian ones would be fostered. The use of networks to promote campaigns would also give community work a major boost in transcending one of its major limitations – its parochialism. Networking can give a campaign an influence beyond the numbers directly involved and provides the opportunity for drawing moral support, additional resources and the involvement of people regionally, nationally and internationally, as has happened with the women's refuge movement. Networking also enables one campaign to influence another.

Community workers following feminist principles of direct action need to be aware of and prepared for a hostile response from individuals, groups and the state (locally or centrally). The state will defend its power, its hegemony over the definition of what is considered legitimate action and the dominant ideology unless that groundwork is done. Indeed, unless the state is permeated by a feminist political presence throughout, only limited progress can be made in providing a more humane world for ourselves and future generations. (Dominelli and McLeod 1989) Only when feminist principles of organising permeate state activities can a more truly egalitarian social order unfold and encompass each and every individual in our society. Ultimately, feminist social action is about the politics of inclusion and the creation of a society free of oppression of any kind.

Section 4
Between the state and the market: the mid-1990s to the 2000s

Introduction

This section reviews the period in which the restructuring of state welfare entered a second phase in its passage through Conservative to three successive (New) Labour governments and on to a Conservative–Liberal Democrat coalition government in 2010, hailed at the time as a break with traditional two-party politics. The natural starting point for this section, therefore, may seem to be the 1997 general election, which saw the first Labour government returned in nearly 20 years. But the making of New Labour, as it rebranded itself, may be as significant as its electoral success in relation to the long-term consequences for community development. This is because 'New' Labour was both a reaction to the New Right politics of the Thatcher government and a product of it. It has been argued that the most significant legacy of Thatcherism, as it came to be known, was the ideological changes it embedded for and in successive governments and the public at large (Butcher, 1993): indeed, Mrs Thatcher herself is alleged to have quipped that her greatest political legacy was Tony Blair. In this sense Thatcherism monopolised the political terrain well after its electoral demise. Among the ideological shifts through the 1980s and 1990s were an appeal to possessive individualism and the promise of (consumer) choice, a belief in the efficiency of the market, and an aversion to the state as service provider of first resort. In this respect the state, regarded in the social democratic period as the primary 'solution' to social problems, was now firmly established as being itself the overwhelming 'problem' in the neo-liberal world. What this signalled was a significant rebalancing of the rights and responsibilities of citizenship, in the process of which 'rights' became negatively associated with 'dependency', and citizenship was stripped of its collective dimension through the construction of 'the consumer'.

Much of the significant raft of legislation that was enacted from the mid-1980s on – in relation to health, education and welfare – was aimed therefore at privatisation of public services where possible, while at the same time introducing market mechanisms, processes and cultures into the public sector in general. The consequences of this process were reflected in practice in three distinct ways: first the ubiquitous 'partnership' model of collaboration between state, private sector and communities shifted the centre of gravity away from democratic debate and towards a kind of corporate consensus in which local government was supplanted by local governance (Glendinning et al, 2002); secondly, the 'contract culture' became endemic, with service agreements creating competition between various kinds of providers sometimes, as in the NHS, in the context of an internal market; thirdly, the performance, audit and measurement culture with its target and inspection regimes fundamentally reshaped the parameters of practice. Work with communities was seriously constrained by all three. The enabling state – steering rather than rowing, as it had been characterised (Rhodes, 1996) – was beginning to reposition community development in new, interesting and deeply problematic ways.

The period from the late 1970s until around the middle of the 1990s, described retrospectively by Davidson (2010) as one of 're-orientation', had involved 'a frontal onslaught on the labour movement and the dismantling of formerly embedded social democratic institutions (roll back)'. This period, he suggests, lasted up until the mid-1990s, to be followed by a second 'regime of consolidation', which 'involved a more molecular process involving the gradual commodification of huge new areas of social life and the creation of new institutions specifically constructed on neo-liberal principles (roll out)'. Both 'roll-back' and 'roll-out' have been endemic in public policy, with serious consequences for community development. For example, recourse to 'the community' has become an alibi for 'rolling back' the welfare system while at the same time the performance and audit culture has been 'rolled out' through various standardised versions of community engagement and 'best practice' regimes as a means of steering or controlling the process.

As New Labour sought to gain electoral ground during the period of late Thatcherism (suffering humiliating General Election defeats in 1987 and 1992, and following the demise of Thatcher herself as Prime Minister in 1990), it moved steadily away from its social democratic roots to embrace the neo-liberal economics of its predecessor, but with a distinctively new 'spin'. 'Third Way' politics, created to transcend the dichotomy between state and market, now sought to reconnect them in policy. This was achieved discursively by smuggling in a misleadingly 'ethical' vocabulary to bolster economic arguments (Judt, 2010). Put somewhat crudely, Third Way politics incorporated progressive social sentiments and aggressive economic objectives as if they were natural allies: 'not only enterprise but also social justice', for example (Fairclough, 2000). The work by Lovett et al (1994) (Ch 4.1, this volume), however, testifies to the difficulties of combining 'enterprise' with community development in ways which did not simply co-opt 'the community movement' against their long-term interests. Popple (1995a) (Ch 4.2, this volume) has tried to capture the essence of different models of practice which represent different responses to the changing context.

Language and discourse has been central to 'rolling out' and 'embedding' the New Labour project and it is emblematic that this Third Way synthesis was constituted in and through language as much as practice, so that it became normalised and regurgitated through everyday use. It was not unusual, for example, for community work to be described in terms of 'delivering empowerment', an oxymoron in educational and political terms. This discursive turn therefore caused particular difficulties for community development, because it suggested that the lexicon of values long associated with community development had been appropriated for rather different purposes, a trend which has continued and shows no sign of abatement (Craig, 2007 – Ch 4.9, this volume).

A central theme of Third Way politics was the necessity of a process of 'modernisation' which would seek to update public services to meet the expectations of the modern consumer in a fast-moving globalised world (Giddens, 1998). Central to this process was the move from government to governance through which 'consumer choice' would be enacted by a newly activated and 'empowered' civil society. The key idea for New Labour as it moved in this direction was a reinvented notion of 'community' which was to become a new mode of regulation and control, at a symbolic level at least. Hoggett (1997) argues that 'community' became for New Labour what 'class' had been for old Labour. In these terms, a remoralisation process was under way, through which certain groups would come to be seen, and in some cases to see themselves and their 'anti-social activities', as responsible for all kinds of social problems, irrespective of the wider structural context which had actually generated the difficulties (Carlisle, 2001, Ch 4.5, this volume). In this process, the term 'welfare' was beginning to suggest everything that was wrong with what would subsequently become expressed politically by the incoming 2010 Conservative-Liberal Democrat coalition as 'the broken society'. Drawing on both discredited pathological explanations and outmoded communitarian solutions, community was coming to stand as both problem and solution in the restructured welfare system (Mooney and Neal, 2009). This has made the community development role particularly problematic in relation to its traditional constituency of place, as community has been recycled in policy as a 'prescription for the poor' (Taylor, 2003).

Community development practice has been implicated in processes of modernisation in two particular ways, first, as a strategic agent of the localised modernisation agenda: facilitating partnership working, applying set standards of community engagement, capacity-building around pre-determined outcomes, managing the performativity culture. Second, it has been subject itself to modernisation processes which have reconfigured its role, and this has renewed longstanding questions as to the appropriate parameters of professional practice. For example, although thousands of new posts may have been created to service the community agenda, such expansion has generated intense concern both about the terms and conditions of practice and the language in which it is framed. Surveys of 3,000 self-defined community workers through the 1990s and 2000s revealed that few had had professional training of any kind, a quarter were appointed to posts where experience or training were not required, most were working on short-term contracts and most were managed by people who also had no experience of, or training in, community development. A government publication of the time suggested that there might be 20,000 community workers in the UK – now anyone could be a community development worker, it seemed (Banks et al, 2003; Glen et al, 2004). This suggested considerable confusion about the tasks facing community work and a potential dilution in the professional focus of community work.

In this sense it can be seen that developments during this period have been systematically linked to the 'new' political lexicon associated with the wider restructuring of welfare. These include active citizenship (Thompson, 2000), capacity-building (Craig, 2007 – Ch 4.9, this volume) and social capital (Taylor, 2007 – Ch 4.11, this volume). Professional reaction has been predictably varied. On the one hand, there have been attempts to create some critical distance and to redefine the distinctive core interests of community development (with the development of national occupational standards in various contexts). On the other hand, there has been an interest in reclaiming the radical potential of community development from a centralising state which, both directly and indirectly, has attempted to colonise the territory (Ledwith, 2005). The 'reality of a recentralisation of political control' (Taylor, 2007) which has characterised many partnership arrangements, for example, raises questions for community workers in their claims to be responsive to the needs and aspirations of those they work with in communities. In addition, the increasing professionalisation of community development as a means of delivering the new governance structures has been accused of eschewing the structural analysis of the origins of deprivation first associated with the Home Office-funded CDP of the 1970s, and contributing to the 'respectabilisation' of community development as an instrument of policy (Miller and Ahmad, 1997 – Ch 4.3, this volume).

In the new welfare order, community development is at least as likely to be funded by non-state actors and agencies as through direct policy initiatives and this has changed the terms of engagement. For example, the growth of the contract culture has attempted to refashion a disparate voluntary sector into a coherent force for service delivery through the rise of the 'third sector'. This term itself reflects the expansion of providers that now occupy the shifting ground between the state and the market, including the private sector. This is an expansion which the 2010 government appears determined to accelerate, albeit without the terms and conditions associated with public sector providers. Such diversification of providers has been accompanied by a managerial turn in the provision of services generally, with community development required to justify itself by the same quantitative measures as other social and welfare services. There has also been a growth in the number of private consultants ready to advise on the transition. This has occurred at the same time as user involvement has become institutionalised in many services, creating potential conflicts of outcome and interest (Cowden and Singh, 2007).

Devolution was a major New Labour commitment and this period saw a new government in Scotland (1999) and National Assemblies in Wales (1998) and Northern Ireland (1998). While there have been some significant divergences in the devolved contexts, however, there has also been a notable convergence in the general move towards modernisation of services and an economistic approach to policy (Mooney and Poole, 2004). Although institutional arrangements may have changed, the relations of power remain stubbornly similar. A new participatory paradigm has also emerged at local level, reflecting the wider decentralisation agenda, with mixed results. Although central and devolved governments have emphasised their commitment to involving local people in a wide range of policy decisions relating to employment, health, crime reduction, education, local government services and regeneration, translating this into meaningful local participation has remained a significant challenge for community development (Foley and Martin, 2000). A key concern has been that, while responsibility for a wide range of governance activities has been pushed downwards to 'the community', overall control of the agenda has been increasingly centralised, leaving many communities doubtful as to whether 'voice' can, in such a managed context, guarantee sufficient influence to make it worthwhile (Cairns, 2003). These tensions were well exemplified in the government's flagship New Deal For Communities, where any attempts by 'the community' to take control of management and spending were met by a centralising response (Dinham, 2005).

At one level, there has been a recognition in policy of the need for government departments and professionals to pursue 'joined-up thinking' in order to achieve greater community participation. On the other hand, by the early 2000s, the 'reality' of top-down versions of empowerment had created a crisis of identity for community development as it was drawn upon increasingly to turn the 'public issues' of the social democratic welfare state into the 'private troubles' of the neo-liberal managerial state – a complete reversal of its traditional claims. Community work surveys across the UK began to consistently show a pattern of target-driven, policy-led work which left little room for engaging with communities on their own terms; that practice was essentially 'dominated by the policy and political context rather than creating it' (Craig, in Shaw, 2004: 24). As the state has gradually become more colonised by the market, therefore, more and more of its activities have been privatised or delegated to depleted and 'responsibilised' communities (Clarke, 2006). In this context, community workers have been increasingly expected to 'enable' those already most disadvantaged communities to take on significant active citizenship roles in service delivery while rights to publicly funded services based on need have become further eroded. In a profound sense, as Martin (2003) suggests, we may have been witnessing 'the *de*construction of welfare through the *re*construction of citizenship', with the unwitting collusion of community development. This is increasingly a global problem as the demands for citizen action in many parts of the world may seriously outmatch the capacity of civil society to deliver (Cooke and Kothari, 2001).

Community development has had to face up, increasingly, to the challenges of globalisation and its localised consequences. In many ways, globalisation has made the local more important. Reversing the usual formulation of 'think global, act local', Gaventa (2001) (Ch 4.6, this volume) argues for the necessity of locating global processes in local conditions and in making common cause through transnational solidarity and the promotion of rights. Making the critical connections between interlinking dimensions of poverty in global and local contexts is also advocated by Ledwith (2007) (Ch 4.10, this volume) if community development is to be more than the 'politics of tokenism' she fears it is in danger of becoming. On the other hand, globalisation has alerted many to the reality that community development is struggling with the same issues worldwide (Budapest Declaration, 2004).

Reference to and reliance on 'the community' in policy has always obscured a more complex reality, and this has become particularly acute in the latter part of this period (Shaw, 2008 – Ch 4.12, this volume). As the management of diversity has become more critical in the context of a more differentiated public, 'communities of interest' have arguably begun to resemble a checklist of all those groups who have been previously excluded from, or marginalised by, '*the* community' of place (Cain and Yuval Davis, 1990). Struggles around identity and difference have therefore reflected a common experience of exclusion and 'othering' as much as of unity and inclusion. The growth of social movements largely outside of state-mediated democratic structures has offered new opportunities and challenges for community development – for example around issues of disability (Cameron, 2007); 'race' (Shukra, 2007 – Ch 4.8, this volume); the environment (Cannan, 1999) and women's organising (Dominelli, 1995). As Shukra (2007) (Ch 4.8, this volume) also highlights, identity politics has taken a rather disturbing turn. Sudden policy interest in 'community cohesion', following the 9/11 and 7/7 terrorist attacks, in New York and London respectively, may create an impression that the cultural identity of immigrants – specifically British Muslims – has been the main barrier to social integration, rather than systemic racism. On the other hand, experience of exclusion has always been instrumental in creating the kinds of solidarity which have enabled marginalised groups to challenge their exclusion and to participate in a more meaningful way.

It is ironic, but none the less true, that, despite the many achievements of New Labour, during their period of office inequalities substantially increased and the excluded have become ever more marginalised (Wilkinson and Pickett, 2009). At the same time those organisations, particularly the labour and trade union movement, that would traditionally have exposed and opposed this reality have themselves been marginalised. The so-called 'victory of capitalism', following the presumed demise of communism as a political system, has been comprehensively debunked by the collapse of the global financial system towards the end of the first decade of the 2000s, but there remains, as yet, no sign of an alternative political project to engage the popular imagination, although there has been a growth in social movement activity and the potential for widespread dissent.

It is clear that community development cannot be expected to take responsibility for resolving the social consequences of wider economic restructuring, address the failings of the banking system or offer a substitute in the absence of an alternative political project. There are, therefore, calls for a renewal of the value base of community development and a reassessment of the dilemmas of practice, given the current contingencies of policy and politics (Hoggett et al, 2008). There are also calls, echoing the analysis of the early 1980s, for a renewed focus on the role of the state as an ambivalent formation which needs to be struggled over rather than simply abandoned to the market (Taylor, 2007 – Ch 4.11, this volume). As ever, community work is essentially linked to political processes and the dynamics of social and political change. This means that continuous critique and analysis will be fundamental to its survival in a form which retains its historical potential for progressive social change.

<h1 style="text-align:center">4.1</h1>

Education, conflict and community development in Northern Ireland

Tom Lovett, Deirdre Gunn and Terry Robson

Introduction

People often think of the word "community" as synonymous with division and strife in Northern Ireland, as in 'the two communities', 'community conflict'. However, there is a positive side to community in this strife-torn region. Over the past twenty years, in urban and rural areas of the province suffering from the worst effects of violence, poverty and deprivation, countless men and women have been engaged in the process of community development. In the face of tremendous odds they have sought to find solutions to the numerous social and economic problems facing their communities. They have fought to participate in the many decisions affecting their daily lives, to build new community structures which would enable ordinary men and women to shape their own social and economic environment.(McNamee and Lovett 1992)

The issues we address here are the extent to which this community development process has provided a 'bridge' across the sectarian divide, the role of government in supporting, assisting and shaping community development in a divided society and the role of education in this process.

Community development in the 1970s

In the early years of the conflict in N. Ireland (the 1970s), when the violence reached a peak and the two communities were deeply divided, there was, in fact, a very energetic and enthusiastic community development movement which did succeed in crossing the sectarian divide. It was very much a 'bottom up' movement assisted by a whole series of events, some peculiar to N. Ireland, others common to western societies in general. (Lovett and Percival 1978)

From: Lovett, T., Gunn, D. and Robson, T. (1994) 'Education, conflict and community development in Northern Ireland', *Community Development Journal*, vol 29, no 2, pp 177-86.

In Northern Ireland there was the impact of massive redevelopment and regional economic policy, resulting in the destruction and dispersal of traditional working class communities (Protestant and Catholic) throughout the province. On top of this were the occasions when government authority seemed about to collapse and local community groups were left to their own devices, e.g., the 'no-go' areas, the internment crises of 1971, and the 1974 Ulster Workers strike. These situations presented enormous challenges to community groups. Many felt that the ordinary structures and services of government had broken down and that they had to assume some responsibility for filling the vacuum.

This movement threw up its own, articulate, leaders (mainly men), many of whom had been active in trade unions or labour politics. They were influenced by events outside Northern Ireland e.g. the civil rights movement, the student movement and the concepts and ideas made popular by radical thinkers like Illich and Freire and by what can only be described as a 'nondirective' approach to community development. (Gunn 1992)

The result was a movement with deep roots in the issues and problems facing Catholics and Protestants in their everyday lives. One Protestant community leader stated: 'The experience of the Greater West Belfast Community Association in the field of community action is at least harrowing and at worst a recipe for violence. Violence in this domain is neither the violence of materialism nor the counter-violence of fear. It is the violence of impotence'. (Lovett *et al.* 1983: 51) Another, Catholic, community leader stressed that it provided a bridge across the sectarian divide, emphasising the problems common to both communities. He hinted that these were as important as the 'National Question'. 'No matter what happens to the national question in the final analysis the community struggle goes on; the struggle against the hopelessness and helplessness of ordinary people to manage to cope in a complex society. We cannot separate politics from the community question'. *(Ibid*: 56)

Common to all those involved in this movement was the belief that radical changes were necessary to enable people to have a greater say in the decisions affecting their everyday lives. There was an emphasis on non–directive methods, participation, community control and a belief that this 'movement' could, somehow, provide a solution to the larger political divisions facing Catholics and Protestants in N. Ireland. (Gunn 1992)

It was, in many respects, a community 'action' as distinct from a community 'development' movement. There was an emphasis on direct action, on 'them and us', illustrated by campaigns against the authorities in both Catholic and Protestant communities. It was also concerned with creating alternative community structures, e.g., co-ops. In many senses it was thus part of a long working class tradition of collective action.

The role of government

The role of government in this whole process was contradictory. On the one hand, through the Community Relations Commission, it adopted a community development approach to community relations, i.e., suggesting that better community relations would come about when both communities had the confidence and experience to engage in dialogue. This would emerge as a result of involvement in community development. This view was strongly held by the first chairman and director.(NICRC 1971)

As a result the Council's community development officers provided a great deal of support and encouragement to the growing community movement. They often acted as the conduit that merged the expression of popular discontent and community action with the theories and practices of community development and radical education. However, the first short-lived power-sharing government in 1974 decided that the community movement was too radical, too likely to usurp the function of elected representatives. The result was the disbandment of the Community Relations Commission, an example of agency conflict with many parallels with American and British experience of government initiatives in community development. (Griffiths 1974)

The reaction of community groups was to press for their own support structures. A number of these were established, most short-lived, some surviving well into the 1980s. However, the movement reached a crisis point at the same time as the demise of the Commission. It was riven with contradictions which, in the end, weakened any impact it might have had on community divisions in Northern Ireland. These were:

i. the fear of a social 'movement' with explicit aims and objectives and clear leadership. Protestant activists were frightened of any possible connection between such a 'movement' and the Northern Ireland Civil Rights 'movement', regarded by many of their co-religionists as a republican front. There was also strong opposition to the idea of 'leading' such a movement and having clear social, economic and political objectives. This ran counter to the prevailing 'non-directive' community development ideology;

ii. conflict within the movement about the nature and purpose of community development. Workshops (Lovett et al. 1983) indicated that, despite the sense of a common movement amongst the participants, they held very different views about the role and purpose of community development vis-a-vis social change and government. At one extreme were those who saw their role as supporting state agencies, at the other extreme those who thought in terms of a radical oppositional movement. In between were a number of different approaches! As American experience has shown, the search for a common ideology amongst community activists produces such divisions. (Perlman 1980)

The end result was that the 'movement' split into its many component parts, some concentrating on local issues, others establishing support and resources for community development within a particular ideological or sectarian standpoint. A cross-community co-ordinating organisation was established (Community Organisations Northern Ireland), very much in the nondirective mould, but it was shortlived. A counter organisation, the Ulster Community Action Group, was also established as an umbrella organisation for Protestant groups. There is evidence that those involved in the latter had some influence on Protestant para-military thinking vis-a-vis a cross-community solution to the Northern Ireland problem. (Gunn 1992)

These developments made it relatively easy for the government to support community activity as a form of self-help and to co-opt leading members onto a Standing Advisory Council of Community Groups to oversee voluntary community work in the province. This was also a short-lived initiative. Community groups had little real influence and the government quickly passed responsibility over to local district councils, most of which were unsympathetic to community development.

The experience of community development in this period was a striking example of the British genius for taking the radical edge off radical community initiatives by creating forms of co-optative machinery, a process assisted by divisions amongst community groups. Thus many community groups, despite their involvement in conflict strategies with elements of the state, and managing their own communities in periods of crisis became, in effect, part of the state welfare system.

Community development in the 1980s and 1990s

Since the 1970s, major changes have occurred in the field of community development in Northern Ireland, some positive, some negative, but all set against a background of continuing violence and sectarianism. Some of these developments are unique to Northern Ireland, others are common throughout these islands. These are:-

i.   the growth of issue-based work, and the increasing involvement of the voluntary (as distinct from the community) sector, working on issues like crime, vandalism, drugs, homelessness. These large voluntary organisations are, with some exceptions, province-wide, as distinct from community-based organisations, with professional workers and the ethos which goes with the latter;

ii. major extension in the government's involvement in the local community through its Action for Community Employment scheme (ACE). This is a scheme to provide limited work experience for the unemployed. Because of its original emphasis on 'contribution to the Community', it was taken up by hundreds of community groups across the province. At the present moment there are over 10,000 employed under this scheme by a range of voluntary and community organisations;

iii. the emphasis on 'community' care and services by the Health and Social Services Boards and, like the voluntary sector, their involvement in the community, seeking partnerships with the latter to deliver such services;

iv. a realisation that community development has been very urban-oriented in theory and practice and the need to encourage community development in the empoverished rural areas of Northern Ireland. A Rural Development Council has recently been established by the government to work in this field; (Kilmurray 1989)

v.   the increasing role of women, and women's groups, in community development and community relations. This has been assisted by the tremendous changes in social values and attitudes in both communities, primarily, but not entirely, affecting women. However, despite their prominent role in community development and cross-community work, recent research confirms that women in Northern Ireland have not been able to translate this into the political arena; (Rooney 1992)

vi. the growing emphasis on community economic regeneration and the support available for such work from government, the European Community and the International Fund for Ireland (IFI). This again has produced strains between the desire of the funders for a community enterprise approach, encouraging local small businesses, as distinct from a more collective approach linking community development principles and practices to community regeneration; (Nicholls 1991)

vii. the establishment of a new Community Relations Council as a quasigovernment body to promote community relations in the province. This new Council, unlike its predecessor, does not take a community development approach. Instead the emphasis is very much on straightforward community relations work with a strong 'cultural' flavour, i.e., working with the two cultural traditions. However, there is a recognition that community development is a necessary, and major, foundation for community relations work. (Fitzduff 1991)

These changes have resulted in an enormous growth in the number and range of people involved in community development e.g. local activists, professional community development workers, civil servants, social workers, youth workers, community enterprise workers. They have also produced a more complex, widespread, and diffuse community development base where community development principles and processes are often neither understood nor practiced. (CDRG 1991)

This is all against a background where a number of significant events since the 1970s have created deep divisions between the two communities making contact between community groups very difficult and often dangerous.

The first major event was the Provisional Irish Republican Army's hunger strike in 1981 and the subsequent involvement of Sinn Fein (the IRA's political wing) in politics, with an emphasis on 'community politics'. This community politics was often nothing more than extension of advice work into local communities and an emphasis on local issues and problems. (Rolston 1984) However it did raise a fear in government circles of paramilitary involvement in, and control of, community groups in nationalist areas. It also increased fears in the Protestant community about such involvement. The other major event was the signing of the Anglo-Irish Agreement. This was greeted with total opposition from the Protestant community and the inevitable violence which followed brought community contact to a low ebb.

The end result of all these developments was that during the 1980s community development was, as a recent report confirms, in a 'hiatus'. (CDRG 1991) This is not entirely true. The number of people involved in community development grew, as indicated above, but they lacked any coherent, shared strategy and philosophy. Community development work was fragmented and increasingly co-opted by the state as a vehicle for alleviating unemployment or divesting itself of its responsibilities for community services and community care.

The ACE scheme in particular has, whilst assisting many community groups to resource and expand their work, set the agenda in terms of education and training. It has also increased the power of the churches in this field. The government views the latter as a safe alternative to the possible financing of terrorist involvement in community development. As a result, a number of community groups have had their funds withdrawn with no evidence offered of such involvement. (Robson 1992) This is the stick to complement the carrot.

The same can be said regarding the present emphasis on community economic regeneration. The province is dotted with such schemes, often generously supported by the IFI and Government Departments. However, the emphasis is very much on 'enterprise' and economic regeneration and not on community development. The end result is that they are often 'topdown' schemes with little community involvement and run by a combination of clergy and businessmen.

In many respects these schemes would appear to have effectively co-opted the community movement. They represent, in varying degrees, the apparent success of state hegemony over what appeared to be a counter-hegemonic force. However, as always, there is room within such 'hegemony' for community groups to devise their own agendas and to make use of the opportunities provided by increased financial support. There are, in fact, some positive developments which offer community development an opportunity to counteract this increasing co-option and to strengthen its independence. The major one is the increasing emphasis, from the European Community, on an integrated approach to community regeneration and on forming real partnerships between local people, voluntary organisations and government departments and agencies.

People in local communities have been well ahead of the EC and then local political representatives, in recognising the essential links between social, economic, health and environmental issues affecting their everyday lives. (Lovett 1992) They have campaigned for years for such co-ordination; for decentralisation and flexibility; for real participation in the decision-making process. They have had to struggle against the bureaucratic, uninformed and often irresponsive nature of government agencies and departments. That situation is slowly changing as large voluntary organisations, statutory bodies, government departments and agencies become, of necessity, involved in local community regeneration. However, as indicated above, those concerned have little or no knowledge of community development principles and practices. They often have their own, conflicting, agendas.

The role of education

The major problem today remains the need for resources to support the community development process; to give it coherence and to provide the necessary training and education. The Community Development Review in Northern Ireland has recommended the need for such resources whilst a recent report from the same body has stressed the need for a coherent and effective training and education programme to counteract the prevailing government ACE scheme. (CDRG 1992) Such training and education must recognise that community education and community development are two sides of the same coin, and an integral part of any effort to support community regeneration. The process of local development is also a process of education and training. Adult education is this context is geared to, or relevant to, the requirements of the overall development of the community, which integrates innovate learning into social, cultural and economic progress.

Some organisations, e.g., the Ulster People's College, have attempted to provide such education and training. It is one of the educational initiatives which arose out of the community movement of the 1970s and has managed to survive as an independent, popular community education centre. In co-operation with the Community Education Centre at the University of Ulster, it has attempted to bridge the sectarian divide emphasising that 'community' education is education *for* the community *about* the community.

Thus its work is concerned with the links between culture, community studies and community development. This is particularly important (though not exclusively so) for Protestant activists. They realise that community development is more prevalent in Catholic areas. In a recent report, on a conference on Protestants and Community Development, (O'Hadhmaill 1991) this imbalance is attributed to the closer relationship between Protestants and the state and a subsequent dependence on the latter which is not typical of Catholics. Of course, as the analysis outlined above indicates, the situation vis-à-vis Catholics and the state is much more complex. Nevertheless, except for the short period in the 1970s, when, as indicated above, Protestant leaders emerged from the labour and trade union movement, it is the case that community development is predominantly a Catholic activity. That same report suggested that, if Protestants were to be encouraged to become active, then it is necessary to start where people are, looking critically at their community and culture.

This sums up what the College is trying to do in all its educational work: an examination and exploration of people's communities in all their complexity in order to encourage the embracing of options which improve people's sense of identity, integrity, security and dignity. An emphasis on these manifestations of popular culture and politics from the base of Northern Irish society gives the People's College a specifically important function. (Lovett 1993)

It is important to note that the Ulster People's College arose out of a specific context. The explosion of community activity during the early part of the 'troubles' led, as suggested above, to the belief that there was an alternative to traditional politics which could transcend the sectarian divide. It was a growing awareness that this transcendence was an illusion which led the College's founders to establish a cross-community education centre in the province. Without an opportunity to explore precisely the issues that divide local communities it was felt that continuing antagonisms would prevent coherent and effective campaigns on all levels in relation to pressing issues affecting working class communities.

Conclusion

There was a time when the conflict in Northern Ireland was viewed as a purely Irish phenomenon. That is no longer the case. Ethnic and sectarian conflict are now regarded as major problems facing many European societies as they enter the last decade of the 20th century. Are there any lessons to be learnt from the experience of community development in Northern Ireland in terms of its contribution to the search for peace?

It is obvious for all the reasons outlined above that it has not been a major influence on events here. It has failed to translate its concerns and vision into a coherent social philosophy, or to influence the agenda in the political process. However, this is not simply because of the role of the state in this process, manipulating players for its own ends. Such an analysis ignores the ability of these players to use the system; the conflict *within* communities about the role and purpose of community development; the conflict *between* communities about the legitimacy of the state.

Nevertheless, community development has provided a bridge across the community divide. It has acted as a form of social cement preventing Northern Ireland from sliding into a Bosnian situation. Obviously, the ideals of the 1970s were over-ambitious in terms of the contribution of community development to a political solution. However, it has a role to play in easing conflict here, stressing its concern with equality, democracy and empowerment. That contribution may be assisted by the present emphasis in the European Community on the role of communities, and community development, in an integrated approach to urban and rural regeneration with such communities as real partners in the process.

But, if community development is to play a major role in such a 'partnership', then education and training have an essential part to play in encouraging that reflective process which will eventually empower people here to move beyond their own ditches into the political arena.

4.2

Models of community work

Keith Popple

Here, we analyse the models which constitute contemporary community work practice, to distinguish community work from other forms of intervention. An extensive review of the community work literature fails to provide an agreed number or the exact scope of different community work models. What has been developed here, includes the models most readily agreed upon: community care, community organization, community development, social/community planning, community education and community action, together with models developed from feminist community work theory and the black and anti-racist critique. These models have evolved often in an uncoordinated manner to address a particular difficulty or concern, or as the application of a particular theory or approach. Aspects of these models are not entirely discrete; there is a degree of overlap between them. The models are, however, an important method of categorizing central approaches to the activity we call 'community work'. They are ordered on a continuum from those concerned primarily with 'care' to those known for their emphasis on 'action'.

Community care

Community work, focused on the model of community care, attempts to cultivate social networks and voluntary services for the welfare of residents, particularly older people, persons with disabilities, and young children. This concentrates on developing self-help concepts to address social and welfare needs and uses paid workers who encourage people to care and to volunteer. Professional involvement in community care can be on one of three levels. At one level, professionals are expected to fulfil a more or less permanent supportive or monitoring role, using volunteers and low-paid helpers. A second level is where the activity is initiated by professionals who plan to be (briefly) supportive, so that community care can be continued withoutIthem.

From: Popple, K. (1995) 'Models of community work' in *Analysing community work: Its theory and practice*, Buckingham: Open University Press, pp 54-74.

A third level reflects community care as an activity undertaken by laypeople with relatively little help from professionals.

Community care policies have been criticized by social policy writers, pointing to the dominance of familist ideology, and its links with the wider ideology of possessive individualism. (Finch and Groves, 1985; Dalley 1988) Dalley argues that community care has been actively promoted by the Right for a number of reasons. These usually revolve around the need to avoid the expense of institutional care, but also because this form of care is perceived as the most 'appropriate' and 'natural' form of care for the dependent, a view derived from the residualist or anti-collectivist approach to welfare, whereby the family is seen as the locus of care, and the role of the statutory sector only comes into play when that unit has broken down in some way. The Barclay (1982), Griffiths (1988) and Wagner (1988) Reports developed the policy and practice of community care models, endorsing the early development of localizing social work services that had been taking place in some areas, while hastening the development of community-based social work in local authorities elsewhere. The intention throughout was for social services departments (SSDs) to deliver their services in the changing political, social and economic climate. (Hadley *et al.* 1987)

The community care model rapidly developed as a significant and relatively well-resourced form of community work which had clear connections with the ascendancy and influence of the New Right ideology of the same period. (Levitas 1986; Loney *et al.* 1991) However, since the 1960s, a number of social scientists have developed a critique of the failure of institutional care to provide people with humane treatment (Goffman 1961; Townsend 1962; Foucault 1967, 1977), while more recently the UK disability movement has stressed the desire of disabled people for independent living in mainstream housing rather than institutional care. (Morris 1990)

Community organization

Community work formulated on the community organization model has been used widely to improve co-ordination between different welfare agencies, helping to avoid duplication of services and poverty of resources while attempting to provide an efficient and effective delivery of welfare. Examples of community organizations are councils of voluntary service, older person's welfare committees, and 'similar organizations engaged in the coordination, promotion and development of the work of a number of bodies in a particular field at local, regional or national levels'. (Jones 1977: 6) The community organization service-orientated model has been engaged in pioneering work often leading to the state funding and managing services developed by such organizations.

Most critics of the community organization model underpin their arguments with theories from the radical and socialist approaches. Dearlove (1974) cites the role of community organizations in employing 'expert' professionals whose job it is to offer advice to working–class people in an attempt to stifle the anger felt in a particular community. The role of the 'expert' in this model is to channel these feelings into acceptable structures. The Community Development Projects (CDPs) were also critical of the community organization model, arguing that the Urban Deprivation Unit created by the Department of Environment in 1973 operated with managerialist methods, ignoring the concerns of people living in the communities they professed to serve. (CDP 1977) Feminists similarly criticized the community organization model (Dominelli 1990: 10), although there has been evidence of feminists developing new styles of community organization. (Adamson *et al.* 1988)

Community development

The community development model of community work is concerned with assisting groups to acquire skills and confidence to improve the quality of the lives of its members. With its emphasis on promoting self-help by means of education, this model is thought to reflect the 'uniqueness of community work'. (Twelvetrees 1991: 98) The community development model, championed in North America by Biddle and Biddle (1965), evolved in Britain from the work initiated by Batten (1957; 1967) deriving from his experiences when working in the colonies. This model of community work was used as a tool by British administrations overseas to manipulate local communities within colonial domination; a similar approach is taken in the United Nations statement on community development in developing countries. (UN, 1959: 1) This has been criticised by Ng (1988), who documents how the model was used in the colonies to integrate black people into subordinate positions within the dominant colonizing system.

The experience of community development in Britain has been characterized by work at the neighbourhood level, focusing upon a process whereby community groups are encouraged to articulate their needs. The expectation is that this will lead to collective action in the determination and meeting of these needs. The typical worker in this model has been described by Dominelli (1990: 11) as 'usually a man who helps people learn by working on problems they have identified. He is typically a paid professional interested in reforming the system through social engineering' although there are, of course, numerous examples of women being employed as community development workers.

In his analysis of Strathclyde Regional Council's programme of community development, Barr (1991) concludes that community development workers would be more effective if they laid more emphasis upon social planning approaches. This was a concept established by Rothman (1970), who placed community development alongside social planning and since developed by Twelvetrees (1991). He argues that, whereas community development is involved in working alongside a particular community (whether locality or community of interest), social planning involves the community worker 'liaising and working directly with policy-makers and service providers to improve services or alter policies'. In some typologies of community work, (Rothman 1970; Jones 1977; Thomas 1983; Twelvetrees 1991), social planning is considered to be a discrete model of community work.

Social/community planning

The social/community planning model of community work is considered to be similar to community development and has been described as

> the analysis of social conditions, social policies and agency services; the setting of goals and priorities; the design of service programmes and the mobilisation of appropriate resources; and the implementation and evaluation of services and programmes. (Thomas 1983: 109)

This model is believed to be the most common of community work models. However, as Twelvetrees (1991) points out, this is complicated by the breadth of the term, which can include economic planning and national planning. This means that although most community workers are engaged in social/community planning, not all those involved in this activity can be termed 'community workers'.

One of the advocates of social/community planning, which he calls simply 'community planning', is Marris (1987), arguing that it should be possible to incorporate the demand for open, democratic planning into political struggles for social justice. Marris believes that the failure of the CDPs was due in part to their classical Marxist analysis of class relations which failed to recognize the subtle, complex and changing nature of working-class communities. He also believes that this focus on class antagonism led to an inability to work within the state to achieve improvements for the people who lived in the neighbourhoods the projects were intended to assist. Marris argued that if community work is to effect anything more than marginal change it needs to find common ground with the government even if the ideologies of the two are at variance. Marris suggests that social/community planning is one strategy that can be used to help protect working-class communities from the uncertainty and lack of control they suffer when redevelopment takes place in their locality.

The main criticism that can be levelled at this view is that it assumes that the knowledge gained by community workers will be used by decision-makers in a rational manner for the benefit of members of the community. Evidence from Marris is not convincing. He cites the redevelopment of London's Docklands and the evolution of the Docklands Strategic Plan which attempted to involve and take account of the people living in the affected area. He later admits, however, that the plan actually had little effect because

> plans are so often ignored, whenever they attempt to set priorities ... in the interests of the most vulnerable, or constrain the freedom of action of those more powerful so as to reach some resolution which is both fair and practicable, [so that] planning even at its best often comes to seem merely a distraction from more effective forms of political protest, and so co-optive. (Marris 1987: 160)

However, Marris continues to believe in the potential of the social/community planning model because political struggle without it leads only to 'competitive bargaining between different kinds of interests, and that cannot protect the weaker and more vulnerable members of society.' (*Ibid*)

Community education

The community education model of community work has been described as 'a significant attempt to redirect educational policy and practice in ways which bring education and community into a closer and more equal relationship.' (Allen *et al.* 1987: 2) Community education has a long tradition in the UK which has evolved from three main strands. (Martin 1987) The first is the school-based village and community college movement initiated by Henry Morris in Cambridgeshire during the late 1920s, (Morris 1925) followed by the establishment of similar integrated educational provision in Leicestershire under the guidance of Mason during the following decade. (Fairbairn 1979) The second strand comprised the experiments developing from the Educational Priority Area projects (1969-72) which attempted to provide 'compensatory education' in selected disadvantaged inner-city areas as recommended by DES (1967). (Halsey 1972; Midwinter 1972) The third strand was working-class adult education work undertaken by a number of the CDPs in the early 1970s. (Lovett et al. 1983)

Community education has been further analysed as having three 'qualitatively different ideologies': consensus, pluralism, and conflict. (Martin 1987: 22) Martin argues that the consensus or universal model is focused around the secondary school/community college; the pluralist or reformist model is linked to primary schools and their neighbourhoods; and the conflict or radical model is focused around working-class action. To this can be added the feminist analysis of community education articulated by Rogers. (1994) The conflict or radical model shares with community development an emphasis on innovative, informal, political education, and has been greatly influenced by the Brazilian adult educator, Paulo Freire, whose work has served as a significant challenge to school-based education.

In its place Freire developed an 'education for liberation' where learners and teachers engage in a process in which abstract and concrete knowledge, together with experience, are integrated into praxis (which can be defined as action intended to alter the material and social world). The fundamental features of this praxis are critical thinking and dialogue (as opposed to discussion) which seek to challenge conventional explanations of everyday life, whilst at the same time considering action necessary for the transformation of oppressive conditions.

Community action

The community action model of community work was both a reaction to more paternalistic forms of community work and a response by relatively powerless groups to increase their effectiveness. The CDPs were initiated as a government-supported community work venture based upon the community organization and community development models. Soon after their commencement this direction changed, with the Projects evolving on the lines of the community action model.

The community action model of community work has traditionally been class-based and uses conflict and direct action, usually at local level, in order to negotiate with power holders over what is often a single issue. Early writings on community action by, among others, Lapping (1970) and Leonard (1975), together with the influential books published by Routledge in conjunction with the Association of Community Workers (ACW) (Jones and Mayo 1975; Mayo 1977; Curno 1978; Craig et al. 1979, 1982; Smith and Jones 1981; Ohri et al. 1982), and other significant writings (Cockburn 1977; Cowley et al. 1977; O'Malley 1977; Curno et al. 1982; Lees and Mayo 1984) provide a rich source for the practice and debates surrounding the model up to the early 1980s, as does some of the North American community work literature (Alinsky 1969, 1971; Piven and Cloward 1977; Lamoureux et al. 1989).

An important strand of community action has been that linked with trade union activity. (Corkey and Craig 1978; Craig et al. 1979) This has often been a direct result of the work of the CDPs in a particular locality. Examples of the projects that arose from such an intervention include the Coventry Workshop, the Tyneside Trade Union Studies Unit, and the Joint Docklands Action Group. This type of action was further developed in the 1980s/90s by municipal socialism, based on a broad political group described as the 'new urban left'. Towards the end of the existence of the Greater London Council there were a plethora of supported community projects. However, Goodwin and Duncan (1986) argue that such policies are most effective in terms of political mobilization and that policy-makers on the left should be aware of the limitations of policies promising large-scale job creation and local economic regeneration. With rising unemployment, the problems faced by people without employment became a concern during the early 1980s and have continued to be so to the present day, whilst the development of co-operatives has also been an important theme. (Roof, 1986)

The role of the community worker in the community action model is an interesting one and highlights the tension within the state towards community work. Much of the literature notes that the majority of community work is sponsored by the state which, through its agencies, will define and regulate the work of practitioners. However, community action, by its very nature, is often engaged in conflict with the employers of community workers, the local authorities. A wider debate on the contradictions surrounding this position is addressed in *In and Against the State*. (LEWRG 1980) It is for this reason that community action is usually seen as an area of practice undertaken by campaigners and activists not employed, directly or indirectly, by the state. Thomas argues that one cannot conflate the role of community worker with that of community activist. They are, in his view, different, and clearly reflect his own adherence to the pluralist approach and practice theories.

Feminist community work

Feminist community work theory evolved from the development, since the 1960s, of feminist theory. Female community workers have applied these theoretical understandings to practice (Dixon *et al.* 1982), both in feminist campaigns and in permeating existing community work practice and principles. (Dominelli and McLeod 1989) While there is no agreed single theoretical feminist position, there is a consensus that the central aim of feminist community work practice is the improvement of women's welfare by collectively challenging the social determinants of women's inequality. Although much practice is focused at the personal, local or neighbourhood level, it is linked practically and theoretically with wider feminist concerns. For example, women have been active in many localities in providing accommodation, usually in the form of emergency housing, for battered women. This securing of safe accommodation is a response to the immediate suffering experienced by individual women at the hands of violent men, to the inadequate provision made by the state for such women, as well as presenting a stand against male violence. (Wilson 1977; Pahl, 1985a)

The use of women-only groups, whether in specialist consciousness raising or in more general ways, is a central feature of feminist community work. Among its advocates, Hanmer and Statham argue that the quality of the group process is likely to be improved in a single-sex group, because the intimate and interpersonal problems are likely to be confronted more quickly. The authors claim that the realization that their problems are not unique should help to reduce women's feelings of personal inadequacy, and thus start to alleviate isolation and stigmatization. Similarly, research has shown that men take over and influence community groups by controlling the 'introduction and pursuit of topics, the use of available time, the lack of emotional content in conversation'. (Hanmer and Statham 1988: 131) This is confirmed by Gallacher (1977), who notes that men hold key positions in community associations.

Feminist community workers have engaged in a variety of creative attempts to develop non-hierarchical structures and more participatory ways of working. Criticisms of traditional forms of organization as being alienating and inaccessible initially resulted in attempts to develop structureless groups. However, there is a recognition that it is 'a mistake to equate structure with hierarchy'. (Freeman 1984: 62) This has led Barker to argue that 'the quest for a structure which is genuinely participatory, which does not alienate people, and yet achieves the goals which the group has set itself must be central to feminist practice within the women's movement and in community work'. (Barker 1986: 87) Process models in group work have been of concern to feminist community workers who indicate that they can function to exclude and to intimidate group members. Process models are concerned with both the different stages a group moves through (for instance reflection, planning and action) and the development individual group members achieve. Previously, the importance of process has been overlooked by radical community work because of the dominance of the former model. Dixon et al. (1982: 63) argue, for instance, that this non-political approach was reflected in the writings of early theorists such as Batten. However, as they go on to state, 'Feminist analysis shows clearly that process is political, and needs urgent consideration if our campaigns are to achieve their aims'.

The concern with regard to feminist community work is that the flow of written work in this area has been reduced to a trickle. The lack of recent feminist community work literature is commented upon by Dominelli (1990: 8), who highlights the fact that two of the main exponents of community work literature, Thomas and Twelvetrees, have 'virtually ignored the implications of gender'. Similarly, more radical texts appear to have included little on gender. (Brandwein 1987; Lee and Weeks 1991) When one considers the role women play in community work, whether as activists as described by Campbell (1993), or in administering a community work project as discussed by Brandwein, it is clear that women have played a highly significant part in the practice. Dominelli (1990: 122) argues that women's contribution to community work has been undervalued. For instance, while there are texts that track the campaign work women have been engaged in (Mayo 1977; Curno *et al.* 1982), the perception of women themselves has rarely been considered. The paucity of literature in this field indicates the need for further research and dissemination of results.

Black and anti-racist community work

Traditional forms of community work have failed both to meet the particular needs of the Black community and to challenge institutional and personal racism. Here we examine the response to this by the Black community and those community workers who are engaged in developing an anti-racist critique. Historically there is evidence that the Black community has not passively accepted racism and racist policy and practice. Since their arrival in Britain, Black people have been active in their communities, supporting each other and organizing to resist discrimination and defend their rights. (Bhat *et al.* 1988; Solomos 1989) The focus of discrimination has varied, although frequently it has appeared as if Black people have been and continue to be besieged in a number of areas including education, housing, immigration, health, employment, and police relations. Similarly, a range of different and overlapping responses has developed: campaigns; self-help groups; direct action; alternative and supplementary provision. At times these have required coalitions to be built and alliances forged, at others autonomous organization has been preferred. Unfortunately, few studies have been made of these community-based organizations and campaigns. At the time of writing, a detailed survey of the nature of Black voluntary groups, their activities, sources and level of funding, composition and organization, is being undertaken by the National Council for Voluntary Organisations. Those studies that have been made tend to be limited in their scope. (Solomos 1989: 149) There is also evidence of Black people being excluded from mainstream political life in Britain, leading to migrants launching a number of local and national groupings including the Indian Workers' Association and the West Indian Standing Conference. (Carter 1986; Jacobs 1986) Anwar (1986) argues that racial disadvantage and discrimination will only be solved when Black people are included in the political process and in British public life.

The establishment of community projects by the Black population is often a response to exclusion from white-dominated provision as well as providing opportunities to develop and strengthen cultural, social and political ties. Although Black people do not form a homogeneous group within Britain, they share with each other the experience of racism and of colonization which, as noted earlier, has given them certain strengths and perspectives. Community work projects funded by the Commission for Racial Equality and Racial Equality Councils have, however, met with criticism from two different sources. One argues that public funds should be given to projects that are for the whole community and not one particular group. This argument fails, however, to recognize structural racism, which leads to Black people being excluded from mainstream organizations and the need for them to have separate provision. The other source of criticism has come from Black radicals such as Sivanandan (1976; 1990), who believe that such projects dissolve and co-opt Black protest. Within white-dominated community work, the activity has only gradually addressed the issue of racism and it is felt in a number of quarters this has only been partial. (Ohri *et al.* 1982; Dominelli 1990) According to Loney, the central issue that needs to be addressed by white community workers is the continuing failure of institutions to provide equal treatment of Black people while recognizing the specific needs of ethnic minorities. (Loney 1983: 54)

On a wider level, since the passing of the 1948 British Nationality Act, and up to and since the 1988 Immigration Act, 'race' and immigration have been central issues in British political life. During the early 1980s, a number of mainly Labour-controlled local authorities attempted to operate and implement racial equality policies and practices. In at least one study these were to prove that the local political scene was an important site of struggle, particularly for local organizations committed to racial equality. (Ben-Tovim *et al.* 1986) The abolition of the Greater London Council in 1986 was believed to have serious implications for Black residents of the capital since it left no city-wide commitment to support the Black community and no agreement to tackle racism. There has been some criticism by Black writers that well-intentioned white people incorporated the Black struggle into the local authority anti-racist strategies of this period. (Bhavnani 1986; Gilroy 1987) These writers and others (Mullard 1984; Troyna and Carrington 1990) criticize multi-cultural education strategies which emphasize cultural pluralism and equality in a setting of economic and social inequality. With these limitations recognized, it is important not to overlook the contribution from white anti-racists in community work to the struggle for equal opportunities and for the provision of more resources for the Black community, and in 'confront[ing] racism, sexism and other forms of discrimination both within ourselves and within society'. (ACW 1982)

Finally, Ohri *et al.* (1982) argue that the primary issue for the Black community and the one which community work must address if it is to remain relevant to the needs and concerns of Black people, is resistance to racism.

Conclusion

In conclusion, we can see that although there is overlap between the models discussed, particularly in terms of techniques and skills, the models reflect different traditions and ideologies. Community care, community organization, community development and social/community planning represent the pluralist tradition in community work. The community action model and the emerging models from feminism and the Black and anti-racist critique reflect a radical and socialist approach. Different aspects of community education fit into different approaches. The radical strand of the model is epitomized in the work of Freire and of Lovett. The work of school-based community education, including the compensatory education programmes, is, however, an example of the pluralist approach. Certain models, for instance community care and social/ community planning, are centred upon the premise of delivering a service in a more efficient and often cost-effective manner. Other models, such as those from the radical and socialist approaches, are focused around certain ideological positions and commitments. Together with the remaining models the above offers us a framework in which to understand community work practice.

4.3

Community development at the crossroads: a way forward

Chris Miller and Yusuf Ahmad

Introduction

Until recently, community development, as an occupational activity, was confined to a relatively marginal, fragmented, but often irritatingly radical group of workers. For some 20 years (1968-87) there existed a degree of connectedness between those employed as community workers and those seeking social transformation via political action in civil society. Today, as part of a restructuring of welfare provision, community development, underpinned by such concepts as empowerment and partnership, is being 'talked-up' as a respectable, indeed essential, process and mechanism for social integration and the delivery of public services. Instead of being the sole province of a struggling and insecure occupation, community development has become one of the cornerstones of social welfare intervention strategies. It is to be incorporated into the working practices of a wide range of health and welfare professionals, and its values are to permeate the organisations of public welfare. This appears to be almost a universal trend as global agencies of economic and social development, such as the World Bank and the United Nations (UN), adopt at least the language of what was a radical tradition.

Whilst the virtues of community development have been central to the policy debates, this has not always been matched by significant shifts in the process of policy implementation. Although community development, which remains a contested activity, is being promoted as a central mechanism for social legitimation, opportunities still exist to go beyond the goals of social cohesion in what remains a highly unequal world. Whilst this article is directed at all those concerned with community development, it is especially concerned with those who have been drawn to it for its emancipatory potential.

From: Miller, C. and Ahmed, Y. (1997) 'Community development at the crossroads', *Policy & Politics*, vol 25, no 3, pp 269-84.

Community development at the crossroads

Butcher suggests three distinct levels of analysis to explain the adaptation or incorporation of what was once a marginal and sometimes radical policy alternative, into the mainstream of policy-making and delivery. First, he argues that the community development approach can be adopted if it has the potential to solve pressing problems. It thus arises as a short -term response to the, policy-makers' needs to find workable alternatives to existing patterns of decision-making, provision and practices.' (1993: 56) A second approach explains it in terms of state responses to a series of crises confronting it since the mid-1970s, induding 'performance', 'legitimation' and 'fiscal'. Finally, a third level of analysis, which allows us to reflect more generally on the overall context, points to wider changes in economy and society referred to variously as reflecting a shift from modernity to post-modernity, from Fordism to post-Fordism, characterised by an emphasis on the recognition of societal pluralism and diversity, flexible labour markets, specialised production and new modes of regulation.

If Fordism is viewed as a mode of regulation (Stoker 1989), then the welfare state in general, and the local state in particular, has played a central role. At a structural level it provided both the mechanisms of regulating and planning economic growth, as well as providing institutions for managing an expanding range of welfare services. At a strategic level, the local state was the key site where political consensus was both constructed and experienced. However, as capitalism attempts to create new forms of production, so the forms of regulation also need to change and a new regime is required, 'with appropriate institutional forms, social relations and balance of social forces within the power bloc and among the people.' (Jessop 1986) This involves the creation of a new historic bloc, a new set of social relationships between state, economy and civil society. Conservative governments since 1979, it is argued, have attempted to create just such a new formation. New social institutions and relations are needed that legitimise the new production regime, create new and lower expectations about what the state can deliver, and attempt to anticipate and control potential social unrest. With growing social polarisation, community development is seen as an effective mechanism to ensure local populations are not totally excluded from social life. The rhetoric of community development, with empowerment and partnership as central organising principles, has thus been harnessed at least at the symbolic level to both facilitate these organisational changes, and to provide legitimacy to emergent forms of the local state.

Some have viewed such societal changes more positively as ushering in their wake new thinking about the structure and purpose of government at both central and local levels. (Bums et al. 1994) The new paradigm is seen as providing possibilities for decentralisation and greater responsiveness to local conditions and needs, the devolution of policy-making and extension of local democracy, as well as the means by which the local state can effectively regulate the delivery of services, the production over which it now has very little control. The current emphasis on plurality and diversity, can, it is argued, lead to more effective responses to differential need, an aspect neglected by the traditional welfare state. Thus, attempts by community development progressives to develop an emancipatory practice have coincided with, or been facilitated by, other demands on the state, which as Cochrane (1994) suggests, could facilitate the growth of a more challenging politics, releasing users from their status as supplicants.

Structure and agency: the role of practitioners

All three of Butcher's explanations have something to offer, but ignore a fourth dimension: the active role of occupational networks in furthering their own interests. Irrespective of why community development might now be seen as an effective welfare strategy, the need to credentialise and professionalise the practice has been central to the process. Its leading advocates from academia, policy-making and professional practice have progressively moved closer as a policy network. (Rhodes 1981) This occupational sub-group not only provides a coherent and influential voice, but has often been strategically placed to shape both policy formulation and implementation. Additionally, some of those involved have retained values and interests that are opposed to the dominant approaches within the state. (Gyford 1985; Lansley *et al.* 1989). For this group of professionalised intellectuals, the promotion of community development has been conducted in a variety of situations as their careers have taken them across different sectors, employers, roles and functions. For some this has meant moving from very localised grassroots work to city-wide, regional or national activity, into more direct policy-making roles, often operating from within key strategic positions within local and central government, and then perhaps to academic roles. The latter have been either research-oriented or teaching, linked directly to a training responsibility for community development, or located within the broader fields of social and urban policy. Additionally, the theoretical discourse about community development in academic publications, professional bodies and policy statements, has been produced by those with a stake in the advancement of its practice. Such horizontal mobility between roles and agencies, whilst making for a lively interchange between theory and practice, can result in confusion between prescriptive viewpoints on community development and a more detached analysis of its meanings, practice and outcomes. The need for such detachment is particularly important given that much of its work has been state-sponsored.

Unlike its counterpart, social work, the professionalisation of community development has been slow to emerge. From the late-1960s, state-employed workers appeared in growing numbers via the expanding Urban Programme and social services departments. Nevertheless, the primary employment base, supported by a significant amount of unpaid input, remained solidly within the non-profit sector. Such paid and unpaid employment within civil society has left a further legacy for the growth of the occupation in that a significant number of those entering the field did so from a critical perspective. Indeed, a neo-Marxist analysis has been central in the development of research and theoretical literature. Moreover, Bryant (cited Miller and Bryant 1990) reminds us that, for a period, community development contained a 'healthy anti-professional' approach. This meant that the potential and desire for local activists to gain, or retain, control of local organisations, and indeed the whole community development process, was a cherished value. Paid workers would declare that their intention was to work themselves out of a job: their effectiveness could ultimately be judged by their own unemployment.

Although the non-profit sector was increasingly dependent upon state funding, their attachments to state policies continued to be fairly loose and did not prevent many such agencies adopting a critical stance towards their own paymasters. Indeed, the local state was often the primary focus against which community organisations would mobilise. This process was no doubt made more possible by inadequate systems for monitoring and evaluating as well as the relatively poor levels of communication and strategic planning within and between state agencies. Bryant reminds us that the core values within community development, of participation, democracy, and working for change, do not belong exclusively to any one occupational group, and that a key task has always been building alliances with other like-minded groups. Such a perspective enabled community development to resist the temptations of professionalisation and credentialism and, indeed, these remain contested arenas amongst practitioners.

Many of the current influential spokespeople within the occupation either entered, or progressed within, metropolitan local government during the early 1980s, at a time of conflict between local and central government. They had developed their theoretical base and practical skills during the preceding decade, working in the third sector, state-managed projects (especially the ill-fated Community Development Projects), or as part of the general expansion of practitioners within local government. With this experience behind them and committed to a progressive approach, they secured strategic managerial positions, often in areas of corporate decision making, or took up the role of elected representative. They were thus able to play an active part within local policy-making at a time when a number of key Labour-controlled 'new urban left' authorities (Gyford 1985) were rediscovering their political, as opposed to their administrative, role via new initiatives in decentralisation, equal opportunities and local economic development.

Community development quickly became adopted as both the practical and theoretical springboard from which to launch such initiatives in developing new organisational structures, providing more effective consumer-oriented services, inter-agency and local partnership arrangements, and building new consultative and democratic structures. Thus the fluid language of community development continued to provide an opportunity to defend or preserve what were identified as best practices and to promote progressive policies, as well as offering a mechanism to reduce costs or engage with local and influential agencies to facilitate the shift to a mixed economy of welfare.

Community development as the new vision

The AMA (1989) developed one of the first policy responses, since the Labour Party's defeat in the 1987 general election, for those local authorities hopeful of building an oppositional base to central government. Community development is explicitly located within the context of a critique of bureaucratic paternalism, the deepening financial crisis, and the ideological and material victories of the new Right. It is made clear that there is to be no return to the old and discredited ways of local government, that indeed government has to be 'reinvented'. The need for change is identified in relation to service provision, workforce practices and relationships with service users and local citizens. This is both an attempt to recapture some of the initiative, lost to the new Right, and a statement of what some progressives now think is possible. They seek both to defend and protect local government services, and the principle of collective provision, and to promote a new role for the local state in meeting social needs. The intention is to maximise any opportunities there might be within the restructured, and admittedly, hostile environment.

Yet what is significant, compared with strategies of a decade earlier, is what is missing. The most notable absence is the possibility of radical transformation of the social, political and economic structures. Similarly, little mention is given to other key players in the urban left strategy, such as the public service trade unions, new social movements, and the broad range of non-welfare oriented groups within civil society. (Lansley *et al.* 1989) It appears too, that a number of the lessons of earlier initiatives are also ignored (Green and Chapman 1992) as is any reference to alliances and joint action across local authorities, or the need for national political leadership from within the Labour Party, the absence of which seriously undermined the urban left project. (Miller 1996) The focus is again on the most disadvantaged or marginalised, a strategy of 'last resort for poor communities' (MacArthur 1993), and ignoring the view that the connections between the poor and the non-poor have to be made, as do the relationships between spatially disadvantaged neighbourhoods and patterns and opportunities in the wider economy. (Donnison 1993) At best then it is only a partial strategy but may also reflect the growing overlap between advancing the market position of community development professionals, via further credentialism, and the pursuit of radical political objectives through state employment or sponsorship.

We do not suggest that community development has no role to play in addressing issues such as poverty and disadvantage. Indeed, one can agree with the AMA view that it can 'form an effective element in any local authority's anti-poverty and equal opportunities strategies'. (AMA 1993: 11) Others, such as Cochrane (1986) have also argued convincingly that community politics has already posed a significant challenge from below to the managers of the urban system, and that some credit for the support of such politics must go to community development programmes. Fordham (1993), focusing on the concerns of effective policy implementation, suggests that local programmes help ensure that major services reach the parts that would otherwise not be reached. Others (MacArthur 1993) have been able to offer a sound checklist for good practice in relation to welfare policy formulation, implementation and evaluation as it relates both to poverty and disadvantage and, indeed, across the complete spectrum of health, social welfare and economic regeneration. Yet, given the impact of new Right policies and increasing societal polarisation, community development strategies of the kind outlined, can also lead to the incorporation of community organisations, as they become increasingly service-oriented, bound by contracts and short-term funding. Such pressures almost inevitably lead to an internal restructuring within community organisations themselves. This usually includes a growth in managerialism, the extension of professionalisation, a decline in risk-taking for fear of losing valuable funding, and an altogether more respectable organisational persona.

What future for community development

We have argued that within the policy debates, community development has assumed a significant role in the effective delivery of a new model of welfare. However, the implementation of such proposals has been somewhat more problematic and uneven, not least as a consequence of resource shortages and a lack of understanding about how to proceed. Indeed, the trends are contradictory; for example, as Labour talks of decentralisation and community development it increasingly adopts a centralised approach to decision- making. Community development is at a crossroads and we suggest four specific areas where we believe it can progress. First, we suggest there is a need to refocus on individual learning, and how individuals might respond to or initiate a process of social change in an increasingly complex environment. Second, we endorse the AMA's central theme of the introduction of a community development strategy and approach within all aspects of public provision. The third concerns the democratisation of social and political life, with a specific focus on strengthening the civil rights and status of particular social groups. Finally, we argue for the development of public spaces that are outside and independent of the state.

Change and the individual

Our starting point is that of the individual. With the exception of some feminist writers (Barker 1986; Dominelli 1995; Hanmer and Rose 1980), radicals within community development have given a low priority to a focus that prioritises individuals, their needs, and capacities for identifying and pursuing the possibilities for change. (Thomas 1983; Waddington 1983) Such concerns are said to belong to other helping occupations – social work, advice and advocacy, counselling or care. Indeed to prioritise individual needs, rather than those of collectivities, would mean locating oneself within a conservative and largely discredited model of change, that fails to address the structural causes of people's circumstances. Moreover, it might suggest that community development was colluding with a process of deception, that implied it was the absence of social skills, knowledge, and personal qualities that lay at the root of personal and social problems, ensuring that people remained in their subordinate positions.

However, it is increasingly evident that social divisions have widened, with long-term economic security a reality for only a minority. In a globalising economy it is not uncommon to feel powerless to influence key decisions that fundamentally effect our current and future lives. Those public services that can effectively respond to social needs continue to decline. In such circumstances, the burden of ensuring a reasonable level of physical and psychological survival for self and others close to oneself, can often be achieved only at a considerable individual price. Consequently, there is much that needs to be done to enable people to regain or experience some sense of self-confidence and self-worth. In this context, those strategies should not be under-valued that explicitly provide for personal attention and affirmation, offering a sense of achievement gained from meeting specific and concrete, albeit limited, goals. These should be developed along with opportunities to share experiences, concerns and understandings, to ask questions, to challenge and be challenged, to provide and receive mutual support. Such strategies, aimed at developing personal capacities and sense of self, can clearly be achieved indirectly, as a by-product of some other developmental or concrete activity, and indeed this has been the position most often adopted within community development. However, we would retain as a core value that one must begin with people's immediate and current concerns, knowledge and understanding.

Community development as a process for welfare intervention

Next, we endorse the position adopted by the AMA that community development workers need to demonstrate the value of their approach in other areas of social welfare, and indeed to the very organisation of regional and local government. There is increasing recognition that effective services are those where there is some consent between service users and providers about the nature of the problem, the role of the state in tackling the issue, and the identification of appropriate strategic responses. Moreover, ongoing and appropriate opportunities for feedback and dialogue are required, over the implementation and evaluation of chosen policies, with evidence that this is valued and acted upon. (European Foundation 1995) This is reflected in the sometimes rhetorical emphasis that is given to concepts and working practices such as partnership, participation, 'consumer-driven' and 'community-focused'. These now appear across a range of welfare interventions, in areas such as urban policy and economic regeneration, community care, social work and community health.

All of this should be fully exploited by community development practitioners. Similarly, the growing calls for inter-professional and inter-agency work across traditional welfare boundaries requires the very organisational skills that community development has acquired, if this is to go much beyond a mere exchange of information.

Progressive community development has long been critical of both the overall Fabian welfare paradigm and of specific approaches adopted by different welfare occupations in response to immediate circumstances. Equally, it has been convinced that the values and methods it embodies are more likely to yield effective policy outcomes. Community development offers the possibility of a transformation of the user – provider transaction. It acknowledges conflict and competing interests amongst different stakeholders, and attempts to ensure that there are democratic structures in place in order to resolve these. Similarly, it has emphasised a needs-led service, one that discovers and respond to unmet needs and draws in the non-service user to wider welfare debates, as well as reflecting upon current provision, and advocates on behalf of user and non-user alike. In relation to colleagues, community development promotes working relations that are problem-solving, emphasises teamwork, are inter-professional and seek collective solutions. Community development workers can demonstrate their effectiveness and justifiably argue for the adoption of such values and methods across a range of welfare work.

However, such an approach is likely to meet with considerable resistance from within the occupation. Despite what was argued earlier about the influence of a small group of professionalised intellectuals, frontline community development workers have tended to view themselves as separate from, and indeed marginal to, other welfare occupations. Similarly, their roles have been seen as involving processes and objectives distinct from other interventions. Community development has not freed itself entirely from practices constructed around a critique of local public service provision and the consequent emphasis given to enabling local groups to campaign against the local state, or develop their own service provision in response to the perceived failings of state services. Thus, workers often display what is at best an ambivalent attitude towards the concept of professionalism and to other professions. This can be understood as reflecting their commitment to both the promotion of bottom-up strategies for social change, and a desire to acknowledge and value that experience, knowledge and skills, and ways of acquiring these, usually dismissed by other professionals. However, it can also have the effect that community development workers undervalue themselves and feel less confident and assertive in relation to their welfare colleagues, more comfortable with the traditionally superior mask of professionalism.

Explanations for this are complex but no doubt relate to the occupation's structural position within organisations, the social origins of those involved, and the commitment to a particular set of values. Thus, most community workers find themselves physically isolated from other colleagues, literally on the agency's margins, disconnected from mainstream practices and policy-making. They are often working against rather than with other welfare professionals, more closely identified with service users.. Even the professionalised intellectuals remain largely scattered and need actively to create opportunities to express their interests. The social background of many of those recruited into the occupation has militated against the assumption of an assertive position. Although this has been undergoing some profound changes a significant proportion of those engaged in frontline work remain and will continue to be solidly in a community activist or volunteering background. Finally, the occupation has been influenced by an ideological position that is both suspicious of professionalism as an occupational strategy, concerned that the price of adopting the symbolic signs of being a professional is to lose touch either with one's personal roots or with the lives of those with whom one is working.

The extension of democracy

In addition to working to improve the quality of public service provision, a third key area is to engage in the bigger task of extending democratic processes. A number of authorities during the 1980s acknowledged the need to once again promote local government as the focus of local democracy, and community development was seen as a key method to facilitate and develop the process. (Burns *et al.* 1994; Miller 1996) However, by the end of the decade such initiatives were either struggling to maintain their momentum or had been curtailed. Yet the need to strengthen both the representative and direct democratic processes at local level has not diminished. Indeed, there is even greater urgency to pursue this given the increased centralisation and marketisation of social welfare.

The shift in the local authority role from service provider to service enabler and the growth of the mixed economy in welfare provision has recently led some writers to refer to a switch from local government to local governance. In this context, community development has a role at a variety of levels. Perhaps the area which is most familiar is in supporting local organisations to develop and maintain appropriate management structures that are both accountable to their membership and able to represent their interests to external organisations. Similarly, there is a need to initiate and strengthen user-management structures, along with geographic and interest-based networks. Finally, there is an urgent need to develop, and experiment with, a variety of consultative and decision-making mechanisms to ensure that the state sector, including quangoes, along with private and non-profit sector service-providing agencies are more transparently accountable and able to communicate effectively. Community development workers have relevant, if under-used, skills and knowledge in these areas. They should learn to promote these and exploit those opportunities that emerge in the shifting climate.

The repoliticisation of public life

Although community development has an important role to play in ensuring more effective service provision and enabling local government to become more accountable, perhaps the real challenge, in sharp contrast to the current emphasis on consumer feedback, is the extent to which it can play a role in the repoliticisation of public life within civil society. There is a growing need for the creation of public fora at local, city and regional level where the focus is on both the politics of everyday life and the management and organisation of the social world, rather than the important but more restricted concern with the politics of welfarism. Opportunities for creative public debate need to be reopened to ensure vigorous engagement in public life. Without embarking on this wider agenda there is a danger that the current revival of interest in community development will result in it losing any links it had previously with local politics and being transformed into being the primary strategy for managing Britain's decline. (Cochrane 1994) Yet whilst the possibilities remain for the incorporation of progressive movements, community development could offer some hope that new avenues can be opened up to enable different interests and commonalities to be articulated.

Similarly, community development needs to re-examine its focus on the most disadvantaged. This has fallen too easily into an agenda for highlighting and isolating the disadvantaged and marginalised, as being in need of social management. It is an approach that has generated major conflicts and disunity, based upon the creation of artificial hierarchies of disadvantage, within community development itself, and amongst more progressive political forces. Again, it must be acknowledged that whilst the local neighbourhood, or other communities of interest and attachment (Willmott 1986) continue to be significant both in relation to people's sense of identity, and as a base for the formulation and implementation of policy, that we do indeed live increasingly in an interdependent global society. Whilst community development has focused primarily on the local, it would be a mistake to ignore the need for parallel developments in the promotion of national international voices. Such voices should be nurtured and given avenues of expression.

Those who practice and theorise about community development, as well as vigorously tackling social divisions, need to respond to the polarisation of social life by identifying and promoting values and processes that acknowledge our dependence and interdependence, focusing on what interests there are in common, as well as our diversity. To this end, a more refined or detailed analysis of social categories is needed. Too often community development has been prepared to accept loose generalisations that make assumptions based on biological ascriptions about interests, attributes and politics. A key task is to create more opportunities for the poor and the non-poor to come together to identify common interests, find ways to address internal differences and conflict and re-engage in the simple but essential process of speaking to each other about needs, issues and concerns, avoiding the erection of artificial barriers but forging alliances across social boundaries and thereby resisting further decay and polarisation. The extent to which community development workers will be able to engage in this process of repoliticisation will vary according to both the circumstances of the moment and specificity of their particular employment situation. No doubt, there will continue to be some ambiguity as to whether they are essentially welfare professionals or agents of political change. The extent to which their networks extend beyond the functions of the local state to encompass new social movements, protest politics and the labour movement both within and beyond national boundaries, will help to determine their effectiveness in this respect, as indeed will the development of truly independent non-profit organisations.

4.4

When 'active citizenship' becomes 'mob rule'

Jane Thompson

As the children of the Paulsgrove Estate in Portsmouth go back to school, and their teachers ask them what they did during their summer holidays, they will be able to say that they joined the vigilantes. They will have learned that sometimes men want to have sex with young children in ways that must have set them thinking about what kind of 'sex' this could possibly be. They will have painted banners saying 'kill the pervs' and 'hang the scum'. They will have watched their mothers – and a few of their fathers – baying for blood. They will have learned to sing the battle song from older – less contradictory – protests ... *'we shall not, we shall not be moved ...'* as they too sat down in the road. They will have learned to spell paedophile.

Local working class people, and their children, taking to the streets to express their views, to speak with confidence to the media and register their anger, does not happen often. In debates about 'political apathy', 'the democratic deficit' and 'neighbourhood renewal', the prospect of locally-led and locally owned interventions to resist unpopular state policies, and to argue for changes in the law, would seem to be the answer to every earnest capacity builder and community regenerator's prayer. Except that these protests had the characteristics of a witch-hunt. They depended on media provocation, fuelled by emotion. They operated on hearsay and suspicion, frightening other residents who felt unable to disagree for fear of being associated with paedophilia. They appear to have harassed and terrified 'the wrong men', forcing some 'innocent' families to flee and resulted in at least one named paedophile committing suicide.

It was not long, of course, before the women themselves came in for public condemnation. As one commentator put it, *'if this is the alternative, I'd rather live next door to a paedophile'*. If these had been mothers of public-school children, they would have been 'concerned parents'. If they didn't have tattoos, pale faces, peroxide hair, and didn't look so obviously working class, they would never have been called a mob.

From: Thompson, J. (2000) 'When "active citizenship" becomes mob rule', *Adults Learning*, September, pp 23-4.

235

In press interviews, the women talked wildly of castration, hanging and the putting down of 'animals'. While their language might have made the chattering classes wince, no one who listened to them could be in any doubt that they were frightened for their children's safety, that they resented their estate being used as a 'dumping ground' for paedophiles, and that 'something else' was also going on.

It was also obvious that the *News of the World* – in pursuit of profit – knew more about how to galvanise the 'active citizenship' of working-class people on impoverished estates than any number of community development workers and adult educators with their mapping exercises, needs analyses and drop-in taster sessions.

If nothing else, the activities of the Paulsgrove vigilantes should remind us that the National Strategy for Neighbourhood Renewal and the attention of the Social Exclusion Unit, which focuses on those living in the worst estates, needs a more nuanced analysis of what constitutes social exclusion and deprivation especially in relation to the social and educational intervention that is most likely to be appropriate.

These residents are not 'hapless victims' who need to be rescued by better information and guidance services and mentoring schemes, designed to lead them gratefully towards social inclusion. Their standpoints cannot be easily be normalised according to middle-class values via training for employment or by participating in 'worthwhile' activities like voting or family learning. They do not appear to lack confidence or need their capacity for leadership developing.

These protesters are, especially the women, quite capable of making their presence felt. Indeed they do it all the time. Here – as elsewhere – women's activism comes out of their radicalism in the domestic sphere, and especially in relation to housing, health and children. Fighting local authorities about tenant's issues; campaigning for play facilities; tackling vandalism and drugs; targeting women's health care, isolation and depression, all provide examples of militant self-help activities undertaken by women at the crisis point where class and sexual oppression meet. (Thompson 2000) Taking to the streets to remove paedophiles from their estate is part of this same tradition carried through in ways that have left those with authority shocked by the enthusiasm for rough justice, and quite unable to stop them in their tracks. It is the kind of activism which is best understood as defiance and as resistance to traditional (and middle-class) constructions of femininity, participation, respectability and subordination.

If missionary intervention is inappropriate in these circumstances, there must be something else education can contribute to local action like this – especially when it seems that paedophiles are merely the scapegoats for concerns that are actually about something else. So let us consider the bigger picture.

This present moral panic was a direct consequence of the disappearance and murder of Sarah Payne, and of the efforts to use the media in order to find her, and later her killer. This disappearance of a small, blonde-haired girl playing in a cornfield coincided with the start of the summer holidays and spoke directly to the worst fears of every parent in the country. When the *News of the World* decided to 'stretch the story' by publishing the names and addresses of known paedophiles, it was against the advice of the police, probation service, sex counsellors and the government. At the time of writing, the police have still not disclosed information about a sexual assault on the child. Neither has the *News of the World's* 'moral outrage' on behalf of children and in pursuit of paedophiles put a halt to their habitual story lines and photo opportunities promoting the sexualisation of women and young girls which, by its very nature, helps to set the social context for sexual abuse.

In the period between Sarah Payne's disappearance and the Paulsgrove protests, 10 other children in Britain were murdered. None of their deaths received more than token media attention in the press. Possibly this was because their killers were quickly identified. Possibly it was because they were killed by one or other of their parents – in most cases, their fathers. The statistics relating to child murder confirm this pattern. Currently five or six children a year are murdered by a stranger. Between 80 and 100 are murdered by someone they know – most often a parent, or someone close to the family. All of the experts now accept that the incidence of child sexual abuse and domestic violence is higher than any other kind of violent crime. It is also on the increase. The Home Office now accepts that recent official figures are only the tip of the proverbial iceberg.

However politically and socially appropriate it may be to compile a register of paedophiles, it should not be assumed that this record constitutes anything other than a list of those who have been prosecuted. The disturbing truth of the matter is that children are much more likely to be at risk from those they live with than from a dangerous stranger with a police record for previous sex crimes against children.

Perhaps the women of Paulsgrove know this. I cannot imagine that they do not. The women will include among their number those who have experienced sexual abuse or domestic violence. Some of the men marching with them will be culpable of the very crimes they claim to condemn. The fact that the women have been prepared to extend their vigilante activity – on the basis of word-of-mouth information – against those whom the police describe as 'innocent of any crime' is some recognition of the prevalence and ordinariness of child sexual abuse in the community.

And 'dumping paedophiles', if it is true, in areas of cheap social housing like Paulsgrove is not so surprising. These are precisely the places where those who are 'socially excluded' for a variety of reasons are concentrated. It does not mean to imply that child sexual abuse only occurs in deprived neighbourhoods or working class communities. There is no evidence to suggest that richer men are less likely to abuse and murder children than poor men. But they are less likely to come under the scrutiny of Social Services and much less likely to end up in prison.

It remains to be seen how the government will respond to the aftermath of Paulsgrove and to the *News of the World's* tacit incitements to violence. At the start of an election year, the appeal to populism at the expense of a universally despised minority will be a cheap, comfortable solution. Launching a more serious debate, with the promise of action, about the much greater risk children face from those whom they know, will constitute a much braver, more principled response. But it will be a response that will benefit from joined-up thinking. If the government is prepared to act on the evidence of recent crime figures about the prevalence of domestic violence, and pay serious attention to what makes unacceptable numbers of men commit acts of domestic violence and abuse children, they will also derive some insight into the alleged 'crisis in masculinity' – what Tony Blair refers to as the 'yob culture': the reasons why many men exclude themselves from learning (McGivney 1999); use football matches as any excuse to fight each other and the police; and – like William Hague – take pleasure in boasting about their laddish capacity to drink vast amounts of alcohol as an indication of their masculinity.

So far as adult learning is concerned, the evidence of Paulsgrove speaks of agency and outrage on the part of the protesters and also of ignorance. It reveals the fine line between people power and 'mob rule'. Education cannot cancel outrage but it can confront ignorance. If educators are not prepared to struggle alongside learners to create useful and democratic knowledge based on reason and emotion, shaped in the context of ethical and political considerations, which link personal troubles to public issues, the local to the bigger picture; and in which every one of us has something to learn and something to teach, then the field is left clear for the *News of the World* and their like to do their worst.

The residents of deprived estates deserve better than 'mob rule' and rough justice. Gender violence sustained by power and secrecy will not be dented by creating scapegoats. Only when those with the least power – women and children – regain confidence in those supposed to love and help them; only when they have access to gender equality, knowledge, critical thinking and proper influence, will they settle what they see as gross injustice in way that do not do injustice to themselves or others.

4.5

Inequalities in health: contested explanations, shifting discourses and ambiguous policies

Sandra Carlisle

Introduction

The political context of health inequalities research

Natural scientific disciplines such as public health and epidemiology have their roots in the presumptions of modernism and the Enlightenment – notably the existence of externally verifiable realities that can be uncovered through rational thought and scientific study. (Watson 2000) Although such assumptions may be challenged by social scientists espousing less positivist perspectives (Popay *et al.* 1998), scientific research is seldom explicitly aligned with political issues. The value of research findings is linked to their neutral status and presentation of the facts observed and hypotheses verified. (D'Andrade 1995) Yet political ideology has a crucial role in shaping the commissioning of research, the type of evidence that gets accepted and subsequent policy action. The UK Working Group on Health Inequalities (widely known as the Black Report) provides a well-known exemplar: originally commissioned under a Labour administration, the Report (DHSS 1980) encountered a hostile reception from an incoming Conservative administration. The fiscal implications of the structuralist-materialist explanations for health inequalities supported by the report's findings led to their outright rejection by a new government committed to an ideology of reductions in public spending.

The research community responded by defending the field of social inequalities in health against charges that they did not exist, or were not increasing. Macintyre (1997) suggests that much research energy was thus spent in (successfully) keeping health inequalities on the political agenda, rather than on investigation of the processes by which such inequalities are generated and

From: Carlisle, S. (2001) 'Inequalities in health: contested explanations, shifting discourses and ambiguous policies', *Critical Public Health*, vol 11, no 3, pp 267-79.

239

maintained, and that less attention has been paid to specific recommendations for much the same reason. This paper argues that the field of inequalities in health research is unavoidably politicized—through the political context in which such research is conducted, through the competing explanatory frameworks advanced, and through the linked discourses that propose or imply particular solutions to the problem.

The health inequalities debate

There is a lengthy tradition in the UK of contested explanations for inequalities in health. Macintyre (1997) has suggested that, in the latter part of the nineteenth and early part of the twentieth centuries, debates about the causes of inequalities in health were shaped by three different explanatory discourses. Hereditarian explanations for class variations in disease argued that people's social position depended on biologically-determined natural capacity. Variations in health were therefore inevitable and little could be done about them. Behavioural explanations viewed the high infant mortality rate found in the labouring classes and bad health of poorer sections of the population as a consequence of working-class maternal ignorance and generally unhealthy or feckless ways of living. Education was seen as the appropriate measure to improve health. Environmental explanations regarded the widespread poverty and material conditions of urban industrial life as central to the social distribution of disease and premature death. From this perspective, social reform was urgently needed.

In their review of the contemporary research field, Popay *et al.* (1998) have argued that two main constructions continue to dominate research on health inequalities: first, the view that individual behaviours and lifestyles are principally responsible (e.g. Hattersley 1999); second, the view that inequalities in health are a mirror for wider social inequalities and injustice. (e.g. Bartley 1994; Davey Smith 1996; Wilkinson 1997a, 1997b, 1998a, 1998b) There is thus a historical continuity between nineteenth-century environmental explanations and contemporary models based on poverty and deprivation. There are also elements of continuity between behavioural/hereditarian models and contemporary explanations that posit the pathology of lifestyles and 'cultures', the determining impact of biological factors, or the endemic nature of inequality in all societies. There are apparent differences in the social values and political ideology underpinning these different explanatory discourses, all of which have implications for a policy response.

Contemporary models: overlaps and discontinuities

From the perspective of the twenty-first century, the evidence for continuing inequalities in the social patterning of health is beyond doubt and the research literature is now vast. It has been estimated that about 800 empirical and conceptual papers have been devoted to this topic over the last two decades in Britain alone. (Macintyre 1997). The explanatory models outlined here are thus inevitably an over-simplification of a highly complex and constantly developing research field. They do *not* constitute an adequate review of this field: rather, it is suggested that they are broadly indicative of three influential contemporary discourses around: poverty/deprivation, psychosocial stress and individual deficits. There are obviously some conceptual overlaps between these three broad-brush explanatory types.

The psychosocial stress model acknowledges the problem of an inequitable social structure but sees the generative mechanism for health inequalities in the relationship between social structure and individual psyche. The individual deficit model similarly acknowledges social inequity but is less focused on restructuring society than on tackling the problem at the level of individuals and their 'culture'. The boundaries between types of explanation tend to be fluid rather than clear cut, explanations remain incomplete and contested, and theoretical diversity stimulates the ongoing debate. (Health Education Authority 1999) Although such diversity facilitates increasingly sophisticated theoretical and methodological development and refinement within the multidisciplinary research community concerned with the issue of health inequalities, it also seems to provide policy-makers with a dauntingly complex field from which to construct remedial action. Does this matter? In order to address this question we first need to consider the types of discourses that are deployed around potential solutions.

Discourses of inequality

The term discourse draws attention to the importance of understanding how language is used to construct the social world in various ways. In discussing the language of politics, Levitas (1998: 3) argues that a discourse constitutes ways of acting in the world, as well as a description of it: a discourse both opens up and closes down possibilities of action. From this perspective, discourse analysis:

> underlines the fact that the matrix of concepts through which we understand the world and act in it profoundly affects those actions and thus the world itself, *without denying the material character of social relations.*

The discourse model outlined below was originally developed by Levitas (1986, 1998) to tease out the various meanings of social exclusion embedded within current political debate. She identifies three different discourses around social exclusion: RED (a redistributionist discourse); MUD (a 'moral underclass' discourse related to 'pathological' culture/behaviour); and SID (a social integrationist discourse); the latter overwhelmingly associates social inclusion with being in paid work. Although developed for a different context, Levitas's discourse model is a useful conceptual tool for considering the debates around inequalities in health, which involve both the language of research and the language of politics, and which are closely intertwined in any case with debates around social exclusion. Levitas's RED, MUD and SID model is applied in the following section as a way of exploring a number of approaches to tackling health inequalities and some of their limitations.

Redistributionist discourse (RED)

The RED approach to health inequalities is unmistakably linked to the poverty/ deprivation explanatory model. From this perspective (normally located amongst writers on the political 'left') a more equitable distribution of resources in society and the restructuring of socioeconomic policy is required. (Bartley 1994; Townsend 1998; Wilkinson 1998b; Davey Smith et al. 1999):

> There is *one central and fundamental* policy that should be pursued: the reduction of income inequality and consequently the elimination of poverty. Ending poverty is the key to ending inequalities in health. (Davey Smith et al. 1999: 163: emphasis in original)

The redistributionist discourse frames the problem as one of wealth, as well as poverty. It acknowledges the role of relative inequality in its focus on 'downward' redistribution through reformed welfare policies. It rejects welfare dependency arguments and argues for the strengthening rather than the reduction of the welfare state. (e.g. Bartley et al. 1997) This perspective is also found in the report of the Independent Inquiry into Inequalities in Health (the Acheson Inquiry), which states that:

> We consider that without a shift of resources to the less well off, both in and out of work, little will be accomplished in terms of a reduction of health inequalities by interventions addressing particular 'downstream' influences. (Department of Health 1998a)

One problem with the deprivation/redistributionist approach is the related belief (particularly in some of the debates around health promotion and health education) that increases in income will be accompanied by an increase in 'healthy' types of expenditure. Poverty as a determining factor for health-related behaviour and expenditure is challenged by the social anthropological conceptualization of the class-related 'habitus'. (Bourdieu

1984) Bourdieu argues that the tastes, behaviours and preferences of any socioeconomic group are not only shared, but become internalized as 'natural'. We cannot predict that increases in income will lead automatically to 'healthy' tastes and behaviour because preferences in such things as diet or physical activity cannot be simply mapped onto a simple healthy/ unhealthy dichotomy. They carry social meanings that need to be understood and related to the physical, social, economic and cultural context within which they occur.

Moral underclass discourse (MUD)

This type of discourse may be deployed as part of a neo-liberal or new right political discourse. The concept of a 'moral underclass' resonates with explanations of health inequalities that focus on individual irresponsibility for health, given the profound associations between perceived moral turpitude and illness in contemporary society. (Blaxter 1997) MUD-type approaches believe the solution to lie with individuals themselves, who should change their reprehensible behaviour and accept responsibility for their own health. From the MUD perspective, social and health inequalities are endemic in all societies; recommendations for action therefore tend to be cast in terms of individual adaptation to inevitability rather than social change. This type of discourse is related to the individual deficit model of health inequalities outlined above. The solution is to increase the margin of resources at individual or community levels by increasing resources or reducing needs. One way of achieving this is through a conventional health promotion/empowerment approach, providing adaptive skills and reducing needs through increasing lower-socioeconomic groups' understanding of and resistance to advertising techniques and peer pressure. (Charlton and White 1995) A community development approach to the creation of mutual help networks, for example food co-ops and credit unions, would have the additional benefit of leaving financial input virtually unchanged.

From the egalitarian instincts perspective of evolutionary psychology, macro-scale action fails to tackle the real problem. (Charlton 1997) Policy goals should therefore address the subjective experience of inequality at the level of individuals, which is where its effects are felt. A pragmatic, if admittedly second-best solution is to create a 'step-like' inequality — a stratification of classes, with egalitarianism within strata. This type of encapsulation would provide a protective insulation from invidious comparisons with more advantaged social groups as differentials between strata may be compatible with equality within strata:

> If resource differentials are indeed a reliable consequence of a delayed-return, surplus economy, then inequality might be regarded as an endemic injustice which cannot be eradicated but

> must nevertheless be negotiated . . . the inequity of inequality therefore requires containment, compensation and compromise at the 'capillary' social level — the family, the workplace and the community. (Charlton 1997: 422)

The casualty approach implied by an individualistic discourse fails to acknowledge the role of structural inequalities in facilitating or preventing access to basic components of health such as adequate housing, decent food, education, transport, income and employment. It also carries unacceptably stigmatizing undertones of personal social, economic and moral failure.

Social integrationist discourse (SID)

A social integrationist discourse dominates the New Labour approach to social problems. (Levitas 1998) SID approaches in response to explanations for health inequalities claim the causal effects of social polarization, social exclusion and resultant psychosocial inequalities. There are parallels with the psychosocial stress model. Social integrationist discourse around health inequalities is closely related to the perceived relevance of social capital and social cohesion to health. Social capital sees the community rather than the individual or the social structure as the unit of analysis. It has been defined variously in terms of the existence of trust in one's fellow human beings, active community networks, participation in civic activities, and shared objectives. (Gillies 1998) Some argue that low social capital is a key causal factor in health inequality and that income inequality only exerts its effect through this variable. (Lomas 1998) Building social capital has been seen as a relatively inexpensive means of tackling the structural determinants of health and disease and offsetting the most abrasive effects of health inequalities. (Gillies 1998) SID-type solutions suggest that creating and sustaining social cohesion or social capital at the community level is the most appropriate way to tackle the problem.

Despite its obvious appeal, Muntaner *et al.* (2000) argue that social capital is being conceptualized in unsophisticated ways and that care needs to be exercised in making such claims. They suggest that the concept is being used as an alternative to materialist-structural explanations for inequalities and invokes a romanticized view of communities. SID-type solutions tend to assume that material circumstances are without significant influence after certain threshold levels are passed but this remains doubtful. Elstad (1998) reminds us that the evidence for relative inequality still does not explain why individual or household income is closely related to mortality risk within most present-day affluent societies.

Table 1 presents a simple heuristic framework, encapsulating the different perspectives on problems, solutions and action found within the RED,

MUD and SID discourses on health inequalities. The explanations and proposed solutions to health inequalities delineated here all recognize the role of broader social inequalities: the key point is that their focus for action differs.

Table 1: Problems, causes, solutions and actions

Discourse level	Source of problem	Explanatory level	Causal mechanism	Solution	Action level
Redistribution (RED)	Concentration of resources in higher socioeconomic groups	Social structure	Inequitable social distribution of resources	Relieve poverty by redistributing resources downwards	Socioeconomic policy
Social Integration (SID)	Social polarization of socioeconomic groups	Interaction between individual and social structure	Relative inequality and social stress in disadvantaged groups	Reduce and increase social integration	Community
Moral underclass (MUD)	Lower socioeconomic groups	Individual experience and action	Narrow resource margins	Help poor people develop coping strategies	Individual

Shifting discourses

It is argued that the contested nature of the various explanations around health inequalities facilitates political flexibility and is compatible with complex ideological shifts between different types of discourse. One result of this is ambiguous policy initiatives that place responsibility for action at the community and/or individual level, rather than at that of national government strategy. The majority of workers in the fields of health services and community development would justifiably reject suggestions that they knowingly utilize a 'moral underclass discourse'. Nevertheless, government initiatives based on 'empowering' types of health promotion and community development activities can unwittingly be a thinly disguised veneer for the classic victim-blaming approach and the social marginalization of the problems of poverty, relative deprivation and poor health. Work on developing social integration and cohesion at the community level and combating social exclusion is currently being undertaken in many communities as 'bottom-up', grass-roots initiatives have experienced a steady rise in popularity over the last couple of decades. However, promoting social citizenship as one of the principle responses to inequalities and other difficulties in society is unsustainable without adequate social welfare safety nets. (Hutton 1996; Bartley *et al.* 1997) Critics have also pointed out that encouraging communities to develop their own strategies for combating social problems is a less than admirable way for the Government to solve pressing problems with regard to social order and the increasing costs of the welfare state. (Wainwright 1996) Farrant (1991) has documented the underlying contradictions and tensions of community development work, drawing attention to the historical roots of community development in colonialism where, far from being inherently radical, it was employed to safeguard and further the interests of the ruling class and reduce the burden on colonial administrators. From this perspective, the drive for social integration can be viewed as part of a political prescription for community manipulation.

The identification of discourses is both an analytical device and a means of empirical description. (Levitas 1998) RED, MUD and SID provide three potential strategic approaches but they remain partial, like the contested explanatory frameworks on which they are based. In the UK, government policy documents have stressed the importance of individual health behaviours and lifestyles, based on the assumption that individuals control their own lifestyles and that approved changes will improve health outcomes. (Department of Health 1992) More recent policy documents have begun to acknowledge the role of poverty and social inequality in shaping life circumstances and impacting on health. (Department of Health 1998b,1999) There are similarities between redistributionist and social integrationist approaches in seeking to narrow the gap between rich and poor, but the latter type of discourse is arguably dominant in contemporary social policy. Utilizing RED-type solutions aimed at poverty elimination is undoubtedly an uphill task as this approach requires political will to action that extends beyond the life of any one parliament. Such policies are likely to meet with considerable resistance on both ideological grounds (e.g. accusations of nanny state-cum-social engineering tactics) and pragmatic grounds (e.g. unpopularity with certain sectors of the voting population).

Contemporary initiatives include an emphasis on reducing 'pathological' lifestyles, e.g. by eating a better diet, quitting smoking and increasing physical activity; these can be categorized as a MUD-type solution. Although most UK policy documents now acknowledge the impact of poverty and deprivation on health, a redistributionist discourse is rarely explicit and many policy initiatives aimed at tackling health inequalities provide a better fit with a social integrationist discourse model. A plethora of community-based initiatives are founded on the explicit assumption that multi-level, multi-sectoral partnership working at community level, e.g. through Healthy Living Centres and Health Action Zones, is the best way to tackle the problem (a SID-type solution). In particular, work is seen as the best route into a healthier life, principally through the New Deal and Welfare to Work initiatives, even though being in paid employment guarantees neither freedom from ill-health and poverty for the individual nor cohesion for the community. Although the weight of evidence indicates that inequalities in health can only effectively be tackled by policies that reduce poverty and income inequality (Shaw *et al.* 2000), individualistic explanations and solutions to health inequalities will probably continue to be highly acceptable to any government. Such approaches are inevitably less costly (in economic and political terms) than redistribution of resources through increased welfare benefits for the poor and progressive taxation for the wealthy.

In summary, it seems likely that the complexity and lack of consensus inherent in the discourses surrounding health inequalities provides the flexibility and ambiguity cherished by policy-makers. Ambiguity facilitates claims of government leadership in tackling the issue through the publication of consultation and policy documents, whilst simultaneously avoiding dramatic action at the level of the social structure. At the same time, the increasing popularity of community development initiatives, and political emphasis on social integration rather than equality, enables the government to devolve responsibility for action to the community and individual level. Awareness of health inequalities is now central to contemporary political debates but responsibility for any failure to reduce the health divide will be shared by many throughout society.

4.6

The significance of global citizen action

John Gaventa

Across the globe, citizen action is widely recognized as part of the discourse and practice of democratic politics and social change – at least at the local level. (Barker 1999) Through community organizations, social movements, issue campaigns, and policy advocacy, citizens have found ways to have their voices heard and to influence the decisions and practices of larger institutions that affect their lives. A number of writers have documented this rise in civic action empirically, even referring to a 'global associational revolution that may prove to be as significant to the latter 20th century as the rise of the nation–state was to the latter 19th century'. (Salamon 1994) Theorists of democracy also have given renewed recognition to the role and importance of civil society in governance itself: For many, democratic governance includes the role of citizen action outside of, and in relation to, the formal political sphere, not participation by citizens in government alone. (Minogue 1994; Rhodes 1996).

Our argument goes beyond citizen action at the local level into relatively new territory – that of 'global citizen action.' The broadening of citizen action into the global sphere recognizes a new contemporary reality in which power relations at local and global levels are increasingly intertwined and in which 'governance involves more than the state, community involves more than the nation, and citizenship involves more than national entitlements and obligations'. (Scholte 1999: 22)

Since the 1970s, many activists have been guided by the adage 'think globally, act locally.' Our argument suggests the reverse: Think locally about the impacts of global institutions and global forces. Act globally on them. The first part of this equation – the local effects of global institutions and forces – has received a great deal of attention in the burgeoning literature on globalization. Public understanding is growing of the ways in which our daily lives and choices are affected by the practices of transnationals, world trade and financial flows, the global media, and the policies of multilateral institutions. But what does it mean to

---

From: Gaventa, J. (2001) 'Global citizen action: lessons and challenges' in M. Edwards and J. Gaventa (2001) *Global citizen action*, London: Earthscan, pp 275-89.

act globally? We provide several suggestions. In one sense, global action is action on or against global institutions, whose policies and programs have significant impact at the local, national, and regional levels. In recent years, such citizen action has been dramatically illustrated in a series of large public protests, such as those at the G8 meetings in Birmingham, UK in1998, where 60,000 people joined hands against world debt; in Hydrabad, India, in 1998 where 200,000 largely peasant farmers protested the policies of the WTO; in Seattle in 1999, where workers, environmentalists, and others protested over trade and 'global capitalism'; and in the similar protests at the World Bank and IMF meetings in 2000.

These and other struggles and campaigns have sought not only to organize around specific issues and policies but also to make these suprastate institutions more accountable, democratic, and transparent.

In another sense, the literature suggests that global action occurs when citizens link across borders in campaigns on issues of mutual concern. While global in the sense of covering the entire planet would be too grandiose a term for many of these examples, they illustrate the importance of solidarity and support across national borders. Sometimes, such campaigns focus on collective action on a specific issue – such as the practices of a multinational. Where globalization makes it harder for nation-states to regulate large multinationals for fear of capital flight or relocation of industries, transnational civil society organizing helps to fill the void by providing checks and balances against the behavior of otherwise unaccountable suprastate organizations. In other cases such as the Slum/Shack Dwellers movement or the spread of participatory methods and approaches, transnational solidarity takes the form of horizontal sharing, learning, and support through which global linkages can help to empower local voices.

In yet a third sense, citizens act globally in order to realize or promote a set of rights offered to them by global treaties or agreements. In numerous historical and contemporary examples, global forms of action have contributed to greater awareness and understanding of rights, which have in turn led to new international agreements or conventions. The Jubilee 2000 campaign articulated the right to freedom from debt, global movements led to the UN Declaration for the Elimination of Violence Against Women, and campaigns for conventions to regulate landmines have had success. These campaigns continue a long and pivotal history of citizen action on human rights, such as the antislavery movements and the international movement for women's suffrage. (Keck and Sikkink 1998) Global citizen action is also critical to the enforcement and implementation of existing international treaties and convenants. With reference to the United Nations Convention on the Rights of the Child, it is only through citizen action at the local level, reinforced by global networks, that the promise of such international agreements can be realized. Further, we have seen that global declarations of human rights offer important spaces and levers around which other mobilization efforts can occur.

The appeal to universal human rights takes us, however, to another concern about the concept of global citizen action. What do we mean by 'citizenship' at the global level? The debate is a complex one, which raises thorny issues of universalism and particularity, global governance and national sovereignty. To some, citizenship is a bundle of rights and entitlements gained in relationship to a nation–state. The absence of a clear government at the global level makes the concept of a global citizen a non sequitur. To others, however, universal rights are already established in documents like the Universal Declaration of Human Rights and other international legal instruments. In a recent strategy paper, British Secretary of State for International Development Clare Short argued that human rights are essential to the achievement of international targets to reduce poverty because 'they provide a means of empowering people to make effective decisions about their own lives'. (DfID 2000) Moreover, she argues, such rights must be extended on a global scale to include those of participation, inclusion, and obligation (that is, assurance that obligations to protect and promote rights are fulfilled). An understanding of citizenship as participation puts less emphasis on rights as entitlements, to be bestowed by a nation–state or another form of government, and more emphasis on citizenship as something that is realized through responsible action. (Lister 1998; Cornwall and Gaventa 2000)

From this perspective, global citizenship is the exercise of the right to participate in decision-making in social, economic, cultural, and political life, within and across the local, national, and global arenas. This is true especially at the global level: where the institutions and authority of global governance are not so clear, the rights of citizenship are made real not only through legal instruments but through the process of citizen action, or human agency, itself. Rights to participation in global decision-making also carry with them a set of responsibilities, which, in the absence of external rules and standards, must be self-developed and self-imposed, a challenge that many global civic actors have yet to fulfill.

Even if we accept this conception of global citizenship, another important set of empirical questions remain to be answered: Can global citizen action really make a difference? Under what conditions? Much is known about the possibilities and limits of citizen action at the local and national levels. How can citizens go further to influence powerful actors in distant places? One line of argument might be that effective global citizen action is desirable but impossible – global decisions are shaped by structures and forces beyond the reach of action by ordinary people. But there is another story. As civil society actors have linked together around the world, their influence on the global stage has been impressive. We have seen the utility and impact of citizen organizing on numerous issues including landmines, housing, sustainable tourism, dams, children's rights and labor, violence against women, fair trade, and infant health. Global citizen action has contributed to large-scale cancellation of third world debt, to the democratization of foreign policy, and to the challenging of power relationships at multiple levels. To some degree, global citizen action has helped to change – or at least restrain – the practices of large institutions ranging from the World Bank, IMF, and WTO to multinational corporations; and it has clearly affected international treaties and conventions including those relating to nuclear weapons, human rights, and the environment. Beyond specific policy changes, global citizen action has made a number of other contributions to global governance, including encouraging civic education, magnifying citizen voice to policymakers, stimulating public debates, increasing transparency and accountability, legitimizing and democratizing global institutions, building social cohesion, and promoting ecological integrity.

Lessons for good practice

Global citizen action implies – and must embrace – a diversity of approaches and outcomes. There is no single blueprint, no universal path, through which global citizen action can occur. At one level, this lesson has to do with choices about strategies and tactics. As the analysis of campaigns to influence the World Bank points out, 'Different goals require different kinds of coalitions.' The goals and strategies that are possible will vary from context to context, based on differences in values, organizational forms and capacities, leadership, and political space. A campaign that assumes that one size fits all, that one solution or approach is best in all cases, may mean domination by more powerful actors who design the size and shape of the campaign.

Recognizing diversity does not mean ignoring commonality. Rather, affirming diversity while working for common or universal goals has proven critical to a form of global citizen action that is more inclusive than the one-size-fits-all approach. In a case study of international work for the rights of women, Bunch observes that campaigns that universalize the category of woman may suppress attention to power and inequality among women and 'impose a limited agenda on all women on the basis of experience of some – usually white, middle class, and living in the north.' Building on Mohanty's (1991) concept of common differences, they describe the importance of understanding how women in different parts of the world and in differing circumstances may experience oppression differently, even though they do so 'in relation to common systems of power and domination.'

An intellectual understanding that global citizen action needs to affirm difference within a framework of commonality has significant organizational implications. (Edwards 1999) The international movement for women's human rights balanced the tension between commonality and particularity through a form of networking at the local, national, and international levels that allowed 'for decentralized, co-ordinated and non-hierarchical action around common goals'. In the process, it 'developed a model that affirms the universality of human rights while respecting the diversity of particular experiences.'

Global citizen action implies action at multiple levels-local, national, and international – which must be linked through effective vertical alliances. The most effective and sustainable forms of global citizen action are linked to constituency building and action at the local, national, and regional levels. It is equally important that such actions be 'vertically aligned' so that each level reinforces the other. One of the clearest examples of 'vertical alignment' is the case of the Uganda Debt Network. Here, participation in a global campaign (Jubilee 2000) led to a favorable decision on debt relief for Uganda. At the same time, advocacy by civil society at the national level contributed to greater budget transparency and to greater government responsiveness to the needs of poor people, including the establishment of the Poverty Action Fund. Through projects such as the Ugandan Participatory Poverty Assessment Process (involving Oxfam, other NGOs, and the Ministry of Finance), attention was paid to national budgeting processes that would help to ensure that debt relief funds were used to meet the needs of poor people. (McGee and Norton 2000) At the same time, active education and mobilization work at the local level helped to strengthen the awareness and voice the priorities of poor people throughout the process. In this case, no level would have been fully successful without action at each of the others.

Building strong vertical alliances also has implications for redefining the links between Northern and Southern organizations. A number of case studies address the challenge of how to create and sustain more equitable, democratic, and accountable relationships among NGOs based in the North, which often campaign and speak 'on behalf' of the South, and those in the South, which must organize to affect the centers of power and decision-making in the North. The case study of ALOP, a network of Latin American NGOs, points to the importance of regional associations as a 'bridge' between South and North. The experience of Jubilee 2000 also reflects on the North-South imbalances that have characterized the campaign in terms of access to resources, information, and global decision-making. It points to the national (as well as global) campaigning and to South-South sharing of experiences as steps that can be taken to remedy these problems.

Vertical links are also strengthened through 'horizontal' networks and partnerships, which themselves are strongly linked to local realities. While case studies have focused on the process of building vertical links between ordinary people and global decision-makers, others focus on the strength that comes from horizontal sharing and network building. Slum dwellers, for example, were able to build an international movement through community exchanges that started slowly and gradually spread across eleven countries. South-South sharing and training contributed to the global spread of participatory approaches in research and development planning. In the case of the landmines campaign, the emergence of a 'network of networks' was critical to success.

In developing and promoting these horizontal links, almost every case study refers to the valuable role of rapid communications – especially the Internet – in supporting information sharing and coordinated action. This is consistent with other studies that have analyzed the role of globalized forms of communication for social movements, such as the use of the Internet by the Mexican Zapatistas in their human rights campaign. (Schulz 1998). However, the Internet is insufficient: face-to-face communication is critical for developing mutual trust. In the case of cross-border organizing on free trade for example, a series of direct dialogues allowed activists in the United States, Mexico, and Canada to agree on common principles and clarify differences, forging a strong foundation for success. Other examples show how successive UN world conferences provided critical arenas in which dialogue occurred and where personal relations of trust were formed, facilitating subsequent collaboration.

In addition to face-to-face contacts at global conferences and events, community-based, people-to-people exchanges are also important in building global networks. Both the case of the Slum/Shack Dwellers International and of the spread of participatory research experiences point to the importance of direct exchanges for accelerating the process of learning, and for providing significant events wherein local people can express and share their knowledge and expertise. In both cases, the rapid spread of knowledge and practices at the local level also affected policies by setting precedents and creating models that then attracted attention and influenced the practices of larger institutions. In the case of the Slum/Shack Dwellers International movement, horizontal exchanges also contributed to changing the locus of power between Southern and Northern NGOs by circumventing the filtering of resources and information that often occurs when networks are coordinated through the North. In other cases, direct people-to-people exchanges have contributed to new forms of North-South interaction based on mutual learning and solidarity. (Gaventa 1999)

Global citizen action is strengthened by participatory forms of research, increasingly sophisticated policy analysis, and continuous organizational learning. To be credible, effective and accountable, global citizen action must pay attention to its own knowledge and learning strategies. Knowledge strategies can be important tools for linking micro and macro realities, for policy advocacy on complex issues, and for building continuous organizational responsiveness and flexibility.

One of the key issues facing the legitimacy of international NGOs is that of voice. How do they link their own voices as advocates with the knowledge and voices of local people on whose behalf they sometimes claim to speak? Whose realities are represented? (Chambers 1997; Holland 1998) One important strategy that is emerging to answer this question is the use of participatory research methods to ensure a stronger link between the views and realities of local people and those being articulated by global policy actors, be they NGOs or international organizations. In Mozambique for example, the Agenda for Action for Children took the view that children had a right to be heard on issues that affect them and sought to include children in the rights assessment and visioning process. In Uganda, the use of participatory poverty assessments helped to link poor people's voices to national and international debates. More recently, a large scale Consultations with the Poor exercise in twenty-three countries (in which a number of international NGOs were involved) has used participatory research to influence both national debates on poverty and the World Development Report 2000. (Narayan et al. 2000)

While more inclusive and increasingly sophisticated research approaches are required by civil society actors to maintain legitimacy on international issues, they also must be able to create internal learning strategies that allow them to be responsive to differing voices and constituencies and constantly to improve their own practices. Grounding learning in the concrete realities and experiences of poor people creates a capacity for global movements to self-correct and to sustain themselves when the international advocates or 'experts' have left the scene. NGOs must also be able to strengthen their participatory processes for monitoring and assessing their own effectiveness and to use the results of such exercises for organizational learning. (Gaventa and Blauert 1999)

Global citizen action requires constant attention to internal forms of governance that are participatory, transparent, and accountable. There are numerous examples wherein the legitimacy, credibility, and effectiveness of global citizen action is affected not so much by the quality of external strategies and linkages as by attention to the ethics and consistency of internal behaviors and practices. In an era of globalization, when messages and symbols are created and transmitted almost instantaneously, corporations and other global actors have learned that one or two examples of socially irresponsible practice can do enormous damage to their credibility on other issues and in other places. As a result, they are committing greater resources to monitor and improve the quality and ethics of their work. International civil society actors must be willing to do the same. Edwards (2000) has argued that civil society must continue to promote innovations in three crucial areas:

The principle of 'a voice not a vote', structured to give every interest in civil society a fair and equal hearing and building from the bottom up so that global campaigns are built on strong local foundations. One way to do this would be through a set of compacts among governments, businesses, and NGO networks that layout the roles and responsibilities of each set of actors around particular issues or institutions.

A seat at the global negotiating table in return for transparency and accountability on a set of minimum standards for NGO integrity and performance, monitored largely through self-regulation. Codes of conduct may be the best way to enforce a sense of self-discipline in global citizen action, perhaps with an international ombudsman to arbitrate in particularly difficult disputes.

A 'level playing field' for NGO involvement, with special backing for voices that are currently left out of the global debate. That means additional support for capacity building, economic literacy, and financial autonomy among NGOs and other civil society groups in developing countries, and more opportunities to guarantee their direct participation in the international arena.

Challenges for the future

Despite its successes, global citizen action is still in the early stages of its evolution, and numerous challenges lie ahead. A first set of challenges arise partly from civil society's success: the increasing legitimacy and opportunities for civil society participation in global debates and in global institutions also pose risks of cooptation. Global civil society actors may find themselves spending more time and resources on servicing the participation agendas of global agencies rather than furthering the demands of grassroots constituencies. Given their new-found acceptance as global players, international NGOs may find themselves lulled into an overestimation of their own importance.

To ensure that new opportunities for civil society participation in global decision making are genuinely widened, a second set of challenges must be addressed. These involve strengthening the capacities of civil society to participate fully, inclusively, and effectively at the global level. In many parts of the world, the opportunities and demands for citizen action now outmatch the capacity of civil society to deliver. In the absence of strong, accountable organizations and the experience and skills to engage effectively, the openings for greater civil society participation risk being filled with unaccountable and ill-equipped actors.

Increasingly, the rush to participation mandated from above – as seen, for example, in new World Bank policies such as the Poverty Reduction Strategy Paper that requires national participatory poverty planning as a condition for debt relief – risks contributing to poor quality practices that simply relegitimize the status quo or dilute the possibilities for more authentic bottom-up participation in the future. Greater attention must be paid to minimum standards of quality in civil society participation, both for civil society's own internal practices, and the ways in which civil society consultation and participation is used in larger policy processes. (McGee and Norton, 2000)

However, the responsibility to extend and ensure the breadth, depth, and quality of global citizen action does not rest with civil society alone. A third set of challenges has to do with institutional change. National experiences in scaling up participation over the last decade show that the greatest obstacles may rest, not with the capacity of those who are seeking to participate, but in the ability of large institutions to adopt and embrace participatory approaches to change. For global policy institutions to embrace participatory approaches fully will mean radical organizational transformation, whether in international NGOs, multilateral or bilateral agencies, donors, or corporations. Only when large-scale institutions alter their internal incentives and rewards, decision-making structures, and knowledge systems will decision-making at the global level become truly inclusive and participatory.

Finally, the most fundamental challenge for global citizen action hearkens back to the need to address the theory and practice of global citizenship. What level of civil society participation and power are possible and desirable in the global arena? Where do the rights and responsibilities of global citizenship intersect with other rights and responsibilities in the household, in local and national governments, and in the marketplace? How can citizen voice in global debates be structured in ways that promote a genuine sense of equality and democracy in global civil society itself? These questions are demanding, and their answers are as yet unclear. However, a century ago we could not have imagined the extent to which citizens across the world have since succeeded in their struggles for more complete and inclusive democracies in their localities and national polities. In the twenty-first century, the globalization of power demands a new form of global citizen action that extends the theory and practice of democracy still further.

4.7

Whose problem? Disability narratives and available identities

Colin Cameron

Oppressive images

> So often do they hear that they are good-for-nothing, know nothing and are incapable of learning anything – that they are sick, lazy and unproductive – that in the end they become convinced of their own unfitness. (Freire 1996:45)

Paulo Freire's words may have referred originally to the situation of Brazilian peasants in the 1960s, but they have a universal quality and may legitimately be applied to the experience of disabled people in Britain in the first decade of the 21st century. When the discourses of dominant culture present disability in terms of personal tragedy, dependence, and incapacity, it is to be expected that many disabled people come either to accept poverty, unemployment, restricted life chances and social exclusion as the consequences of their own individual characteristics as not-quite-good-enough human beings. (Oliver 1996); or to distance themselves from the term, avoiding contact with other disabled people for fear of being discredited through association. (Titchkosky 2006: 224) I use the term 'culture' here to refer to everyday social practice and interaction as well as to the arts. It is the practice through which people make sense of themselves as actors in their own cultural worlds. (Willis 2000)

Mainstream cultural texts, past and present, provide a negative and narrow range of stereotypes and representations upon which people with impairments can draw in order to make sense of their own experience and from which to construct personal and social identities. Disabled people are overwhelmingly represented as either pitiable and pathetic; sinister and evil; or tragic but brave. (Rieser and Mason 1992: 98) Thomson (1997) has drawn

From: Cameron, C. (2007) 'Whose problem? Disability narratives and available identities', *Community Development Journal*, vol 42, no 4, pp 501-11.

attention to the fact that within literature disabled characters are usually one-dimensional and passive. Paul Darke (1998: 184) has identified the existence of a 'normality genre' in film, in which disabled characters fulfil the same function as 'Red Indians' in westerns or aliens in sci-fi movies: representing a threat to the fabric of normal decency which has to be resolved (usually in the case of normality films through the disabled character being killed or cured) in order that normality can be preserved or restored.

This oppressive representation reflects values and assumptions in a cultural context in which disability is conceptualised through what is known as the medical model. The medical model of disability is most clearly identified in the World Health Organisation's 1981 International Classification of Impairments, Disabilities and Handicaps. Impairment here is defined as 'any loss or abnormality of psychological, physiological or anatomical structure or function'; while disability is recognised as 'any restriction or lack of ability (resulting from an impairment) to perform an activity in the manner or within the range considered normal for a human being'. (Barnes *et al.* 1999: 23) In other words, disability is regarded as an individual problem, emerging as a result of something 'wrong' with the bodies of people with impairments, to be responded to by making normalising, compensatory, or therapeutic interventions in the lives of people with impairments.

In terms of industrialised capitalism, this way of thinking about and representing disability has a fairly lengthy history but shows little sign of disappearing. It is easy to find these stereotypes in Victorian classics where we would expect to find them. There is the poor, pathetic victim, Tiny Tim in Dickens' 'A Christmas Carol' (2003); the bitter and twisted monster, Blind Pew in Stevenson's 'Treasure Island' (1998); and the plucky, determined cripple, struggling against adversity, Klara in Spyri's 'Heidi' (1995).

What is revealing is to discover how little distance has been travelled in over a century. In contemporary cultural texts including literature, film, and charity advertising, for example, the same negative messages about disability and disabled people circulate. Disabled people are either objects of pity and wonder or freaks, never just ordinary people looking to get on with their lives.

Caravanning for the Disabled informs us that:

> a disability need not hinder someone's enjoyment of touring and sightseeing, but rather enhance the pleasure of the experience and allow them to enjoy it more intensely. They also realise more clearly how limited their lives would be without the stimulus touring and travel provide. (Caravanning for the Disabled, 2006)

In Andrew Collins' autobiography, *Where Did It All Go Right? Growing up normal in the 70s*, Collins tells us that:

> Mrs Munro had a mentally and physically handicapped son called Steven whom she occasionally brought into school just to scare the life out of me. (Collins 2003: 67)

The website report by *Thurrock Council News* of its Citizen of the Year Awards includes a list of descriptions of various of the town's disabled citizens saturated with words like *bravery, overcoming, living life to the full despite illness, special, inspiring courage, the face of adversity, overcoming personal difficulties,* and *sheer determination to overcome his disability.* (Thurrock Council 2005)

Images and representations such as these reflect and reinforce expectations which accept as common sense the idea that impairment is an undesirable attribute that blights the lives of those it affects: rather than being a relatively commonplace and usual part of human experience.

Disability arts

> Disability Arts are art forms, art works and art productions created by disabled people to be shared with and to inform other disabled people by focussing on the truth of disability experience. (Masefield 2006: 22)

Disability arts emerged during the 1980s as the cultural expression of the disabled people's movement, a self-organised democratic social movement which campaigns for equality for people with impairments within a disabling society. The organising principle around which this movement united itself was the social model, which re-defined the problems of disability. In the social model impairment is identified as 'the loss or limitation of physical, mental or sensory function on a long-term or permanent basis'; while disability is 'the loss or limitation of opportunities to take part in the normal life of the community on an equal level with others due to physical and social barriers'. (Barnes 1994: 2) Disability is not a flaw that individuals *have.* Rather, it is a relationship experienced by people with impairments in a society in which the distribution of resources and opportunities has been organized without taking their needs into account. People with impairments have experienced relegation to the margins of society and been provided with segregated 'special' services in a 'sheltered' world of 'care'.

As Thomas (2002: 20) notes, disability is 'the active and purposive social exclusion and disadvantaging of people with impairments, involving the social imposition of restrictions of activity and the socially-engendered undermining of their psycho-emotional well-being.' The disabled people's movement has argued that the problems of disability can be resolved if attention is shifted from attempting to cure or rehabilitate people with impairments to removing barriers so that they can participate on their own terms as equals within the social mainstream.

Hambrook (2005) has suggested that the activities of the disability arts movement can be divided by decade:

> During its origins in the 1980s cabaret and performance were prevalent. Throughout the 90s theatre and dance became a force to reckon with, with the emergence of companies like Graeae, Heart'n'Soul and Candoco. Over the past five years or so, film, media and the visual arts have seen a blossoming of work by disabled artists.

Disability cabaret created a point of connection and awakening for disabled people who, up until then, had been encouraged to believe that the most creative activities they could hope to pursue were dominoes and basket weaving. Johnny Crescendo's 'Choices and Rights' or 'Disabled People Aren't Allowed to Say 'Fuck'' (Holdsworth 1989); Simon Brisenden's 'Scars' or 'Battle for the Elephant and Castle' (DAIL 1992); Sue Napolitano's 'Hump' or 'Disabled Apartheid' (Napolitano 1993); Ian Stanton's 'Chip On Your Shoulder' or 'We've Got Each Other' (Stanton 1997): these songs, poems and performance pieces were the cultural accompaniment to a new political narrative on disability, a narrative written by disabled people which said that disabled people were not sad and pathetic but angry. 'In a world that tells us we're shit because we're disabled, it's especially important that we have a unique place that provides peer group pressure and support,' writes Mat Fraser (2004). The emergence of organisations such as the London Disability Arts Forum, the National Disability Arts Forum, the Northern Disability Arts Forum, and the North West Disability Arts Forum supported and developed this activity.

Disability arts developed during the 1990s, taking on a professionalism which had little to do with performers wanting to 'overcome and prove themselves' and a lot to do with disabled artists being professional about their work. Common Ground Sign Dance Theatre, a company of Deaf and hearing performers, gained recognition for inventive and elaborate pieces using the gestures and textures of British Sign Language as foundations for works exploring Deafness – identified as an aesthetic experience – and the rejection of deafness as perceived by a majority culture restricted to thinking/communicating through the spoken word. Power, respect and control were the key themes underlying the work of Heart'n'Soul, a reggae band and performance group of people with learning difficulties. 'Some people watching us are disabled people and they'll be thinking 'I wish I could do that'. We're teaching people how to be strong, and it's important for us to show other people that they can create their own stuff'. (Delin 1997:176)

Disability arts continues to flourish across a diversity of art forms: visual artists Cathy Woolley, Colin Hambrook, Lyn Martin, Aidan Shingler, Fatma Durmush, and Phil Lancaster; mixed media artists Tony Heaton, Brenda Cook, Juan delGado and Mark Ware; film makers Aaron Williamson and Philip Ryder; performance artists Deborah Williams, Jeni Draper, Jean St Clair, and Claire Cunningham; writers and stand-up comics Penny Pepper and Laurence Clark – and many others – contribute to the deepening of the exploration of the experience of disability which suggests that this is far from being simply about personal tragedy.

For many disabled people, attendance at a disability arts cabaret, performance or exhibition has been a moment of revelation. To begin to understand that the negative experiences you thought were yours alone are shared and understood by others and to begin to understand that it is not you but the social environment around you that needs to change is a powerful awakening. When an artist can communicate these things in words or music or through dance or image, a sense of connection and solidarity is established.

Many disabled people who would never countenance handcuffing themselves to a bus or throwing themselves out of their wheelchairs to block traffic have, nevertheless, become engaged with the broader politics of disability through disability arts. Campbell and Oliver (1996: 199) have likened the disabled people's movement to a jigsaw, 'each piece vital for the true picture to emerge'. At the Leonard Cheshire Red Feather celebrity ball in Manchester in 2002 a group of twenty disabled activists took over the party, letting off stink bombs and filling the banqueting suite with feathers whilst singing 'The bus driver abused me' and other disability rights protest songs. (Cameron 2007). In this scene, two pieces of the jigsaw, disability arts and the direct action network are seen coming together as part of a wider movement.

An affirmative model of disability

Current charity slogans – 'Turning disability into ability' (Capability Scotland 2006) or 'Looking through disability' (Playback 2009) – reinforce the idea that disability is an unfortunate individual condition that can be overcome with caring intervention. It is implied that imprisoned inside the afflicted body of each disabled person there is a healthy, 'normal' person – the 'true' person – struggling to break free.

A colleague of mine who has cerebral palsy tells of how, growing up, he identified positively with the self within – the inner self through whose senses he experienced and through whose cognitive processes he rationalized – and rejected his condition as something with which he was burdened but that had nothing to do with making him *who he was*. As an adolescent

I recognized myself as somebody who had been in a serious road accident, who had experienced brain injuries, talked slowly and had a bit of a limp, but I responded with anger to any suggestion that I was disabled. (Swain and Cameron 1999) Disabled artist Eddie Hardy tells of how, as a teenager he was 'still in denial about being disabled... and if I saw anyone who was disabled I didn't want to talk to them, and if I did talk to them it was as if I was able-bodied, doing the old patronising bit'. (Shakespeare *et al.*: 1996: 51) Through coming into contact with the disabled people's movement and the social model, each of us is now able to say, with pride, 'This is who I am.'

But things might have happened otherwise. Twenty-five years further down the line, young disabled people I worked with as a trainer recently made statements at the outset of the course along the lines of: 'I'm not disabled, me. I'm normal.' 'You feel sorry for the disabled kids. You want to help them'. (LCIL 2005) Subjection to dominant discourses means that people with impairments, rejecting disability identity, continue to struggle as individuals against structural barriers, believing both the cause and the solution to the discrimination they experience to lie within themselves. Very often this leads to disillusionment.

Through the development of the culture of resistance that is disability arts, disabled people have developed a discourse which rejects personal tragedy narratives and which identifies impairment as part of human experience to be valued on its own terms. A recent development in Disability Studies, which builds upon both the social model and upon insights generated within the disability arts movement, is an affirmative model which redefines impairment as: 'physical, sensory, emotional and intellectual difference divergent from dominant cultural norms but which is to be expected and respected on its own terms in a diverse society'; and disability as 'a personal and social role which simultaneously invalidates the subject position of people with impairments and validates the subject position of people identified as unimpaired'. (Cameron 2008)

Conclusion

The challenge to workers in the fields of community development and community arts is to identify which models of disability inform their own practice. What is required is not an avoidance of the term 'disability' or an uncomfortable, unconvincing pretence that everyone is the same; but an acceptance and equal valuation of difference and a recognition of and determination to address the barriers inherent in social environments. This means going beyond simply accepting people with impairments as individuals to acknowledging the ways in which disability is created through interactions, expectations, assumptions, remarks, ways of doing things. Not viewing people with impairments as being 'just like the rest of us'(only not quite as good), but recognizing their impairments as an important part of who they are. Not compensating so that they can participate in what everyone else does (only not quite so well), but in changing the things everyone else does. It means allowing people with impairments to do things differently when they want without having to feel that doing things differently is second-rate or not quite as good as conforming. (Thomas 1999: 43)

Much use has been made within disability cabaret of Augusto Boal's Theatre of the Oppressed. (1979, 1997) Forum theatre addressing disability issues is a good idea, though there are dangers involved in going down the simulation route. (Swain and Lawrence 1994) Focus on barriers rather than on impairment. Disability arts represents disabled people as strong, knowing, angry, proud, sexual, funny. It provides us with more positive representations upon which people with impairments can draw. Visit disability arts websites for ideas. Disability Arts Online (http://www.disabilityartsonline.org) is a good example.

There is an important role for community development/community arts informed by the social model in acknowledging and exploring disability as a social construction in order to enable people with impairments and those alongside them to develop perspectives and identities which resist those offered by dominant culture. Community arts informed by the affirmative model is reflective practice which examines and challenges its own knowledge and understanding in order to break free of the shackles of normality and embrace difference.

The changing terrain of multi-culture: from anti-oppressive practice to community cohesion

Kalbir Shukra

The management of ethnically diverse areas under New Labour is now framed by its cohesion agenda. To accommodate this agenda, many in community and youth work have rejected the anti-oppressive and anti-discriminatory practice paradigm. Special editions of *Youth and Policy* (1995) and *Community Development Journal* (1997) were dedicated to understanding the anti-oppressive approach that was rooted in the social movements of the 1970s and 1980s and interpreting what it could mean for practice. Community cohesion is the new touchstone in political, policy and practice debates of how best to shape and maintain an acceptable multi-ethnic Britain. What has produced this change? Can community cohesion be progressive? Is there still a role for anti-oppressive and anti-discriminatory practice?

Models of anti-oppressive and anti-discriminatory practice were developed from the early 1980s. By the 1990s they were sometimes called 'perspectives' as in 'black perspectives' or 'feminist perspectives' (Williams 1989; Thompson 2003) because they represented the voices of particular movements. As far as youth work and minorities were concerned, the broad black and anti-racist movement provided an alternative perspective to the assimilationist state-commissioned Inquiries. The latter was concerned with how to manage minority youth and how to encourage immigrants to fit in. The Hunt Report (DES 1967) on 'Immigrants and the Youth Service' was one of the first of these. By contrast, the key voices from the black and anti-racist movement between the late 1960s and 1980s sought to build a black consciousness that would challenge state racism. The militant campaigns around policing, the workplace and schools between the 1970s and 1980s (Ramdin 1987) were not publicly funded, but independent campaigns that organised against state racism and drew primarily on what was understood to be a principle of independent black and Asian self-organisation. (Shukra 1998)

From: Shukra, K. (2007) 'The changing terrain of multi-culture: from anti-oppressive practice to community cohesion', *Concept*, vol 17, no 3, pp 3-7.

Crucially, none of the struggles was based on working with the state – indeed 'no-reliance on the state' and 'self-determination' were core campaigning slogans of the time. Independent black self-organisation died in the 1980s when black radical activists decided that they needed to take the grants, the jobs and positions on committees that would bring them closer to a new site of struggle: the local state. Despite the criticisms at the time that multiculturalism was too focused on cultural difference and not enough on rights, it nevertheless became the basis of state-funded youth and community work amongst minority communities. This was the heyday of the saris, steelbands and samosas youth work (Chauhan 1996) alongside some separate provision, new projects and campaigns.

The diversity agenda borne of the late 1990s (Martin, 2006) has been accompanied in this decade by a growing debate about the state of the nation's connectedness. It has centred on Goodhart's (2004) view that Britain has gone too far in multiculturalist diversity for the good of social cohesion. The concept of social cohesion took off after inquiries into riots in the north of England in 2001. Reports authored by Cantle (2001), Denham (2001) and Ouseley (2001) respectively, concluded that minority and white communities are divided and live parallel but separate lives that are in part shaped by social policy and in part by the values and attitudes of Asian communities. The consequences of the local divisions were viewed as the source of local tensions and youth alienation. The solution was to be found in imbuing social policy with the intent of building cohesive communities locally. The intended outcomes were 'a common vision and a sense of belonging for all communities', an appreciation and positive valuing of difference in backgrounds and circumstances, similar life opportunities for people from different backgrounds and positive relationships between people from different backgrounds. (Local Government Association 2002)

Community cohesion is now a key policy driver in regeneration programmes, local authorities have community cohesion strategies and a new industry devoted to community cohesion has emerged to enable professionals to use the language and framework of community cohesion rather than anti-discrimination/oppression. Cohesion strategies in practice, however, have produced ever better ways of helping minorities to be or become better people: learning English, becoming politically literate, socialising with other minorities, understanding other faiths are key in the cohesion consultant's repertoire. The focus of cohesion practitioners is on modifying communities ideologically and behaviourally rather than empowering communities to change social structures that hold them back. Ideologically, community cohesion is little more than a reconstruction of 1960s and 1970s 'assimilation', assuming that cultural differences obstruct integration and that those who are different need to adjust in some way. (Back *et al.* 2002)

Central to the Local Government White Paper *Strong and Prosperous Communities* (TSO 2006) for England and Wales, community cohesion has now moved into managing diversity as a way of 'tackling extremism'. The White Paper confirmed previously implied links following 9/11 and the London bombings between 'diversity' and 'extremism'. It notes that tackling and preventing extremism is 'core business' for central and local government, as well as other partners including the third sector. For community and youth work practitioners, then, it will be almost impossible to avoid. Indeed, the Home Office already has a funding stream devoted to preventing extremism that is so explicit that some community and youth workers have refused to engage with it.

The White Paper poses a distinction between the ideas of the vast majority of muslims who share British values and a tiny minority who justify terrorism with extremist ideologies. Local government is seen as having a role in preventing extremism by winning hearts and minds and working with the right organisations. The acceptable organisations, of course, are ones that can be policed in a zone of moderation acceptable to New Labour. (Back *et al.* 2002) In this process, youth participation becomes less about enabling young people to develop a voice and more about filling a 'vacuum' that might otherwise be 'exploited by extremists'.

The discourse around 'diversity', 'segregation' and 'extremism' in the 2006 White Paper translates into British Asians or muslims deliberately setting themselves apart from majority communities and allowing their youth to fall prey to extremists who may encourage them to become terrorists. As such, they are seen not as the victims of discriminatory housing and employment policies, but as perpetrators of home-grown terrorism. Therefore the issue is not one of tackling racism but of changing the attitudes and lifestyles of British Asians and muslims in particular. Many of the new cohesion initiatives seek inter-community dialogue with the aim of increasing understanding of difference and therefore greater tolerance. Tolerance, of course, does not address racism as it is 'passive'. (Quirk 2006) Barry Quirk, Chief Executive of London Borough of Lewisham suggests that in order for local government to 'create the conditions where local political citizenship and local civil society can flourish amid ethnic, religious and cultural diversity', we need to move from closed communities to open communities. Whether commentators write of 'closed' or 'segregated' communities, their focus for change remains the behaviour of Asian – particularly muslim – communities and not rural or white communities. That is perhaps due to the policy focus on the 'incivility, rather than the civility, of urban life'. (Fyfe *et al.* 2006) The calls for greater tolerance, open communities and removing the veil (Ramadan 2006) are all about promoting civility and curbing incivility by encouraging ethnic minority groups to engage with and conform to a 'common language' (Fyfe *et al.* 2006) or a 'common culture'. (Eagleton 2007)

Under New Labour, organisations and voluntary associations that cannot be relied on to support the common culture are treated as extreme or criminal as they 'contribute little or nothing to a society's stock of civility' and at worst are 'bearers of incivility'. (Boyd 2006) The allocation of blame and responsibility for riots, home grown terror and other urban social problems results in Asian muslims and new migrants being viewed as destructive. Their closedness or self-segregation is seen as a problem because their 'behaviours are less easily regulated by the approbation or sanction of others'. (Fyfe *et al.* 2006) Their attachment to a different way of life in a British context is portrayed not as a source of richness – which would imply valuing diversity – but as an alien threat.

By contrast, social movements that produced models of anti-oppressive practice have understood closed communities to be a potentially positive development, in the sense that they foster solidarity and collective forms of organisation. The all-important 'us' against a perceived 'them' is vital to building a movement – not automatically a negative development. We must ask ourselves why and how communities became closed in the first place. Is it a symptom of their incivility, or is it a rational response to their experiences of oppression and discrimination? The social movement analyses have not only sought to understand 'why' people look inwards but have also recognised that there are structural reasons. By contrast, the community cohesion agenda identifies those who self-exclude and are not part of the common culture as the source of urban problems.

Histories of minority community organisations demonstrate that newness, hostility and fear produce informal networks of support (Shukra 1998) or what the social capital theorists call 'bonding' capital. (Putnam 2001) Hostility in the form of police raids, racist attacks, anti-muslim public discourse is unlikely to produce the trust needed to open up already closed or segregated communities. Equally, demanding that people speak English at home, remove their veils and open up their communities is unlikely to produce the desired results, just as Sennett (2003) noted that 'treating people with respect cannot occur simply by commanding it should happen'.

It is on this basis that some community cohesion projects seek to create the opportunities for people to mix, socialise and celebrate together. To build bridges, dialogue, civility or openness across communities, however, a precursor to success is tackling the symptoms and sources of oppression and discrimination. It may be naively idealistic for us to believe that we can successfully facilitate long-term openness before we live in a world where everyone is equal, because the structural oppressions are likely to send people back to their closed corners, their alienated responses and their incivility, to seek shelter, strategies of survival or to organise separately. Without prioritising the dismantling of oppressive socio-economic and ideological structures, policy-makers and practitioners remain at risk of doing little more than scolding Asians for not having white friends or neighbours, for not speaking English when in England, and for not fitting in.

This shift from tackling structural problems like racism to focusing on the way that diverse communities should live together in the framework of a common culture has taken place as a result of two key developments in the 1980s. One of these was a shift from the state being seen as the source of racism to becoming the site of anti-racism. This process transferred the focus from building a wider social movement against structural discrimination and oppression into changing policies and organisations.

A second development was a political settlement by the 1990s between the state and the black and anti-racist movement. The settlement centred on the integration of Black and Minority Ethnic (BME) professionals and politicians into the mainstream, to create a process through which potentially militant activists emerging from community action could be emasculated. Crudely, minority professionals and politicians entered the mainstream in exchange for resources, influence and representation for minorities. (Shukra 1998) They became representatives of minority civility: the respectable BME communities. Meanwhile they distanced themselves from trouble-makers and 'incivility' – those 'undesirable elements' outside their sphere of influence.

As the normative settlement developed on the basis of jointly agreed notions of what constituted civil or acceptable/respectable behaviours and responses and what did not, middle England has been able to support respectable BME people, even when this pits them against the incivility of 'unrespectable' white people. This explains why Stephen Lawrence and his family, who symbolised new black British civility, received widespread support against unrespectable white youth who are believed to have killed Stephen Lawrence. It also explains the antagonism to white Jade Goody in Channel 4's Big Brother house and the overwhelming support for respectable Indian celebrity, Shilpa Shetty.

In return for endorsing respectable minorities, the state is allowed free rein to attack unrespectable minorities. Thus it has become open season on unrespectable ethnic minorities whether they be those classified as illegal immigrants, terror suspects or criminals of some other sort. As perceived 'bearers of incivility' they are deported, detained, jailed or, since 9/11, kept in Belmarsh and Guantanamo or shot in police raids. Those trying to get into Britain by whatever means are equally treated as criminals rather than as people who seek refuge in a state of desperation.

The ideological process of creating support for the normative settlement has involved the construction of recognisable agents of incivility. Stuart Hall (1978) identified the process by which black youth in the 1970s were turned into 'folk devils' through the creation of 'mugging' as a new crime which in turn received widespread media coverage, producing a 'moral panic'. The same processes can be seen at play today with Asian youth being turned into the new folk devils as home-grown terrorists or rioters. The criminalisation process makes them difficult to defend. Similarly, the new moral panics focus on the myriad dangers and strangeness of others in our midst – from veil-wearing women to bearded Asian men who become stereotyped as potential suicide bombers. They are all seen to fall outside mainstream values of what is acceptable as either respectable or part of a common British culture.

Despite the work of some refugee groups, the National Civil Rights Movement, National Assembly Against Racism and others, mainstream youth work is driven by the citizenship and participation agenda, onto which cohesion is now being grafted. Some of the work shaped by these policy concerns in schools and youth clubs aims to train young people to be what Bernard Crick (1998) calls 'politically literate' citizens. For Crick, political literacy is about a 'compound of knowledge, skills and attitudes'. Participation in youth parliaments, youth councils or OBV-style initiatives learning how to use institutions is the way to develop political literacy. (Shukra et al. 2004) This fits well with the community cohesion framework.

I would argue that an anti-oppressive model of citizenship education would need to expand Crick's definition so that 'politically literate' citizens can recognise and challenge racism as an anti-democratic force. This might draw on Freire's notion of political education and so be more consistent with youth and community work that has a focus on deliberative democracy, developing critiques of structures and advocating social change rather than voting and conformity. These could be the basis of new community solidarities built on fighting discrimination and oppression. In the process, communities might themselves arrive at compromises through their everyday interactions, rather than relying on New Labour institutions to define 'citizenship' and 'Britishness' and then coercing people to sign up to it as a condition for staying in the country. The language and framework of community cohesion is a managerial one that seeks to contain and direct people's lives by reducing difference. It is at the expense of people's freedom to forge their own identities, relationships and solidarities in the process of challenging oppression and discrimination.

4.9

Community capacity-building: something old, something new...?[1,2]

Gary Craig

Introduction

Fifteen years ago, the term 'community capacity-building' (CCB) was not to be found anywhere within the policy literature. Now it is ubiquitous, particularly in the context of urban policy, regeneration and social development. In 2000, a UK report described CCB as 'the New Holy Grail', (Duncan and Thomas 2000:15), noting that the government's national regeneration programme contained more than 3000 separate CCB initiatives. Increasing use of the term seemed, however, to raise more questions than it answered. Why is this, what does the term mean and is there anything truly distinctive about the practice of community capacity-building? It may seem strange to address audiences probably more concerned with global and local challenges, when many people are preoccupied with such important issues as terrorism, with poverty alongside obscene wealth, with global climate change or with the growth of racism, on what appears to be a linguistic nicety. However, the use of language in the field of community development is critical since it goes to the heart of what community workers are all trying to do, to empower people to take more control over their lives. The language of community development underpins or, more often obscures, issues of power and ideology and it often is used – or should we say misused – by those in power to promise much and deliver little to the communities with which we work, communities of people who are disadvantaged in so many ways.

---

[1] The full (English) epigram is 'something old, something new, something borrowed, something blue'. Given the association of blue with right-wing political parties, community capacity-building might be said to incorporate all these dimensions.
[2] A longer version, which applies the arguments here to a range of service provision, is available as E. Noya *et al.* (2010).

From: Craig, G. (2007) 'Community capacity-building: something old, something new ...?', *Critical Social Policy*, vol 27, August, pp 335-59.

273

The nature of 'community'

Debates about language in community development are not, in fact, new. Look at the term community itself: this is to be found everywhere in the language of policy and politics, particularly, it seems, where politicians wish to engender a sense of wellbeing and consensus. Yet it remains a term loaded with contradictions and ambiguities. Hillery (1964) examined the literature fifty years ago, identifying several hundred meanings, arguing that the only distinctive common characteristic was that of social interaction. Stacey's influential 1969 paper, 'The Myth of Community Studies' indeed challenged the notion that there might be an entity which sociologists could recognise as 'community'. In the early 1980s, one commentator viewed the-then enthusiasm within many national governments for the word 'community' as a cynical and superficial gloss on policy programmes, describing community as a 'spray-on additive'. (Bryson and Mowbray 1987 cited in Craig 1989: 2) Certainly, its usage within very many recent UK public policy programmes – in community safety, community policing, community health, community education – suggests that governments hope that it will convey a sense – if not the reality – of 'community' ownership of such programmes. The idea of 'community' – along with other key concepts such as opportunity, accountability and responsibility – has been central to the development of what New Labour governments from 1997 have regarded as the Third Way approach to social and economic policy. Community appears to have greatest resonance when New Labour talks, in particular, about poverty. However, this continuing focus on small 'deprived' 'communities', 'can run the risk of diverting attention away from the wider political economic forces which cause and maintain the concentrations of poverty and unemployment in these areas'. '"Spraying-on" community as a solution to social problems provides no guarantee of progressive outcomes.'

Those writing about – and practising – community development, have struggled over the past fifty years to define what 'community' means for their practice. It is clear that in the current global discourse about community development, 'community' has three basic meanings: first, it refers to a *geographical community*, a defined and bounded residential area. Community development workers from both North and South however, have come to recognise that seeing 'community' simply as a geographical entity did not adequately deal with the realities of conflict or tensions between different interests within spatially-defined communities. Community thus properly incorporates axes of diversity which may generate conflicts. Much of the language of government fails to acknowledge this, implicitly denying that communities may be the site of contestation as much as of consensus (except, ironically, when the discourse becomes racialised). The second cross-cutting type of community identified by community development workers is thus a *community of identity*. Within and between geographical communities there might be a wide range of communities of identity with differing needs and interests. Seeing community as a site of conflict between competing interests challenges the political approach of communitarianism. Whilst 'community' is of central importance to communitarians, their view of community is characterised by conformity, conditionality and moral prescription, driven by top-down policy solutions rather than developed through democratic dialogue from within communities themselves. Government does not therefore respond to agendas set from below but shapes policy programmes from above, *for* communities, and in terms of its own political agendas.

Thirdly, community workers have often found themselves engaged in relatively short-term work, focused on particular issues such as improving housing or traffic condition working with groups constituting *issue-based communities*.

The practice of community development

Turning to the practice of community development, this is a concept which has also been used to cover a range of differing understandings of practice and outcome. The history of community development can be traced back to the 1950s at least but from the late 1980s, many governments and international organisations 're-discovered' community development, although not always labelling it consistently as such. Thus the World Bank viewed community participation as a means for ensuring that Third World Development projects 'reached the poorest in the most efficient and cost-effective way, sharing costs as well as benefits, through the promotion of self-help'. (Craig and Mayo 1995: 2) Their programmes, better known in reality for fiscal conservatism than for political and social risk-taking, frequently led, however, to the undermining of local community social and economic structures whilst appearing to advocate the importance of 'community', one example of the confusion which surrounds this and related terms such as community empowerment. The United Nations Development Programme commented in 1993 that it had 'people's participation as its special focus, indeed describing it as 'the central issue of our time'. *(Ibid.)* In reality, these international and national agencies have given scant attention to issues of social justice, with respecting the dignity and humanity of the poorest, with their right to participate in decisions which affect them or with mutuality and equality, principles underpinning the philosophy and practice of community development as it is understood by practice-based organisations.

Community capacity-building: scope and definitions

The term community capacity-building has begun to be used widely within both 'developed' and 'developing' countries to describe activities involving work with local deprived communities, to promote fuller engagement with social, economic and political life. As with the term community, there has been little clarity in its use; nor is it clear why it should have emerged so strongly into policy discourse. A detailed literature searches suggests that the earliest sustained references to *capacity-building* in the literature date from the early 1990s, in the work of United Nations agencies but to do with 'building capacity for the formulation of plans and strategies in support of sustainable development … ',(UNDP 1991) for example in the context of water sector capacity-building. However, 'the acknowledgment that the UN needed better capacity in its interface with communities was the point at which the discussion and models of *community* capacity-building for provider organizations and government shifted to a more participative mode' (McGinty 2003:5) and links with community development acknowledged. Capacity-building then elided in policy discourse into *community* capacity-building.

Within Europe, the first major allusion to CCB came in a 1996 report to the European Commission, (EC 1996:68) drawing on American experience, regarding strategies for community economic development in disadvantaged communities. Some Northern thinking was also, however, increasingly influenced by the development literature where what had frequently been 'top-down' project work was increasingly replaced by a recognition of the need to 'strengthen people's capacity to determine their own values and priorities and organise themselves to act on this.' (Eade and Williams 1995: 64) From these contradictory origins, the concept has been adopted in a variety of national and policy contexts, some more concerned with building the strengths and capacities of *organisations* (not always those which worked with 'communities') and others more specifically to do with CCB, that is building the capacity of *communities* themselves. Although CCB is the focus of this discussion, boundaries remain blurred: thus, building the capacity of organisations *within* deprived communities is often seen to be a part of CCB. The use of the narrower term 'capacity-building' also remains common in development literature from both North and South.

By 2001, use of the term CCB had become widespread, so much so that it was becoming the target of sceptical humour. At one UK conference , it was caricatured as 'developing local skills in a way that ensures people are able to know what is missing'. (cited in Beazley *et al.* 2004: 5) Another writer likened it to public participation, referring to an earlier definition by Arnstein as 'like eating spinach, because ultimately it is good for you.' (*Ibid*: 1) The term had come to convey such a range of meanings that it was often seen to increase confusion rather than provide clarity, leading to suggestions it should be dropped altogether. This sense of confusion led to several attempts to interrogate its meaning. In the context of its own need to be seen to be combating poverty, the first New Labour government had claimed to regard CCB as a 'key idea'. However, as two writers noted, 'with every new policy area, there is a new jargon to be invented and learnt ... this perspective applies with particular force in the area of community capacity-building'. (Stoker and Bottom 2003: 6) Their analysis of how New Labour characterised the 'problem' and the need for CCB included 'a lack of formal engagement in politics, lack of capacity to engage in institutions of democracy, reflecting social exclusion, lack of basic infrastructure to support community life, and the need to support individuals so that they can become full members of society.' *(Ibid.)* This analysis may sound familiar to those who have studied New Labour policy and political literature.

The UK Charity Commission, which regulates the activity of charities, decided recently – reflecting increased interest in the concept – to include 'community capacity-building' in its limited list of charitable aims (education and the relief of poverty being the other two). It defined CCB as:

> Developing the capacity and skills of a community in such a way that it is better able to identify and help meet its needs and to participate more fully in society. (Charity Commission 2000: 3)

This is remarkably close to – if shorter than – the definition of community development emerging from the Budapest Declaration.[3] It is significant that the Commission debated at length as to whether to use the term community development instead of CCB, perhaps deciding on the later because of its contemporary popularity with government. The UK Home Office, a key government player promoting CCB, described 'building the capacity of both individuals and groups within communities as central to the process of civil renewal' (Blunkett 2002: 5) and defined CCB as:

> Activities, resources and support that strengthen the skills and abilities of people and community groups to take effective action and leading roles in the development of their communities. (Home Office 2003: 15)

---

[3] See www.iacdglobal.org: the Budapest Declaration was the outcome of a conference marking the accession of ten new countries to the European Union in 2004, bringing together community development workers from more than thirty countries.

This accords well with the Charity Commission's definition, in that it stresses the importance of participation, community development and the strengthening of skills, abilities and responsibility. By this time, in the UK, CCB had come however to mean different things to different government departments, another example of widespread linguistic and ideological confusion.

Capacity and partnership

The relationship between partnership working, a key form of local governance promoted by many governmental agencies, which emerged more or less simultaneously alongside the enthusiasm for CCB, has also become a salient issue. There isn't space to argue the case in detail here but it is clear that effective partnership working is frequently undermined by the uneven capacity of partners. CCB, in this context, may often result in a form of organisational strengthening at a level of governance beyond the reach of communities themselves, confirming the difficulties that smaller community groups have in becoming fully involved – on their own terms – in community regeneration programmes. Partnership working has in fact increasingly been criticised for building the capacity of the powerful (and their organisations) or for building the capacity of the weak only insofar as it accords with the interests of the powerful. (Glendinning *et al.* 2002)

A critique of community capacity-building

There clearly remains substantial linguistic and ideological confusion surrounding the term CCB just as there is with the terms community, and community development. This confusion is not helped by the fact that, despite warm official rhetoric, there is little evidence as to whether CCB actually works. The community development literature has recently begun to grapple with questions of its effectiveness but none of this debate appears to have spilled over into analysing the effectiveness of CCB.

CCB as a concept and practice can be criticized from at least four different perspectives. *First*, given the marginal differences between the proclaimed goals and methods of community development and CCB, it may seem superfluous to introduce a new concept into the policy lexicon. It seems probable that the elision between the two concepts, from capacity-building's initial focus on developing the strengths of organizations into a catch-all term covering a range of activities at 'community' level, was accelerated by political fashion: new governments wishing to introduce apparently new policy programmes often adopt new terminology to distance themselves from their predecessors' programmes.

The *second*, related, critique is that, as with the term 'community', the concept of CCB is applied uncritically – as the 'spray-on additive' – to a very wide range of activities, many of which have little to do with the development – with community control of the skills, knowledge, assets and understanding of local deprived communities – at the heart of the definition of community development. Thus CCB is used in a contemporary context by international organizations such as the World Bank and by national governments to describe what are effectively 'top-down' interventions where local communities are required to engage in programmes with pre-determined goals – such as the privatization of public services within a context of tight fiscal control – as a condition for receiving funding, approaches far removed from 'bottom-up' community development interventions.

Thirdly, those working with local communities question the motives of those promoting CCB 'from the top'. For example, CCB is seen as being pursued by powerful partners to incorporate local communities into established structures and mechanisms rather than having to face the challenges to those structures which effective working with deprived communities presents, challenges which go to the heart of the reasons for deprivation and inequality. Government programme managers seek to co-opt local activists and individualize rather than collectivize local communities' experience, much in line with the Third Way approach of New Labour.

A critique of the CCB programme of the Government of Victoria in Australia comes to similar conclusions. Government here effectively ensured that any activities which might be regarded as political (such as advocacy by community members) were excluded from the framework of the initiative, and claimed credit for the action plans of participating communities. The ability of the community to act on its own behalf, to work on issues which it identified, and at a pace and in a manner which it determined itself, was compromised by the government's need to promote its own social and political agendas. (Mowbray 2005: 263)

A study of CCB projects working with Aboriginal Koori people in Australia noted:

> This new capacity-building jargon signifies an entrenchment of notions of what constitutes capacity, who defines capacity and what constitutes the relationship between the dominant culture *capacity-builders* and those identified as *capacity deficient*. ... The term community capacity-building will have little meaning to the peoples of Central Australia. Supporting, helping, sharing, giving of time and resources, cultural affirmation and taking care of country are responsibilities not viewed as special individualised effort but as cultural competencies. Discussions of community capacity-building

in indigenous contexts must avoid the paternalistic construction of a 'deficit' in the Aboriginal domain. (Tedmanson 2003: 15)

And an Aboriginal respondent argued:

> To restore capacity in our people is to be responsible for our own future. Notice that I talk of restoring rather than building capacity in our people ... we had 40 to 60,000 years of survival and capacity. The problem is that our capacity has been eroded and diminished [by colonialists] – our people do have skills, knowledge and experience ... (*Ibid.*)

The fundamental argument here – appropriate to other groups representing the powerless – is that 'cultural difference is viewed as a weakness and not a strength, a capacity deficit to be rebuilt or a problem to be "solved".' (*Ibid.*) This story is a familiar one to many community development workers and those in the communities – in North and South – with which they have worked. Responding to a government review of CCB, the body representing UK community development training argued that

> the experience of many communities is that 'community capacity-building' programmes (with a myriad of titles), have been imposed on them; with perceived needs, desired outcomes and preferred methods part of the package which they have not had the opportunity to identify, develop or agree. ....the 'community' (often not self-defined) is exhorted to play its part in an environment where inequalities of resources, power, information and status are not even acknowledged, never mind addressed. (FCDL 2004: 3)

This is the most fundamental critique of CCB, that it is based on the notion of communities being 'deficient' – in skills, knowledge and experience. This approach 'pays no attention to the capacity of institutions to overcome inherent barriers to engagement' (Beazley *et al.* 2004: 6) i.e. the problem lies not with communities but the institutions, structures and processes which affect them; and secondly, definitions of CCB built on the deficit model again 'give no indication of what capacity is being built towards – is it an end in itself?' (*Ibid.*) This is a question that has plagued the theory and practice of community development and is reflected in a continuing emphasis from governments on measuring programmatic outputs in terms of narrow quantitatively-defined goals rather than on community process and outcomes. Essentially, although it is possible to identify the characteristics of 'strengthened' or 'resilient' communities (skills, knowledge, organisation etc), the fundamental aim of community development is –

consonant with its value base – to ensure that greater political power lies with local communities. The endpoint might thus be 'less comfortable, more empowered and awkward but self-determined communities'. (*Ibid.*) Might the lack of capacity not also apply to the ability of powerful partner agencies to listen to, engage with and share power with communities effectively, to 'cope with residents' decisions going against them?'

This 'deficit' approach to CCB assumes a social pathology approach to communities lacking skills and abilities: these qualities would allow local community residents to be 'good citizens' in terms identified by government and 'for those in power, this model of capacity-building is useful. It poses no threat. It is top–down, paternalistic, and deflects attention away from the need to change the existing institutional and economic structures. It is a view that supports the status quo.' (Beazley *et al.* 2004: 3) Such an analysis of CCB from the perspective of the values of community development, would suggest that a view of communities as somehow deficient in certain skills and capacities to enable them to engage effectively with other actors in local governance misses the point. Communities have skills, ideas, capacities: but these are often latent or unacknowledged. Local and central governments often come with their own agendas which they attempt to impose, however subtly, through partnership working, or more crudely, directly on local communities, often using funding as a lever for compliance. The task for powerful partners in this kind of CCB partnership working should be to listen to communities' demands and respond appropriately, most of all when what local communities are demanding may be in conflict with external agendas; and for the former not to continue with predetermined goals and programmes. This may not just be difficult for powerful partners, it may be precisely what – despite the rhetoric of CCB – they are not interested in. For example, there can be little doubt that the UK government's understanding of CCB is linked to its desire to have more stable, organised communities with which it can more easily engage to pursue its own ideas of community cohesion (particularly given the increasing racialised impacts of the so-called 'war on terror'), community safety, family policy and criminal justice. The 'carrot' of funding is key in getting community groups to 'buy in' to government agendas. Much CCB at a local level can be seen as a way of creating structures fitting with government funding requirements.

Conclusion

It is clear that CCB can be seen as none other than our old friend community development. Under this new umbrella term, however, not only has a similarly wide range of activities found shelter, many of which have little to do with the goals and values of community development, but that many of the old tensions and difficulties of community development – of manipulation of communities, misappropriation of terminology, co-option of activists, conditional funding and state-controlled power games such as divide and rule – have emerged. Local, regional and national governments and international bodies – particularly those of a centre-right disposition, including New Labour – thus buy themselves continuing political space enabling them not to respond to the demands of the dispossessed, or to obscure the structural reasons for continuing poverty and inequality. To respond effectively to local communities' demands would mean giving up much of the power which these bodies enjoy. We may well ask: who defines the capacities which communities need and why? What control do local communities exercise over the capacity-building process? And who defines what a strong community would look like? Community capacity-building is essentially not a neutral technical process: it is about power and ideology and how these are mediated through structures and processes. As with the terms community and community development, the term CCB is used to hide a false consensus about goals and interests. In reality they are all arenas for political contestation. And, as with these earlier terms, CCB has been manipulated by governments to give a false sense of community ownership and control.

Reclaiming the radical agenda: a critical approach to community development

Margaret Ledwith

Introduction

These ideas arise out of a concern that we have allowed education to be seen as synonymous with training, and there is a subtle and dangerous difference. One is about thinking and the other is about doing, neither of which is much good without the other. Paulo Freire says, 'action is pure activism' unless it involves critical reflection (Freire 1972: 41), and what he calls *authentic praxis* is the bedrock of community development. It simply means that for our practice to have a social justice outcome, it is essential that every project that we undertake is planned, developed and evaluated within an emancipatory, anti-discriminatory framework.

Heavily influenced by state policy, the skills-driven approach to education in which our work is now embedded is tailored to feed the needs of the economy, and therefore founded on the worldview of western capitalism. Critical education, designed to encourage questioning and action for change, is founded on a different worldview, that of participatory democracy forged out of principles of cooperation and equality. Our work is the 'practice of freedom' (Freire 1976) not maintenance of the *status quo*, so therefore I suggest that in failing to be vigilant about changes in the political context we run the risk of developing practice that reinforces discrimination whilst still waving the banner of social justice. This is a dangerous path to tread!

It is my opinion that the full collective potential of community development is threatened by a resistance to praxis, a theory-practice divide which results in 'actionless thought' on one hand, and 'thoughtless action' on the other. (Johnston cited in Shaw 2004: 26) If we fail to generate theory in action, and move towards a unity of praxis where theory and practice

From: Ledwith, M. (2007) 'Reclaiming the radical agenda: a critical approach to community development', *Concept*, vol 17, no 2, pp 8-13.

are synthesised, we give way to anti-intellectual times which emphasise 'doing' at the expense of 'thinking'; we react to the symptoms rather than root causes of injustice – and leave the structures of discrimination intact – dividing people through poverty, creating massively different life chances by blaming the victims of an unjust system. This is what I refer to as 'a politics of tokenism'.

The policy context

The policy context is fascinating. In the process of devolution within the UK, community development has come into public prominence, yet the bewildering array of policy initiatives emerging from government, frustrated by short-term funding, work counter to the concept of *development*. This presents a fundamental threat to the overriding purpose of community development, still poorly understood, with its long-term, social justice intentions. Principles of participatory democracy call for an understanding of power and discrimination at every stage of our practice. Critical education, the process which runs through community development, is expressed through the myriad of practical projects that are relevant to everyday issues in local communities. This is where people learn to question their everyday reality, and to act together to bring about change for a fair and just future. But, by concentrating on the practical projects, rather than the education for which they are the vehicles, we allow ourselves to operate on principles of amelioration rather than transformation. We are distracted by the symptoms of injustice and fail to reach the root causes, and in doing so give free reign to the *status quo*. These are the ways in which an emphasis on training can mask the purpose of community development, and give us the illusion that we are making a difference.

The Blair Government has signalled its commitment to devolution and local governance, as expressed in the Local Government White Paper *Strong and Prosperous Communities* which emerged from the newly-formed Department for Communities and Local Government in October 2006. It is an unsurpassed opportunity for community development to assume a prominence in the public eye and take the lead in creating communities for a fair and just future. Yet, the evidence suggests that we are allowing ourselves to be redefined as a tool of government policy at the expense of our transformative purpose. Here, I attempt to identify the weaknesses in our armour.

A radical agenda

Community development has always had a radical agenda. (Ledwith 2005). By this, I mean that our practice is inspired by a vision of social and environmental justice. It is fundamentally committed to bring about social change which contributes to this end. So, our practice starts in people's everyday lives, 'extraordinarily re-experiencing the ordinary'. (Shor 1992:122). This calls for a critical approach – situating local practice within the wider political picture. In other words, unless we have an analysis of power, of the structures of oppression in the world that reach into our local communities and impact on personal lives, our practice is likely to be tokenistic at best.

Critical approaches to community development locate grassroots practice within that driving vision of a just and sustainable future. The well-defined ideological base that connects with our vision provides us with a framework through which to evaluate every stage of the community development process. It is what I loosely term an ideology of equality informed by such values as mutual respect, reciprocity, dignity, mutuality, trust and cooperation. This offers a system of checks and balances to examine the validity of our practice, testing that what we are doing is what we say we are doing, echoing a jarring dissonance if we have slipped off track. For example, if I say my practice is committed to social justice, what evidence is there that it is making a difference to the oppression that people experience in their lives? If I say that my practice is based on values of mutual respect, is there evidence that there is an increase in the health, confidence and autonomy of the people with whom I work? These questions needs to be set in collaboration with everyone involved in any aspect of the process, from policy to project, but most particularly with the local people with whom we work together in partnership. In these ways, the practical projects that we develop with people in community provide the context for critical consciousness, the 'teaching to question' that is at the heart of Paulo Freire's (1972) critical pedagogy and which makes the connections with structures of discrimination. In turn, critical consciousness becomes the basis for collective action, generating the confidence and the analysis to bring about change for social and environmental justice on a bigger scale than the community group. Personal issues become local projects, projects become causes, and causes become movements for change (Sivanandan cited in Cooke 1996) as we network and form alliances that reach out beyond the perimeter of our communities.

Globalised times

Discrimination needs to be understood in relation to how personal lives are shaped by changing political forces. (Ledwith 2005) The process of globalisation has accelerated over the past two decades, creating a human crisis as well as a threat to the entire planet. (Cannan 2000) Cannan (2000) cites evidence of a five-fold increase in economic growth since the Second

World War at the same time as poverty gaps between nations and within nations have doubled. In relation to our children, one example of this outrageous contradiction is the way that a rich nation like the UK is divided within, with one-third of its own children still growing up in poverty (a rise from one in ten in 1979), whilst at the same time it is more divided than ever from the developing world, with immunity and distance from other realities, say, Ethiopian children starving to death. This argument is central to sustainability and to social justice. We cannot operate on a naïve interpretation of social justice which aims to lift the standards of living of the poorest in line with the artificially created greed of the rich, when the world is not able to support such excesses.

This becomes a human rights issue when set alongside the well-rehearsed understanding we have of poverty-related morbidity and mortality. We know that poverty creates ill-health and premature death; for example, in the UK, children of those in the bottom social class are five times more likely to die from an accident and 15 times more likely to die in a house fire than those in upper social classes. (Flaherty *et al.* 2004) Yet evidence points to the fact that escalating child poverty during the Thatcher period was a political choice rather than an inevitability. Bradshaw, investigating international trends, provides evidence that out of 25 countries only Russia and the USA had higher rates of child poverty than the UK. In 16 years, 1979-1995, child poverty increased more in the UK than in almost all other industrial countries, and in Europe only Italy had a sharper increase than the UK. Important to note is that this included countries facing similar demographic and economic trends. 'Nearly half of all countries had no increase or a reduction in their child poverty rates'. (Bradshaw 1999: 16)

Even a relatively superficial glance at the statistics reveals that children at risk of poverty correlate with social groups targeted by poverty, a critical factor in this analysis:

- Lone-parent households
- Low paid households
- Households without an adult in paid work
- Minority ethnic families
- 'Dis'abled children or those with a 'dis'abled parent

and that children who grow up in poverty are more likely to:

- Underachieve at school
- Experience unemployment and low wages
- Have low self-esteem
- For girls, become pregnant in teenage years
- For young men, to be at risk of suicide

- Have low expectations
- Be suspended, excluded or truant from school
- Have low birthweight, leading to infant death or chronic disease later in life
- Suffer from malnutrition
- Die prematurely (mortality)
- Suffer from long-term debilitating illness (morbidity)

Critical connections like this provide us with a complex picture of the interlinking dimensions of poverty which target some social groups much more than others. The correlation between unemployment, poor mental health, homelessness, school exclusions, children in care/leaving care and the escalation in youth suicide are important critical connections for community development (Howarth *et al.* 1999), as is the connection between increasing concentrations of poverty on council housing estates (Page 2000) and the gendered and racialised dimensions of child poverty which link to growing up in lone-parent families and in families of non-white ethnicity, compounded by ill-health and low income. (Gordon *et al.* 2000) We must be concerned, both in terms of its profound injustice and its cost to society as a whole.

Our consciousness remains partial if we focus our analysis on a personal/local level and fail to notice the ways in which these are social trends that are linked to structural injustices. Our practice will address the symptoms and overlook the causes. In this sense, it is vital that these trends are set within wider issues of world poverty and its gendered and racialised dimensions. Peter Townsend, as a critical commentator on world poverty and on behalf of UNICEF, talked about the UK escalation in child poverty as a 'neglect-filled Anglo-American model which unless there is massive investment in children will head for economic catastrophe.' (Townsend 1995: 10-12)

His comments were made before New Labour came into power in the UK and went public on poverty, but the issues remain the same. Important to remember here is that community development practice needs to be informed by an incisive analysis of the discriminatory nature of poverty in society at large, and an understanding of how these trends affect the communities with which we work. For example, relative poverty within a country has a massive impact on issues related to social exclusion. Setting this within an understanding of world poverty and environmental justice gives insight into the ways in which the problems lie with disproportionate levels of consumption in Western societies which the earth cannot sustain. Therefore, a critical approach to practice has to be based on the notion of a redistribution of wealth that reduces the divisions cleaved by poverty which affect the life chances of people both *within* nations and *between* nations. Globalisation's acceleration has resulted in what Peter Reason (2002) calls the twin global crises of our times – *social justice*, with the most vulnerable of the world exploited for the greed of western markets, and *sustainability*, with ecosystems that sustain our world being destroyed by exploitation and pollution. In these ways social justice and environmental justice become inextricably linked, and naïve notions of increasing the levels of consumption of the poorest in our society will simply accelerate these crises for the world as a whole.

Critical praxis

At the same time, a parallel but related process of anti-intellectualism is encouraging uncritical practice. So, while we are failing in 'being critical', social injustices are escalating as globalisation creates more complex oppressions within and between nations. In these ways, the issues of the world at large become issues for our communities. In other words, in the name of a free market economy, not only is labour exploited in the interests of class, but the same structures of oppression which subordinate groups of people according to 'race', gender, age, sexuality, ethnicity, 'dis'ability … are being reproduced on a global level. In the words of Fisher and Ponniah: 'Capitalism, imperialism, monoculturalism, patriarchy, white supremacism and the domination of biodiversity have coalesced under the current form of globalisation' to form a major threat to a just, equal and sustainable future. (2003: 11) This is precisely why the practice of community development, rooted as it is in anti-discriminatory analysis, cannot justify an approach to practice which focuses on the local and overlooks global dimensions of oppression.

We need to be vigilant and stay critical if we are to prevent our practice getting distracted and slipping into some feel-good, ameliorative, sticking plaster on the wounds of injustice. We need to reclaim our radical agenda from attempts to hijack and dilute it into a rhetoric of self-help – neatly placing the blame for social divisions at the feet of the victims. For example, concepts like participation, empowerment, social justice, equality are not just pleasant and friendly ideas but come from a participatory worldview – one which is founded on cooperation and true democracy rather than competition and free market politics.

Here, I would like to tell you a story to illustrate my point:

> 'Tell them that I love all the children of the world as my own.' The microphone echoed the quiet voice of Gandhi as he stood before the angry, unemployed millworkers of Lancashire in the 1930s. He had taken the train from London, against the advice of Winston Churchill, to explain why he had put an embargo on English-woven cotton being exported to India. 'I am sorry for your suffering, but

millions of people in my country are unemployed.' Community action in the form of the Bombay bonfire of English-woven cotton, had been followed by community development, teaching local people to spin and weave for their own needs. The strident Lancashire voice of the man with the microphone echoed, 'Mr Gandhi says he loves all the children of the world'. 'That is not what I said; I said I love all the children of the world *as my own'*. The quiet but insistent tones of Gandhi were picked up almost imperceptibly, but made a big impact on me. His simple statement reflected an alternative worldview, one of co-operation and connectedness, one in which all children are loved because we are all woven together by the common web of humanity. My point is that a participatory worldview calls for a paradigm shift, a radical perspective framed by an ideology of equality which is never distorted by a politics of tokenism.

If we fail to be vigilant, we become distracted and our truth becomes distorted. Gary Craig captures some of the consequences of this when he says:

> Community work is too often drawn into the latest fashions of government policy agendas because that is where the funding is, rather than developing and maintaining a clear analysis to inform action. Increasingly, the emphasis on training seems to be on skills to the exclusion of thinking about the theory and politics of community work: government now provides a community development employment base which is fragmented, short-term and insecure with the result that practice is dominated by the policy and political context rather than creating it. (Craig in Shaw 2004: 42)

The result is that, despite the plethora of policy initiatives and increased funding targeting community-based interventions, there is little evidence in the UK that any sustainable difference is being made to the lives of people in poverty. This has led to a renewed government drive for devolution, as expressed in the Home Office-led *Together We Can* initiative to get departments working together across boundaries to achieve greater community participation. The recent White Paper *Strong and Prosperous Communities*, from the newly-formed Department for Communities and Local Government, together with consultation papers *Removing the Barriers to Community Participation* and *The Community Development Challenge*, in which I have been involved, indicates an ongoing commitment to community participation, but also alerts us to the fact that the term 'community empowerment' is being used as synonymous with improved service delivery – which is just a small part of the community development agenda. Nevertheless, we can still seize it as a real opportunity to make a difference to the lives of marginalised communities. My point is that, without vigilance, community development will be diverted into a different role – one which focuses primarily on service delivery and fails to analyse and act on the structures of power which continue unabated to create and recreate oppression and marginalisation.

Action for change

So, my challenge is for us to get better at weaving theory into our practice, enabling us to explain why we are doing what we are doing at any stage of the community development process, and so creating knowledge-in-action based on practical experience. Without theory, practice is in danger of being reduced, at best, to a self-help, local activity.

Taking a critical approach gets us to the heart of what is creating social and environmental injustice by developing practice which:

- Contributes to change for a peaceful, just and sustainable future.
- Develops anti-discriminatory analyses that reach from local to global, identifying the ways in which personal stories are political.
- Builds practical local projects with people in community.
- Teaches people to question their reality.
- Forms strategic alliances for collective action across difference.
- Remains true to its radical agenda, with social and environmental justice at its heart.
- Generates theory in action, practical theory based on experience which contributes to a unity of praxis.

The time has come for urgent action on the part of us all!

Community participation in the real world

Marilyn Taylor

The recent shift from government to governance has created new opportunities for people from disadvantaged communities to participate in decisions that affect them. However, the weight of evidence over the years suggests these communities have remained marginal to partnerships and similar initiatives.

This article explores challenges and opportunities characterising past participation policies and the potential for change. It uses governmentality theory as a framework, discussing how state power is reproduced in new spaces, but also allowing for the possibility of 'active subjects' shaping and influencing the exercise of government. (Morison 2000: 119) It draws on studies of community participation in neighbourhood renewal programmes in England and beyond to consider implications for both government and communities, if community participation is to move from rhetoric to reality.

The theory: from government to governance

Governance theory analyses power not as 'social control' but as 'social production'. It moves away from fixed ideas about power as a commodity rooted in particular institutions to more fluid ideas of power developed and negotiated between partners. Governance discourse includes propositions about an 'enabling' state, 'steering' not 'rowing' (Osborne and Gaebler 1992); new combinations of markets, hierarchies and networks; the opening up of decision-making to greater participation; rescaling and multi-level governance; and decentralisation and devolution. It is also associated with normative concepts of community, social capital and civil society as integrating forces built on networks and trust. The emphasis on communities resonates with ideas of devolution and partnership, suggesting new sets of relationships between citizens, policy-makers and service agencies.

Some governance theorists hail its self-organised inter-organisational networks as 'the ultimate in hands-off government'. (Rhodes 1997: 110) But

From: Taylor, M.(2007) 'Community participation in the real world', *Urban Studies*, vol 44, no 2, pp 297-317.

others ....have criticised the failure of much of the governance discourse to address issues of power, agency and accountability (Gittell 2001; Newman 2001) and fundamental inequalities in bargaining positions different partners bring to the table. (Jones 2003: 586) These new governance spaces, as Cornwall observes (2004a), are spaces into which communities/citizens are invited by the state, created and defined by it ('invited spaces'), as opposed to spaces created and defined by citizens ('popular spaces').

Like governance theory, governmentality theory, drawing on Foucault (1979) but developed by other scholars, is based on an analysis of power as 'social production' rather than 'social control'. It replaces the notion of zero sum power and 'docile bodies' upon which power is inscribed (Morison 2000: 120) with the idea that state power is decoupled from the state as 'government' and is instead produced through a range of sites and alliances 'at a distance from' or 'beyond' the state. Governing has thus become a domain of strategies, techniques and procedures through which different forces and groups attempt to render their programme operable. (Rose and Miller 1992)

Governmentality theorists warn, however, that forms of power beyond the state can often sustain and enlarge the state more effectively than its own institutions. (Foucault 1980:73) This is not achieved through coercive control, but through a more complex and subtle diffusion of techniques and forms of knowledge through which communities 'can be mobilised, enrolled, deployed in novel programmes' and 'techniques which encourage and harness active practices of self-management and identity construction, of personal ethics and collective allegiances'. (Rose 1999:176)

Somerville (2005:125) summarises three routes through which elite power is reinforced and reproduced: recentralisation, responsibilisation and privileged access to decision-making: 'All governing coalitions tend to favour their own people (privileged access), to exercise control from the centre (recentralisation) and to mould citizens in their own image and likeness (responsibilisation).'

Recentralisation

Newman contrasts the almost utopian emphasis in some governance literature on decentralised, network forms of governance with the reality of a recentralisation of political control, limiting considerably 'the scope for participation to contribute to a more open and reflexive style of governance'. (2001:163) This control extends beyond partnership spaces to the everyday life of communities and citizens. Thus Raco (2003:78) describes how, 'across whole areas of state action, there is an increased concern with defining and shaping "appropriate" individual and community conduct, regulation and control'. The 'community discourse', meanwhile, has hi-jacked a 'language of resistance and transformed it into an expert discourse and professional vocation'. (Rose 1999:175) Communities, Rose argues, have become zones to be investigated, mapped, classified, documented and interpreted. The state thus reaches out beyond new governance spaces into communities themselves.

At the same time, recentralisation manifests itself in the dominance of an audit culture, through which surveillance 'has become institutionalised and routinised into every aspect of economic and social life'. (Flynn 2002:163) Auditee organisations, Power argues, need to be reformed to make them 'auditable'; the auditor thus becomes an explicit change agent rather than just a neutral verifier. (2003: 188-9) Similarly, Atkinson describes how, in developing technologies required of them by government programmes, community participants 'restructure themselves' and are forced to 'demonstrate that they are capable of governing themselves, collectively and individually, in ways that reflect these wider demands'. (2003: 118)

In this way, Morison argues (2000:129) that 'what might be presented as increased autonomy, a chance to govern oneself, can also be seen as a reconfiguration of rationalities so that the self-interest of the sector aligns with the interest of a state seeking to mobilise a reserve army of support effectively and on its own terms'. The emphasis on performance then depoliticises partnerships, mainstreaming participation as technical rather than as political. (Taylor 2003; Hickey and Mohan 2004:11)

Transferring responsibility downwards

While power is increasingly vested in global corporations, responsibility for welfare is pushed down the line to local, community and individual level, with risks borne by those least able to bear it. The withdrawal of the state can thus be deciphered as a technique for government, shifting the costs and responsibilities of the state onto communities and 'responsible and rational individuals', absolving the state of its own responsibility for addressing social injustice. (Hickey and Mohan 2004) But as communities accept a responsibility to seek ways of transforming their position themselves, 'the danger is that, having signed up to achieve the unachievable, they will end up being condemned as the authors of their own exclusion.' (Atkinson 2003: 102)

Privileged access

Governing 'beyond the state' doesn't take place in a vacuum. The existing distribution of power is inscribed in the new sites and spaces. Swyngedouw (2005) thus draws our attention to ways in which governing beyond the state privileges certain actors, through entitlement and status, the mobilisation of discourse alliances which ignore or silence alternatives, and new forms of governance established as regulatory frameworks for managing a beyond-the- state policy. The 'rules of the game' continue largely to be framed by government actors, with regulatory techniques enshrined in central guidance, cultures of decision-making, procurement protocols and auditing requirements.

Community participants are also disadvantaged by power and resource differentials. Cornwall (2004b) argues that, generally speaking, 'invited spaces are transplanted onto institutional landscapes in which entrenched relations of dependency, fear and disprivilege undermine the possibility of the kind of deliberative decision-making they are to foster'. Citizens are constructed as subjects, clients and consumers rather than as citizens of equal worth and decision-making capacity.

Active subjects?

To summarise: governmentality theorists describe a contradictory process whereby on the one hand, responsibilities are driven down into new governance spaces at local state and, increasingly, sublocal level, involving new non-state players but where, at the same time, power and control is recentralised at nation-state and supranational level. The new governing spaces can thus be characterised as arenas of co-option and colonisation, inscribed with rationalities, technologies and rules of engagement internalised by non-state actors which create privileged pathways for more powerful actors.

Nonetheless, there is in Foucault's notion of power the possibility of resistance, allowing the articulation, and implementation of alternative agendas. (Atkinson 2003: 117) Self-steering actors outside the state can thus become 'active subjects' in new governance spaces, not only collaborating in the exercise of government, but shaping and influencing it. (Morison 2000: 119) Thus, Raco (2003: 79), applying governmentality theory to devolution, argues that, while 'neighbourhood governance could be seen as a way of relegitimising the state' by reorganising state practices in line with the 'imagined places of subject populations', 'new domains and territories of state action provide new platforms and opportunities for the articulation and implementation of alternative agendas'.

Social movement theorists use the concept of a 'political opportunity structure' to highlight ways in which changes in the political context create or deny opportunities for social action. They remind us (Tarrow 1994: 99; Caniglia and Carmin 2005: 204) that the opening up of political power in new governance spaces creates opportunities that can be exploited, offering:

- institutional provisions for participation;
- external resources for people who lack internal ones;

- alliances that did not previously seem possible; and
- realignments that can bring new groups to power.

Even when social movements collapse and advances are reversed, Tarrow argues, 'they leave behind them incremental expansions in participation, changes in popular culture and residual movement networks'. (1994:190)

Governmentality theorists argue that new governance spaces beyond the state are still inscribed with a state agenda. This is evidenced in both the 'what' and the 'how' of neighbourhood renewal. In terms of the 'what', successive studies of UK regeneration programmes have illustrated how agendas can be dominated by the priorities of developers. (Anastacio *et al.* 2000) and business interests. In terms of the 'how', the dominance of the audit culture is well-evidenced in studies of neighbourhood renewal. At the most simple level, the demands of monitoring crowd out other activities and shape the way in which activities are legitimated. The dominance of the audit culture, however, is demonstrated not only through conformity with external demands. At both community and partnership level, the heavy demands of monitoring reinforced a risk-averse culture, leading to underspend, stifling innovation and placing a premium on conformity with 'tried and trusted' methods, or initiatives which conformed to government's current definitions of 'best practice'. This in turn sets up more pressure, as failure to spend quickly enough or to deliver high-profile changes saps political support for community-led programmes.

In the field of neighbourhood renewal, early policy documents did underline the structural causes of neighbourhood decline. (SEU 1998) Nonetheless Atkinson (2003: 102) detects 'a strong undercurrent within New Labour's policies towards urban areas and "excluded spaces" in particular, that those living there bear some responsibility for their situation'. Indeed, once neighbourhoods have been classified as sites of intervention, even a decision not to participate is loaded with meaning. The intransigent problems of social exclusion are put down to apathy, 'dependency and a "poverty of expectations"' (Newman (2001: 152-3) and solutions to the need for individuals to become active citizens, gain the right skills and adapt to a flexible labour market.

There is a considerable resource imbalance between communities and their partners in new governance spaces. The evidence from many studies suggests that community voices are also excluded by the 'rules of the game' and 'traditional routines', taken-for-granted by public sector partners. (Taylor 2000a; Coaffee and Healey 2003) Traditional cultures of decision-making are further entrenched by considerable resistance to community participation. Even where communities are given entitlement and status, it is often only a minority of acceptable voices which get heard. This is exacerbated by the fact that community participants are often dependent on their partners for funding. Furthermore, the promise of increased powers to local authorities through devolution is taking place against a background of centrally defined targets and continued constraints on mainstream local government funding.

For some local state actors, community participation is seen as a form of discipline and limitation of their powers and legitimacy. (Lowndes and Sullivan (2004: 55) In these circumstances, it is perhaps unsurprising that they hang onto their remaining power. This capacity for resistance to change permeates the literature. In the US, the evaluation of the Empowerment Zones initiative argues that 'reforms that devolve power to state and local governments without changing the participants, fail to produce more responsive policies or contribute to the revitalisation of the democratic process'. (Gittell 2001: 92) It describes how each city's historical power structures reassumed control of decision-making as programmes progressed and how directors of the initiatives declared themselves frustrated by having to include communities in decision-making.

Another route by which existing power is maintained in these new spaces is by the ways in which the public and community themselves are 'constructed' in these new spaces and by which legitimacy is conferred on community representatives by other players. Many accounts point to the way in which power-holders construct 'the community' in their own image, recruiting people like themselves into their partnerships. In addition, the 'rules of the game' limit the number of people who can take up this role by demanding certain skills and knowledge and by placing practical limitations on who can participate. The demands of the representative role mean further that they risk becoming 'professionalised', detached from their constituency by the demands of their representative role and internalising the values and purposes of their new peers. It is also easy for partners to diminish the 'community' contribution by questioning the legitimacy of representatives. This does not diminish the need for communities to take accountability and legitimacy seriously. Shirlow and Murtagh are highly critical of community representatives who determine what is best for their neighbourhood without any meaningful consultation. (2004: 63)

Becoming active subjects

So how can new community players can become active subjects and exercise power? UK neighbourhood renewal experience suggests that recentralisation, earlier criticised as disempowering, can act to strengthen community empowerment. Central government's performance management requirements have also acted as an incentive to take communities seriously. A second positive message from empirical evidence is that colonisation and 'responsibilisation' are more complex processes than the critique suggests. Many communities have made conscious choices to take on responsibility for local programmes and diversify funding in order to retain their independence, assert their ownership of community interventions and ensure that new resources meet community needs. Thus, one community's 'responsibilisation' can be another's community empowerment. Some of the best-known community initiatives in the UK have used central government funding to acquire and develop their own assets. This, in turn, increased their leverage in local partnerships, giving some of them access to central government policy-making arenas as valued advisers.

Some political opportunities identified by social movement theorists were cited earlier. It is possible to find evidence of most of these: new institutional provisions have been accompanied by new resources and made possible new alliances and realignments of power, having the potential to shift existing privileged access to power. These opportunities can certainly be found in the neighbourhood renewal field, as central government has swung its weight behind communities and marginalised groups, as leaders in the voluntary and community sector (VCS) have been seconded into government to assist the development of new policies; and through the setting up of a National Community Forum at central government level to bring policy-makers into direct contact with people on the ground.

Hickey and Mohan (2004: 15) remind us that the state is not a homogenous entity, that 'not all local elites and power relations are inherently exclusive and subordinating'. This suggests that central government discourses of 'community' and 'participation' have strengthened the hand of allies – agents within the system who want change. It has also brought together players who have not been in the same spaces before, increased understanding between them, providing incentives for those who had not worked in this way to do so. Recent research on local strategic partnerships (LSPs), meanwhile, suggests that an increasing, though still small, proportion of these are now chaired by VCS representatives. (ODPM 2005) The presence of new community players on LSPs and the creation of thematic subgroups also creates new spaces for dialogue between sectors at different levels.

Colonisation and co-option?

Fung and Wright (2003: 264) argue that democracy-enhancing collaboration is unlikely to be sustained without effective countervailing power. However, 'outsiders' have argued that years on the outside of policy processes has not improved their situation (Craig *et al.* 2004) and that they needed to argue on the inside to make any headway; a combination of both insider and outsider strategies was in fact likely to be most effective. Insiders benefited from the fact that outsiders were continually placing items and arguments on the agenda that would otherwise be ignored; outsiders benefited because there were insiders prepared to follow issues getting onto the political agenda through to implementation and, where claims fail, rescue what can be rescued to mitigate the impact of regressive legislation. Navigating tensions within these new governance spaces is not easy. Community players can, however, generate their own power, exploiting ambiguities in the new 'messy' governance spaces where government respondents also acknowledge uncertainty about how to operate.

While evidence emphasises the problems faced by communities participating in new governance spaces, there have been small gains. Even modest changes can make a huge difference to individual lives – and may also have unforeseen consequences, like the 'butterfly's wing' of chaos theory. (Kooiman 2003) The recreation of state power in new governance spaces may not thus be as thorough-going or inevitable as the earlier analysis suggested. Even when immediate gains seem few, a longer-term perspective offers a more optimistic assessment. When social movements collapse and advances are reversed, Tarrow argues, 'they leave behind them incremental expansions in participation, changes in popular culture and residual movement networks.' (1994: 190)

The implications for government and communities

In summary, although new governance spaces emerging recently are suffused with state power, there are still opportunities for communities to become 'active subjects' within them, to influence the exercise of government. This suggests that 'governing-beyond-the-state' (Swyngedouw 2005) is a fluid and dynamic process where there is a possibility both of power becoming more transparent (hence more accountable) and of new circuits of power opening up. There are contradictions within processes of governing that can be exploited, alliances to be struck, small gains to be made that may start off processes of more fundamental change. However, if these opportunities are to be maximised, there are many implications for both government and communities themselves.

Communities

Communities don't have to enter new governance spaces. Morison reminds us there will always be organisations and communities that will (2000:13) remain 'incompletely domesticated'. There are choices between having voice within the new invited spaces, or building countervailing power, creating independent 'popular' spaces and exiting the formal democratic system altogether.

We know (Craig *et al.* 2004) that community empowerment is likely to require both insiders and outsiders, those who choose to enter invited spaces and those who prefer to operate in their own 'popular' spaces. Indeed,

citizens need their own popular spaces to develop their own independe
narratives and voices, whether or not they then decide to enter invited spac
(Cornwall 2004a) Gaventa argues further (2004: 38) that progress is m
likely at the interstices between popular spaces and invited spaces.'Navigati
the intersections of relationships may in turn create new boundaries
possibility for action and engagement'. But operating effectively in tl
way requires community players in these new spaces to be sophisticat
about their engagement and understanding of power. Engaging effective
as an 'active subject' requires considerable skills; whilst this is sometimes tl
case (Jones 2003), there are also instances where community participar
jeopardised their chances of being taken seriously in the governance spac
where they had chosen to engage.

At one extreme, Shirlow and Murtagh (2004:68), writing in Norther
Ireland, refer to the VCS there as shaped by 'victimhood'. Indeed, mar
writers, internationally as well as in the UK, have commented on tl
difficulty of making the transition from a politics of opposition to one (
engagement. However, both Gittell (2001) in the US and Greer (2001) ii
the UK argue that government funding programmes themselves encourage
this narrow perspective through an emphasis on specific projects rather than
more comprehensive approaches to community development. Many urban
initiatives also foster intra-community conflict – capacity building projects,
as Shirlow and Murtagh (2004: 68) point out, remain tied to inherently
conflictual and contradictory processes with groups competing for limited
resources and political attention.

Government

The focus here has been on communities. In analysing community
engagement it is, however, important to appreciate the three-way
relationship between central government, the local state and the VCS. For
many voluntary and community organisations, their primary relationship
is with the local state but, in a country where local government is not
constitutionally independent and raises only a small proportion of its income,
it is central government policy which creates the parameters and controls the
resources which shape local relationships. In this situation, local state actors
are both subject and object, able to manipulate power through privileged
access but also disciplined by the central state through communities and
other means and being given new responsibilities without resources to fulfil
them. While this creates opportunities and ambiguities for communities to
exploit, it also fuels resistance from local state players who see their own
powers ebbing away.

Proposals for 'double devolution', pushing powers and resources down to
local level, along with a parallel commitment to 'proportionate and risk-

based accountability' (Miliband 2006), aim to change the balance of power and allow policy to respond more effectively to local need and capacity. However, evidence suggests that, unless there is a significant shift in local authority culture, devolved power will stick at this level in many authorities and the power gap between citizens and the institutions of governance that current policy seeks to address will remain.

This is a conundrum for central government. In keeping with its commitment to subsidiarity, it has devolved funding for community participation and for neighbourhood management into a local Safer and Stronger Communities Fund under local authority control. In doing so, it has lost some significant levers and incentives for promoting community engagement, especially in the most resistant authorities. There are still community involvement targets to be met, but these will compete with conflicting service-driven targets and are, at best, a blunt tool. Indeed, a performance-driven culture discourages risk, encouraging blame-avoidance, especially where results are likely to take time to achieve. Nor is it clear, with the reorganisation that this devolution entails, what skills and capacity will remain in regional government offices to support the community engagement agenda. Meanwhile the community empowerment infrastructure that has been built up at local level looks vulnerable.

Community development and the politics of community

Mae Shaw

The problem of community

Much has been written about the problematic nature of 'community', emphasising its distinctive character as an historically situated and theoretically contested idea. As Mayo (1994:48) observes:

> It is not just that the term has been used ambiguously, it has been contested, fought over and appropriated for different uses and interests to justify different politics, policies and practices.

This tells us something about the elusive nature of the term. But it also tells us something about its wider social significance and the way in which it continues to be appropriated to legitimate or justify a wide range of political positions which might otherwise be regarded as incompatible. (Stacey 1969) This potential for providing competing legitimacies for very different interests and purposes is, of course, part of the theoretical problem for policy analysis in this field, but it is also problematic for a practice which is predicated on values such as community empowerment and social justice. Plant's (1974) advice that it is necessary to 'explore a meaning' before 'espousing a cause' is therefore particularly apposite.

Although the word has been in the English language since the fourteenth century, Williams (1976) suggests that, in thinking about community today, we are essentially heir to two particular and opposing traditions of political theory. On the one hand, the liberal tradition regards the individual as prior to all other forms of social life, positing the basis of all social experience in contract and reason, not custom and practice. On the other hand, the communitarian tradition stresses 'rootedness, a sense of locality, identity of interests, fraternity and co-operation and a sense of identity communally mediated' as the only means of achieving individual liberty and equality.

From: Shaw, M. (2008) 'Community development and the politics of community', *Community Development Journal*, vol 43, no 1, pp 24-36.

(Plant 1974: 29) The relationship between individual freedom and the common good is of course one of the central concerns of social and political theory, but for community development it produces particularly sharp ideological tensions which have been explored over time in various typologies that have sought to define and locate it. (Barr 1982; Thorpe 1985; Popple 1995b; Taylor 2003)

From the nineteenth century on, the term 'community' became imbued with evaluative meaning, embodying two distinct and competing visions. Over time, it can be seen that these competing visions have produced two separate discourses which continue to vie for loyalty and legitimacy in policy and in practice – 'backward-looking romanticism and forward-looking socialism' (MacGregor 2001) – although these have to some extent been fused in Third Way ideology. (Kenny 2002)

Raymond Williams (1976:66) famously summed up the problem thus:

> Community can be the warmly persuasive word to describe an existing set of relationships, or the warmly persuasive word to describe an alternative set of relationships.

It is important to remember that the contradictory provenance of community development with its roots in both benevolent welfare paternalism and autonomous working-class struggle (Baldock 1980) has created a curiously hybrid practice which has awkwardly (and sometimes unconvincingly) embodied *both* of these meanings simultaneously. This capacity to conflate two largely opposing rationalities has unsurprisingly resulted in the kind of 'functional ambiguity' which has made community development so difficult to pin down – and so useful to so many different interests. (Martin 1987) Part of the problem of course is that, whilst the socialist discourse of transformation and empowerment has tended to operate at a rhetorical level, it has generally concealed a much more conformist and conservative reality. (Barr 1991)

Such a fusion (or, indeed, confusion) of conflicting notions of community is arguably at the root of one of the longstanding preoccupations of community development – whether it can (or should) be called a profession at all, 'professionalisation having been posed as potentially undermining to community activism and autonomous community movements'. (Mayo 1998: 164). This has resulted in a kind of schizophrenic approach to the development of practice theory which, far from reconciling the tensions, has been in danger of reinforcing the problem by constructing and sustaining a spurious dichotomy between political and professional dimensions of practice.

Specht (1978), for example, distinguished between 'passion vs responsibility'; between community work as a social movement and as a profession. The former he regarded as 'ideological' whilst the latter was 'objective'. In similar terms, Twelvetrees (1991) contrasted the 'professional' approach with the 'radical' approach. Whilst these distinctions may have some merit, they are also inherently problematic because the inference is that any alternative to the professional approach is unprofessional or, indeed, incompetent. Conversely, professionalism is deemed, from this standpoint, to be non-ideological and non-political. Keith Popple identifies what he sees as two broad 'camps': 'those who are keen to increase community work's professional status (the technical school)' and 'those who see the potential of community work as part of a movement for greater social change (the radical school)'. (in Shaw 2004) Since 'radical' has become such a problematic term, particularly in light of its appropriation by the neo-liberal agenda, Mayo's (1998) distinction between 'technicist' and 'transformational' approaches to *professional* community development may be more helpful by suggesting that different purposes can and should be contested, as the legitimate scope of professionalism. In other words, community development is both a professional practice *and* a political practice. It is therefore important to emphasise that the distinction is a conceptual tool for analytical purposes, rather than a dichotomy in which one has to choose sides. There are different ways of talking about community development and why it matters and the way we understand community in these terms is central to our analysis of what community development might be 'for' at any time, in any given context.

Community as 'fact' and 'value'

In his theoretical exploration of community, Plant (1974) argues that we can only understand its meaning through 'its actual use in language and thought, in the description, interpretation, organisation and evaluation of behaviour'. In other words, we need to look at what function it fulfils in particular contexts in order to understand its meaning. Therefore, if we look for *the* definition of 'community' we miss the critical connection between value and meaning.

All conceptions of community are necessarily premised on some normative account of 'the good life', though this is rarely made explicit. This is a clue to how it can be claimed with equal moral and political legitimacy across the ideological spectrum, '[building] credence for projects which may be inherently controlling ... and projects which may be liberating'. (Mayo 1994: 57) Such ambiguity is further compounded, however, when what community *should be* is conflated with what is often a very different reality, and the idea of community becomes an ideal. It is possible to see how this normative account – of what community ought to be – can all too easily obscure the social reality of communities and pre-empt the necessity to locate community in its wider socio-economic context. Resort to pathologising and moralising is a more politically expedient and economically defensible approach, and the ideological function of 'community' has been used to good effect by successive governments to re-present persistent structural problems as local problems susceptible to local or individual solutions. (Craig 1989)

However, it is vital to recognise the ways in which structural location, material circumstances, position within the division of labour, gender, age, ethnic identity and so on structure community relationships. (e.g. Oakley 1992; Harvey 1989) Without an adequate understanding of the ways in which power relations construct and constrain community life, we are left clutching at the straws of idealised and sentimental versions. If we take a fairly typical kind of a loosely communitarian formulation, the problem becomes clear immediately. Clark (1992:125), for example, identifies 'a sense of security, a sense of significance and a sense of solidarity' as 'the essentials of community'. Yet if we analyse these 'essential' features, we may find that they are not always or necessarily compatible. For example, security for some may be achieved only by the exclusion of others; the 'belongingness' associated with solidarity may be constituted through the not-belonging of others; significance may actually signify the reproduction of unequal roles and relations.

Cohen (1985) argues that boundaries are essential to the definition and meaning of community. One of the classic ironies of the term, of course, is that the assumed unity it implies cannot help but draw attention to such boundaries, and the discriminations they signify – between who is 'in' and who is 'out'. For Brent (1997) 'community formation is intrinsically about creating difference ... a site of division'. The idea of community as a process of differentiation is also taken up by Bauman (2001) who argues that communal identities can be 'after-effects or by-products' of boundary drawing. For example, black people in the UK were imbued with communal identity only when their currency as 'units of production' became devalued as a result of wider economic change. (Sondhi 1997)

This exposes the way in which boundaries can be extended (often temporarily or conditionally) to integrate former 'strangers' or indeed 'enemies' when economically necessary or politically expedient. Historically, for British black people – more recently, economic migrants and refugees – the 'after-effects' of antagonism and exclusion may express much more accurately their communal identity. (Gilroy 1987) Similarly, where normative accounts of community have consistently constructed disabled people as the 'other' – to be tolerated as conditional members only – disabled peoples' organisations have forged their identities in opposition and resistance to the conditions of their 'inclusion' as much as their experience of exclusion. (Oliver 1990) Furthermore, some of those who might be otherwise be regarded as amongst the included, such as young Asian women, may reluctantly exclude themselves if membership demands obedience to unacceptable norms. (Gupta 2003) In the end, Cain and Yuval-Davis (1990: 7) are compelled to ask:

> Is 'the community' everybody who lives in a certain area, is 'the community' a particular grouping conscious of itself as a grouping or is 'the community', paradoxically, all those who have been excluded from feeling part of 'the community?'

These questions suggest that, far from generating harmonious social relations, community can create, or at least reinforce, social polarisation and potential conflict; differentiation rather than unity. They also throw into sharp focus the way in which those 'communities of interest' targeted in many policy initiatives may in fact be delineated by their very status as 'other' in relation to the community of locality – with potentially exclusionary consequences. What is clear is that while the internal dynamics of communities are complex in themselves, meanings and boundaries can also be imposed from outside, by those responsible for policy interventions. (Miller 2004) In other words, communities can be constructed or contrived in and through policy itself.

The contrived community

The tendency to romanticise 'neighbourhood' is strong in community studies. Young and Willmott (1957), for example, in their seminal study *Family and Kinship in East London* painted a vivid picture of the demise of close neighbourhood bonds as mass redevelopment and relocation dispersed long established inner-city communities. However, as they also discovered, despite the undisputed ties of family and kinship, 'community' was no substitute for decent living conditions when there was a choice. It could indeed be argued that the massive expansion of council housing in the post-war period offered a means of escape from the entrapment of community for many, particularly women for whom 'place' has always been double-edged. (e.g. Bulmer 1987; Williams 1993) Sentimentalised notions of 'natural' communities are therefore to be treated as suspect. It may be the case that a kind of mutuality existed in traditional working-class areas up to and immediately after the Second World War, but even this cannot be assumed to have been in any way a 'natural' phenomenon. In fact, Abrams (1980) regards the close-knit community networks of the past as entirely 'unnatural' – a set of instrumental associations arising from 'chronic collective deprivation' rather than mutuality or solidarity: 'instrumental collectivities … [which] … settle on an identity and a set of boundaries which oversimplify their reality in order to gain resources'.

In this case, communities can be understood as contrived rather than organic or indeed authentic – playing the part even when this depends upon adherence to a negative identity in order to make themselves eligible for increasingly selective or targeted funds. (MacGregor 2001) The distinction between 'traditional neighbourhood' and 'modern neighbourhoodism' made by Abrams is very useful in this respect for signalling the way in which the contrived community has become increasingly instrumental in policy. In any case, most so-called 'traditional' communities on closer inspection can be seen to have come out of economic rather than social needs. (Suttles 1972) Those almost iconic (and now all but disappeared) communities of weavers, miners or shipyard workers are cases in point.

In his critique of 'neighbourhood as community', Harvey (1989: 236-7) argues that the construction of community functions simultaneously to obfuscate and to manage the social relations of class-based spatial segregation. In other words, communitarian approaches constitute a 'masking ideology' by concealing those very capitalist relations which actually divide communities. Those areas which continue to be the dubious beneficiaries of 'modern neighbourhoodism' are invariably characterised by social and economic decline – increasingly 'ghettoes of the excluded'. (*Ibid.*) In this case, it is easy to see why the assertion of the 'natural' community is attractive to politicians and policy-makers alike because 'it suggests a process in which communities [are] more nearly the products of personal and human nature than the contrivances of planners, bureaucracies, and depersonalised institutions'. (Suttles 1972: 9) In other words, unproblematic resort to 'community' can conceal the rather more complex reality that policy is active both in contriving and managing communities. Policy is not simply a neutral mediator of diverse community interests.

As the balance between rights and responsibilities has shifted, community is increasingly invoked to imply individual responsibility and social obligation. (Humes 2004/5) In fact, it could be argued that 'community' has almost become a synonym for the dispersed state, charged with responsibility for service delivery, social control and even surveillance. (Mooney and Neal 2009) In this context, the creation of an 'alternative set of relationships' as signalled by Williams has been appropriated to reinforce a market vision to which there is, ironically, claimed to be no alternative.

Community as possibility

> Community has the capacity to forge a union between the community as supplied from above with its basically unequal social structures and community created from inside with its supportive and more ethical human relations. (Yeo and Yeo 1988)

This quote captures well the ambivalence of community and helps, in part, to locate community development as the product of two sets of forces and interests which reflect the changing context of political relations in society. The first is pressure from above, reflecting the changing needs of the state and broader economic and political interests, the second from below, which stems broadly from democratic aspiration (latent or manifest). (Cooke and Shaw 1996) The practitioner is dialectically and strategically positioned between these competing demands.

One way forward is to think of community as an intermediate level of social reality in which people collectively experience both the possibilities of human agency and the constraints of structure – between, in Wright Mills' (1970) terms, the micro politics of 'personal troubles' and the macro politics of 'public issues'. (Martin 2003) It is in the dialectics of community, understood in this way, that citizens may conceivably be able to analyse and articulate their own often contradictory experience of policy, to express new forms of collective identity and interest or to revive old ones. If this potential is to be realised, however, it may be necessary to create some critical distance between 'community as policy' and 'community as politics'. (Shaw and Martin 2000) On one hand, community as it is deployed in policy discourse and practice to pursue the objectives of government can create a spurious unity which makes managing communities more straightforward. (Cochrane 1996) On the other hand, community as politics can create a public space in which people can come together to collectivise their own experiences and aspirations in ways which may make managing them more difficult. Community development should be concerned to develop people's potential as active subjects in politics even when they are simultaneously constructed as objects of policy. When community as politics confronts community as policy, there can be an opportunity for a form of community development which is both relevant to people's real interests *and* which engages with and may even change policy.

Paradoxically, for many groups, 'the context in which … demands have been spontaneously articulated has been supplied by a political language premised on notions of community'. (Gilroy 1987: 233) This suggests that policy is active in constructing 'new' communities through contradiction as much as intention; that different kinds of solidarity can be generated through the language of community in ways which can strengthen collective interests in opposition to social exclusion or, indeed, to fight against limited (and limiting) forms of inclusion.

The distinction between 'space' and 'place' helps us to see how recourse to community can open up the potential for experience to be articulated and politicised – or the reverse. Fiona Williams (1993) argues that community defined by 'place' can simply:

seek to promote integration based upon people's acceptance of their 'place' as subordinate or superior whereas 'space' is derived from a sense of community representing a collective striving for communal values based on principles of co-operation.

In this sense, the dialectics of community provides a means of seeing how 'confinement, marginalisation and exclusion can themselves create the bonds that turn place into space'. In an important way, these ideas connect back to the ambivalence of community with its reactionary and radical potential, and turn an historical contradiction into a theoretical resource for current and, indeed, future community development.

Conclusion

It is clear that community development has been, and continues to be, subject to competing rationalities, inhabiting a position at the intersection of a range of opposing ideas, traditions, visions and interests – claimed by right, left and centre with equal enthusiasm. Undoubtedly, part of its continuous attraction as mediator between the state and particular 'problem' constituencies lies precisely in its professional versatility and political adaptability. This is both its strength and its weakness because, although it can be appropriated to maintain the *status quo* and preserve privilege, it can also create an increasingly rare public space for the expression of various forms of common position and collective identity or, indeed, dissent. This capacity to synthesise different, often incompatible, interests may go some way towards explaining why 'community seems to be subject to a rolling contract' (Bauman 2001), always provisional, but always there.

In the end, creating, sustaining or where necessary defending the creative 'spaces' in which people can assert, celebrate or contest their 'place' in the world is what defines progressive community development practice. However, this also means engaging with the politics of community in ways which offer the possibility of talking *back* to power rather than simply delivering depoliticised and demeaning versions of community empowerment.

Afterword

We are now at a point in the history of UK community development that may prove to be a significant milestone, not only for community development, but also for UK social policy more generally. Soon after it came to power in May 2010, the UK coalition government made a series of pronouncements that could have huge significance for community development policy and practice in the future. It is possible that these policy pronouncements have more rhetoric than substance to them in terms of their long-term impact on practice. While community development activists are curious and not a little alarmed about what the move to a 'Big Society', proposed by the 2010 Coalition government, might mean for their practice, who, now, after all, talks of the Third Way, which generated so much political heat but little policy light in the first term of New Labour at the end of the twentieth century? It may also be, given the robustness of community development, that it is able, as at previous significant milestones, to adapt to a changing policy context while holding on to its basic values. Nonetheless, and however current political rhetoric manifests itself in policy, it is clear that public expenditure will be under immense pressure for the foreseeable future, which will have significant implications both for community development and the communities it serves. For all these reasons, this brief Afterword has to be highly speculative. But, as the account given in the Introduction shows, this changing context is likely to bring both new possibilities and new dangers for community development practice.

The Afterword offers the opportunity for reflecting back on the themes that were set out in the Introduction, together with those developed in each section of this book. As the Introduction explained, we set out to explore the history of community development in the UK context. But this was not intended as a definitive history, offering any one 'true' version of community development as an occupation. Rather, the aim has been to explore the competing definitions and varying perspectives that have informed community development, over time, against the continuing benchmark of community development values. While the selections of the editors represent something of a consensus as to what the key literature has been, that consensus is broad enough to have incorporated a wide range of perspectives.

Community development has been defined and promoted by differing governments and other public bodies, just as it has been defined and developed through collective action, by communities and social movements from the 'bottom up'. As the chapter extracts in the book illustrate, these differing approaches have impacted in various ways, over time, with significant implications for the development of community work, in terms of its (contested) professional status and training requirements. While – we hope – those involved in promoting community development share common values, in terms of participation, empowerment, social inclusion and social justice, these values have often been blurred in policy and political pronouncements and thus interpreted in differing ways, their potential ambivalence enabling them to be mobilised for widely differing economic, political, social and cultural agendas.

Although the book has been concerned with community development in the UK, these agendas have been affected by wider debates, internationally, too, set in the context of the shifting boundaries between the state, civil society and the market, with varying pressures from social movements of differing strengths and ambitions, as well as similarly varying pressures from governments at different levels. How, then, might this type of contextualisation assist us in analysing the current scenario for community development in a rapidly and very fundamentally changing context? And how, more specifically, might this include taking account of the changing boundaries between the market, the state and civil society, in the context of capitalist globalisation processes – processes that have become very significantly more fully developed over the period that has been covered in this book?

There may be parallels but also differences with previous periods of significant change. The obvious comparison, on the basis of discussions in this book, would be the changes associated with the years after 1979, when neo-liberal approaches became dominant, similarly building on trends emerging from previous governments. The introduction to Section 3 of the book illustrates these potential parallels, with the public expenditure cuts of the Callaghan government marking the beginnings of public policies to 'roll back the state', which accelerated under the 1979–90 Thatcher administrations. This was the period in which the roles of the state and the market began radically to be redefined, with major implications for civil society in general, and for community development more specifically. The scale of the changes that are being considered now take these processes much further, however, marking a step change of potentially massive significance.

Future predictions are almost certainly unhelpful (and almost equally certainly going to become dated rapidly). At the time of writing, the political future is extremely uncertain with potentially enormous pressures on the Third Sector, despite the apparent opportunities that are also being offered. Given the extent of the public expenditure constraints, there are also major concerns as to community development's future role, concerns partly captured by the Community Development Foundation's post-election initiative to review the status of and prospects for community development. Will community development be promoted predominantly as a means of compensating for increasing gaps in public service provision?

Will community development workers come to be replaced by community organisers, operating on a voluntary basis? And what might be the impact of such changes in terms of training and continuing professional development for community development workers? Waddington (1979), as we have seen, argued that there will always be a need for community development workers, to manage the tensions between governments and those that they govern, in democratic societies. But what forms might this take, if the welfare state, as we know it, is radically transformed if not actually dismantled? Clearly it is too early to tell.

The post-World War II 'consensus' would seem to be fundamentally challenged, then, with major implications and dilemmas for those concerned with community development. In these circumstances, this book demonstrates the relevance in revisiting previous debates, recognising that community development workers are both 'in and against the state', while also acknowledging the changing relationships between the state, civil society and the market. Without progressive public policies, neither community development workers, nor indeed civil society organisations, more generally, stand much chance of being effective, on their own, when it comes to addressing issues of equalities and social justice – issues that are central to community development values (however these are interpreted). In this sense, community development may be argued to involve being *for* the state as well. Rather than being either 'in or against' the state, such an approach would also see the state as a contested sphere for communities and their allies to work for policies and practices that promote social inclusion and social justice.

These questions of social justice and equalities relate to wider changes too, both in Britain and elsewhere. In some ways it can be argued that equalities issues have been mainstreamed, despite the fact that most mainstream organisations, including government departments, are at best insipid in their pursuit of the policies that they have developed. Conversely, it can be argued that the impact of equalities issues (like community development itself) has been effectively incorporated or neutralised, while being mainstreamed. During the period covered by this book, social movements have mobilised to promote equalities and social justice for women, for black and ethnic minorities, for people with disabilities and for gays, lesbians, bisexuals and transsexuals. These movements have been central to the changing context for community development, along with social movements to promote equalities and social justice for older people and for younger people, for migrants, refugees and asylum seekers. Without such pressures from social movements, equalities and social justice can be hijacked, like the term 'community' itself, losing their socially transformative edge.

Meanwhile 'communities' themselves have also been undergoing fundamental changes in the context of globalisation. 'Communities' were never homogeneous, of course. There were always inherent conflicts and tensions between groups, ages, genders, ethnicities and other forms of social divisions and interests. But 'communities' are becoming increasingly diverse – super-diverse in the UK, in fact. Active citizenship has come to include active citizenship across as well as within nation state boundaries with the development of transnational, and even to some extent, global notions of citizenship. It is one way in which refugees, for example, have managed to maintain a sense of community despite being scattered across the world. For many, although not of course all migrants, for example, 'community' may be defined in varying and supranational ways, with active engagement in their communities of origin as well as within their differing communities of locality and interest in the UK. This all poses new challenges while opening new possibilities for linking the local with the global, whether at European or indeed at international levels.

There are, in addition, new possibilities for linking the local with the global through the use of new technologies, without in any way suggesting that these can substitute for face-to-face contact within and beyond the framework of the nation state. Globalisation thus offers problems but also opportunities. There is increasing awareness of how to develop such opportunities in relation to local/global struggles to challenge poverty, to improve working conditions, to promote access to basic rights such as education and health and to advance social justice more generally. There are also, of course, significant examples of action linking global and local struggles over environmental issues and climate change – issues, regretfully, that are barely represented in the community development literature.

There are potentially relevant issues here, too, in relation to the history of community development, North and South. The first sections of the book explored the colonial legacies, while more recent chapters have been exploring the scope for South/North learning – learning from the global South as well as learning within and between these differing contexts. In recent years, citizen engagement and community participation programmes in Britain have increasingly explicitly drawn from such experiences.

At this point, the experiences that have been and are being shared via the International Association for Community Development (IACD) should also be noted. Although launched as an organisation in 1953, IACD barely featured in community development debates in Britain in the 1960s. Since its relaunch, in the 1990s, however, IACD has played an increasingly active role internationally. The Association is now more relevant than ever in terms of facilitating that transfer of experience, as the report 'What in the world?' (Burkett and Bedi, 2008) illustrates. IACD has reflected learning from rural as well as urban contexts, learning that has been under-represented in this book, despite increasing recognition of its importance in the UK, as well as elsewhere. And IACD has also been providing global solidarity for those concerned with community development and active citizenship, as the 2004 Budapest Declaration has been demonstrating, providing benchmarks for community development, particularly in contexts with very different histories in East and Central Europe.

This book has reflected continuing debate over the years about the nature of community development itself, whether as a profession, an occupation, or a practice underpinning various forms of activism. Who actually owns it and from which perspective do they promote it? Where is community development currently located? Ownership would seem to be dispersed between a range of organisations, with varying bases and priorities, as we note in the Introduction. This fragmented context for community development stands in some contrast with the late 1960s when the Association of Community Workers was effectively the only game in town (although social work continued then to try to claim it for its own). However, at that time there were a number of university-based and other training opportunities for community development. Most of the former have long since disappeared, and been replaced by continuing contestations in relation to training (or the absence of training) for community development. How will this be defined and managed, in terms of overall aims, orientations and objectives, as well as in terms of quality controls? These questions remain despite recent attempts to define the parameters of practice through national occupational standards in various parts of the UK (see, for example, www.fcdl.org.uk; www.paulo. org.uk; www.cldstandardscouncil.org.uk). While these uncertainties pose challenges, however, there may be significant advantages associated with this situation of relative fragmentation and dispersal. Whatever the future holds in these uncertain times, it seems reasonable to suggest that community development will continue to be contested, from varying perspectives, rather than having been 'captured' by any one owner. Given our starting aim, to represent continuing debates, rather than to capture community development's 'true' meaning, this would seem a positive note on which to conclude, whatever the challenges to come.

References

Abel–Smith, B. and Townsend, P. (1965) *The Poor and the Poorest*, London: Bell.

Abrams, P. (1980) 'Social change, social networks and neighbourhood care', *Social Work Service* 22.

ACW (1982) *ACW Definition of Community Work*. London: Association of Community Workers.

Adamson, D. (2003) 'Community Regeneration in Wales', *Journal of Community Development Work* 4: 79-97.

Adamson, N., Briskin, L. and McPhail, M. (1988) *Organizing for Change: The Contemporary Women's Movement in Canada*. Oxford: Oxford University Press.

Alinsky, S. (1969) *Reveille for Radicals*. New York: Vintage Books.

Alinsky, S. (1971) *Rules for Radicals*. New York: Random House.

Allen, G., Bastiani, J., Martin, I. and Richards, K. (eds) (1987) *Community Education: An Agenda for Educational Reform*. Milton Keynes: Open University Press.

AMA (1989) *Community Development: The Local Authority Role*, London: Association of Metropolitan Authorities.

AMA (1993) *Local authorities and community development,* London: Association of Metropolitan Authorities.

Ambrose, P. and Colenutt, B. (1975) 'Office Development: Rents, Values and Profits' in P. Ambrose and B. Colenutt, *The Property Machine*, Harmondsworth: Penguin.

Anastacio, J., Gidley, B., Hart, L., Keith, M., Mayo, M. and Kowarzik, U. (2000) *Reflecting Realities: participants' perspectives on integrated communities and sustainable development*, Bristol: The Policy Press.

Anthias, F. and Yuval-Davis, N. (1992) *Racialized Boundaries: Race, Nation, Gender, Colour and Class and the Anti-Racist Struggle*, London: Routledge.

Anwar, M. (1986) *Race and Politics, Ethnic Minorities and the British Political System,* London: Tavistock.

Armstrong, J. and Key, M. (1979) 'Evaluation, change and community work', *Community Development Journal*, 14(3): 210-23.

Arnstein, S. (1969) 'A ladder of citizen participation', *Journal of the American Planning Association*, 35(4), July: 216-24.

Atkinson, R. (2003) 'Addressing urban social exclusion through community involvement in urban regeneration', in R. Imrie and M. Raco (eds) *Urban Renaissance? New Labour, Community and Urban Policy*, Bristol: The Policy Press: 109-119.

Back, L., Keith, M., Khan, A., Shukra, K., and Solomos, J. (2002) 'New Labour's white heart: politics multiculturalism and the return of assimilationism', *Political Quarterly*, 73(4): 445-54.

Baldock, P. (1977) 'Why community action? The historical origins of the radical trend in community work', *Community Development Journal*, 12(2).

Baldock, P. (1980) 'The origins of community work in the United Kingdom' in P. Henderson, D. Jones and D. N. Thomas (eds) *The Boundaries of Change in Community Work*, London: Allen & Unwin.

Banks, S. and Gallagher, A. (2008) *Ethics in Professional Practice,* Basingstoke: Palgrave Macmillan.

Banks, S. and Vickers, T. (2006) 'Engineering communities through active learning, *Journal of Community Work and Development* 8: 83-104.

Banks, S., Henderson, P., Butcher, H. and Robertson, J. (2003) *Managing community Practice,* Bristol: Policy Press.

Barclay, P.M. (1982) *Social Workers: Their Role and Tasks (The Barclay Report)*, London: Bedford Square Press.

Barker, H. (1986) 'Recapturing sisterhood: a critical look at 'process' in feminist organising and community work', *Critical Social Policy* 16: 80-90.

Barker, J. (1999) *Street-Level Democracy: Political Settings at the Margins of Global Power*, West Hartford: Kumarian Press.

Barnes, C. (1994) *Disabled People in Britain and Discrimination*, London: Hurst.

Barnes, C., Mercer, G. and Shakespeare, T. (1999) *Exploring Disability: A Sociological Introduction*, London: Polity.

Barr, A. (1982) 'Practice models and training issues' in Bidwell, L. and McConnell, C. (eds) *Community Education and Community Development*, Dundee: Northern College of Education.

Barr, A. (1991) *Practising Community Development: Experience in Strathclyde.* London: Community Development Foundation.

Barr, A. and Hashagen, S. (2000) *ABCD Handbook: A Framework for Evaluating Community Development,* London: Community Development Foundation.

Barr, A., Hashagen, S. and Purcell, R. (1996) *Monitoring and Evaluation of Community Development in Northern Ireland*, Glasgow: Scottish Community Development Centre.

Barr, A., Stenhouse, C. and Henderson, P. (2001) *Caring communities*, York: Joseph Rowntree Foundation.

Bartley, M. (1994) 'Health costs of social injustice', *BMJ* 309: 1177-78.

Bartley, M., Blome, D. and Montgomerie, S. (1997) 'Socioeconomic determinants of health', *BMJ* 314: 1194.

Batten, T.R. (1957) *Communities and their Development*. London: Oxford University Press.

Batten, T.R. (1962) *Training for Community Development: A Critical Study of Method.* London: Oxford University Press.

Batten, T.R. with M. Batten (1967) *The Non-directive Approach to Group and Community Work,* London: Oxford University Press.

Bauman, Z. (2001) *Community: Seeking Safety in an Insecure World*, Cambridge: Polity Press.

Beazley, M., Griggs, S. and Smith, M. (2004) *Rethinking Approaches to Community Capacity Building*, Birmingham: University of Birmingham (mimeo).

Bell, C. and Newby, H. (1972) *Community Studies: An Introduction to the Sociology of the Local Community*. New York: Praeger.

Benington, J. and Donnison, D. (1999) 'New Labour and social exclusion: the search for a Third Way or just Gilding the Ghetto again?' in H. Dean and R. Woods (eds) *Social Policy Review 11*, Luton: Social Policy Association.

Ben-Tovim, G., Gabriel, J., Law, I. and Stredder, K. (1986) *The Local Politics of Race:* London: Macmillan.

Berry, L. (1988) 'The rhetoric of consumerism and the exclusion of community', *Community Development Journal*, vol 23, no 4: 266-72.

Beynon, H. (1985) *Digging Deeper: Issues in the Miners' Strike*, London: Verso.

Bhat, A., Carr-Hill, R. and Ohri, S. (eds) (1988) *Britain's Black Population: A New Perspective* (2nd edn), Aldershot: Gower.

Bhavnani, R (1986) 'The Struggle for an Anti-racist Policy in Education in Avon', *Critical Social Policy*, 16: 104-8.

Biddle, L. and Biddle, W. (1965) *The Community Development Process: The Rediscovery of Local Initiative*, New York: Holt, Rinehart & Winston.

Blaxter, M. (1997) 'Whose fault is it? People's own conceptions of the reasons for health inequalities', *Social Science & Medicine*, 44(6): 747-756.

Blunkett, D. (2002) Speech at the Relaunch of the Active Community Unit, Home Office: 29 May.

Blunkett, D. and Jackson, K. (1987) *Democracy in Crisis: The Town Halls Respond*, Sheffield: Hogarth Press.

Boal, A. (1979) *Theatre of the Oppressed*, London: Pluto.

Boal, A. (1997) *Games for Actors and Non-Actors*, London: Routledge.

Bourdieu, P. (1984) *Distinction: A Social Critique of the Judgement of Taste*, London: Routledge & Kegan Paul.

Boyd, R. (2006) 'The value of civility?', *Urban Studies*, 43(5/6): 863-878.

Bradshaw, J. (1999) 'Comparing Child Poverty', *Poverty*, No 104, Autumn.

Brandwein, R.A. (1987) 'Women and Community Organisation' in Burden, D.S. and Gottlieb, N. (eds), *The Woman Client*, London: Tavistock.

Brayne, F.L. (1945) *Better villages*, Bombay: Oxford University Press.

Brent, J. (1997) 'Community without unity' in Hoggett, P. (ed) *Contested Communities: Experiences, Struggles, Policies*, Bristol: The Policy Press.

Brockensha, D. and Hodge, P. (1969) *Community Development: An Interpretation*, New York: Chandler.

Brown, A. (1986) *Groupwork*. London: Heinemann Educational Books.

Bryant, B. and Bryant, R. (1982) *Change and Conflict: A Study of Community Work in Glasgow*, Aberdeen: Aberdeen University Press.

Bryson, L. and Mowbray, M. (1981) '"Community": The Spray-on Solution', *Australian Journal of Social Issues* 16: 4: 255-67.

Budapest Declaration (2004), www.iacdglobal.org/BudapestDeclaration.

Bulmer, M. (1987) *The Social Bases of Community Care*, London: Allen and Unwin.

Bunch, C.D. (1990) 'Women's rights as human rights', *Human Rights Quarterly*, 12(4): 486-98.

Burns, D., Hambleton, R. and Hoggett, P. (1994) *The politics of decentralisation*, London: Macmillan.

Butcher, H. (1993) 'Why community policy? Some explanations for recent trends', in Butcher *et al* (eds) (1993) (*op. cit.*)

Butcher, H., Glen, A., Henderson, P. and Smith, J. (1993) *Community and public policy*, London: Pluto Press.

Cain, H. and Yuval-Davis, N. (1990) 'The equal opportunities community', *Critical Social Policy* 10(2).

Cairns, T. M. (2003) 'Citizenship and regeneration: participation or incorporation?' in P. Coare and R. Johnston (eds) *Adult Learning, Citizenship and Community Voices: Exploring Community-based Practice*, Leicester: NIACE.

Calouste Gulbenkian Foundation (1968) *Community Work and Social Change. A report on training*. London: Longman.

Calouste Gulbenkian Foundation (1973) *Current Issues in Community Work* (the Boyle Report), London: Routledge and Kegan Paul.

Cameron, C. (2007) 'Whose problem? Disability narratives and available identities', *Community Development Journal*, 42(4): 501–11.

Cameron, C. (2008) 'Further towards an affirmation model', in Campbell, T., Fontes, F., Hemingway, L., Soorenian, A. and Till, C. (eds) *Disability Studies: Emerging Insights and Perspectives*, Leeds: The Disability Press.

Campbell, B. (1993) 'Stand of a heroine', *Guardian*, 25 January.

Campbell, J. and Oliver, M. (1996) *Disability Politics: Understanding Our Past, Changing Our Future*, London: Routledge.

Cameron, C. (2007) 'Whose problem? Disability narratives and available identities', *Community Development Journal*, 42(4): 501–11.

Caniglia, B. and Carmin, J. (2005) 'Scholarship on social movements', *Mobilization*, 10(2): 201–12.

Cannan, C. (2000) 'The environmental crisis, Greens and community development', *Community Development Journal*, 35(4): 365–76

Cantle, T. (2001) *Community Cohesion – A Report of the Independent Review Team*, London: Home Office.

Capability Scotland (2009) Accessed at http://www.capability-scotland.org.uk

Caravanning for the Disabled (2006), http://www.caravansitefinder.co.uk/ features/ disabled

Carlisle, S. (2001) 'Inequalities in health: contested explanations, shifting discourses and ambiguous policies', *Critical Public Health*, 11(3): 267–79.

Carter, T. (1986) *Shattering Illusions*, London: Lawrence & Wishart.

CDF (2007) *The Community Development Challenge*, London: Community Development Foundation.

CDP (1976) *The costs of industrial change*, London: Community Development Project Inter-project Editorial Team.

CDP (1977) *Gilding the Ghetto: The State and The Poverty Experiments*, London: Community Development Project Inter-project Editorial Team.

CDRG (1991) *Community Development in Northern. Ireland: Perspectives for the Future*, Belfast: Community Development Review Group.

CDRG (1992) *Education and Training for Community Development*, Belfast: Community Development Review Group.

Chambers, R. (1997) *Whose Reality Counts?*, London: Intermediate Technology Publications.

Chanan, G., West, A., Garratt, C. and Humm, J. (1999) *Regeneration and Sustainable Communities*, London: CDF.

Charity Commission (2000) *The Promotion of Community Capacity-Building*, Taunton: Charity Commission.

Charlton, B.G. (1997) 'The inequity of inequality: egalitarian instincts and evolutionary psychology', *Journal of Health Psychology* 2(3): 413–25.

Charlton, B.G. and White, M. (1995) 'Living on the margin: a salutogenic model for socio-economic differentials in health', *Public Health* 109: 234–43.

Chauhan, V. (1996) *Beyond Steel Bands 'n' Samosas*, Leicester: National Youth Bureau.

Clark, D. (1992) 'Education for community in the 1990s: a Christian perspective', in Allen, G. and Martin, A. (eds) *Education and Community: The Politics of Practice*, London: Cassell.

Clarke, J. (1996) 'The problem of the state after the welfare state' in May, M., Brunsdon, E. and Craig, G. (eds) *Social Policy Review 8*, Canterbury: Social Policy Association.

Coaffee, J. and Healey, P. (2003) '"My Voice: My Place": Tracking Transformations in Urban Governance', *Urban Studies* 40(10): 1979-1999.

Coates, K. (1973) 'Socialists and the Labour Party', *Socialist Register* 10: 55-79.

Coates, K. and Silburn, R. (1970) *Poverty: The Forgotten Englishman*. Harmondsworth: Penguin.

Cochrane, A. (1986) 'Community politics and democracy', in Held, D. and Pollitt, C. (eds) *New forms of democracy*, London: Sage.

Cochrane, A. (1994) 'Restructuring the welfare state', in Burrows, R. and Loader, B. (eds) *Towards a Post-Fordist Welfare State*, London: Routledge.

Cochrane, A. (1996) 'From theories to practices: looking for local democracy in Britain' in King, D. and Stoker, G. (eds) *Rethinking Local Democracy*, Basingstoke: Macmillan.

Cockburn, C. (1977) *The Local State*, London: Pluto Press.

Cockburn, C. (1991) *In the Way of Women: Men's Resistance to Sex Equality in Organizations*, Basingstoke: Macmillan.

CoE (1985) *Faith in the City*, Archbisop of Canterbury's Commission on Urban Priority Areas, London: Church of England.

Cohen, A.P. (1985) *The Symbolic Construction of Community*, London: Tavistock.

Colenutt, R. (1979) 'Community action over local planning issues' in G. Craig, M. Mayo and N. Sharman (eds) *Jobs and Community Action*, London: Routledge and Kegan Paul, pp 243-52

Collins, A. (2003) *Where Did It All Go Right? Growing Up Normal in the 70s*, London: Ebury Press.

Community Development Project (1977) *Gilding the Ghetto: The State and the Poverty Experiments*, London: CDP Inter-project Editorial Team

Community Development Journal (1997) 32(3), June, Oxford: Oxford University Press.

Connolly, C. (1990a) 'Washing our Linen: One Year of Women Against Fundamentalism', *Feminist Review*, 1990: 68-77.

Connolly, C. (1990b) 'Splintered sisterhood', *Feminist Review* 36: 52-64.

Cooke, B. and Kothari, U. (eds) (2001) *Participation: The New Tyranny?*, London: Zed Books.

Cooke, I. (1996) 'Whatever happened to the class of '68? The changing context of radical community work practice' in Cooke, I. and Shaw, M. (eds) (1996) (*op. cit.*)

Cooke, I. and Shaw, M. (eds) (1996) *Radical Community Work: Perspectives from Practice in Scotland*, Edinburgh: Moray House Publications.

Cooper, C. (2008) *Community, Conflict and the State*, Basingstoke: Macmillan.

Corkey, D. and Craig, G. (1978) 'Community Work or Class Politics?' in Curno, P. (ed) (1978) (*op. cit.*)

Cornwall, A. (2004a) 'New Democratic Spaces? The Politics and Dynamics of Institutionalised Participation', *IDS Bulletin* 35 (2): 1-10.

Cornwall, A. (2004b) 'Spaces for Transformation? Reflections on Issues of Power and Difference in Participation in Development', in Hickey, S. and Mohan, G. (eds) *Participation: from Tyranny to Transformation*, London: Zed Books: 75-91.

Cornwall, A. (2008) 'Capacity participation', *Community Development Journal* 43(3): 269-83.

Cornwall, A. and Gaventa, J. (2000) 'Repositioning Participation in Social Policy', Background paper prepared for the IDS conference 'The Future of Social Policy', October 28-29, Brighton (mimeo).

Cowden, S. and Singh, G. (2007) 'The "user": friend, foe or fetish? A critical exploration of user involvement in health and social care', *Critical Social Policy* 27(1): 5-23 (online).

Cowley, C., Kaye, A., Mayo, M. and Thompson, M. (1977) *Community or Class Struggle,* London: Stage 1.

Craig, G. (1989) 'Community work and the state', *Community Development Journal,* 24(1): 1-19.

Craig, G. (2002) 'Measuring empowerment', *Journal of the Community Development Society* 33(1): 123-46.

Craig, G. (2007) 'Community capacity-building: something old, something new...?', *Critical Social Policy* 27(August): 335-59.

Craig, G. and Mayo, M. (eds) (1995) *Community Empowerment,* London: Zed Books.

Craig, G., Derricourt, N. and Loney, M. (eds) (1982) *Community Work and the State: Towards a Radical Practice: Community Work Eight.* London: Routledge & Kegan Paul in association with the Association of Community Workers.

Craig, G., Derounian, J. and Garbutt, R. (2005) *Training for rural community development activists,* Dunfermline: Carnegie UK Trust.

Craig, G., Mayo, M. and Sharman, N. (eds) (1979) *Jobs and Community Action: Community Work Five,* London: Routledge & Kegan Paul in association with the Association of Community Workers.

Craig, G., Popple, K. and Shaw, M. (eds) (2008) *Community Development in theory and practice,* Nottingham: Spokesman Books.

Craig, G., Taylor, M., Monro, S., Parkes, T., Warburton, D. and Wilkinson, M. (2004) *Willing Partners?,* Final Project Report to ESRC, Swindon.

Crick, B. (1998) *Education for Citizenship and the Teaching of Democracy in Schools,* York: Qualifications and Curriculum Authority.

Croft, S. and Beresford, P. (1992) 'The politics of participation', *Critical Social Policy* 25, Autumn: 20-44.

Curno, A., Lamming, A., Leach, L., Stiles, J., Ward, V. and Ziff, T. (1982) *Women in Collective Action,* Newcastle upon Tyne: Association of Community Workers.

Curno, P. (ed) (1978) *Political Issues in Community Work: Community Work Four.* London: Routledge & Kegan Paul.

DAIL (1992) *Disability Arts in London: the First Five Years,* London: Disability Arts in London.

Dalley, G. (1988) *Ideologies of Caring: Rethinking Community and Collectivism,* London: Macmillan.

D'Andrade, R. (1995) 'Moral models in anthropology', *Current Anthropology,* 36(3): 399-407.

Darke, P. (1998) 'Understanding Cinematic Representations of Disability' in Shakespeare, T. (ed) *The Disability Reader: Social Science Perspectives*, London: Cassell

Davey Smith, G. (1996) 'Income inequality and mortality: why are they related?', *British Medical Journal*, 312: 987-8.

Davey Smith, G., Dorling, D., Gordon, D. & Shaw, M. (1999) 'The widening health gap: what are the solutions?', *Critical Public Health* 9(2): 151-170.

Davidson, N. (2010) 'What was Neoliberalism?', in Davidson, N., McCafferty, P. and Miller, D. (eds) *Neo-liberal Scotland: Class and Society in a Stateless Nation*, Cambridge: Cambridge Scholars Publishing.

DCLG (2006) *Strong and prosperous communities*, London: Department for Communities and Local Government.

DCLG (2010a) *Improving outcomes? Engaging local communities in the NDC programme*, London: Department for Communities and Local Government.

DCLG (2010b) *The New Deal for Communities Experience: Final assessment*, London: Department of Communities and Local Government.

DCLG (2010c) *Involving local people in regeneration*, London: Department of Communities and Local Government.

Dearlove, J. (1974) 'The Control of Change and the Regulations of Community Action' in Jones, D. and Mayo, M. (eds) *Community Work One*, London: Routledge and Kegan Paul.

Delin, A. (1997) 'Heart'n'Soul' in Pointon, A. and Davies, C., *Framed: Interrogating Disability in the Media*, London: British Film Institute.

Demuth, C. (1977) *Government Initiatives on Urban Deprivation*, London: Runnymede Trust.

Denham, J. (2001) *Building Cohesive Communities – A Report of the Ministerial Group on Public Order and Community Cohesion*, London: Home Office.

Dennis, N. (1958) 'The popularity of the neighbourhood community idea', *Sociological Review* 6(2).

DES (Department of Education and Science)(1967) *Immigrants and the Youth Service* (The Hunt Report), London: HMSO.

DES (1967) *Children and their Primary Schools*. Report to the Central Advisory Council for Education, No. 1 (Plowden Report). London: HMSO.

DES (1967) *Children and Their Primary Schools*. Report to the Central Advisory Council for Education, No. 1 (Plowden Report), London: HMSO.

DES (1969) *Youth and Community Work in the 1970s. Proposals by the Youth Development Council* (Fairbairn-Milson Report). London: HMSO.

DfID (2000) 'Strategies for Achieving the International Development Targets: Human Rights for Poor People', London: Department for International Development.

DH (Department of Health) (1992) *The Health of the Nation: A Strategy for Health in England*, Cm 1968, London: HMSO.

DH (1998a) *Independent Inquiry into Inequalities in Health: Report* (Chairman: Sir Donald Acheson), London: TSO.

DH (1998b) *Our Healthier Nation: A Contract for Health*, Cm 3852, London: TSO.

DH (1999) *Saving Lives: Our Healthier Nation*, Cm 4386, London: TSO.

DHSS (Department of Health and Social Security) (1980) *Inequalities in Health: Report of a Working Group* (Black Report), London: DHSS.

Diamond, J. (2004) 'Local regeneration initiatives and capacity building: whose "capacity" and "building" for what?, *Community Development Journal*, 39(2): 177-205.

Dickens, C. (2003) *A Christmas Carol*, London: Penguin.

Dinham, A. (2005) *Another Deal for what Community?*, Unpublished PhD, Goldsmiths College, University of London.

Dinham, A. (2007) 'Raising expectations or dashing hopes?', *Community Development Journal*, 42(2).

Di Stefano, C. (1991) 'Who the Heck are We? Theoretical Turns Against Gender', *Frontiers: A Journal of Women's Studies* XII(2): 86-108.

Dixon, G., Johnson, C., Leigh, S. and Turnbull, N. (1982) 'Feminist Perspectives and Practice' in Craig, G *et al* (eds) (1982) (*op. cit*).

Dominelli, L. (1990) *Women and community action*, Birmingham: Venture Press.

Dominelli, L. (1995) 'Women in the community: feminist principles and organising in community work', *Community Development Journal* 30(2): 133-43.

Dominelli, L. (2006) *Women and Community Action* (revised 2nd edn), Bristol: The Policy Press.

Dominelli, L. and McLeod, E. (1989) *Feminist Social Work*, London: Macmillan.

Donnison, D. (1993) 'The challenge of urban regeneration for community development', *Community Development Journal*, 28(4).

Driver, S. and Martell, L. (1998) *New Labour: Politics after Thatcherism*, Cambridge: Polity Press.

Du Bois, W. (1971) *The Seventh Son*, New York: Vintage.

Duncan, P. and Thomas, S. (2000) *Neighbourhood Regeneration: Resourcing Community Involvement*, Bristol: The Policy Press.

Dwyer, P. (2000) *Welfare rights and responsibilities*, Bristol: The Policy Press.

Dyen, M. (1989) 'Organize the Activists', *Social Policy*, Spring: 27-33.

Eade, D. and Williams, S. (1996) *The Oxfam Handbook of Development and Relief*, Oxford: Oxfam.

Eagleton, T. (2007) 'Those in power are right to see multiculturalism as a threat', *The Guardian*, February 21.

EC (1996) *Social and economic inclusion through regional development, the community economic development priority in European Structural Funds programmes in Great Britain*, Luxembourg: European Commission.

Edwards, M. (1999) *Future Positive: International Cooperation in the 21st Century*, London: Earthscan and Sterling, Virginia: Stylus.

Edwards, M. (2000) *NGO Rights and Responsibilities*, London: Foreign Policy Centre.

Edwards, J. and Batley, R. (1978) *The Politics of Positive Discrimination*, London: Tavistock.

Edwards, M. and Gaventa, J. (2001) *Global Citizen Action*, London: Earthscan.

El-Salahi, Z. (2010) 'Preventing violent extremism through community work? Essentialism and Manipulation' in Emejulu, E. and Shaw, M. (eds) *Community Empowerment: Critical Perspectives from Scotland, The Glasgow Papers*, Edinburgh, Community Development Journal.

Elstad, J.I. (1998) 'The psychosocial perspective on social inequalities in health', *Sociology of Health and Illness* 20(5): 598-618.

Erasmus, C. (1968) 'Comment', *Human organisation*, 27(1): 65-74.

Etzioni, A. (1993) *The Spirit of Community*, New York: Crown.

European Foundation (1995) *Public Services and Social Exclusion*, Dublin: EFILWC.

Fairbairn, A. (1979) *The Leicestershire Community Colleges and Centres,* Nottingham: Nottingham University/National Institute for Adult Education.

Fairclough, N. (2000) *New Labour, New Language?* London: Routledge.

Farrant, W. (1991) 'Addressing the contradictions: health promotion and community health action in the United Kingdom', *International Journal of Health Services,* 21(3): 423-39.

FCDL (2004) *Building Civil Renewal: A Review of Government Support for Community Capacity Building and Proposals for Change,* Submission from Federation for Community Development Learning, Sheffield: Federation for Community Development Learning.

Federation of Community Work Training Groups (1990) *Annual Report,* Sheffield: Federation of Community Work Training Groups.

Finch, J. and Groves, D. (1985) 'Community Care and the Family: A Case for Equal Opportunities' in Ungerson, C. (ed), *Women and Social Policy: A Reader,* London: Macmillan.

Fisher, W.F. and Ponniah, T. (2003) *Another World is Possible: Popular Alternatives to Globalization at the World Social Forum,* London: Zed Books.

Fitch, B. and Oppenheimer, M. (1968) *Ghana: End of an Illusion,* London: Monthly Review Press.

Fitzduff, M. (1991) *A Typology of Community Relations Work and Contextual Necessities,* Community Relations Council, Pamphlet No 1, Belfast: Community Relations Council.

Flaherty, J., Veit-Wilson, J. and Dornan, P. (2004) *Poverty: The Facts,* London: Child Poverty Action Group.

Flint, J. and Robinson, D. (2008) *Community Cohesion in Crisis?,* Bristol: The Policy Press.

Flynn, R. (2002) 'Clinical Governance and Governmentality', *Health, Risk and Society* 4(2):155-73.

Foley, P. and Martin, S. (2000) 'A New Deal for community? Public participation in regeneration and local service delivery', *Policy & Politics,* 28(4): 479-92.

Foot, P. (1969) *The Rise of Enoch Powell: An Examination of Enoch Powell's Attitude to Immigration and Race,* Harmondsworth: Penguin.

Fordham, G. (1993) 'Sustaining local involvement', *Community Development Journal,* 28(4): 299-304.

Foucault, M. (1967) *Madness and Civilisation,* London: Tavistock.

Foucault, M. (1977) *Discipline and Punishment: The Birth of the Prison,* Harmondsworth: Allen Lane.

Foucault, M. (1980) *Power/Knowledge,* Brighton: Harvester Press.

FPSC (1989) *Family Policy Bulletin,* no 6, London: Family Policy Studies Centre.

Francis, D. and Henderson, P. (1992) *Working with rural communities,* London: Macmillan.

Fraser, M. (2004) http://disabilityarts.com/archive/features/mat-fraser/

Freeman, J. (1984) *The Tyranny of Structurelessness.* London: Dark Star and Rebel Press.

Freire, P. (1970) *Cultural Action for Freedom,* Harmondsworth: Penguin.

Freire, P. (1972) *Pedagogy of the Oppressed,* Harmondsworth: Penguin.

Freire, P. (1976) *Education: The Practice of Freedom,* London: Writers and Readers.

Freire, P., Horton, M., Bell, B. and Gaventa, J. (1990) *We Make the Road by Walking*, Pennsylvania: Temple University Press.

Fung, A. and Wright, E. (2003) 'Deepening Democracy: Innovations in Empowered Participatory Governance', *Politics and Society*, 29(2): 5-41.

Fyfe, N., Bannister, J. and Kearns, A. (2006) '(In)civility and the City', *Urban Studies*, 43(5/6): 853-861.

Gallacher, A. (1977) 'Women and Community Work' in Mayo, M. (ed) (1977) (*op. cit.*).

Gaventa, J. (1999) 'Citizen knowledge, citizen competence and democracy building' in Elkin, S. (ed) *Democracy and citizen competence*, Philadelphia: Penn State Press.

Gaventa, J. (2001) 'Global citizen action: lessons and challenges' in M. Edwards and J. Gaventa (eds) *Global citizen action*, London: Earthscan, pp 275-89.

Gaventa, J. (2004) 'Towards Participatory Governance: Assessing the Transformative Possibilities', in Hickey, S. and Mohan, G. (eds) (*op. cit.*): 25-41.

Giddens, A. (1998) *The Third Way: The Renewal of Social Democracy*, Cambridge: Polity Press.

Gilchrist, A. (1995) *Community Development and Networking*, London: CDF.

Gillies, P. (1998) 'Effectiveness of alliances and partnerships for health promotion', *Health Promotion International* 13(2): 99-120.

Gilroy, P. (1987) *There Ain't No Black in the Union Jack. The Cultural Politics of Race and Nation*, London: Hutchinson.

Gittell, M. (2001) 'Empowerment Zones: An Opportunity Missed: A Six-City Comparative Study', New York: City University of New York.

Glass, N. (2005) 'Surely some mistake', *The Guardian*, January 5.

Glen, A., Henderson, P., Humm, J., Meszaros, H. with Gaffney, M. (2004) *Survey of Community Development Workers in the UK*, Sheffield: CDX.

Glendinning, C., Powell, M. and Rummery, K. (eds) (2002) *Partnerships, New Labour and the Governance of Welfare*, Bristol: The Policy Press.

Goetschius, G. (1969) *Working with Community Groups: Using Community Development as a Method of Social Work*, London: Routledge and Kegan Paul.

Goffman, E. (1961) *Asylums*, New York: Doubleday.

Goodhart, D. (2004) 'Discomfort of strangers', *The Guardian*, 24 February.

Goodwin, M. and Duncan, S. (1986) 'The Local State and Local Economic Policy: Political Mobilisation or Economic Regeneration', *Capital and Class* 27(Winter): 14-36.

Gordon, L. (1991) 'On difference', *Genders* 10: 91.

Gordon, D., Adelman, L., Ashworth, K., Bradshaw, J., Levitas, R., Middleton, S., Pantazis, C., Patsios, D., Payne, S., Townsend, P. and Williams, J. (2000) *Poverty and Social Exclusion in Britain*, York: Joseph Rowntree Foundation.

Green, J. and Chapman, K. (1992) 'The British Community Development Project', *Community Development Journal* 27(3): 242-58.

Greer, J. (2001) 'Whither Partnership Governance in Northern Ireland?', *Environment and Planning C: Government and Policy*, 19: 751-70.

Griffiths, H. (1974) 'Community development in Northern Ireland', Occasional paper on social administration, Belfast: New University of Ulster

Griffiths, Sir Roy (1988) *Community Care: Agenda for Action*, London: HMSO.

Gunn, D. (1992) 'Review of community development during the '70s', Unpublished paper, University of Ulster.

Gupta, R. (ed) (2003) *From Homebreakers to Jailbreakers*, Southall Black Sisters, London: Zed Books.

Guttentag, M. (1972) 'Children in Harlem's community-controlled schools', *Journal of Social Issues*, 28(4): 18.

Gyford, J. (1985) *The Politics of Local Socialism*, London: Allen and Unwin.

Hadley, R., Cooper, M., Dale, P. and Stacey, G. (1987) *A Community Social Worker's Handbook,* London: Tavistock.

Hall, S., Critcher, C., Jefferson, T., Clarke, J. and Robert, B. (1978) *Policing the Crisis: Mugging, the State and Law and Order*, Basingstoke: Macmillan.

Halmos, P. (1970) *The Personal Service Society*, London: Schoken Books.

Halsey, A.H. (e) (1972) *Educational Priority,* London: HMSO.

Hambrook, C. (2005), accessed at www.disabilityartsonline.org.uk/colin_hambrook_gallery

Hanmer, J. and Rose, H. (1980) 'Making sense of theory' in Henderson, P., Jones, D. and Thomas, D. (eds) *The Boundaries of Change in Community Work,* London: Allen & Unwin.

Hanmer, J. and Statham, D. (1988) *Women and Social Work: Towards a Woman-Centred Practice,* Basingstoke: Macmillan.

Harris, V. (ed) (2010) *Community Work Skills Manual* (5th edn), Newcastle upon Tyne: ACW.

Harvey, D. (1989) *The Urban Experience*, Oxford: Blackwell.

Hattersley, L. (1999) 'Trends in Life Expectancy by Social Class: an update', *Health Statistics Quarterly* 2(Summer): 19-24.

HEA (1999) *Inequalities in Health: A Series of Seminars held by the HEA*, eds S. Waller, A. Crosier and D. McVey, London: Health Education Authority.

Heginbotham, C. (1990) *Return to the Community: The Voluntary Ethic and Community Care,* London: Bedford Square Press.

Henderson, P. and Kaur, R. (eds) (1999) *Rural Racism in the UK*, London: SIA/CDF.

Henderson, P and Salmon, H (1995) *Community Organising: the UK Context,* Community Development Foundation, London.

Henderson, P. and Thomas, D. (2002) *Skills in Neighbourhood Work* (5th edn), London: Routledge.

Henderson, P. and Vercseg, I. (2010) *Community Development and Civil Society*, Bristol: The Policy Press.

Henderson, P., Jones, D. and Thomas, D. (eds) (1976) *The Boundaries of Change in Community Work,* London: Allen & Unwin.

Henderson, P., Wright, A. and Wyncoll, K. (eds) (1982) *Successes and Struggles on Council Estates: Tenant Action and Community Work,* London: Association of Community Workers.

Hickey, S. and Mohan, G. (2004) 'Towards Participation as Transformation: Critical Themes and Challenges', in Hickey, S. and Mohan, G. (eds) (2004) (*op cit.*): 3-24.

Hickey, S. and Mohan, G. (eds) (2004) *Participation: from Tyranny to Transformation*, London: Zed Books.

Hillery, G.A. (1964) 'Villages, cities and total institutions', *American Sociological Review* 28: 32-42.

HMSO (1968) *Report of the Committee on Local Government and Applied Personal Social Services*. Cmnd 3703 (Seebohm Report), London: HMSO.

HMSO (1969) *People and Planning* (Skeffington Report), London: HMSO.

HMSO (1973) *The Russell report on Adult Education in England and Wales*, London: HMSO.

HMSO (1975) *Adult Education: The Challenge of Change* (The Alexander Report), London: HMSO.

Hobsbawm, E. (1994) *The Age of Extremes: The Short Twentieth Century*. Harmondsworth: Penguin.

Hoggett, P. (ed) (1997) *Contested Communities,* Bristol: The Policy Press.

Hoggett, P., Mayo, M. and Miller, C. (2009) *The Dilemmas of Development Work: Ethical Challenges in Regeneration*, Bristol: The Policy Press.

Holland, J. (1998) *Whose Voice?*, London: Intermediate Technology Publications.

Holden, T. (2005) *Queen Coal: Women of the Miners' Strike*, Nottingham: Sutton Publishing.

Holdsworth, A. (1989) *Johnny Crescendo revealed*, Manchester: Holdsworth.

Home Office (1960) *Children and Young Persons* (Ingleby Report). London: HMSO.

Home Office (1979) *The Funding Register for Ethnic Minority Self-Help Groups,* London: HMSO.

Home Office (2003) *Building Civil Renewal*, London: Home Office.

hooks, b. (1991) *Yearning: Race, Gender and Cultural Politics*, London: Turnaround.

Horton, M. and Freire, P. (1990) 'The difference between education and organizing' in P. Freire, M. Horton, B. Bell and J. Gaventa (eds), *We Make the Road by Walking*, Philadelphia: Temple University Press: 115-29.

Howarth, C., Kenway, P., Palmer, G. and Miorelli, R. (1999) *Monitoring Poverty and Social Exclusion 1999*, York: Joseph Rowntree Foundation/New Policy Institute.

Humes, W. (2004/5) 'The discourse of community in educational policy', *Education in the North* No 12.

Hutton, W. (1996) *The State we're in*, London: Vintage.

IACD (2004) The Budapest Declaration, www.iacdglobal.org/BudapestDeclaration

Jacobs, S. (1976) *The Right to a Decent Home*, London: Routledge.

Jacobs, B. (1986) *Black Politics and the Urban Crisis in Britain,* Cambridge: Cambridge University Press.

Jacobs, S. (1994) 'Community work in a changing world' in Jacobs, S. and Popple, K. (eds) *Community Work in the 1990s*, Nottingham: Spokesman.

Jessop, B. (1986) 'Regulation, post-Fordism and the state' in W. Bonefeld and J. Holloway (eds) *Post-Fordism and social form*, London: Capital and Class: 69-91.

Jones, D. (1977) 'Community Work in the United Kingdom' in Specht, H. and Vickery, A. (eds), *Integrating Social Work Methods,* London: Allen & Unwin.

Jones, D. and Mayo, M. (eds) (1975) *Community Work Two,* London: Routledge & Kegan Paul.

Jones, K. (1991) 'The Trouble with Authority', *Differences,* 3(1): 104-27.

Jones, P. (2003) 'Urban Regeneration's Poisoned Chalice: Is there an Impasse in (Community) Participation-Based Policy?, *Urban Studies,* 40 (3): 581-601.

Jubilee 2000 website, www.oneworld.org/jubilee2000/ or (in the United States) www.j2000use.org/j2000

Judt, T. (2010) *Ill Fares The Land*, Harmondsworth: Allen Lane.

Keck, M. and Sikkink, K. (1998) *Activists Beyond Boarders: Trans-National Advocacy Networks in International Politics*, London: Cornell University Press.

Kenny, S. (2002) 'Tensions and dilemmas in community development: new discourses, new Trojans?', *Community Development Journal* 37(4): 284-99.

Kilmurray, A. (1989) 'The Rural Action Project in N. Ireland', *Scope* (December). Kumarian Press.

Kooiman, J. (2003) *Governing as Governance*, London: Sage.

Kuenstler, P. (ed) *Community Organization in Great Britain*, London: Faber.

Lamoureux, H., Mayer, R. and Panet-Raymond, J. (1989) *Community Action*, Quebec: Black Rose Books.

Lansley, S., Goss, and Wolmar, C. (1989) *Councils in Conflict, the Rise and Fall of the Municipal Left,* Basingstoke: Macmillan.

Lapping, A. (ed) (1970) *Community Action* (Fabian Tract 400), London: Fabian Society.

LCIL (2005) *It's Your Life,* Lothian Centre for Integrated Living, Edinburgh.

Leaper, R. (1968) *Community Work*, London: National Council of Social Service.

Leat, D. (1975) 'Social theory and the historical construction of social work activity: the role of Samuel Barnett', in Leonard, P. (ed) *The Sociology of Community Action*, Sociological Review Monograph, University of Keele.

Ledwith, M. (2005) *Community Development: A Critical Approach*, Bristol: The Policy Press.

Ledwith, M. (2007) 'Reclaiming the radical agenda: a critical approach to community development', *Concept* 17(2): 8-13.

Lee, B. and Weeks, W. (1991) 'Social Action Theory and the Women's Movement: An Analysis of Assumption', *Community Development Journal,* 26(3): 220-26.

Lees, R. (1972) *Politics and Social Work*, London: Routledge and Kegan Paul.

Lees, R. and Mayo, M. (1984) *Community Action for Change,* London: Routledge and Kegan Paul.

Lees, R. and Smith, G. (1975) *Action-research in Community Development,* London: Routledge and Kegan Paul.

Lenin, V.I. (1966) *Imperialism: The Highest Stage of Capitalism,* Moscow: Progress Publishers.

Leonard, P. (ed) (1975) *The Sociology of Community Action,* Sociological Review Monograph 21, Keele: University of Keele.

Levitas, R (1998) *The Inclusive Society? Social Exclusion and New Labour,* Basingstoke: Macmillan.

Levitas, R. (ed) (1986) *The Ideology of the New Right,* Cambridge: Polity Press.

Lilley, R. (1989) 'Gungarakayn Women Speak: Reproduction and the Transformation of Tradition', *Oceania*, 60, 2: 81-98.

Lister, R. (1998) 'Citizen in Action: Citizenship and Community Development in a Southern Ireland Context', *Community Development Journal* 33(3): 226-35.

Litwak, E. and Meyer, H. (1966) 'A balance theory of co-ordination between bureaucratic organizations and community primary groups', *Administrative Science Quarterly* 11.

LGA (2002) *Guidance on Community Cohesion,* London: Local Government Association.

Lomas, J. (1998) 'Social capital and health: implications for public health and epidemiology', *Social Science and Medicine* 47(9): 1181–8.

London Edinburgh Weekend Return Group (1980) *In and Against the State,* London: Pluto Press.

Loney, M. (1983) *Community against Government.: The British Community Development Project 1968-78: A Study of Government Incompetence,* London: Heinemann.

Loney, M., Bocock, R., Clarke, J., Cochrane, A., Graham, P. and Wilson, M. (eds) (1991) *The State or the Market: Politics and Welfare in Contemporary Britain* (2nd edn), London: Sage, in association with Open University Press.

Lorde, A. (1984) *Sister Outsider,* New York: The Crossing Press.

Lovett, T. (1992) 'Ligoniel: A Case Study in Community Development', *Scope* January.

Lovett, T. (1993) *Bridging the Sectarian Divide in N. Ireland,* Belfast: The Ulster People's College, Studies in Adult Education, Spring.

Lovett, T. and Percival, P. (1978) 'Politics, Conflict and Community Action in N. Ireland', in P. Curno (ed) (*op. cit.*)

Lovett, T., Clarke, C. and Kilmurray, A. (1983) *Adult Education and Community Action,* London: Croom Helm.

Lovett, T., Gunn, D. and Robson, T. (1994) 'Education, conflict and community development in Northern Ireland', *Community Development Journal* 29(2):177-86.

Lowndes, V. and Sullivan, H. (2004) 'Like a Horse and Carriage or a Fish on a Bicycle: How well do Local Partnerships and Public Participation go together?, *Local Government Studies,* 30(1): 51-73.

Lugard, F. (1922) *The Dual Mandate in British Tropical Africa,* London: Cass.

Lukes, S. (2005) *Power: A Radical View,* 2nd edn, Basingstoke: Palgrave.

MacArthur, A. (1993) 'Community partnerships: a formula for neighbourhood regeneration in the 1990s', *Community Development Journal* 28(4): 305-15.

MacGregor, S. (2001) 'The problematic community' in May, M., Page, R. and Brunsdon, E. (eds) *Understanding Social Problems: Issues in Social Policy,* Oxford: Blackwell.

Macintyre, S. (1997) 'The Black Report and beyond: what are the issues?', *Social Science and Medicine* 44(6): 723–45.

Mandel, E. (1972) 'The changing role of the bourgeois university' in T. Patement, (ed) *Countercourse,* Harmondsworth: Penguin.

Mani, L. (1990) 'Multiple Mediations: Feminist Scholarship in the Age of Multinational Reception', *Feminist Review,* 135: 24-41.

Manning, B. and Ohri, A. (1982) 'Racism – the response of community work' in Ohri, A., Manning, B. and Curno, P. (eds) *Community Work and Racism, Community Work* 7, London: Routledge and Kegan Paul, pp 3-33.

Marris, P. (1987) *Meaning and Action: Planning and Conceptions of Change,* London: Routledge & Kegan Paul.

Marris, P. and Rein, M. (1967) *Dilemmas of Social Reform,* New York: Atherton Press.

Martin, I. (1987) 'Community education: towards a theoretical analysis' in Allan, G., Bastiani, J., Martin, I. and Richards, K. (eds) *Community Education: An Agenda for Educational Reform,* Buckingham: Open University Press.

Martin, I. (2003) 'Inflections of "community" in educational work and research' in Centre for Research in Lifelong Learning (CRLL), *Experiential – Community: – Work-based: Researching Learning outside the Academy,* Glasgow: Glasgow Caledonion University/University of Stirling.

Martin, I. (2006) 'Diversity, difference and justice', *Concept* 16(2): 4-8.

Masefield, P. (2006) *Strength: Broadsides from Disability on the Arts,* Stoke-on-Trent: Trentham Books.

Matthews, N. (1988) 'Surmounting a Legacy: Explanations of racial diversity in a Local Anti-rape Movement', *Gender and Society,* 3, 4: 518-553.

Mayer, A.C. *et al* (1958) *Pilot project India,* mimeo.

Mayo, M. (1975a) 'Community development as a radical alternative?' in R. Bailey and M. Brake (eds) *Radical Social Work,* Edward Arnold, pp 129-43.

Mayo, M. (1975b) 'The History and Early Development of CDP' in Lees, R. and Smith, G. (eds), *Action Research in Community Development,* London: Routledge & Kegan Paul.

Mayo, M. (ed) (1977) *Women in the Community, Community Work Three,* London: Routledge & Kegan Paul.

Mayo, M. (1994) *Communities and Caring: The Mixed Economy of Welfare,* Basingstoke: Macmillan.

Mayo, M. (1998) 'Community work' in Adams, R., Dominelli, L. and Payne, M. (eds) *Social Work: Themes, Issues and Critical Debates,* Basingstoke: Macmillan.

Mayo, M. (2005) *Global Citizens,* London: Earthscan.

Mayo, M. and Jones, D. (eds) (1974) *Community Work One,* London: Routledge & Kegan Paul.

McConnell, C. (1996) *Community Education: The Making of an Empowering Profession,* Edinburgh: Scottish Community Education Council.

McGee, R. and Norton, A. (2000) 'Participation in Poverty Reduction Strategies: A Synthesis of Participatory Approaches', IDS Working Paper 109, Brighton: IDS.

McGinty, S. (2003) 'Community capacity-building', Paper presented at Australian Association for Research in Education conference, Brisbane, Australia (www.aare. edu.au).

McGivney, V. (1999) *Excluded Men: Men Who are Missing From Education and Training,* Leicester: NIACE.

McNamee, P. and Lovett, T. (1992) *Working Class Community in N. Ireland* (2nd edn), Belfast: Ulster People's College.

Meade, R. and Shaw, M. (2006) 'Editorial Introduction, Community Development Journal Special Issue on Community Development and the Arts', *Community Development Journal* 42(4): 413-21.

Meekosha, H. (1993) 'The bodies politic: equality, difference and community practice', in H. Butcher, A. Glen, P. Henderson and J. Smith (eds) *Community and Public Policy,* London: Pluto Press, pp 171-92.

Meekosha, H. and Pettman, J. (1991) 'Beyond Category Politics', *Hecate,* 17(2): 75-92.

Meekosha, H. *et al.* (1987) *Equal Disappointment Opportunity: a Report to the Department of Community Services on Programs for Immigrants and their Children,* Canberra: Department of Community/ Services and Health.

Mercer, K. (1990) 'Welcome to the Jungle: Party and Diversity in Post-Modern Politics' in J. Rutherford, (ed) *Identity: Community, Culture, Difference,* London: Lawrence and Wishart.

Midwinter, E. (1972) *Priority Education,* Harmondsworth: Penguin.

Miliband, D. (2006) 'Empowerment and the New Deal for Devolution', Speech by the Minister of Communities and Local Government to the Annual Conference of the New Local Government Network, 18th January.

Miliband, R. (1994) *Socialism for a Sceptical Age,* Cambridge: Polity Press.

Miller, C. (1996) *Public Service Trade Unionism and Radical Politics,* Aldershot: Dartmouth Press.

Miller, C. (2004) *Producing Welfare: A Modern Agenda,* Basingstoke: Palgrave.

Miller, C. and Ahmed, Y. (1997) 'Community development at the crossroads', *Policy & Politics* 25(3): 269-84.

Miller, C. and Bryant, R. (1990) 'Community work in the UK: Reflections on the 1980s', *Community Development Journal* 23 (4): 315-323.

Miller, S.M. and Rein, M. (1974) 'Community participation: past and future' in D. Jones and M. Mayo (eds) *Community Work Two,* London: Routledge and Kegan Paul, pp 3-24.

Mills, C.W. (1970) *The Sociological Imagination,* Harmondsworth: Pelican.

Minh-Ha, T. (1989) *Women, Native, Other: Writing, Post-Colonialism, and Feminity,* Bloomington, Indiana: Indiana University Press

Minogue, M. (1994) 'The Principles and Practice of Good Governance', British Council briefing, Law and Governance, Issue 4. Manchester: British Council.

Mohanty, C.T. (1991) 'Cartographies of struggle' in C.T. Mohanty, A. Russo and L. Torres (eds) *Third World Women and the Politics of Feminism,* Bloomington, IN: University of Indiana Press.

Mooney, G. and Neal, S. (eds) (2009) *Community: Welfare, Crime and Society,* Maidenhead: The Open University Press.

Mooney, G. and Poole, L. (2004) 'A land of milk and honey? Social policy in Scotland after devolution', *Critical Social Policy* 24 (4).

Moore, B. (1966) *Social Origins of Dictatorship and Democracy,* Harmondsworth: Penguin.

Morison, J. (2000) 'The Government–Voluntary Sector Compacts: Governance, Governmentality and Civil Society', *Journal of Law and Society* 27(1): 98-132.

Morris, H. (1925) *The Village College: Being a Memorandum on the Provision of Educational and Social Facilities for the Countryside, with Special Reference to Cambridgeshire,* Cambridge: Cambridge University Press.

Morris, J. (1990) *Pride without Prejudice,* London: Women's Press.

Morris, J. (1991) 'Us and Them: Feminist Research, Community Care and Disability' *Critical Social Policy,* 11, 3, 33: 22-29.

Mowbray, M. (1984) 'Localism and Austerity – The Community Can Do It', *Journal of Australian Political Economy,* 16, March: 3-14.

Mowbray, M. (2005) 'Community capacity building or state opportunism?', *Community Development Journal* 40(3): 255-64.

Moynihan, D. (1969) *Maximum Feasible Misunderstanding: Community Action in the War on Poverty,* New York: Free Press.

Mullard, C. (1984) *Anti-Racist Education: The Three O's,* Cardiff: National Antiracist Movement in Education.

Muntaner, C., Lynch, J. and Davey Smith, G. (2000) 'Social capital and the third way in public health', *Critical Public Health,* 10(20): 107–124.

Napolitano, S. (1993) *A Dangerous Woman,* Manchester: GMCDP.

Narayan, D., Chambers, R., Shah, M. and Petesch, P. (2000) *Voices of the Poor: Crying Out for Change,* Washington, DC: World Bank.

Nehru, P. (1957) *Speeches on Community,* Delhi: Ministry of Community Development.

Newman, J. (2001) *Modernising Governance: New Labour, Policy and Society*, London: Sage.

Ng, R. (1988) *The Politics of Community Services: Immigrant Women, Class and the State*, Toronto: Garamond Press.

Nicholls, P. (1991) 'Who Should Run Community Enterprise?' in NEWSVIEW, Issue 2, Belfast, November.

NICRC (1971) *First Annual Report*, Belfast: Northern Ireland Community Relations Commission.

Nisbet, R. (1953) *The Quest for Community: A Study in the Ethics of Order and Feedom*, Oxford: Oxford University Press.

Nisbet, R. (1966) *The Sociological Tradition*, New York: Basic Books, Inc.

Noya, A., Clarence, E. and Craig, G. (2010) *Building a Better Life Together*, Paris: OECD.

O'Hadhmaill, F. (1991) 'Community Development in Protestant Areas', *Scope*, November.

O'Leary, T. (ed) (2008) *Asset-based Approaches to Rural Community Development*, Fife: International Association for Community Development.

O'Malley, J. (1977) *Politics of Community Action*, London: Russell.

Oakley, A. (1992) *Social Support and Motherhood*, Oxford: Basil Blackwell.

ODPM (2005) *LSP Evaluation: Interim Report*, London: Office of the Deputy Prime Minister.

Ohri, A., Manning, B. and Curno, P. (eds) (1982) *Community Work and Racism: Community Work Seven*, London: Routledge & Kegan Paul.

Oliver, M. (1990) *The Politics of Disablement*, Basingstoke: Macmillan.

Oliver, M. (1996) *Understanding Disability: From Theory to Practice*, London: Macmillan.

Osborne, D. and Gaebler, T. (1992) *Reinventing Government: How the Entrepreneurial Spirit is Transforming The Public Sector*, Reading, MA: Addison Wesley.

Ouseley, H. (2001) *Community Pride, Not Prejudice – Making Diversity Work in Bradford*, Bradford: Bradford Vision.

Page, D. (2000) *Communities in the Balance: The Reality of Social Exclusion on Housing Estates*, York: Joseph Rowntree Foundation.

Pahl, J. (ed) (1985) *Private Violence and Public Policy: The Needs of Battered Women and the Response of the Public Services*, London: Routledge & Kegan Paul.

Parmar, P. (1990) 'Black Feminism: The Politics of Articulation' in J. Rutherford (ed) *Identity: Community, Culture, Difference*, London: Lawrence and Wishart

Parry, G.B. (1964) 'Individuality, politics and the critique of paternalism' *Political Studies* 12: 163-77.

Perlman, J. (1980) *Seven Voices from One Organisation. What does it Mean?*, Unpublished paper, University of Southern California.

Pettman, J. (1992) *Living in the Margins: Racism, Sexism and Feminism in Australia*, Sydney: Allen and Unwin.

Phelan, S. (1991) 'Specificity beyond Equality and Difference', *Differences* 3(1): 128-43.

Pitchford, M. (2008) *Making Spaces for Community Development*, Bristol: The Policy Press.

Piven, F. and Cloward, R. (1977) *Poor People's Movement: Why They Succeed, How They Fail*, New York: Vintage Books

Plant, R. (1974) 'Community as fact and value', in *Community and Ideology: An Essay in Applied Social Philosophy*, London: Routledge and Kegan Paul.

Playback (2009), http://www.playbacktrust.net/

Popay, J., Williams, G., Thomas, C. and Gatrell, T. (1998) 'Theorising inequalities in health: the place of lay knowledge', *Sociology of Health and Illness* 20(5): 619–44.

Popple, K. (1995a) 'Models of community work' in *Analysing Community Work: Its Theory and Practice*, Buckingham: Open University Press, pp 54–74.

Popple, K. (1995b) *Analysing Community Work: its theory and practice*. Buckingham: Open University Press.

Popple, K. (2006) 'The first forty years of the CDJ', *Community Development Journal*, 43(1): 1–18.

Poplin, D. (1972) *Communities: A Survey of Theories and Methods of Research*, New York: Macmillan.

Powell, E. (1968) 'Text of speech delivered in Birmingham, 20 April, 1968', *Race* X(1): 80–104.

Power, M. (2003) 'Evaluating the Audit Explosion', *Law and Policy* 25 (3): 185–202.

Putnam, D. (2001) *Bowling Alone: The Collapse and Revival of American Community*, New York: Simon and Shuster.

Quirk, B. (2006) 'The three 'Rs': Respect, reason and rights' in *Complexity and Cohesion*, SOLACE Foundation Imprint, December: 21–33.

Raco, M. (2003) 'Governmentality, Subject-Building and the Discourses and Practices of Devolution in the UK', *Transactions of the Institute of British Geographers:* 75–95.

Radford-Hill, S. (1986) 'Considering Feminism as a Model for Social Change' in T. De Lauretis (ed) *Feminist Studies:*157–72.

Ramadan, T. (2006) 'Europe and Islam: local initiatives for global change' in *Complexity and Cohesion*, SOLACE Foundation Imprint, December: 21–33.

Ramdin, R. (1987) *The Making of the Black Working Class in Britain*, Aldershot: Gower.

Reagon, B. (1983) 'Coalition Politics: Turning the Century' in B. Smith (ed) *Home Girls: A Black Feminist Anthology*, New York: Kitchen Table.

Reason, P. (2002) 'Justice, sustainability and participation: inaugural lecture', available from <p.w.reason@bath.ac.uk>

Rhodes, R. (1996) 'The New Governance: Governing Without Government', *Political Studies* 44: 652–67.

Rhodes, R. (1997) *Understanding Governance*, Buckingham: Open University Press.

Rhodes, R.W. (1981) *Control and Power in Central-Local Relations*, Aldershot: Gower.

Rieser, R. and Mason, M. (1992) *Disability Equality in the Classroom*, London: Disability Equality in Education.

Robson, T. (1992) *The State, Community Action and Employment in N. Ireland*, Unpublished paper, Community Education, Research and Development Centre, Belfast: University of Ulster.

Rogers, V. (1994) 'Feminist Work and Community Education' in Jacobs, S. and Popple, K. (eds) *Community Work in the 1990s*, Nottingham: Spokesman.

Rolston, B. (1984) 'Whatever happened to Community Politics', and A. Pollock, 'Sinn Fein Moves into Community Arena', in *Fortnight Magazine*, Belfast, July/August.

Roof (1986) 'The Penny Drops at Coin Street', *Roof*, March/April: 6–7.

Rooney, E. (1992) *Women, Community and Politics in N. Ireland: Interim Report*, Belfast: Community Education Research, Development Centre, University of Ulster

Rose, N. (1999) *Powers of Freedom: Reframing Political Thought*, Cambridge: Cambridge University Press.

Rose, N. and Miller, P. (1992) 'Political Power beyond the State: Problematics of government, *British Journal of Sociology*, 43: 173-205.

Ross, M. (1955) *Community Organisation: Theory, Principles and Practice.* New York: Harper and Row.

Rothman, J. (1970) 'Three Models of Community Organisation Practice' in Cox, F., Erlich, J., Rothman, J. and Tropman, J. (eds), *Strategies of Community Organisation,* Itasca, IL: Peacock Publishing.

Rowbotham, S. (1990) *The Past is Before Us: Feminism in Action since the 1960s.* Harmondsworth: Penguin.

Salamon, L. (1994) 'The Rise of the Non-profit Sector: A Global Associational Revolution', *Foreign Affairs* 73(4).

Sartre, J-P. (1970) *Preface to Frantz Fanon, 'The Wretched of the Earth',* Penguin: Harmondsworth.

SCCVO (1984) *The Garnock Valley Community Project: Final Report,* Edinburgh: Scottish Council for Community and Voluntary Organisations.

Scholte, J. A. (1999) 'Global Civil Society: Changing the World?', Centre for Study of Globalisation and Regionalisation Working Paper No. 31/99, University of Warwick, Warwick, UK.

Schultz, M. S. (1998) 'Collective Action Across Borders: Opportunity Structures, Network Capacities, and Communicative Praxis in the Age of Advanced Globalization', *Sociological Perspectives* 41: 587-616.

SED (Scottish Education Department) (1975) *Adult Education: the Challenge of Change* (The Alexander Report), London: HMSO.

Segal, L. (1987) *Is the Future Female?,* London: Virago.

Sennett, R. (2003) *Respect: The Formation of Character in an Age of Inequality,* Harmondsworth: Penguin.

SEU (1998) *Bringing Britain Together,* London: Social Exclusion Unit.

Shakespeare, T., Gillespie-Sells, K. and Davies, D. (1996) *The Sexual Politics of Disability,* London: Cassell.

Shaw, M (1996) 'Out of the quagmire: Community care – problems and possibilities for radical practice', in Cooke, I and Shaw, M (eds) (*op.cit.*).

Shaw, M. (2004) *Community Work: Policy, Politics and Practice,* Hull: Universities of Hull and Edinburgh.

Shaw, M. (2008) 'Community development and the politics of community', *Community Development Journal* 43(1): 24-36.

Shaw, M. and Martin, I. (2000) 'Community work, citizenship and democracy: re-making the connections', *Community Development Journal* 35(4): 401-404.

Shaw, M., Dorling, D., Gordon, D. and Davey Smith, G. (2000) *The Widening Gap: Health Inequalities and Policy in Britain,* Bristol: The Policy Press.

Shirlow, P. and Murtagh, B. (2004) 'Capacity-Building, Representation and Intracommunity Conflict', *Urban Studies* 41(1): 57-70.

Shor, I. (1992) *Empowering Education: Critical Teaching for Social Change,* London/Chicago, IL: University of Chicago Press.

Shukra, K. (1998) *The Changing Pattern of Black Politics in Britain,* London: Pluto Press.

Shukra, K. (2007) 'The changing terrain of multi-culture: from anti-oppressive practice to community cohesion', *Concept* 17(3): 3-7.

Shukra, K., Back, L., Keith, M., Khan, A. and Solomos, J. (2004) 'Race, Social Cohesion and the Changing Politics of Citizenship', *London Review of Education*, 2(3), November, London: Taylor Francis.

Sivanandan, A. (1976) *Race, Class and the State,* London: Institute of Race Relations.

Sivanandan, A. (1990) *Communities of Resistance: Writings on Black Struggles for Socialism,* London: Verso.

Skinner, S. (1997) *Building Community Strengths,* London: Community Development Foundation.

Skinner, S. and Wilson, M. (2002) *Willing Partners?,* Leeds: Yorkshire Forum.

Smith, A. (1981) *The Ethnic Revival,* Cambridge: Cambridge University Press.

Smith, L. and Jones, D. (eds) (1981) *Deprivation, Participation and Community Action. Community Work Six,* London: Routledge & Kegan Paul.

Solomos, J. (1989) *Black Youth, Racism and the State: The Politics of Ideology and Policy.* Cambridge: Cambridge University Press.

Somerville, P. (2005) 'Community Governance and Democracy', *Policy and Politics*, 33(1): 117-44.

Sondhi, R. (1997) 'The politics of equality or the politics of difference? Locating black communities in western society', *Community Development Journal* 32(3): 223-232.

Specht, H. (1978) 'The dilemmas of community work in the United Kingdom: a comment', *Policy & Politics*, September.

Spender, D. (1976) *Man-made Language,* London: Routledge.

Spyri, J. (1995) *Heidi,* Harmondsworth: Penguin.

Stacey, M. (1969) 'The myth of community studies', *British Journal of Sociology* 20(2): 134-47.

Standing Conference on Community Development (1991) *SCCD Charter: A Working Statement on Community Development,* Sheffield: SCCD.

Stanton, I. (1997) *Rolling Thunder,* Stream Records. London.

Steiner, C. (1974) 'Radical psychiatry and movement groups' in The Radical Therapist Collective (ed), *The Radical Therapist,* Harmondsworth: Penguin.

Stevenson, R.L. (1998) *Treasure Island,* Oxford: Oxford World Classics.

Stoker, G. (1989) 'Creating a local government for a post-Fordist society: the Thatcherite project', in Stewart, J. and Stoker, G. (eds) *The Future of Local Government,* London: Macmillan.

Stoker, G. and Bottom, K. (2004) *Community Capacity-building,* Lecture given at Lorne, 25 July (mimeo).

SRC (Strathclyde Regional Council) (1978) *Policy Review Group on Community Development Services,* Glasgow.

Suttles, G. D. (1972) *The Social Construction of Communities,* London: University of Chicago Press.

Swain, J. and Cameron, C. (1999) 'Unless Otherwise Stated: Discourses of Labelling and Identity' in Corker, M. and French, S. (eds), *Disability Discourse,* Buckingham: Open University Press.

Swain, J. and Lawrence, P. (1994) 'Learning about Disability: Changing Attitudes or Challenging Understanding' in French, S. (ed) *On Equal Terms: Working with Disabled People* Oxford: Butterworth-Heinemann.

Swyngedouw, E. (2005) 'Governance Innovation and the Citizen: The Janus-Face of Governance-Beyond-The-State', *Urban Studies* 42(11): 1991-2006.

Tarrow, S. (1994) *Power in Movement: Social Movements, Collective Action and Politics*, Cambridge: Cambridge University Press.

Tasker, L. and Wunnam, A. (1977) 'The ethos of radical social workers and community workers', *Social Work Today* 8(23).

Taylor, M. (2000a) 'Communities in the Lead: Power, Organisational Capacity and Social Capital', *Urban Studies* 37(5-6): 1019-35.

Taylor, M. (2000b) *Top Down Meets Bottom Up*, York: Joseph Rowntree Foundation.

Taylor, M. (2003) *Public Policy in the Community*, London: Palgrave Macmillan.

Taylor, M.(2007) 'Community participation in the real world', *Urban Studies* 44(2): 297-317.

Tedmanson, D. (2003) 'Whose capacity needs building? Open hearts and empty hands, reflections on capacity building in remote communities', Paper given at the 4th International Critical Management Studies Conference, University of South Australia (mimeo).

Thomas, C. (1999) *Female Forms: Experiencing and Understanding Disability*, Buckingham: Open University Press.

Thomas, C. (2002) 'A Journey around the Social Model' in Corker, M. and Shakespeare, T. (eds) *Disability/Postmodernity: Embodying Disability Theory*, London: Continuum.

Thomas, D. (1978) 'Community work, social change and social planning', in Curno, P. (ed) (1978) (*op. cit*).

Thomas, D. (1983) *The Making of Community Work*, London: George Allen and Unwin.

Thomas, D. and Henderson, P. (1976) *Skills in Neighbourhood Work*, London: NISW.

Thomason, G. (1969) *The Professional Approach to Community Work*, London: Sands.

Thompson, J. (2000) *Women, Class and Education*, London: Routledge.

Thompson, N. (2003) *Promoting Equality: Challenging Discrimination and Oppression*, Basingstoke: Palgrave Macmillan.

Thomson, J. (2000) 'When "active citizenship" becomes mob rule', *Adults Learning*, September, pp 23-4.

Thomson, R.G. (1997) *Extraordinary Bodies: Figuring Physical Disability in American Culture and Literature*, New York: Columbia University Press.

Thorpe, R. (1985) 'Community work and ideology' in Thorpe, R. and Putruchenia, A. (eds) *Community Work or Social Change: An Australian Perspective*, London: Routledge and Kegan Paul.

Thurrock Council (2005) 'Thurrock's Heroes Honoured', http://www.thurrock. gov.uk/news/content.php?page=story&ID=1614

Titchkosky, T. (2006) *Disability, Self and Society*, Toronto: University of Toronto Press.

Tonnies, F. (1955) *Community and Association*, London: Routledge and Kegan Paul.

Townsend, P. (1962) *The Last Refuge: A Survey of Residential Institutions and Homes for the Aged in England and Wales*, London: Routledge & Kegan Paul.

Townsend, P. (1995) 'Poverty: Home and Away', *Poverty*, No 91, Summer.

Troyna, B. and Carrington, B. (1990) *Education, Racism and Reform*, London: Routledge.

TSO (2006) *Strong and Prosperous Communities, The Local Government White Paper*, London: The Stationery Office.

Twelvetrees, A. (2009) *Community Work* (5th edn), London: Macmillan.

UN (1953) *Report of the Mission on Rural Community Organisation and Development in the Caribbean area and Mexico*, New York: United Nations.

UN (1958) *Evaluation of Indian Community Development*, New York: United Nations.

UN (1959) *European Seminar on Community Development and Social Welfare in Urban Areas*, Geneva: United Nations.

UNDP (1991) *Symposium for water sector capacity building*, Amsterdam: United Nations Development Programme/International Institute for Hydraulic and Environmental Engineering.

UNDP (1993) *Human Development Report*, Oxford: Oxford University Press.

Waddington, P. (1979) 'Looking ahead – community work into the 1980s, *Community Development Journal*, 14(3): 224-234.

Waddington, P. (1983) 'Looking ahead: community work into the 1980s', in Thomas, D. (ed) (1983) (*op. cit.*)

Wagner, G. (1988) *Residential Care: A Positive Choice*, London: National Institute for Social Work/HMSO.

Wainwright, D. (1996) 'The political transformation of the health inequalities debate', *Critical Social Policy* 49(16): 67–82.

Walker, R. and Craig, G. (2009) *Community Development Workers for Bme Mental Health: Embedding Sustainable Change*, London: Department of Health.

Wallace, A. (2010) *Remaking Community?*, Aldershot: Aldgate.

Warburton, D. (ed) (1998) *Community and Sustainable Development*, London: Earthscan.

Washington, B. T. (1967) *Up from Slavery*, New York: Airmont.

Watson, J. (2000) *Male Bodies: Health, Culture and Identity*, Buckingham: Open University Press.

Weisberger, B. (1972) Booker T. Washington, New York: Mentor Books.

Wilkinson, R.G. (1997a) 'Commentary: income inequality summarises the health burden of individual relative deprivation', *British Medical Journal*, 314.

Wilkinson, R.G. (1997b) 'Socio-economic determinants of health: health inequalities: relative or absolute material standards?', *British Medical Journal*, 314.

Wilkinson, R.G. (1998a) *Unhealthy Societies: The Afflictions of Inequality*, London: Routledge.

Wilkinson, R.G. (1998b) 'Long term effects of deprivation increase health's sensitivity to current policies', *British Medical Journal*, 317 (letters): 4.

Wilkinson, R. and Pickett, K. (2009) *The Spirit Level: Why More Equal Societies Almost Always Do Better*, London: Bloomsbury Press.

Williams, F. (1989) *Social Policy: A Critical Introduction to Issues of Race, Gender and Class*, Cambridge: Polity.

Williams, F. (1993) 'Women and community' in Bornat, J., Pereira, C., Pilgrim, D. and Williams, F. (eds) *Community Care: A Reader*, Milton Keynes: Macmillan in association with the Open University, Milton Keynes.

Williams, R. (1961) *Culture and Society*, London: Penguin.

Williams, R. (1965) *The Long Revolution*, London: Penguin.

Williams, R. (1976) *Keywords: A Vocabulary of Culture and Society*, London: Fontana.

Willis, P. (2000) *The Ethnographic Imagination*, Cambridge: Polity.

Willmott, P. (1986) *Social Networks, Informal Care And Public Policy*, London: Policy Studies Institute.

Wills, J., Datta, K., Evans, Y., Herbert, J., May, J. and McIlwaine, C. (2010) *Global Cities at Work*, London: Pluto Press.

Wilson, E. (1977) 'Women in the Community' in Mayo, M. (ed) (1977) (*op. cit.*).

Wilson, M. and Wilde, P. (2003) *Benchmarking Community Participation*, York: Joseph Rowntree Foundation.

Wirth, L. (1957) *The Ghetto*, Chicago: University of Chicago Press (first published 1928).

Yeo, E. and Yeo, S. (1988) 'On the uses of community', in Yeo, S. (ed) *New Views of Co-operation*, London: Routledge.

Young, M. and Wilmott, P. (1957, 1962) *Family and Kinship in East London*, London: Institute of Community Studies.

Younghusband, E. (1959) *Report on the Working Party on Social Workers in the Local Authority Health and Welfare Services*, London: HMSO.

Youth and Policy (1995) Summer, no 49.

Zavela, P. (1991) 'Reflections on Diversity among Chicanas', *Frontiers: A Journal of Women's Studies* XII(2): 73-85.

Index

Note: Abbreviations used in index headings are NI=Northern Ireland; UK=United Kingdom; US=United States.

community organisations as model of
community work 212-13
Community Organisations Northern
Ireland 204
community planning *see* social planning/
community planning
'community politics' in Northern Ireland
206
Community Relations Commission (NI)
203
Community Relations Council (NI) 205
Community Work (book series) 29
community workers *see* professional
community workers
conflict
and community education 215, 216
competition for funding 299
consensus and community education
215-16
Conservative-Liberal Democrat coalition
195, 309
consumerism 7, 287
consumer choice 115, 193, 195
contract culture 193, 196
contrived communities 305-6
controversy and community organisation
in US 61-3
Cornwall, A. 292, 294
Craig, Gary 273-82, 289, 297
Crescendo, Johnny 262
Crick, Bernard 272
critical education approach 283-90
Croft, Suzy 163-9
Crossroads approach 137
cultural representations of disability 259-61
culture/cycle of poverty 79, 84, 92, 94-5,
240
Curno, A. 186
Cutler, Ivor 125

D
Dalley, G. 212
Darke, Paul 260
Davey Smith, G. 242
Davidson, N. 194
Dearlove, J. 213
debt relief and global citizen action 253
decentralisation 197, 224-5, 228, 292
deficit model
and community capacity-building 280-1
and health inequalities 241, 243-4, 246,
247
deliberative democracy 272
Delin, A. 262
Delivering Race Equality (DRE) 13, 15

democracy
and citizen action 249
and community development in colonies
75-6, 81
deliberative democracy 272
democratisation of social and political life
229, 231-2
failure of state mechanisms in western
democracies 80, 96, 97, 112
participatory democracy 283, 284
and price of freedom 59-60
Denham Report (2001) 268
Department for Communities and
Local Government: *The Community
Development Challenge* 10-11, 12, 14
Derricourt, Nick 113-14
Development Trusts Association 5
devolved administrations 13, 17, 197, 284,
289
devolved responsibility 14, 245-6, 247,
293-300, 306
difference/diversity 115, 198, 225
and boundaries of 'community' 304-5
as deficit 280
and equality 171-83
and feminist principles 188-9
and global citizen action 252
increasing diversity of communities 312
New Labour and changing approaches to
multi-culturalism 267-72
understanding women's experience
252-3
'dignity of the individual' 63-4
directive approach to community work
33-4, 38-42
disability
and boundaries of 'community' 304
and community development 8, 17
disability movement and community care
model 212
and essentialist debate 175-6
narratives and identities 259-65
Disability Studies: affirmative model 264
disabled people's movement and disability
arts 261-3, 264, 265
disagreements: community worker's role
36-7
discourse
governance theory and participation
291-2
and health inequalities 241-7
and New Labour 194-5
management of ethnic diversity 269-72
see also language of community
development; social exclusion
discourse

health inequalities 239-47
Hegel, G.W.F. 66, 70
Henderson, Paul 20, 111-12, 125-35
Herder, Johann Gottfried 66
hereditarian explanation of health
    inequalities 240
heterosexual norms and community work
    190
Hickey, S. 293, 297
Hill, Octavia 186
Hillery, G.A. 274
Hobbes, Thomas 72
Hodge, P. 77
Hoggett, P. 163, 195
Home Office
    'areas of special social need' 92-3
    black self-help groups 153-4
    and capacity building 277
    policy for tackling extremism 269, 271-2
    Together We Can initiative 289
    see also Community Development
    Projects
Horton, Myles 157-61
housing associations and group work 48-9
housing development and need for
    community 3, 25-6
human rights and global citizen action
    250-1, 252-3
Hunt Report (1967) 267

I

identity-based communities 8, 10, 115,
    274-5
    disability narratives and identities 259-65
    equality and difference debate 171-83,
    188-9
    and essentialist approach 174-6, 177-8,
    181-2
    identity politics and separatism 179, 180,
    198
    ethnic minorities and community
    cohesion 269-71
Illich, Ivan 30, 202
independence in colonies 25, 75-6, 81
Independent Inquiry into Inequalities in
    Health 242
India: community development
    programme 76
indigenous leaders 43-4
indirect leaders 45
individual/individualism 193
    and community care model 212
    'dignity of the individual' 63-4
    and health inequalities 240, 241, 243-4,
    246, 247

and loss of community tradition 72-3
    and need to 'rediscover' community 68
    prioritisation and social change 229-30
    and responsibility 306
    and Thatcherism 112, 115
    whole man and community 66-7
Industrial Areas Foundation 30
inequality *see* equality; health inequalities
inexperienced indigenous leaders 43-4
Ingelby Report (1960) 27
Inner Area Study reports 93, 95, 96
inner city decline
    Community Development Projects and
    state solutions 91-100
    and Education Priority Areas 215
    new approaches in 1980s 114-15
    'structural analysis' approach 6-7, 28, 79,
    94, 95-6, 96-7
    and war on poverty in US 78-9, 81
insider/outsider strategies 132-4, 297-8
Institute for Community Studies 25
institutional change
    agency adjustment and group work 50-3
    and global citizen action 256-7
    and participation 84-5
    and social planning approach 137-9, 140
institutional racism 149, 150-6, 220
integration and group work 49
inter-agency working 52, 230, 289
interjacent role of community workers
    125-35, 299
International Association for Community
    Development (IACD) 312-13
    Budapest Declaration 9-10, 19, 277, 313
Internet and global citizen action 254
Islam and policy 14, 269, 271-2, 281
issue-based communities 9, 10, 204, 275

J

Jessop, B. 224
Jones, David 20, 125-35
Joseph Rowntree Foundation 19
Jubilee 2000 campaign 250, 253

K

Kuenstler, P. 4

L

language of community development
    273-82
    see also discourse
Latin America and social action 30
Lawrence, Stephen 271

dissatisfaction and radical tendencies 80-1, 101-7
effective organisers in US 61-4
and feminist principles 189-90
and group work 46-50, 53
and institutional racism 150-6, 220
interjacent role on boundaries 125-35, 299
number of 'community work' posts 13, 14-15
present-day dilution in focus of role 15-16, 195-6, 289
 in Northern Ireland 205-6
professionalisation and potential of 225-7, 231
social planning and local community action 139-41
socialist struggle of state workers 101-7
see also education and training in community development
programme development and group work 47-8
property development and community action 117-23
psychosocial stress model and health inequalities 241, 244
public expenditure
 cuts in 1970s 97, 310
 expansion of welfare in 1960s 97-8
 present-day coalition cuts 309
 see also funding and resource allocation
public service delivery
 community development potential for 230-1, 232
 participation as mechanism for 15-16, 197-8, 289-90
 and participation in US 86-90

Q
Quirk, Barry 269

R
race issues
 and community development 8, 10, 17, 164
 black and anti-racist model of community work 219-21, 267, 271
 community work responses to racism 147-56
 strategies to combat racism 155-6
 riots 26-7, 268
 terminology problems 149
 see also black and minority ethnic communities
Raco, M. 292, 294

radical community development 29, 130
 Alinsky's rules for radicals 55-64
 as facet of whole 303
 and incorporation into mainstream policy 220, 223, 228, 271, 279
 need for critical approach 226, 283-90
 and professional dissatisfaction 80-2, 101-7
 radical left critique of community action 141-5
 see also activism; community action
Ramadan, T. 269
Rathbone, Eleanor 186
Reagon, B. 182
Reason, Peter 287-8
recentralisation discourse 196, 292-3, 296
Redcliffe-Maud Report 96
'rediscovery' of community 66, 68, 72
'rediscovery' of community development 9, 275
redistributionist discourse (RED) and health inequalities 242-3, 244-5, 246
reformation and revolution 58-9
regeneration see urban renewal/regeneration
Rein, Martin 79, 81, 83-90
rejection of group workers 50
representations of disability 259-61
research
 and health inequalities 239-47
 see also action research; participatory research
resilience 29
resistance and participation 295-6
resources see funding and resource allocation
responsibility
 and community group work 52
 devolution to community level 14, 245-6, 247, 293-300, 306
 New Labour's rights and responsibilities 193, 197
revolutionary approach 79-80
 Alinsky's rules for radicals 57-60
Rhodes, R. 291
rights and responsibilities 193, 197
 see also responsibility
Robson, Terry 201-9
Rogers, V. 216
'roll-back' policy approach 112, 114, 194, 310
'roll-out' policy approach 194
Roosevelt, Franklin D. 59
Rose, N. 292-3
Ross, M. 29
Rothman, Jack 29, 214

in Northern Ireland 202, 205
user involvement 115, 164-6, 166, 196
  see also participation

V

values and standards
  conflicts in community group work 52-3
  failure to incorporate 15
vertical alignment and global citizen action
  253-4
vigilantism and paedophile panic 235-8
'voice' of communities 10, 166, 298-9
  and global citizen action 255-6, 257
  government reluctance to listen 12, 15,
  197
  in unequal partnerships 295-6
  see also participation
voluntarism
  Community Development Project
    suggestions 99-100
  and confusion with community
    development 7
  and devolution of responsibility 297, 299
  expansion of sector in Northern Ireland
    204
  third sector and service delivery 196
  youth organisations 4-5, 28

W

Waddington, P. 111, 114, 311
Wagner Report (1988) 212
Wales 13, 197
War on Poverty in US 27, 28, 78-9, 81
'war on terror' 14, 271-2, 281
Washington, Booker T. 78
'we-feeling' and non-directive approach
  37-8
Welfare Rights Movement (US) 86
White, M. 243
whole man and community 66-7
Williams, Fiona 307-8
Williams, Raymond 70-1, 301, 302, 306
Williams, S. 276
Willmott, P. 305
Wilson, E. 185
Wilson, Harold 91
Wirth, L. 66-7
women
  active citizenship and 'mob rule' 235-8
  and diversity of experience 252-3
  role in community development 30, 131,
    205
  and feminist principles 185-90, 217-19
  and socialist struggle against state 101-2,
    104-5

under-representation in public life 165
  see also feminism; gender
Working Group on Health Inequalities
  239
World Bank 9, 223, 252, 256-7, 275, 279
Worthington Report (1978) 114
Wright, E. 297
Wright Mills, C. 307
Wunnam, A. 130

Y

Yeo, E. 306
Yeo, S. 306
Young, M. 305
Young Volunteer Force Foundation
  (YVFF) 4-5, 28
Younghusband, Dame Eileen 26, 73
Youth and Policy (journal) 267
youth work
  political literacy 272
  and prevention of Muslim extremism
    269, 271-2
Yuval-Davis, N. 305